THE
CULTURE OF
COLONIALISM

AFRICAN SYSTEMS OF THOUGHT

Ivan Karp, editor

CONTRIBUTING EDITORS

James W. Fernandez
Luc de Heusch
John Middleton
Roy Willis

THE
CULTURE OF
COLONIALISM
THE CULTURAL SUBJECTION
OF UKAGURU

T. O. BEIDELMAN

Indiana University Press

Bloomington & Indianapolis

This book is a publication of

Indiana University Press
601 North Morton Street
Bloomington, IN 47404-3797 USA

iupress.indiana.edu

Telephone orders   800-842-6796
Fax orders   812-855-7931

Manufactured in the United States of
America

Library of Congress Cataloging-in-
Publication Data

Beidelman, T. O. (Thomas O.), [date]
  The culture of colonialism : the cultural
subjection of Ukaguru / T. O. Beidelman.
    p. cm. — (African systems of thought)
  Includes bibliographical references and
index.
  ISBN 978-0-253-00215-0 (cloth : alk.
paper) — ISBN 978-0-253-00208-2 (pbk.
: alk. paper) — ISBN 978-0-253-00220-4
(e-book) 1. Kaguru (African people)—
Ethnic identity. 2. Kaguru (African
people)—Politics and government.
3. Great Britain—Colonies—Africa—
Administration. 4. Great Britain—
Colonies—Africa—Cultural policy.
5. Tanzania—History—To 1964. I. Title.
II. Series: African systems of thought.
  DT443.3.K33B435 2012
  306.08996391—dc23

2012001252

1 2 3 4 5   17 16 15 14 13 12

To those I knew in the colonies
and to the memory of Ivan Karp

Why is it that civilized humanity
Must make the world so wrong?
In this hurly-burly of inanity
Our dreams cannot last long. . .

NOËL COWARD, "TWENTIETH CENTURY BLUES"

CONTENTS

PREFACE

This work is the product of over fifty years pondering the nature of one East African society, the Kaguru. When I commenced fieldwork in 1957, Kaguru society was located in what was termed Tanganyika, a British United Nations mandated territory that was in most respects virtually a British colony. That was a social world now gone. Yet the impact of that lost world, the world of colonial life, remains an important influence on Kaguru and many other East Africans. When I later did more fieldwork from December 1961 until mid-1963, Kaguru society was located in a Tanganyika newly independent of colonial rule but still mainly run locally by the same British and African colonial officials who had managed things earlier. Still later, in 1965 and 1966, I briefly worked in Tanganyika, after it had become Tanzania. By then almost all formal vestiges of colonial rule were gone, and British officials had been entirely replaced by local Africans. While the impact of colonial rule remained, the way of life itself had profoundly altered from what I had originally encountered. This study is about my experiences during my first two field trips, when Kaguru society was still essentially ruled along a colonial model. In an epilogue I briefly mention some of the many changes that took place after that period. This is mainly to show how much has vanished but, ironically, also to show how modern Tanzania has still not entirely escaped the colonial imprint.

I considered writing this volume while I was first doing fieldwork in Ukaguru (1957–58). I attended court hearings, local moots, and political meetings. I spoke to numerous Kaguru leaders and to British colonial officials and examined what local government records I was allowed to see. When I wrote my doctoral dissertation at Oxford, I included a section on colonial rule. In large part, this book is an expanded and revised version of my doctoral dissertation (1961e). I later published some of these findings in articles on Kaguru government and law and on Kaguru political movements (1961a, 1961b, 1961d, 1966, 1967a, Winter and Beidelman 1967). None of these works attracted much interest from my colleagues, so I abandoned colonial topics and concentrated on writing about Kaguru traditional beliefs and social organization. When I again wrote about colonialism, it was about the local Christian missionaries and their impact on Kaguru life, and about the impact of life in Ukaguru on the missionaries themselves (1982a, 1982b, 1999). I neglected the piles of data I had collected on the colonial Kaguru Native Authority. I now return to this colonial political material, partly because colonialism has always interested me, but also because colleagues assure me that a study of colonial life in Ukaguru would interest others, that indeed colonialism is a topic of renewed interest to scholars in the social sciences, including anthropologists (A. Smith 1994). Since this book aims at creating a picture of local colonial political rule, I have provided little material on Christian missions or on colonial economy. Of course, I consider these important and relevant topics, but I have already published extensively on colonial missions (Beidelman 1974a, 1982a, 1982b, 1999) and on the economy of colonial Ukaguru and Tanganyika (Winter and Beidelman 1967).

Before embarking on writing this book, I examined much of the current writings on colonial societies in the course of teaching a graduate seminar on colonialism. Some writing was provocative and interesting, but much struck me as mechanistic, narrow, shrilly self-righteous, and unduly doctrinaire, especially that by authors who seem keen to condemn the entire colonial endeavor in the name of liberal political correctness. It also struck me that almost none of these more negative critics had ever actually lived in a colonial regime. I realized then with surprise that I must be one of the few anthropologists still working who actually experienced colonial life. That seemed an added reason to write this work. I do not mean to argue that those of us who lived in a colonial society are necessarily better analysts than those who did not. It might even be argued, wrongly I think, that our very experiences may cloud our vision. Yet I believe that first-hand experiences provide a vividness and insight lacking in accounts by those who did not have those experiences. At the least, I can provide another point of view. For these reasons I emphasize grassroots descriptions of the local surroundings, everyday activities, etiquette, recreation, and gossip within one small colonial area. I make no claims that the Kaguru case is typical, even for East Africa, but this is an ethnographic slice of life as I experienced it first-hand and therefore has as much value as the other accounts by administrators and travelers that are prized today as resources by scholars of colonialism. As a social anthropologist I provide some analysis, but the chief value of this account is its ethnographic description of everyday affairs. In this I try to appreciate the views of all the protagonists I encountered, but in large part this remains a personal view.

One reason I think that this account may be of special value is that even many colonial old-timers who wrote about their experiences tended to omit much about everyday routine, apparently assuming that their readers only wanted to be diverted by reports of dramatic, exotic, or humorous materials. They wrongly assumed that much that now interests historians, sociologists, and anthropologists would seem humdrum.

I first set foot in East Africa in August 1957, in Nairobi. Kenya was still under a state of emergency due to Mau-Mau; barbed wire, gun emplacements, and armed patrols gave a bellicose aura to the city. Africans were required to show government passes. I saw Africans detained and searched on the streets by soldiers or police. In the countryside I saw detention camps of Africans surrounded by stockades and gun towers. I was told these camps were for displaced and dissident Kikuyu. In 1957 much that I saw in Kenya recalled my grim military experiences in wartorn Korea, only a few years before (see Beidelman 1998).

Later, in Arusha, Tanganyika, I was introduced to a government anthropologist (Phil Gulliver) by my research supervisor (E. H. Winter) who had taken me to East Africa. As they drank and reminisced, the two anthropologists swapped stories about their past experiences and about the adventures of fieldwork. I listened and felt ignorant, intimidated, and awed. My supervisor then spent several weeks driving me about eastern Tanganyika so I could pick a place to work. We finally decided on Ukaguru, mainly because I thought the countryside beautiful, because I had always wanted to study matrilineal people, because I found an empty house I could rent at a local mission station, and because I would be only 70 miles from where my supervisor planned to work in the town of Kongwa. That seemed important at the time, since I had no transportation other than a bicycle. As it turned out, I made use only once of my supervisor's transport and rarely saw him. Being without an automobile turned out to be an excellent way to do fieldwork. Lacking ready transport, I was forced to spend long periods in Ukaguru since I was unable to leave easily even when I was depressed, bored, or sick. I relied for advice and help almost entirely upon local Africans, except for the few local Australian Christian missionaries with whom I had little in common. I developed stamina while hiking and cycling and skill at wheedling rides from African and Asian lorry drivers, who turned out to be very informative—the Asians about local trade and the Africans about the local Native Authority, for which most had worked at some time. On later field trips I drove a Land Rover and then spent more time visiting British colonial administrators some 60 miles to the south at the district headquarters in Kilosa. That proved helpful, but it probably would have hindered my fieldwork during the first two years. At that time Kaguru were deeply hostile toward the local colonial administration on account of an unpopular forestry project that had led to considerable abuse of ordinary Kaguru by some local Kaguru officials. Kaguru repeatedly told me how pleased they were that I was not British and not part of the colonial establishment. My lack of an automobile proved to many of them that I was some kind of outsider or misfit, at least in part, since they did not know of any other European so poor and uninfluential as to be without an auto.

My view of the local colonial system changed over the years. When I first arrived in Kilosa District, where much of Ukaguru is located, I stayed at the local Church Missionary Society (locally usually called C.M.S.) station at Berega. After about six months I found the missionaries difficult, and it appeared that they likewise hoped I would leave. They were unhappy with anyone who danced and drank, and I spent many hours doing both, especially at Kaguru initiations and marriage celebrations. I also frequented Kaguru beer clubs because there I collected more gossip and news than anywhere else. Later I moved to Mgugu, a settlement two miles from the mission, renting a house from the mission's African archdeacon, who covertly ran a shop and beer club off mission property despite mission disapproval of such secular pursuits by church-men. Later still I moved 30 miles northwest to a more remote Kaguru settlement at Idibo, where I rented a house from a subchief through whom I met many people. Most of the Kaguru court cases I use come from his court, which I regularly attended. In my later field trips, when I had a Land Rover, I spent much time at this same more remote settle-ment, which I got to know well. With a Land Rover I was able to tour all of Ukaguru, but my findings mainly come from Berega, Mgugu and Idibo where I resided the longest.

During my fieldwork I got to know two different district commis-sioners and several of their assistants or district officers. My best friends among the colonials were the British medical officer and his wife, who was an American. I also early on became a friend of a local agricultural officer, a labor officer, and a veterinary officer, all of whom were about my own age. I never got on well with any of the district commissioners. My relations with the first district commissioner were so difficult that I must briefly describe them. They do not reflect well on either of us—not well on him because he was an arrogant and authoritarian prig, not well on me because I was tactless, needlessly critical, and probably meddlesome.

When I decided to work in Ukaguru, my supervisor took me to meet the district commissioner at the district headquarters in Kilosa. We met several times after that. When the district commissioner asked me to report anything to him that might be helpful for maintaining order among the Kaguru, especially anything that seemed subversive, I haughtily told him that as a fieldworker I was ethically bound to protect all my informants. I had forgotten that I was a guest of the Tanganyikan colonial government. I should have simply agreed with all he said and then gone about my own business. To his credit, he did not cancel my permit to work in the area, though he was clearly annoyed. Later, when I saw local Kaguru being flogged, roped in gangs, and sent off as forced labor in the mountains on a government forestry project, I was asked by Kaguru to write to the district commissioner to complain about such practices, and I did so. I discuss this situation in detail later in the text; here I simply note that this letter led the district commissioner to withdraw all cooperation. He was unpopular, and his ruling never hurt my work. I got access to district records once he went on leave. Later I became good friends with the unpopular forestry officer who had been involved in securing forced labor. (He claimed that he was not aware that anyone had been flogged or roped up in gangs on his account, and to be fair this was done by local Kaguru in the villages where labor was collected, far from where the forestry project was located.) By the time of Tanganyikan independence I was friends with one of the district officers, who gave me access to what material was still available at district headquarters. (Much had apparently been destroyed or sent elsewhere by the time of independence.)

Throughout all these years I spent some time with colonial officials and their families. Yet I always felt I was an embarrassment to them because I socialized too much with Africans, even in town when I was not doing fieldwork. For example, I usually stayed in African rather than European homes in Kilosa (the district headquarters town), though I also spent much time in a local Greek hotel. Later still, when I had become friends with a number of Africans who were involved in nationalist politics, I was repeatedly followed by government agents when I was in towns. This was, however, a fairly amiable situation, and I recall once even buying drinks for such an agent when he followed me from one bar to another. As my familiarity with East Africa grew, I became ever more amazed at the complex overlapping between the lives and experiences of Africans and Europeans. I was a regular at some African town bars and dance halls, and the gossip in these by African servants about their employers was ear-opening, ranging from remarks about adultery and alcoholism to, in one case, rumors about the murder of a wife.

After Tanganyikan independence in December 1961, little changed at first. I had returned the week of independence, and the same old attitudes prevailed. To my surprise Africans, even high officials, were often discouraged entry into some European clubs, and white people still walked about with a sense of privilege. Even when I left in 1963, many of the officials running local and even national government were still Europeans. Indeed, those of my European friends and acquaintances who had opted to remain after so many others had left at independence were sometimes elevated to quite senior government posts, including the district commissioner with whom I had earlier clashed. Some said that they had been preferred over Africans because they, unlike Africans, were not seeking to replace those in power or angling to get jobs for their kin, and thus they were regarded as more trustworthy by senior

Africans. By then I had lived some years in Britain and held a degree from Oxford. I was wisely advised by an English friend to take several of my Oxford college ties with me and to keep some Oxonian-type gentlemanly dress in reserve for formal occasions. To my amazement, wearing these at bars, parties, and hotels often brought warm overtures from some British and Africans. The old boy network was alive and well, not only in Tanganyika but even more so in Kenya and Uganda when I traveled there.

When I returned to Tanganyika (now Tanzania) in 1965 and 1966, matters were far more difficult. In 1966 I was thrown out of Ukaguru by one African district official because I had not immediately petitioned him for permission to reside there. (I had already received oral permission from the highest national government officials in Dar es Salaam, but this proved useless.) Before arriving at the district headquarters to introduce myself to the local African official, I had made the mistake of residing for two days in the camp of some old Baraguyu (Maasai) friends whom I had met on the road. Not having initially sought the African district leader's formal permission, I had affronted his authority and dignity. (I later was told that this same African official had lost his job for drunkenness and peculation of funds and that he was broke and in disgrace. I never found this out for sure.) Leaving Kilosa District, I then spent time studying records at another district headquarters (Bagamoyo) where the African official had welcomed me cordially. I was also welcomed at the provincial headquarters. I mention these ups and downs to point out that over the period covered in this volume, 1957–65, my experiences with both European and African government leaders were complex and varied, sometimes friendly, sometimes hostile. The British colonial and African nationalist officials treated me both well and poorly on different occasions. In contrast, most Kaguru were always cordial and helpful. They even welcomed me at court cases and meetings that were illegal in government eyes. No Kaguru suggested that I would report such rule-breaking to those higher up. Given this, I do not think I have any serious ax to grind one way or the other in recounting the actions of the various officials I consider. In any case, this study does not deal with many events after 1962, when all the local chiefships and native authorities were dissolved and the number of Europeans in Tanganyikan government began to decrease rapidly. This is, after all, a study of colonial rule, and while colonialist influence and thinking did not vanish with African independence in 1961, they were clearly drawing to a close by the time I left in 1963.

I have changed or omitted the names of most of the persons I describe in the text. Yet I suppose anyone who knows colonial Kilosa District could easily recognize many of the characters in my account. One advantage of waiting so long to publish is that most people described are dead, and the few still left probably do not now care.

One incident during my years as a graduate student at Oxford (after my first fieldwork in Ukaguru) remains a sharp reminder of why my account of rather humdrum local Ukaguru affairs may fill a needed niche in understanding colonial life. In 1960 I attended a lecture on the British colonial achievement given by the doyenne of theorists writing on British colonial policy in Africa, Dame Margery Perham.[1] She painted a rosy picture of the benefits of British Indirect Rule. Being a cheeky student, I stood up and said that her account did not correspond to what I had encountered in East Africa. I said I found that the system of Indirect Rule in Ukaguru was disorganized, corrupt, and contradictory. Dame Margery snorted that this was not true and nodded to me to sit down and be quiet. Indirect Rule was a mistaken policy, and while colonialism in Ukaguru was not entirely bad or good, it certainly did not match Dame Margery's conservative, reassuring picture, one echoed in most of her popularly acclaimed writings, at least until very late in her career. Local British colonial administrators were sometimes misguided and ill-informed. Yet sometimes they were pushed into policies that they themselves disliked, urged on by their superiors with less grassroots experience. To be fair, most whom I encountered were dedicated, hardworking, and honest civil servants, not fitting the very negative descriptions of some postcolonial critics.

This is my fifth and final volume on Ukaguru, Tanzania (Tanganyika), East Africa. In the first, I present an account of that society for college undergraduates (1971a). In the second I describe how Christian missionaries colonized Ukaguru (1982a). In the third I describe how key Kaguru values and beliefs created the moral imagination that animated the traditional Kaguru view of social life (1986). In the fourth, I describe how values and beliefs were indoctrinated in Kaguru people by means of the initiation of adolescents, other rituals, and associated lore that Kaguru repeatedly described as the cultural essence of their society (1997). In this present and final work, I note how colonialists encouraged ethnic (tribal) identity among Kaguru and also how Kaguru tried to consolidate and manipulate beliefs and values in order to maintain or even create an ethnic identity that provided them with a sense of local, social solidarity against their local African neighbors and against European colonialists. This identity would, they hoped, enable them to resist broader social forces that threatened to co-opt Kaguru into a wider colonial and later national state, a state that threatened to preempt Kaguru local needs and values. For Kaguru, as for many of us, local rule was important because it seemed the only practical way to meet pressing needs and goals. Kaguru increasingly defined these in terms of their ethnic identity. They did not see themselves as just like other subjects of the colony or later as just like other citizens of the Tanzanian nation-state. Instead, Kaguru saw themselves as people with a particular style and understanding rooted in the landscape about them. They were Tanganyikans and later Tanzanians, but, to them, it was also important that they were Kaguru. These senses of ethnicity and tradition were profoundly encouraged by the colonial policies of Indirect Rule that I recount in this final study. They were also couched in terms of Kaguru needs as an isolated people less advantaged economically and educationally than many other Africans.

In this final volume on the Kaguru, I develop the themes of Kaguru ethnicity and Indirect Rule as these were first used by Kaguru and by Arab, German, and British colonialists in order to construct a local political system, the Kaguru Native Authority. Ironically, for both the Kaguru and their colonial rulers, this Native Authority represented a structure that was both valued and disdained. My study describes many sides of this governing structure with the aim of emphasizing the deeply ambivalent and ambiguous ways that all the people involved viewed this enterprise. The rhetoric and associated beliefs and values mustered to defend and explain colonial rule were seen as inextricably enmeshed in the beliefs and values that provided an ideology to denounce that same regime, the values or disadvantages of African customs and traditions, the values or disadvantages of democracy, and the values and disadvantages of modernization and change. In short, these policies were couched in contradictions, illusions and delusions, but oddly still worked in some muddled ways.

"Kaguruness" was a part of "Africanness," part of what it meant to be the native owners of a land, something that outsiders could never be. "Kagurunness" was also seen by those at the top of government as part of a so-called "tribalism" that had eventually to be transcended, whether that was by creating a viable political unit of the British Empire or Commonwealth or by creating an entirely independent African nation-state. Ethnicity or tribalism was far more respected or tolerated by the British colonialists than by educated, nationalist Africans. That is because the British colonialists found it much more to their advantage to think and operate in local terms than did African nationalists. Yet while Kaguru ethnicity and traditions were sometimes nurtured by colonial life, these were also the outcome of forces opposed to that life. The local resistance Kaguru voiced against colonialism (and later against some sides of African nationalism) was rooted in the modes of Kaguru tradition, but that tradition itself was far from traditional. Rather, it was a product of colonialism, being both a construct by European colonialists and a construct by those local Africans opposed to colonialists. Colonialism fostered both ethnicity and localism, even though colonialists claimed that their system would eventually evolve beyond such parochialism by introducing a more modern way of life.

It is with reference to these contradictory issues of ethnicity, tradition, localism, and colonial intervention and modernity that I chose a preliminary and now discarded title for this volume, *Take Me to Your Leader*. Since the arrival of the first outsiders in Ukaguru, strangers have asked to be taken to the leaders of the Kaguru people so they could conduct business. At first these were questions from those in caravans, those slaving and ivory-hunting, and then later from those collecting taxes and labor and securing a peaceful countryside. That Kaguru did not traditionally have well-defined and permanent leaders, did not have a centralized polity, and did not even feel especially strongly about being of one ethnicity seemed unacceptable and perhaps unimaginable to the Arabs, Germans, and British. Yet it was not long before Kaguru leaders, a Kaguru polity, and a corresponding Kaguru ethnicity were invented and exaggerated by all concerned. It is in these senses that this present volume is a study about a colonial past now gone, but also newly invented. It is a past that still haunts the present problems of Ukaguru and Tanzania in ways that make this study useful not only as an account of the past but as a lens for examining the present and a glass for peering into the future. I hope it is also an interesting, colorful story.

I make a few final points. First, I write most of this in the past tense rather than in the ethnographic present. This is because my account deals mostly with events that occurred fifty years ago and are now more properly considered history rather than conventional anthropology. Second, I use the name Tanganyika with reference to where I worked. That is because Tanganyika did not become Tanzania until 1964. I use the name Tanzania only where discussing events after 1964 and where commenting about the present. I use the names Kaguru for the people I have studied, Ukaguru for the place where they live, and Chikaguru for the language they speak. Other names have been used over the past, sometimes even by Kaguru, but the names I use here are the prevalent ones used today (see Beidelman 1967b, 1986). The name Geiro (a town and a chiefship in western Ukaguru) was used by the colonial regime all during their rule. After independence, the new government began using the name Gairo. I have stuck to the colonial name since that is what appeared during all my fieldwork. I use the new name only for events that took place long after my main fieldwork. I want to thank my friend Professor Ivan Karp for his great help in advising me about this book, from its content and title to providing valuable research sources. He was a huge support for many years in my studies of the Kaguru and other African topics.

Finally, I want to thank the chair of my department, Professor Terry Harrison, who provided the funds to make the maps which clarify my picture of colonial Ukaguru.

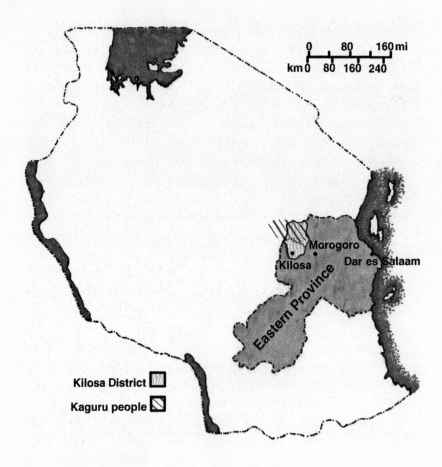

Map 1. Tanganyika Territory Showing Eastern Province,
Kilosa District, and Ukaguru

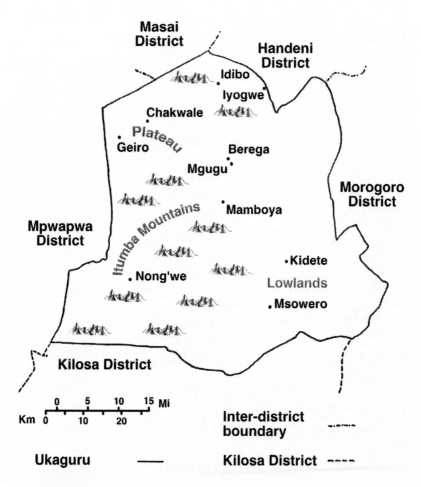

Map 2. Geographical Areas of Ukaguru

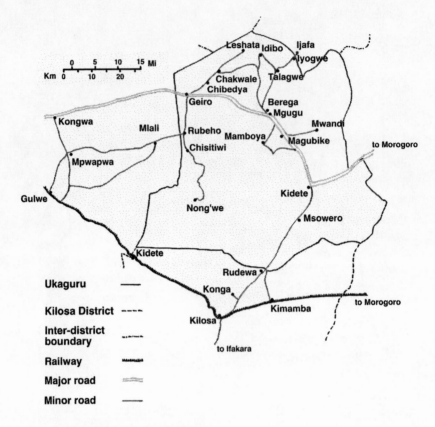

Map 3. Communications in Ukaguru

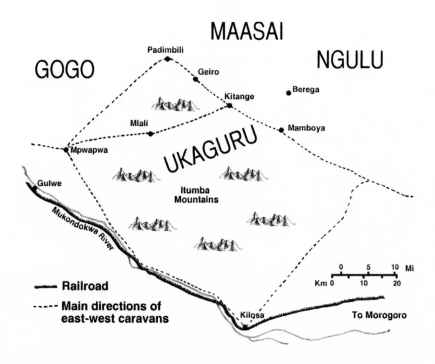

GOGO MAASAI NGULU

Padimbili
Geiro
Kitange
Berega
Mlali
Mamboya
Mpwapwa
UKAGURU
Gulwe
Mukondokwa River
Itumba
Mountains

0   5   10 Mi
Km 0   10   20

Railroad
Main directions of
east-west caravans

Kilosa
To Morogoro

Map 4. Historical Sites in Ukagaru and Its Neighbors

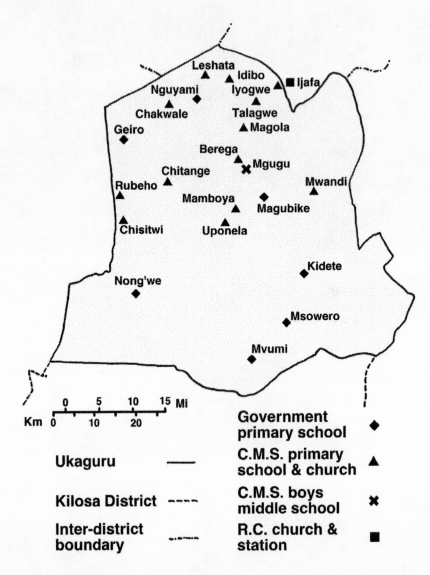

Leshata
Nguyami
Idibo
Iyogwe
Ijafa
Chakwale
Talagwe
Geiro
Magola
Berega
Mgugu
Chitange
Mwandi
Rubeho
Mamboya
Magubike
Chisitwi
Uponela
Kidete
Nong'we
Msowero
Mvumi

0   5   10   15 Mi

Km 0   10   20

Ukaguru ⸺

Kilosa District ----

Inter-district
boundary

Government
primary school ◆

C.M.S. primary
school & church ▲

C.M.S. boys
middle school ✕

R.C. church &
station ■

Map 5. Ukaguru Schools and Missions

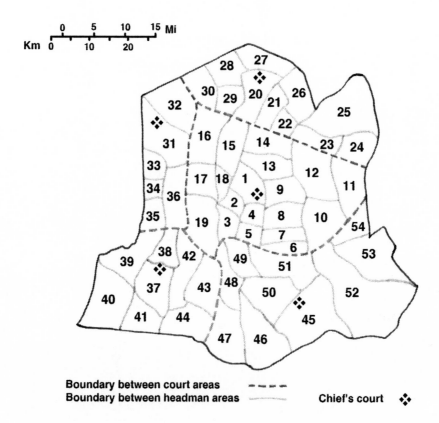

Map 6. Kaguru Native Authority Chiefdoms and Headmanships.
Numbers refer to clans and their homelands indicated in Appendix 12.

INTRODUCTION

Colonialism and Anthropology

This is an ethnographic study of the colonial life of the Kaguru, most of whom lived in Ukaguru, a chiefdom in Kilosa district in east-central Tanganyika, British East Africa. Yet before considering colonial life in Ukaguru, I need to provide some account of the issues that have been raised in the study of colonialism. This is not easy, since even the meanings of terms such as "colony" and "colonialism" are disputed. Given the complexity of the disagreements about these, I focus on only a few key points in this huge scholarly literature. First, I briefly consider some of the ways that colonialism has been broadly characterized and its proper study defined. I then consider how it relates to ethnicity, culture, and "race." I go on to colonialism's relation to power, how it relates to certain forms of hierarchical social organization. This leads to the central feature of this study, British colonial rule at the local level in Africa and the resultant native government embodied in courts, native law, and a cadre of chiefs and other agents that dominated everyday rural life. I use the term "rural" because during the period considered in this book Tanganyika (Tanzania) was mainly a country of uneducated farmers involved in a poorly developed cash economy. Here as elsewhere in sub-Saharan Africa, native government was the most characteristic feature of grassroots British colonial rule. This was usually termed Indirect Rule; it involved an extensive and often acrimonious debate by political scientists, historians, sociologists, and some anthropologists. Before discussing these issues, I want to discuss the original, abandoned title of this book.

The original title of this study was *Take Me to Your Leader*, a phrase familiar to those reading science fiction. It is also a term well-known to anyone acquainted with the popular literature of exploration and first contact. In Africa, the British wrongly assumed that native peoples always had some leader with whom one could negotiate and therefore eventually recruit to help rule a local area for the colonialists.[1] In fact, in many areas of Africa, including Ukaguru, no such unifying leader existed traditionally. It was, however, true that in Ukaguru some opportunistic men had early on made ties with Arab traders and later German adventurers so as to acquire economic and political advantages over others. Some of these opportunistic upstarts were later made chiefs and headmen in subsequent colonial native administrations.

Initially I thought of the title *Take Me to Your Leader* because it conjured up notions of science fiction and a sense of playful irony and unreality in the colonial situation. It was meant to subvert some of the popular colonialist literature and to convey a sense of unreality about the actual legitimacy of supposed native tradition. Most readers of my initial text apparently thought that such a title appeared frivolous, not connoting a proper sense of seriousness to a historical situation that had produced so much suffering and social damage. Consequently, my final title, the one that now appears, employs more serious terms like *culture* and *subjection*. I had first chosen the abandoned, supposedly inappropriate title because early on in my fieldwork I rejected the highly positive official British evaluation of the doctrine of Indirect Rule, a doctrine praised and defended as central to the official writings of the Tanganyikan colonial administration and policymakers. Such views are especially enshrined in the sententious writings of Lord Lugard, Sir Donald Cameron, and Dame Margery Perham. In their works Indirect Rule is repeatedly described as a valuable, even admirable, cornerstone of British colonial hegemony. At best, it was promoted as a seemingly convenient way to rule a large empire cheaply with only a handful of British administrators at the top. Eventually, it became an institution that through time took on a deceptive moral patina that was elaborated by its proponents. I do not doubt that at times some of those involved in justifying British use of Indirect Rule were convinced that this was a liberal and constructive policy. Even many of those who possibly were not entirely under the delusion that this was a good policy still parroted the platitudes associated with Indirect Rule in order to succeed in the co-lonial service. Some who might otherwise have wanted to get rid of Indi-rect Rule thought it career-wise to go along with such policies by writing deceptive, expedient official reports, thereby covering up colonial abuse as well as some of the errors of idle, incompetent, corrupt, and disloyal native agents. Because of such frequent cover-ups, official reports, and complacent memoirs and interviews, potential critics and reformists of this unsatisfactory system were sometimes duped into believing in the delusion that Indirect Rule worked well, socially and culturally, in the ways that its zealous advocates claimed. Some even boasted of Indirect Rule as a benevolent and laudable conception of which the British should be especially proud.

For all these reasons, I wanted my choice of a title for this study to convey a surreal and slightly farcical aura of unreality surrounding the public image, and also a murkier under-life of the colonial world at the grassroots. My previous allusion to science fiction, suggested by my abandoned title of *Take Me to Your Leader*, may have been taking my argument of surrealism a bit too far, but I want here to underscore that my earlier title had a point in its seeming absurdity. I did not want to part utterly from it. This long account of my indecision about just what title to use for this study reflects my continued concern, my turmoil, about the widespread pretense and subterfuge as to just what colonial life actu-ally involved. That colonialists assumed that Kaguru had a single leader who would or should readily collaborate with them outrageously catches something of the misleading half-truths on which the colonial enterprise was based. So too was there an illusion regarding the misguided claim that the early Kaguru had a widespread and consistent sense of ethnic identity, not just an understandably united sense of their all being en-dangered by powerful ethnic and cultural outsiders. Equally unreal, as well as hypocritical, was the British notion that Indirect Rule would eventually educate the Kaguru into being better able to rule themselves. No wonder the local colonial system produced a social life where Eu-ropeans, Africans, and Asians all worked and struggled in a world that often did not make a lot of sense to any of those caught up in it.

The powerful forces of Indirect Rule brought out hugely contra-dictory forms of behavior and sentiments in all of those involved. Of course, it brought hard work and dedication by some, but it also brought frustration and alienation, and finally, for better or worse, it eventually brought malfunction and destruction of the system itself (see Berman 1996:75). The concept and practice of Indirect Rule as embodied in the local African Native Authority, with its chiefs, headmen, courts, and various other staff, constituted the central organizational milieu in which Kaguru experienced colonial life in their homeland. This notion formed a colonial culture of its own (Dirks 1992:3). How far this British approach of Indirect Rule in Ukaguru resembled that of the British elsewhere in Africa or that of other European colonial rulers is debatable. In a famous article, Crowder emphasizes the colonial differences between French and British colonial rule (1964), though others, such as Benton, consider such differences minor when compared to the broader character of colonialism (2002:154). It remains unclear how far understanding the British system will take us in understanding colonial life elsewhere in Africa. Admittedly, the British, French, German, Portuguese, and other colonial rulers each created systems reflecting their particular national character. Yet Benton seems right in maintaining that general cross-cultural structural features of colonialism were in force nearly everywhere. In my work here I concentrate almost entirely on British attitudes and methods.

An examination of British ideas and practices involved in Indirect Rule constitutes the most important part of this introductory chapter to this book about the colonial Kaguru world. Many of the problems revealed by an examination of Indirect Rule continue even today to be sources of difficulties afflicting East Africa now that it has gained some forms of national independence. In some ways, Indirect Rule continues as a force and a delusory assumption in new nationalist political forms. The weight of our past burdens us all.

Some Broad Views of Colonialism in Earlier Writings

Colonialism is an ancient institution, protean in its many particular forms. Finley's account of the varied forms of colonies in ancient Greek and Roman civilizations makes this clear (1976:178). Even the word "colonialism" transcends its descriptive meanings and has been developed as a tool by its political critics (Fieldhouse 1983:7) so that it is now rife with contradictory meanings (ibid.:20). "Colonization is thus a phe-

nomenon of colossal vagueness" (Osterhammel 1997:4). Because of colonialism's long past and wide geographical distribution "only localized
theories and historically specific accounts can provide much insight
into the varied representations and practices " (Thomas 1994:ix). My
concern in this study is with colonialism as it occurred in the recent
past, the second half of the twentieth century, and then only in one
small part of Africa. Yet a few themes brought up by earlier writers are
worth mentioning.

Colonialism always involves economic and political inequality at every level (Smith 1979:384–385). It was "an imperium of commerce" (Nairn
2002:361). It is because of European technological advantages over Africans that Europeans came to dominate them. Europeans' main aim was
economic profit. Walter Rodney describes colonialists as vicious bandits
(1982:205–207), aiming to make Africans sell their labor and goods cheap
and buy European good dear (ibid.:228–229). "The British came into
Africa, according to official history, to abolish slavery; they stayed to
establish wage labour" (Labour Research Department 1926:18–19). European administrators and missionaries often presented their activities
as apart from such economics, but colonialism remained ultimately an
economic endeavor, and all development was gauged at increasing control to secure profits in some way (Rex 1980:135–137; Fieldhouse 1983:74).
Colonialism is synonymous with exploitation. and all forms of exploitation resemble one another (Fanon 1967b:88). Violence lies at the heart of
such domination. Violence enforced social inequalities that few Africans
would otherwise have accepted (Fanon 1963:117). Such violence was not
always overt but was always still implied. Iliffe observes: "Behind the
whole structure, latent and rarely visible, was the underlying violence
of colonial government" (1979:326). "The essence of the colonial system
was despotism" (Mwakyembe 1986:19). Crowder notes that while Africans sometimes appeared seemingly passive in their attitudes toward
colonial rule, this was mainly because they saw resistance as useless in
the face of superior technology (1968:4). Africans rarely saw colonial
rule as moral; colonialist policies appeared repugnant and sometimes
incomprehensible to their own values (Ekeh 1975:93). Yet Africans were
ill-equipped to resist changes constantly imposed upon them from above
due to their overwhelming poverty when compared to their colonial
masters (A. Smith 1994:384–389). Furthermore, colonialism not only

disrupted traditional African economics and politics but also set new and arbitrary boundaries dividing peoples and regions, fragmenting and dislocating indigenous groups (Jerman 1997:61–62; Balandier 1966:55). Finally, colonialists rarely exploited or developed all parts of a colony but instead only favored some areas, thus setting different regions and peoples against one another (ibid.:129).

While the basic motives that sustained colonialism were economic, few colonialists, especially the British, were ready to present colonial ambitions publicly in this light. Instead, such policies of domination were given a more positive, humanistic veneer. They were expressed in terms of social betterment, introduction of higher morality, improving living conditions, and promoting the process of civilization. The voice of modern colonialism was "primarily a middle-class achievement (Gann and Duignan 1978b:3). By most thinking today, there was no respectable reason for colonialism. This consequently prompted elaborate falsification of motives (Hobson 1967:196–198). "Imperialism is based upon a persistent misrepresentation of fads and forces" (ibid.:211). At its worst, British colonialism fed upon inconsistency, double-talk, jingoism, and the whitewashing of motives that masked conquest, economic greed, brutality, racism, bigotry, and injustice in the name of progress (ibid.:198–215). Colonialism distorted political thinking to create a fog of self-delusion, humbug, and absence of self-criticism. Other colonialists were no better (Balandier 1966:38–39). Writing of French colonialism, Césaire blamed "Christian pedantry" for the hypocrisy of Western colonial arguments and capitalism for its basic lack of morality (1970:35); "Wherever the colonizers and colonized met face to face there is force, brutality, cruelty, sadism, violence, and the hasty manufacture, in a parody of cultural training [of] several thousand subordinate officials, 'boys,' artisans, commercial employees, and interpreters who are necessary for the proper functioning of the colonial establishment" (ibid.:40). Césaire's portrayal of colonialism's injustices is stark but accurate; unfortunately, his contrasting portrayal of precolonial life is ludicrously idyllic (ibid.:41). Later critics have also accused colonialists and even some of the anthropologists who studied them of perpetuating a destructive, romantic nostalgia for the past, a nostalgia that impedes modernization and fetishizes backward traditions (Turner 1987:153–154; Bissell 2003:222–226).

In criticizing colonialism, a good case can be made that Africa is the prime example of failed colonialism (Phillips 1989:2–3). Porter describes the British record as particularly "deplorable" (2007:6), though it cannot remotely compare to the horrors of Belgian colonial rule (Hochschild 1998).

This literature on colonialism in Africa is so vast that I mainly examine ethnographic accounts from east and central Africa. Of course, I am familiar with much of the literature from elsewhere and indeed knew many of those writers, such as Max Gluckman, Leo and Hilda Kuper, Isaac Schapera, M. G. Smith, Meyer Fortes, Michael Crowder, Margery Perham, Georges Balandier, Terence Ranger, and others; but I have cited them only where their work relates directly to the material at hand, or indirectly when I cite work such as that of Hugh Macmillan, Ivan Karp, and Jack Goody, who incorporate their works and that of others into their critical writings. After all, this chapter is not a survey of all the literature on colonialism, not even all that for Africa. Instead, as I already mentioned, it is an account to alert the reader to the key issues I consider in my ethnography.

Only a few anthropologists recognized that there was no way fully to comprehend African societies when they studied such systems without also studying the European rulers as well as the ruled. The most striking early argument was made by Balandier (1966:40–44), though he himself failed to provide really detailed material on European colonialists. Balandier did credit Gluckman and Fortes with pioneering work to include whites in a more useful "total" view of the colonial system (ibid.:55). Gluckman had advocated such research, but he provided few details on whites (Macmillan 1995:49–58; Gluckman 1958; A. Smith 1994:384–387; see also, outside of Africa, Firth 1973). Anthropologists from South Africa like Gluckman pioneered in such an approach, although even they little analyzed white views and conduct in detail (Goody 1995:42–43, 115–116). Despite these weaknesses, few anthropologists actively defended colonial regimes. Recently some writers criticized anthropologists' relations to colonialism in Africa (Mamdani 1996, 2001; see Cooper 1997a; Said 1989; Cocks 1995; Asad 1973; D. Lewis 1973:581–584, 590–592). Much of this criticism is poorly situated within the social and historical contexts of the times, and some of it is sanctimonious, glib, and seemingly poorly acquainted with the anthropological literature. Some anthropologists could at times have opposed aspects of colonialism in the field, but one would be unable to do fieldwork if one were to do so strenuously. One was, after all, in the field on the sufferance of those colonialists in power.

Colonialism, Race, and Ethnicity (Tribalism)

Racism is everywhere associated with political and class conflict and exploitation (Cox 1970:383). Almost every writer on European empire-building relates colonialism to racism and ethnicity (Kennedy 1945:308–315, 320; O'Callaghan 1980; Porter 2007:7; Loomba 1998:25, 161–162). European stereotypes of Africans were in place by the 1880s (Curtin 1964:I:xii–xiii). Even after World War II, most British including liberals saw Africans as a child-race (Davis 1973:385–386). The East African settler and novelist Elspeth Huxley described Africans as having a "slave mentality" (1948:153). Others saw them as undependable (Crowley 1968:396–397). Mazrui and Mazrui describe the British colonialists as less arrogant than the French but even more racist (1998:14). Writing from a non-British perspective Memmi, describes Africans as congenitally "lazy" (1965:79–81), and Manoni describes them as inferior (1964:24, 34). Asad credits racism with colonialism's "hysterical intolerance" (1973:45). Race in turn may be tied to notions of "primitivism" (Fenton 1960:160). Some writers tie racism to the capitalism that propelled much of colonial expansion (Ernst 1950:454; Miles 1989:105–111), and, in this sense, comparable discrimination against the working class in the home-country (Kiennan 1992). In most African colonies little dignity was found in manual labor, which was seen as the proper niche to which blacks should aspire (Cox 1970:43), and education of Africans was geared to such lower levels. British colonialists favored the uneducated natives and were suspicious of those Africans lucky enough to be well-schooled; the French seemed a bit more tolerant (Crowder 1968:12–13, 395–398; Kirk-Greene 1970:xvii). With such assumptions, the British saw Africans only fit to serve as supportive cadre in government at the lowest, local levels. Asians were preferred at the next level of service if Europeans could not be found. Kirk-Greene saw British resistance to admitting Africans to the colonial service as the single greatest shortcoming in their rule (1970:xvi–xvii). "The idea that they are incapable of self-government is the key rationalization of the political aspects of colonialism" (Kennedy 1945:312). Racial segregation and discrimination pervaded all sections of East African life, though nowhere was this written into law as it was in South Africa (Goldthorpe 1958:258–273). Many Asians were often even more disdainful of Africans than were Europeans (ibid.:138). Despite the permeation of racism in all sectors of colonial culture and among all groups involved, whites, blacks, and Asians, anthropologists do not have a long or significant record of examining such beliefs and practices in the field (Balandier 1970:25–46), though Malinowski advocated such study (1929:22–23, 1930). In the 1950s and 1960s little likelihood of any change in this situation was considered possible without radical changes on the existing political and economic front, something that almost no one considered likely soon (Rex 1980:120).

In the colonial world race trumped ethnicity in almost all situations, though in East Africa serious divisions existed between various Asians, and class differences, especially between various British, were also important. Among the British, colonial administrators were almost always middle-class and thus formed a coherent and solidary group with very similar attitudes (see Crowder 1968:393, 398–400). The exceptions to this middle-class stereotype were the supplementary services such as clerks, public works, police, and military, who came from a lower class, as well as the merchants and missionaries, who were diverse. Still, as Nairn aptly observes, "The essence of imperial Britain was an unusually intimate 'fit' between society and state, sustained through a partly hereditary class" (2002:73).

In East Africa, what was as important as race was the issue of ethnicity, at least as it concerned Africans. In their everyday dealings most Europeans and Asians generally lumped all black Africans together, as contrasted to the differences they sometimes saw among themselves. However, it was assumed by British administrators that every African belonged to a "tribe" or ethnic group. In British colonies such as those in East Africa, tribal membership was important because it placed Africans under a particular local authority according to the system of Indirect Rule. Tribe became a central feature of how Africans were identified and how they identified themselves, even when and if they did not want to think in such terms. To avoid such tribal labeling was difficult for any African. It was even important when Africans interacted with one another. It was enshrined in censuses, other government surveys, and many certificates of identification.

Throughout their empire the British tended to stress tradition as a part of identity among their subjects (Fieldhouse 1983:33–34; Sklar 1993). Some scholars would claim that this emphasis on tradition and its association with ethnicity promoted a system of divide and rule (Jerman 1997:61–62). Those who have studied British rule in Africa emphasize "tribe" as a rationalization for Indirect Rule, even to the extent that the British created a sense of tribe far stronger than what existed before colonialism (Apthorpe 1968:18; Meredith 2005:153; Mamdani 1996:7–8, 19–22; Stoler and Cooper 1997:11; Rodney 1982:228–229; Ekeh 1990:660–690; Gulliver 1969; Iliffe 1979:323–324). There are good surveys of how the British encouraged East Africans to think and act in terms of tribe (Gulliver 1969; Southall 1970:28–29, 32–33; 1992:100–108). Yet some colonialists argued that this was already an entrenched belief that Africans could not shed (A. Phillips 1955:155), though a better argument could be made that the British created conditions that kept tribalism alive. Some would argue that the British actually created tribalism, at least in the strong form consistent with Indirect Rule (Samuel-Mbaekwe 1986:87–90). Mamdani has gone so far as to describe tribalism as a concept facilitating exploitation by native chiefs (1996:22–24, 43–48, 52–53), while Mafeje has termed it a form of "false consciousness" (1971:259). The ethnic plurality of towns and large agricultural estates (such as those for sisal, tea, and sugar in East Africa) confounded the tribal issue (Osterhammel 1997:89). Promotion of tribalism undoubtedly impeded political development, though writers such as Mamdani (2001) seriously underestimate the importance ethnicity held for many colonial Africans (for criticism of Mamdani, see Cooper 2005). The importance of the concepts of tribe and ethnicity to Indirect Rule is obvious. Unfortunately, an association between the emphasis on these terms and anthropology may be made. Even though few anthropologists actively supported colonial rule, this negative association may be misleadingly implied by the fact that the leading essay in the first issue of the journal *Africa* (the primary scholarly periodical devoted to social studies in that continent) is by Lord Lugard, the reactionary advocate of Indirect Rule who argued for further anthropological research to support such views (1928). Malinowski soon concurred in the same journal (1929, 1930).

In postcolonial times, "tribe" has assumed ambivalent and ambiguous meanings for Africans. Well after independence, Tanzania's President Nyerere used the Swahili term for tribe (*kabila*) in a neutral sense. He drew concepts he associated with tribal life and ethnicity to bolster his promotion of a dubious notion of African socialism (*ujamaa*), "tribal socialism" (1968:11). Yet Nyerere and other African leaders also saw ethnic or tribal loyalties as politically dangerous in dividing African nations (even though many African politicians continued to use tribal loyalties and fears to muster votes). As we now have seen, tribalism has gone on to provide motives for terrible violence and genocide outside Tanzania. Ekeh has provided an excellent account of how the term "tribalism" has been used by modern Africans to signify political and economic favoritism, bribery, corruption, and bad citizenship (1990:660–690). Hugh Macmillan offers the phrase "situational ethnicity" as an alternative (2000:89). Unfortunately, the term "tribe" tenaciously persists with a multitude of meanings, though "tribalism" and "tribalistic" are now terms used in a negative sense by many African intellectuals.

In summary, no useful account of colonial society can neglect notions of race, ethnicity, and tribe. These differences produced "a plural society." In such a colonial world no one could be described as completely meaningful socially except as she or he related directly or indirectly to many groups, some deeply at odds with one another. In East Africa, British administrators, Asian merchants and clerks, and large masses of Africans seemingly pursued vastly divergent trajectories, yet their ideas and actions ultimately made little sense without some reckoning of one another. This may seem obvious, but it is to the credit of Furnivall, who first coined the term "plural society" (1956:239), and followers such as Leo Kuper (1980:239, 246), that we now have a better sense of how colonies worked. In Tanganyika, "plural society" and "multiracialism" took on negative meanings in the years just before independence when the imperialistic Governor Twining tried to promote a multiracial state that profoundly underrepresented the African majority in their own land (Lohrmann 2007:551–558).

Rulers as Masters and Teachers

The most positive models the British presented of themselves as colonial rulers were those taken from an idiom of yesteryear, that of aloof yet benevolent masters, teachers, and parents, though what we know about traditional British life among servants and their masters, public schoolboys and headmasters, or some repressed parents and children is hardly always rosy (Crowder 1968:199). Yet these images were especially evocative for colonial administrations whose members were, at least until sometime after World War II, accustomed to attending public schools and to having had at least one or more servants about their homes back in Britain. These models were hardly a key to how administrators always behaved, but they were notions entertained by such people and do enable one to decipher some of these colonialists' language about their "mission" to rule. "'The Tradition' preserved a system consecrated by wealth, as well as by romantic mythology and pastoral nonsense" (Nairn 2002:36).

The reactionary East African settler and novelist Elspeth Huxley describes Africans as "peasants" and, as such, needing a stern father figure epitomized by a British district officer or settler-master (ibid.:134). A colonial administrator was seen as a paternalistic force who could both protect and guide the supposedly naive natives (Heussler 1963:60; Costa 1999:16), somewhat like a tribal chief or elder, only more god-like for being racially and culturally distant as well as somewhat inscrutable (Apthorpe 1968:19). They were "kings of the bush" (Young 1988:48). The British Colonial Office saw the public school as the ideal producer of such rulers (Tidrick 1993:220). Good colonial officers were like headmasters back home. They were needed for the "character development" of the supposedly childlike Africans (Jones 1970:12–15). Colonialism was seen as a "moral force" that would teach Africans to improve (Brett 1973:60–61). Local colonial rule resembled a school in the sense that colonial district officers had custodial care of supposedly vulnerable, "immature" Africans who required guidance to enter modern life (Heussler 1963:83). (This was a bit like the now outmoded notion at American universities where academic staff were thought to serve as "local parents.") Colonial district officers were thought to know best what should be taught to Africans and what should not. At the invitation of East African colonialists, the personnel from the somewhat racist and conservative Phelps-Stokes Fund sent experts from America to teach the colonial British how to educate their "colored people." Some even visited Ukaguru, and their recommendations were influential in reinforcing the conservative views on education implicit in Indirect Rule. They recommended that Africans be trained in agriculture, crafts, and manual labor, with a strong Pauline Christian emphasis on obedience and resignation to their assigned social lot. Africans should be discouraged from bookish subjects (Jones 1970:xvii–xviii, 36–42, 179–180; Beidelman 1982a:112–123, 231 note 62). This fit with Lord Lugard's own conservative, even racist, notions about how higher Western education would only cause disrespect and insubordination among those Africans to be groomed for possible posts in Indirect Rule (Tidrick 1990:212–213).

The British public school or military academy mentality had many implications for local colonial administration. Corporal punishment and performing service for one's "betters" ("fagging" for upperclassmen) were seen as practices building character. They had been experienced and perhaps perversely enjoyed by middle and upper class British men in the colonial administration and the colonial office. Furthermore, the public school world was a place not giving much attention to women. It is therefore not surprising that African women's roles, work, and significance were rarely topics of concern in local district officers' reports. When women were mentioned, they were often seen as potential sources of disruption and disorder in African society, a problem if they were to get out of hand (Rodney 1982:225–227).

While corporal punishment and work details were common forms of discipline in East African colonial life, their implementation was increasingly delegated to local African agents of Indirect Rule. In this way the British were sometimes able to conceal some of the harsh realities behind their rule. Consequently, they might better claim that they ruled not by crude physical force but by force of moral and personal character, old public-school virtues (Tidrick 1990:213–220). The British liked the image of themselves as so personally commanding that they needed only to advise and suggest what Africans had to do. Onerous rules and orders were sometimes presented as the ideas of African chiefs and hardly those of the British who concocted them (Crowder 1968:211–213). Perceptive Africans, however, could recognize an order when it was given, at least when they wanted to. In this moralistic rhetoric, colonial administrators shared such views with some missionaries and tradesmen, though colonial administrators did not always see eye to eye with such people, especially white settlers (Haynes 1996:25; Beidelman 1982a).

Africans were rarely taught any skills related to commerce. They were usually described as too simple to engage in business, which was thought likely to corrupt them. Sir Donald Cameron, the supposedly liberal and innovative second governor of British Tanganyika, pontificated that the economic advance of the African should never take place at the risk of the African's "moral well-being," implying that the African was too irresponsible and unstable to deal with wealth without close supervision by his white tutorial masters (McCarthy 1982:6). Local administrative policies, from the beginning of British colonial rule, were aimed at teaching skills and attitudes that would facilitate the production of agricultural and animal resources that could be purchased by Europeans and Asians. Administrators were not encouraged to promote Africans going into activities that would make them free of the European job or product markets (McCarthy 1979:12–13). Those Africans who acquired advanced education usually sought to escape from local Indirect Rule by moving to detribalized trading centers or towns (Heussler 1963:63). Similarly, while local administrators often described their concern for public works as proof of their commitment to African social welfare, works such as roads, bridges, markets, schools, and courthouses facilitated the entry of disruptive European and Asian commerce into African areas (Furnivall 1956:319–322). Most district officers' concerns with "native affairs" involved African law, courts, taxation, and collection of fines and fees rather than developing modernizing institutions (Brooke 1954:68).

Local British administrators often described one of their biggest problems to be how to understand local natives, "their people" (Ranger 1976:116). Africans' mentality and culture were sometimes described as inscrutably alien, childlike, illogical, and ungrateful. This was only the other side of the coin. Many Africans viewed British colonial administrators as equally inscrutable and therefore lacking legitimacy in any way that made moral sense to Africans (Samuel-Mbaekwe 1986:93; Barnes 1954:135; Hyden and Williams 1974:174).

The moralistic rhetoric of the master/teacher model that was promoted by colonial officers concealed far more authoritarian and less benevolent policies and practices than were ever acknowledged by most British. Nor did the British actually have a good record educating Africans to enter modern life on terms beneficial to Africans. Still, many local British administrators saw their rule as founded on solid moral, civilizing principles. Many administrators "meant well," and many even tried to lighten harsh, ill-conceived policies dreamed up by the secretariat at the colonial capital or by the colonial office in London. What everyone shared was a rhetoric that obfuscated what actually went on. Kirk-Greene observes: "If we ask whether—and if so where—the Colonial Administrative Service went wrong, the answer, for me lies fairly and squarely in the attitude towards the admission of Africans into the Service" (1986b:xviii).

Indirect Rule: Its Historical Roots

Co-opting local natives to help foreigners rule was a practice common in empires for centuries. It was the only tactic by which so few British could rule millions in Africa and Asia. While Lord Lugard is almost always credited with initiating Indirect Rule in Africa, he really only formalized and published a rationale for earlier policies (Fieldhouse 1983:4; Fields 1985:39–49; Gailey 1974:18; Stephens 1968:53–54; Gifford 1967:351). Indirect Rule was actually based on expediency (R. Brown 1959:50), but it became a formal policy, an almost fetishized doctrine (Collins 1973:83; Tidrick 1990:207–208). When Cameron left Lugard's Nigeria to become governor of Tanganyika, he tried to soften the term to "Indirect Administration," but it was the same thing. Indirect Rule was a seemingly practical, commonsensical policy wherever a handful of Europeans tried to rule masses of natives in Africa, though the British wrote so incessantly about it that one might wrongly assume that it was a great political innovation (Kiwanuka 1970:300–301; Mamdani 1996:49–50; P. Mitchell 1935:xi–xii). Scipio remarks: "A senior British official once described Indirect Rule to me as 'born of nothing else than the dictates of common sense and the local situation and the parsimony of the British Treasury, combined with the British Government's lack of interest in running and paying for an Empire'" (1965:32). One of the main reasons that Indirect Rule was promoted was that it was cheap (Padmore 1969a:315; Gailey 1974:69; Dumbuya 1995:28).

I write extensively about Indirect Rule because arguments defending and criticizing it reveal the values and rationalizations underlying how British thought and felt about colonial rule. In some ways the debates about Indirect Rule reveal the very worst about the humbug and arrogance in the defense of colonial policies.

A phrase repeatedly associated with Lugard's and others' writings about Indirect Rule is "The Dual Mandate." This reflects the assumption that the colonialists governed for two reasons: to preserve and run the British Empire for the glory of the home country, and to provide order, security, and development for the supposedly backward natives. The term "mandate" referred to the belief that the British had a divine right or mandate to that empire, a responsibility or White Man's Burden to civilize non-Europeans (Lugard 1970a:88–102). Unimpressed, Crocker describes the Dual Mandate as a moralistic cover-up for a failed system of domination (1970:113–116). Ironically, the conservative and paternalistic Lugard later served on the League of Nations Mandate Commission that helped supervise British rule in Tanganyika after it was mandated from Germany to Britain. That commission supported the tribalistic policy of Indirect Rule (Dumbuya 1995:141). Lugard's disciple Cameron described Indirect Rule as a "guardianship" (Adewoye 1970:43). For many years Lugard was regarded as an imperial icon, an unquestioned authority on African affairs (Gailey 1974:13–14), even though today many of his observations appear simplistic, wrong, arrogant, and racist. Margery Perham consistently praised him as a visionary. Despite today's criticisms, in earlier decades colonial cadets were told to read Lugard's work before going to the field (Allen 1979:41).

Indirect Rule was assumed to create self-respect among the conquered natives; it allowed the British to feel generous and virtuous for letting subjugated peoples seem to hold some authority over themselves (Tidrick 1990:311–312). Colonialists claimed that Indirect Rule gave local Africans a sense of security (Brown and Hutt 1935:192–193); it fostered British district officers' sentimental view of themselves as helpful teachers and masters (R. Brown, 1959:51). Indirect Rule was also seen as a teaching process where, under the tutelage of the British, untrained Africans could learn to rule in a proper way, viz., a way in keeping with British moral values (Mair 1938:150; Perham 1967c:92, 106). Besides the obvious fact that the British were too few to supervise Africans closely, they needed the help of local people who knew the details of local life, who knew where people lived, to whom they were related, and their positions in local society. Only lifetime residents could know such matters. Besides gathering taxes, such agents were expected to use the leveling of taxes as well as fines and punishments in order to drive local Africans into colonial labor markets and the cash economy (Anne Phillips 1989:11); Labour Research Department 1926:10; Mamdani 1996:52). Rodney maintains that Indirect Rule simply relegated the British dirty work to African chiefs (1982:12–15); his view was held by others (McCarthy 1979:10; Bienen 1967:35; Collins 1970:84; Berman 1996:3–4, 53). It was an "ideology of mediated hegemony" perpetuating British domination (Young 1988:48). It was profoundly contradictory in assuming that rural traditional African society would be stable and yet so-called traditional African leaders would or could help modernize it (Berman 1996:276).

"Tribe" was the key concept underlying this system. It was assumed that Africans belonged to myriad ethnic communities, each unique and requiring its own special rules and rulers. This divide and rule policy inevitably supported traditional, unprogressive policies and inhibited ways such groups could be integrated into a nation-state where citizens held common rights and values. Each ethnic group had its own customs and courts conducted around the language and traditions of that group. Accordingly, native courts became the bedrock of Indirect Rule (Chanock 1985:9). It was through these courts that ordinary Africans could be drawn into the new system under the guise of the old.

Indirect Rule expressed a basic cultural gulf between the ruling British at the apex of the system and the Africans below (Crowder 1978:118–119). While the language of Indirect Rule suggests partnership, careful examination of the system reveals that the British could and did dictate what these local African agents could do. Yet there was considerable room for manipulation on the part of Africans. This was because many British remained ignorant about what actually took place at the grassroots. Consequently, the medial African agents could play off the ruling British and subject natives against each other so that they, the local chiefs and headmen, could gain some influence and power. African chiefs could blame the British for tough laws and taxes even as they used those laws and taxes to extort wealth and favors from their subjects. In turn, chiefs could blame their African subjects when British policies were not effectively carried out. All this subterfuge depended on the linguistic, cultural, and spatial gulf separating the two groups.

Indirect Rule was defended with very muddled arguments reflecting a poor grasp of what Africans were really like. In her rosy picture of the raj in Africa, Perham implausibly asserts that the British only advised African chiefs but rarely interfered with them, presumably influencing them only by hints or setting an example of rectitude sure to inspire emulation (1931:303). In a ludicrously ignorant characterization of African behavior, Perham refers to "that happy and mysterious manner which is the secret of the Bantu, by which without recourse to voting unanimity is attained" (ibid.). Elsewhere she describes the often newly created African courts as "immemorial" and claims that imposing an alternative direct rule would treat Africans as mere marionettes (1967a:15–16), in contrast to Indirect Rule, which was supposedly based on a deep appreciation of local traditions in which Africans would eagerly take part (1967a:26). She does admit that many laws promulgated by African Native Authorities were thought up by the British (ibid.:106).

Perham claims that Indirect Rule actually promoted appropriate modernization: "Once the familiar forms have been restored, the people are free and . . . encouraged to develop and adjust them" (1970:148; Robinson 1950:12–15). She seems unaware of the illogicality of her assertion: why did the "traditional" forms have to be restored unless changing conditions had already led to their being abandoned, if indeed they had even existed earlier? Conservative defenders of Indirect Rule doggedly stuck to their claims that Indirect Rule "took advantage" of social evolutionary processes by drawing on indigenous practices as a starting point (African Studies Branch, Colonial Office 1951:5). Such claims displayed outrageous ignorance of African life, claiming that "Bantu tribal peoples are essentially democrats" (ibid.:8–9). In reality, African traditions were embedded with hierarchies of kinship, ageism, and sexism and promoted considerable coercion. Some Africans sought to escape them when opportunities to migrate to towns were available.

Some armchair experts went so far as to maintain that "the normal peasant wants justice and rain, rather than a say in running his own affairs" (ibid.:21). In short, Indirect Rule was based on a mass of British stereotypes about what African societies, cultures, and persons were supposedly like. Such notions were used to legitimize a dubious local Native Authority administration, but these also permeated all other levels and sectors of a colony, affecting the thinking of colonizers and colonized alike (Chachage 1988:203–215) from British stereotypes of African backwardness and traditionalism to African commitment to a new tribal chauvinism. Some Africans began to take up some of this ethnic and conservative ethos in order to stir up tribal solidarity against neighbors or to construct a supposed African identity opposed to colonial interests (Iliffe 1979:324). In fact, some Africans took the new Christianity, money economy, and modern petty bureaucracy to exploit their fellows.

Almost to the very end of colonial rule, Perham, Cameron, and their followers stubbornly defended Indirect Rule (Crocker 1970:86–89). Perham singled out southeastern Tanganyika as an example of the success of Indirect Rule (1931:308–309), an area Liebenow later described as a huge failure in African government (1971:98–150). Liebenow actually made similar gloomy judgments for other areas of Tanganyika as well (1956a, 1956b).

Did Indirect Rule Work? Its Critics

There were strong criticisms of Indirect Rule from the time Lugard's policies were first formally enshrined in the Colonial Office after he had supposedly demonstrated their value in Nigeria. For example, Charles Temple vehemently opposed Indirect Rule and had far more grassroots knowledge about rule in Africa than did Lugard (Tidrick 1990:201). Temple's criticisms seem especially pertinent, because his judgments are based on his long experience in the emirates of northern Nigeria, areas sometimes claimed to be good examples of successful Native Authorities. In fact, these emirates were steeped in autocracy, corruption, and strong resistance to modern education, liberal social policies, and political change, all processes essential for a successful modern African state, the purported eventual goal of British colonial rule (Gailey 1974:19–20). Fage goes so far as to term Indirect Rule "a philosophic justification of non-action" (1967:699). Present-day life in northern Nigeria is not very appealing to much of the world. Donald Cameron, the first British colonial governor of Tanganyika, generally credited with introducing Indirect Rule to the territory, was earlier an administrator in

Nigeria. There he was especially critical of the Hausa emirates and even some Yoruba rulers. Cameron described Indirect Rule there as impeding modernization and harming the welfare of local Africans (Crowder 1968:200–201, 221). When he introduced Indirect Rule in Tanganyika he sought to avoid such abuses.

Indirect Rule was supposedly based on traditional forms of authority and customs held in African societies. Yet most of the evidence we have indicates that the British who supervised local African affairs had a poor grasp of what Africans either thought or wanted to do (Fields 1985; Gailey 1974:19–21; Achebe 1975:5–6). Tribal groups were assumed to be the building blocks of this new system. Ironically, Indirect Rule probably created more cohesive tribes and a greater sense of ethnic particularism than existed before colonialism (J. Willis 1993:53; Pels and Salemink 1999:2; Tagart 1931:63–68). Colonial administrators' reliance on "tribes" may have created more divisions between African peoples than would have otherwise occurred (C. White 1959). Obviously, none of these features of Indirect Rule fostered the nation-building that the British sometimes claimed they would achieve. It is true that Indirect Rule saved the British money, making use of untrained Africans and paying out little to improve local infrastructures (Pakenham 1985:226). Indirect Rule was based on the "immutable poverty" of the areas where it flourished (Crocker 1970:117); that made short-sighted political sense. It neither met the British claims for social betterment nor did it advance long-term plans for socioeconomic development that might have been to the self-interest of British business.

At the heart of Indirect Rule, at least in terms of the activities of the Africans who served in a Native Authority, were the courts that brought home a sense of order and rule to local Africans. Alexander, a high-court justice in Tanganyika, thought such local courts "barbarously irrational and prejudiced" (G. Alexander 1936:265). For them to work at all required a huge outlay of attention by already over-burdened British district officers (ibid.:203–204). For officials such as Judge Alexander, accustomed to protective divisions in governmental authority, it was disturbing that local African chiefs in Native Authority courts were legislators, judges, and executors of custom and law, all in one (ibid.:206), Surprisingly, Alexander did not seem to recognize that such conflation of duties also characterized British district officers as well.

The cornerstones of Indirect Rule were local Native Authorities, organized around a chief and often subchiefs, headmen, and other agents. When a British administrator first arrived, he asked to see the chief (Austen 1968:155); and where no such chiefs and other leaders traditionally existed, these were created. Where they did exist, they were modified in various ways. Powers to use torture and enslavement were denied. Powers such as the death penalty and long imprisonment were considered too serious to be entrusted to local Africans and were reserved for the British who oversaw such African rulers. Yet in other ways, the powers of chiefs were sometimes enhanced. For example, chiefs could not be removed or punished by their African subjects, as sometimes was possible in the past; only their British masters could do that. Furthermore, chiefs were given powers to enforce rules that were often alien to the traditional community, though enforcing such rules was sometimes circumvented by clever chiefs (Austen 1968:200).

In some cases, chiefs arbitrarily interpreted such rules so as to reward and punish local friends and enemies, though obviously that was not what the British had envisioned. Chiefly abuses were not easily criticized or opposed by local Africans. Consequently, chiefs often embraced and abused these political advantages (Chanock 1985:33; Berman 1996:209–210). This was also true of many government clerks, police, and messengers employed by chiefs (G. Alexander 1936:20). The degree to which such corruption and abuse were likely varied greatly from one Native Authority to another (Mackenzie 1954:124–125). In some cases chiefs newly empowered with new rules and agents used their advantages to carry out old rivalries and feuds with fellow tribesmen (Tidrick 1990:554–557). Chiefs were especially effective where they could recruit kinsmen and cronies to share such advantages not available to those unlucky enough to have been passed over when the British selected leaders (Liebenow 1971:98–100). As Chinua Achebe remarks, Indirect Rule made "a dozen mushroom kings grow where there was none before" (1964:70). At its worst, British saw local misrule as an acceptable price for order and peace (Redmond 1971:602). In other cases, Native Authorities were optimistically portrayed in platitudinous terms; their mere appearance as embodied in the titles, written procedures, and formal reports conveyed a facade of local administrative success (when supported by optimistic reports submitted to those above). Consequently, local British administrators made little effort to look beneath the social surface (e.g., Malcolm 1953).

Given such abuses, many Africans felt helpless under local corrupt chiefs (Tidrick 1990:351–353; Tagart 1931:709–774; Mair 1936:305–312; 1958:12–16; Cooper 1997). Mamdani calls such Native Authorities "decentralized despotism" (1996:48). Even conservative colonialists writers such as Fosbrooke admitted that Native Authority chiefs were generally corrupt (1959b:174). A more radical critic, Padmore, termed Indirect Rule "tyrannical" (1969a:317) and "colonial fascism" (ibid.:332). How could it be otherwise when such a system provided no easy means for local Africans to express public opinion and oppositions (Brown and Hutt 1935:193–194)? Such flaws in this supposedly practical and useful system were inevitable because most chiefs and headmen were poorly educated, often far less than the African clerks, technicians, and teachers employed in the Native Authorities. Furthermore, they were poorly paid, thereby encouraging bribery and extortion (Richards 1960:344–376; Gann and Duignan 1967:222–224; Berman 1996:212–213). On account of all these difficulties local British district officers kept ultimate control of the Authority funds and held chiefly power in check against the worst abuses, at least when they were aware of them (Woodroffe 1957:26). With time some Native Authorities grew into rather large bureaucracies, but numbers have never guaranteed competence or efficiency (Furnivall 1956:447).

In many cases the British themselves, especially before World War II, were poorly trained as administrators and therefore ill-suited to supervise Africans (Fieldhouse 1983:43). Scathing judgment has been leveled against Sir Ralph Furse, who oversaw recruitment in the colonial service. For the snobbish Furse, there were no written rules or tests for selection, but rather informal, subjective interviews to admit "the right kind of people," meaning upper-middle-class public schoolmen with a general arts degree, an interest in team sports, and an aversion to bookish behavior (Tidrick 1990:212–214; Kirk-Greene 2006:39–40; Berman 1996:97–104; Herbert 2002:21; Kirk-Greene 1986b:xii). Before World War II and sometimes even after, recruits to the African colonial administration were chosen for a public school spirit that rated "character" over intelligence or business, technical, and administrative skills (Gifford 1967:358, 369–370). They were "prefects," not specialists. The ideal was to get an "Oxbridge-trained gentleman amateur 'all-rounder'" (Berman 1996:98). Unmarried candidates under 25 were preferred, so men with little experience had to be taught on the job (ibid.:201).

At the core of a Native Authority were the local courts presided over by a chief and his cronies. Despite lip service to tradition, such courts were essentially arenas for the implementation of laws and rules consistent with British orders and opinion and far less embodiments of African tradition (Chanock 1985:61). Local chiefs and elders were pressed to give British administrators the "customary laws" that they thought that the British wanted, promulgating laws so they could keep in favor (ibid.:17). As Killingray notes, Indirect Rule was not so much conceived with traditional African laws as with supporting the colonial structure. As such, Native Authority courts produced "hit or miss" rule (1986:413–415). Many Africans had far less confidence in local courts than was sometimes claimed by the advocates of Indirect Rule (Tanganyika 1957a:1).

Given the poor education and low salaries of chiefs and headmen, it turned out that Indirect Rule produced a weak and demoralized system (Pratt 1982:246–260). Those Africans who sought posts in such a system in order to get ahead were often those least suited for leadership and unemployable at better jobs elsewhere (Barnes 1954:115). Indirect Rule was not, as Perham and Lugard claimed, a great training ground for future African leaders (Gann and Duignan 1967:222–224; Hailey 1950:5–6). Local chiefs were selected as agents for the British and were not usually good representatives of their people toward their colonial masters (Furnivall 1956:47). With so many flaws, Indirect Rule could never be a means for modernization and change (Mair 1936:305–312; Brett 1973:302; Hughes 1969:23–25; Lohrmann 2007:81–94, 269–270). Some even saw it as preventing any change at all (Adewoye 1970:47): "The incorporation of precolonial structures within the colonial state also presumed a parochial focus for African political activity, and facilitated its local containment within the larger structure of the colony. Indeed, one of the principal political objectives of 'indirect rule' was to prevent the political motivation of African peasantry within the context of a trans-ethnic anti-colonial struggle" (Berman 1996:209). Even sympathetic critics conceded that Indirect Rule had been devised by theorists who had seriously underestimated the speed with which Africa would develop economically and politically (Gann and Duignan 1967:575). Even evaluating Indirect Rule by narrow, less theoretical terms suggests that it prevented improvement because it needlessly consumed local resources. What money the British gave back to Native Authorities from the money they collected in local taxes went mainly to pay the growing number of chiefs, headmen, clerks, and other agents and not for development of the local area (Murray 1967:413; McCarthy 1982:7). The Native Authorities received only 25 to 30 percent of the tax money they turned into the colonial administration. British officials recognized this (African Studies Branch, Colonial Office 1951:40–45).

Considering the published criticism of Indirect Rule (and I have cited only some of the literature), we can understand why educated Africans were frustrated and angry about this system (Fieldhouse 1983:34; M. Bates 1957:336). Educated Africans sought to undermine Indirect Rule whenever possible (Padmore 1969a:224) and saw it as an "imperialistic device" (Akpan 1970:147) and not as an attempt to provide Africans with political learning or an authentic voice for their concerns. "It merely favoured, sheltered and strengthened illiterate, conservative, unprogressive and sometimes autocratic chiefs at the expense of younger educated elements" (ibid.:149). Indirect Rule developed a mood of subjection. It led frustrated, educated Africans to move to towns where they could hope for better opportunities (Scipio 1965:33). It demoralized many Africans and bred "a disquieting cynicism" (Crocker 1970:117). Indirect Rule particularly inflamed sentiments against local chiefs. The fact that chiefs were often used by the British as cat's paws against young radical African politicians only made matters worse. Educated African nationalists were especially hostile to chiefs (Murray 1967; Costa 1999:34; Barnes 1954:36). In Tanganyika chiefs were the first officials to lose their jobs with African independence, even while many British were kept on in government service.

Judgments of Indirect Rule

In general, historians have been hard on colonialism, but they have been even harder on Indirect Rule. It was unsuccessful and inconsistent (Brown and Hutt 1935:56) and essentially a mistake (Murray 1967:402–403; Gann and Duignan 1967:223). It led to "cultural mummification" of African tradition in the name of colonial stability (Fanon 1967a:34). It did not work (Tanganyika 1954:4; Spear 2005:71–72; Austen 1968:255–256; Kiwanuka 1970:310; Graham 1976:1). At the end of colonial rule, even Perham, who had done so much to discourage educated Africans from being admitted into the colonial administration (Stephens 1968:36) belatedly asked why the British were so blind to the growing needs involving African national independence. She concluded it was due to Indirect Rule as a "crystallising of tribalism" (1961:114), which led to Africans being ill-prepared to rule (ibid.:115–121). Hughes describes it as "a disaster" (1969:52). Lord Hailey singles out the Native Authorities in Kilosa district, including Ukaguru, as especially unsuccessful (1950:353).

Indirect Rule was more theoretical than useful (Gann and Duignan 1967:225). It was a public policy at odds with social reality. At its heart it was doomed because its proponents were obsessed with law but did not recognize that the "real law" was economic law, which nowhere figured in how British conceived of courts, chiefs, and protocol (Furnivall 1956:277–285). Indirect Rule was a sham because there was no real political separation between the Africans who occupied local government and the British who ran almost everything (ibid.:267). As I earlier noted, Indirect Rule was based on illusion and delusion, but then "colonialism was not a rational or planned condition" (Fieldhouse 1983:417), and the supposed rationality of Indirect Rule hardly addressed how things turned out.

Indirect Rule as a formal doctrine never grew out of local political and social understandings. It was a concept imposed from above, from colonial governors, from the secretariats that governors usually dominated, and ultimately from the Colonial Office in London, which had bought into Lugard's misconceived and reactionary doctrine. Yet it was not those in London but local British District Officers who had the thankless and impossible task of trying to train local underpaid and poorly educated Africans to become leaders who would fit this alien scheme (Lugard 1970b:104–105). It was their honest and tireless efforts that made any of this work at all, however misconceived and confused. Many colonial officers provided more capable and honest supervision, so far as it went, than what was later demonstrated by African officials who took over after national independence (Mair 1977). For better or worse, local Native Authorities were only the tools of the British central administration (Woodroffe 1957:545), so unsurprisingly one critic termed Indirect Rule the cat's paw of British imperialism (Padmore 1969b:113). Indirect Rule produced a double hierarchical bureaucracy, one white, one black, each poorly articulated with the other, so Indirect Rule was doubly cumbersome and inefficient (ibid.:89). Indirect Rule was "applied with particular zeal" in Tanganyika (Young 1994:149), so there is good reason for devoting so much space to it here. The Kaguru case illustrates some of its most unfortunate features.

Yet how representative is the Kaguru case for understanding colonial Indirect Rule in Tanganyika? The Kaguru are a relatively small ethnic group occupying an area that received little attention from the colonial capital in Dar es Salaam. It is, however, an area with a very long history of contact by European and Asian outsiders. The small sizes of the Kaguru population and area made the chiefship easier to comprehend and survey than larger ones. How "typical" then is the Kaguru case? Is the notion of "typical" itself even useful? I cannot honestly answer. I do know that Ukaguru is very different from rich, populous, more modernized chiefships such as those of the Chagga of the Kilimanjaro area or the rich Haya kingdoms on Lake Victoria. It is also very different from the pastoral Maasai to the north of the Kaguru, a people whose vast lands are difficult to traverse and who have resisted modernization. Ukaguru is also far different from the chiefships of large ethnic groups like the Nyamwezi and Sukuma in central Tanganyika, where the large populations and great size of the areas they inhabit make it difficult to determine how coherent these areas and peoples are as units for social study. Finally, all these groups and areas are far different from the Swahili on the coast, whose complex ties over centuries with the Indian Ocean trade and Islam and their constant familiarity with town life have led them to feel apart from up-country peoples. Of course, all of these areas and peoples were subject to colonial Indirect Rule, and all felt the brunt of economic exploitation, missionization, and the demands of national independence and unity that would discourage ethnic (tribal) diversity. If one considers how much these Tanganyikan cases resemble those from other East African nations, such as Kenya, Uganda, Rwanda, and Burundi, then the question of typicality becomes even more difficult.

I cannot give a simple answer to this problem, but I am reminded of a similar problem I faced many decades earlier when I wrote a book on a colonial mission in Ukaguru (1982b). I aimed that book as a pioneering effort in studying the colonial aspects of missionizing at the grassroots. At that time I noted there was no single type of colonial mission but rather many types. I noted too that each mission had its own particular culture, which seemed a variation on a broader kind of mission culture and society. Both I and an earlier writer, the missionary F. B. Welbourn, observed that if one wants to understand broader aspects of a colonial organization and culture, this would best be gained through detailed reportage and analysis of particular cases (ibid.:3–5, 29–30; Welbourn 1961:196). Since missionizing culture is an important variant of colonial culture, it follows that these same arguments might be applied to other colonial institutions, including those of grassroots government. I assume that such detailed case studies will explain and clarify analyses of all colonial institutions everywhere, though always with an eye on pertinent differences.

All this touches on a central Weberian problem in sociological understanding. This notion of types necessarily transcends specific cases. The divergence between type and the realities of particular cases is the most revelatory aspect of the Weberian concept of type. A theoretical type and an actual case illuminate one another to the degree that they both correspond with and diverge from one another. I recall words from my teacher Evans-Pritchard, who repeatedly told me that the only productive method of social analysis was the comparative method, and that was hopeless. I do not recall that he ever put this into print, but he said it often. (Though Evans-Pritchard expressed disdain for Weber whenever I mentioned the great German, Weber would probably have relished the zen-like irony of E-P's assertion.) I also recall another unpublished but frequent remark by Evans-Pritchard that seems appropriate here: the cultural differences between people are more interesting and rewarding to consider than are their common features.

To summarize, I believe the Kaguru case will help us understand how colonialism did and did not work. I do not believe it will always provide answers to many questions from other areas and other peoples in East Africa, much less elsewhere. What would, other than studying each of them? This study will help in that.

Neglected Aspects of Colonial Research

I wind up my discussion of colonialism and Indirect Rule by considering two further issues.

One important aspect of Indirect Rule has been insufficiently analyzed by anthropologists. This involves how Indirect Rule related to social change either positively or negatively in terms of affecting the African as a person. These effects illustrate some of the delusion, contradiction, and hypocrisy concerning that policy, and indeed concerning the colonial venture in general. Furthermore, promoting Indirect Rule had its impact on the personhoods not only of Africans but also of ruling Europeans. This first topic, while recognized as legitimate, has been poorly discussed. The second topic, however obvious, has rarely if ever even been mentioned. In a provocative and insightful essay, Karp remarks on how little attention has been given to analyzing how British colonial administrators had initially characterized Africans when explaining and defending their policies (2002:82–83). Rural areas were seen as orderly because they remained tribal, administered by "traditional" leaders (ibid.:84–85). British administrators thought "hereditary" tribal rulers and rules were best (Dumbuya 1995:123, 239). Yet from the beginning of British rule, these same local African leaders were described as poorly endowed for promoting modernization (ibid.:109), thereby justifying the British holding the real power in determining all important developmental policies in a local area (ibid.:111).

When the British were criticized by outsiders over the slowness of African political development, the British noted that tribal (i.e., not modern) governments had to be maintained to preserve order or even had to be strengthened to undo some of the earlier damage done to these traditional structures by colonialism (ibid.:112). In 1924 an official government white paper described Africans as being "like children" and therefore incapable of administering their own affairs and needing the care of the British to safeguard their interests (quoted in ibid.:131). The British would be assisted in this by African chiefs who were seen as too uneducated and weak to face modern challenges unguided (ibid.:159). In the era before World War II, the plan of the British administration, supported by the League of Nations Commission, was "to develop the native colony along lines that will not westernize him and turn him into a bad imitation of a European . . . our whole education policy is directed to that end . . . the evolution of the native should take place within the framework of his own institutions" (quoted in Dumbuya 1995:140). The British envisioned an African untroubled and therefore peacefully unengaged in radical changes. At about the same time it was thought that introducing voting and other modern Western customs prematurely would actually backfire and produce a "servile race" (ibid.:141). Africans were encouraged to learn their own traditions and practical skills such as elementary writing, knowledge of Swahili, and abilities in farming, carpentry, and simple bookkeeping. The racist Americans consulted to advise the British (invited presumably because the Southern Americans had longer experience dealing with blacks) discouraged higher education and learning English.

The hypocrisy and circular thinking evident in these views of Africans are reflected in Governor Cameron's reply in 1926 to critics asking why Africans were not allowed to represent themselves even in meetings determining territorial policies that directly affected them. "The Native community cannot be directly represented because for the present natives cannot be found with sufficient command of the English language to take part in the debates of the Council, indeed to understand what is being said" (quoted in ibid.:139). By the time Governor Cameron stated this, the British had few years left in which to teach English to literate Swahili speakers. There was no suggestion that translators be provided or that some discussion would be in Swahili. A serious shortage of Africans who could speak and read advanced English continued right up to independence 35 years later.

Africans were not considered capable of governing themselves because they were not educated, and they were not educated because modern education was thought to alienate them from their "tribal" selves and thereby make them hard to govern. Combined with these racist assumptions were conservative Christian ideas that idle hands led to the devil's mischief; Africans were encouraged to learn about lower-level working skills and required to pay taxes so they would seek employment. Some administrators advocated taxes for just such moralistic reasons (McCarthy 1982:10). Yet Africans would have been more usefully productive had they learned higher skills, ones held by Europeans and most Asians. It was difficult, considering all this, to believe that Indirect Rule or missionizing Christianity were aimed at enabling Africans to enter the modern world and govern themselves, even though that was the professed claim used to justify colonial rule and missionary work.

My first recollection of Africans in East Africa related to "tribal" labels. Local whites often described Africans with some ethnic label, even though it was not always accurate. In meeting and talking to Africans, one almost always raised this "tribal" topic. I was often told that a good way to begin any extended conversation with an African was to inquire where she or he was from—in short, what was that person's tribe or ethnicity. Ethnicity turned up on most official documents issued to or about Africans, such as court records, tax receipts, licenses, police files, labor chits. Many (even some Africans) assigned personal characteristics to certain ethnic groups, such traits often being contradictory or odd depending with whom one spoke. For example, British often described Maasai men as noble and brave yet childishly simple in an attractive way (though Kaguru certainly did not think of them so); Chagga were described as hardworking but also as conniving and sometimes impertinent, especially if they were well educated. Haya were often described as grasping and sensual (many were sophisticated because of the coffee trade, and many Haya women were high-level prostitutes in towns and on the railway). None of these labels was particularly accurate or flattering. Yet the idea that tribal tags were so freely used indicates how difficult it was for many whites to think about Africans outside the tribal rubric. It was a rare European who saw Africans as part of a single nation of people, and British ideas about what Africans should want often conveniently subscribed to such limiting local and ethnic labels (see, for Kenya, Berman 1996:206).

Karp points out how colonial bureaucrats often judged their success by the degree to which they provided modern, foreign "improvements" such as hospitals, schools, roads, bridges, and markets. Such development may have been well meant, but few considered carefully how such changes affected Africans, much less what changes Africans themselves thought they needed most. Change was imposed from above (Karp 2002:84–85). The British worried about whether Africans in their charge were becoming overly ambitious and discontented, whether Africans actually needed some of the material goods they most clamored to have.

A good colonial administrator was judged to have a record of governing a people who were peaceable and paid their taxes. Yet presumably the more money Africans might make, the more they would contribute to taxes and a better local economy, even though such changes related to new aspirations and demands.

If few administrators asked African men what they wanted, then no administrator ever asked women what they wanted. Throughout the colonial enterprise in Tanganyika, women were very rarely mentioned as having needs or priorities at all. Administrative records were astoundingly silent with regard to women in every sense. Women were viewed as extensions of men. In this sense, the British administrators appeared implicitly to be even more sexist than local African men, and that was sexist indeed. If British administrators in Ukaguru had a simplistic and often derogatory view of African men, they had no well-considered view of African women at all. In records and administrative memoirs, I found the neglect of African women as significant persons in the official system to be stunning. Women's most significant appearance was in court cases, and then one needed to know a lot about Kaguru society to figure out what was going on. (Women's only other significant appearance in records was in medical reports regarding pre- and postnatal care, and I confess that I did not pursue that avenue of investigation other than to attend a few sessions at local Kaguru mission and Native Authority clinics.)

One could conclude that British administrators saw success and approval contradictorily. They were uneasy about many changes among Africans where material goods had been introduced. British wanted material changes, but they also wanted social order. They wanted Africans to be peaceful, rural tribalists, but they claimed that they wanted Africans to be more progressive and modern in their thoughts and aims. How could both occur?

British administrators in Ukaguru agreed that Africans needed to change, but contradictorily they viewed almost all change with suspicion and uneasiness. Administrators' views of Kaguru were tied to a view of them as rural, tribal persons. Kaguru were rarely seen resembling townspeople, and indeed few Kaguru moved to towns. That, however, was more due to the poor educational system in the chiefdom than due to lack of ambition. Whenever I spoke with local administrators about

Kaguru, I encountered the stereotype of a rural "peasant." Unfortunately, that was surprisingly accurate, but I was surprised that no one ever thought to question why Kaguru did not ask for and want more. Of course, they did want more, and in a later chapter we shall see how such demands were successful only when they were expressed in a "tribalistic" mode. That was the ideal stereotype of an African living under Indirect Rule (see Berman 1996:73–127).

I do not much discuss town life and townspeople in this study. In the area where I worked, Africans in the two local small towns and in the huge sisal estates that dominated the district's local economy were seen as a potential source of difficulty requiring constant attention to maintain order. When I mentioned this to the local district labor officer, he referred to the fact that colonial administrators were concerned with the peace and order of masses of Africans who fit no visible tribal stereotypes. These were a population almost entirely male, with no visible families, Africans without farms or villages. I did not ask administrators how they pictured these African persons, but administrators pointed out that my exposure to rural Kaguru was vastly different from anything I would experience on the sisal estates. I am sure they were right. All such Africans (migrants, townspeople, estate workers) represented a troublesome picture of an African person, the product of radical social change. These were persons hard to fit into the stereotypes British administrators had of what Africans were or wanted to be. My own field experience left me ill fitted to form any views on such matters, though on subsequent visits to East Africa, I spent many weeks living in African housing in the African section of Kilosa and in Dar es Salaam. Whatever these other Africans were, they were not the rural, tribal, settled African persons that were the favorite picture administrators held of Africans in Ukaguru, Kilosa district or most of Tanganyika. The ethos of British colonial rule was deeply hostile to the kind of African who lived in towns (Berman 1996:63).

I have not yet mentioned the picture the British had of themselves, though I discuss this in chapter 6. I do want to note here that few if any of the British administrators in Tanganyika had a realistic view of how they had changed since they had taken up their work in East Africa. I found those who had recently come out in the last year or two very much like any British I might have met back in Britain. In contrast,

I found those who had spent ten or twenty years in the colonial service very different from any people I had ever met. Even though they repeatedly went home for several months every few years, their views of everything from work, money, and relaxation to ideas about race, retirement, and social class were different from those of anyone I had met since I had lived in England. Even before I went to East Africa, British in England told me this would be so. I mention this to remind the reader that when I write that the British had ideas about what African persons were like, and that these ideas formed a set of stereotypes, they had almost no conception of their own personhood other than the assumption that it was like that of others they had left at home. This was odd, because their arguments about their values and character reflected more on what they had left behind than on how they were expected to think and act in the colonial service, especially if they resided up-country, removed from any large body of other whites and any European infrastructure. They had illusions, even delusions, about how they would fit in and manage in the society they had left behind. They saw themselves as representative of that society, but in many ways this was not entirely so. Problems of contradiction and conflict in personhood involved more than the Africans; they involved everyone in the colonial endeavor.

In this last section I have dwelled on the Kaguru and Kilosa district material rather than on more general information as I did previously. That is because I found it difficult to secure detailed materials touching on how British colonialists regarded the African person or even themselves. One must wonder why so few detailed accounts have been published about how colonial rule worked at the grassroots level in Africa. There are several reasons, but the most obvious is that such studies would not have been allowed. Few ruling groups like being studied; such study might demystify and undermine those in power. Only since the end of colonialism have some colonial administrators been interviewed, though little of value has come of this, at least regarding Tanganyika. In contrast, ethnographic study of subjected native peoples was sometimes encouraged by European rulers with the argument that such anthropological knowledge might provide better means of controlling Africans. After World War II, the Tanganyikan colonial government employed one or more government anthropologists who were assigned to collect

information about Africans on certain projects. The level of their expertise varied. The three that I know were Hans Cory [Koritschoner], Philip
Gulliver, and Henry Fosbrooke. Only Gulliver was a fully trained British
social anthropologist; he later became a well-known university professor elsewhere. All worked on projects assigned to them by the territorial
government, some tied to controversial issues. My impression was that
British administrators did not find most anthropologists' work helpful.
Some British administrators, including one at Kilosa, tried to collect
ethnographic information, though what I read was mainly connected to
problems of determining the possible legitimacy of the Native Authority
chiefs and the ways they could be selected.

A second reason studies of grassroots colonial administration in
Tanganyika were unlikely was that during the colonial era few British
social anthropologists received encouragement to study complex social
organization, such as bureaucracies. When I was a graduate student
in Britain (1960–61), and then later in 1963 after I graduated, I met few
British anthropologists interested in Weber or other European, much
less American, sociologists. Yet Berman rightly states, "The inescapable
focus of any study of the colonial state" is "a bureaucratic apparatus for
the domination and exploitation of the subject population" (1996:32–33;
see also his chapter "The Bureaucratic Dialectic":75–127). For British
anthropologists of the post–World War II era, Marx might have been
allowable and, of course, the French School, which was essentially too
normative and reactionary to provide critical insights into something
like colonial administration and related institutions. Even if they had
been interested in studying their fellow British in Africa (and most
were not), anthropologists would have been ill-trained to do so. Later,
when some ventured into studying life in African towns, the mines,
and other issues, they drew back once they reached the whites—even
though the latter were an integral part of how these systems worked.
The most adventurous social anthropologists and sociologists who approached such work were often not British but outsider Jewish scholars
who had come to Britain from South Africa, or Americans who had
studied in Britain. They were often considered worrisome outsiders and
viewed with considerable unease by both British colonialists and the
anthropological establishment, especially political reactionaries such
as Evans-Pritchard (see Goody 1995:42–57).[2] Given this social-cultural

atmosphere in the colonial era, we should not expect any serious anthropological account of how colonial rule worked.

Colonialism and colonial rule must be recognized as diverse (Cooper and Stoler 1989:699), even within Tanganyika, yet the characteristics I noted seem pervasive. Whatever its form, colonial rule was always inherently unstable, its days ever more precarious and conflicted, its legitimacy and usefulness ever more debated the longer colonialism existed (Fieldhouse 1983:49).

PART ONE

History

ONE

Kaguru and Colonial History:
The Rise and Fall of Indirect Rule

Ukaguru has a special colonial history in that it embodies a number of firsts.[1] Ukaguru is the site of some of the earliest European settlements in mainland Tanzania and is where the first white child was born on the mainland. These settlements involved Church Missionary Society people (CMS), who founded one of the earliest missions in East Africa in Ukaguru. This mission station was founded because it lay on the caravan route that the missionaries took to reach their main goal for conversion, the great African kingdoms far to the west in what is now Uganda. For similar reasons Ukaguru was the site of the first major Arab inland fort set up to protect the caravan trade going westward. Obviously the early precolonial history of Ukaguru was above all determined by the caravan trade. During the era of the great East African caravans in the second half of the nineteenth century, Ukaguru lay along what became the main central route for those setting out from the ports of Zanzibar, Bagamoyo, and Sadani to the great and rich, populous areas around the distant great inland lakes. Most famous early European travelers inland passed through Ukaguru—Stanley, Burton, Speke, and many others. Stanley described the Kaguru as amiable, at least where they had not been frequently raided by Arabs or by other Africans, and provided one of the best accounts of the Kaguru's early appearance (1872:247–249). Misleadingly, the early CMS missionary Roger Price wrote home in 1877 to his supervisors: "If there is anywhere a country so near the equator as this where Europeans can live and enjoy health—this must be it" (quoted in A. Smith 1955:8). The frequent deaths of early missionaries to this area proved him wrong. Early travelers' accounts dwelled on how green and beautiful the Kaguru mountain area was. Stanley called it "picturesque and sublime," comparing it to the Alleghanies (1879, I:91). None of these visitors except the missionaries stayed, so that there are few early accounts of any true sociological value.

The early caravan trade is the key to understanding how Kaguru eventually emerged as a seemingly solidary ethnic group and how Ukaguru took on the form of a chiefdom. From the start of the caravan trade, large groups of outsiders passed through Ukaguru seeking supplies and shelter. In doing so they asked local natives to take them to their leaders, who could guarantee strangers safety and provide supplies. The opportunistic men who stepped forward as leaders were the forerunners in the process by which outsiders found local Africans willing to organize Kaguru to cater to the needs of alien exploitation. These early Kaguru leaders often claimed to have more influence and to rule larger areas than they actually possessed. Consequently, a brief account of that caravan trade and the social processes it generated is the best place to begin my account of how Ukaguru became a chiefdom in a system of colonial rule. Ironically, the ideas of Kaguru as a united people and of Ukaguru as a well-defined country owe their meaning and being far more to colonial contact than to any earlier African traditions that prevailed before the Arabs, Germans, and British arrived. This is what Justin Willis terms "the comic spectacle of the invention of tradition" (2002:135).

Ukaguru, the Caravan Trade, and the Germans' Arrival

Caravans going west across what is now Tanzania were organized on the island of Zanzibar, the place where large European ships docked and the trading center of the region. Once a caravan was formed, a difficult process that often took many weeks, it was put on small boats and sent west to the nearby mainland ports of Bagamoyo or Sadani. From there it was about 130 miles west to the borders of Ukaguru. As a caravan got within sight of the impressive mountains of central Ukaguru, it took one of two routes. A southern route went through the Mukondokwa River Valley, passing by a hill where the Germans later built their fort and headquarters in what would become Kilosa town, later the capital of the local colonial administrative district. This route passed though a thinly populated borderland between Ukaguru to the north and Usagara to the south. The Mukondokwa Valley stretches northwest from Kilosa until it ends in the hills at Mpwapwa in western Ukaguru, which was the last major watering place and source of food supplies before caravans crossed the Marenga Mkali, a dry and treacherous area of Ugogo where they had few chances of securing food or water and where they were likely to be attacked by Gogo and other hostile people. Mpwapwa lies on the western borders of Ukaguru, and while it is mainly inhabited by Kaguru there are many Gogo influences. The alternate northern route was through mountainous central Ukaguru with major stops at Mamboya, and then west to Geiro before moving into drier western Ukaguru at Pandimbili or Mlali, and then on to the hostile Marenga Mkali. This was a more difficult but shorter route winding through valleys and passes between high peaks and hills. Sometimes caravans detoured southwestward after leaving the central Kaguru highlands and stopped at Mpwapwa on account of its better supplies and safer quarters, especially after the Germans built a fort there. Mpwapwa lies about thirty miles southwest of the Kaguru trading settlement of Geiro and about sixty miles northwest of Kilosa.

Both these routes passed through a corridor region of relative safety lying between the warlike Maasai to the north and the warlike Hehe to the south. At the height of the caravan trade the northern route through central Ukaguru was vulnerable to raids by the Maasai and the related Baraguyu as well as local Kamba. The southern route was also sometimes raided by Baraguyu but more often by Hehe. All of these peoples, Baraguyu, Maasai, Hehe, and local Kamba had periodically raided Kaguru for livestock and foodstuffs. Yet Kaguru and Ngulu (the Kaguru's eastern neighbors) also raided caravans, sometimes allied with Baraguyu and Kamba.[2] As a result of all this raiding many Kaguru had retreated to the more mountainous parts of their area where they could better defend themselves. Many Kaguru also fled from the caravans (Moloney 1893:41–42; Burton 1860, I:168–169, II:261–263; Stanley 1879:247). While some caravans traded with Kaguru for food, others simply raided them for what they needed. Some Arabs and the Nyamwezi involved in the caravan trade sought more stable relations with Kaguru, hoping to set up permanent stations where they might receive supplies and be quartered. To do so they traded firearms and other goods with Kaguru and settled some of their own people, especially Nyamwezi from central Tanzania, along the route to aid in providing supplies. As a result, along these two routes settlements grew up that contained Nyamwezi and even a few coastal Africans and rarely a temporarily settled Arab. These stations were often palisaded and well armed and provided safe havens for some of the caravans passing through. Kaguru at these stations used their added wealth, newly acquired firearms, and the prestige of Arabs and later Europeans allied with them in order to augment their own political influence over their neighbors.[3]

The impact of the caravan trade during this period cannot be overestimated. Schmidt estimated that in 1892 about 80,000 people passed through Mpwapwa alone, coming from or going to the coast (1894:185).[4] The largest caravans sometimes had over a thousand members and were financed by Indians or Arabs in Zanzibar. Most were led by Arabs or coastal Africans. The porters were often Nyamwezi from central Tanganyika. Many smaller bands of traders, usually Nyamwezi, carried goods and messages back and forth along the route. The Nyamwezi were not above local raiding: as late as 1888 Nyamwezi made alliances with Kamba in order to raid and burn Kaguru settlements northeast of Mamboya until Kaguru drove the Kamba from the area (Roscoe 1888a).

Ukaguru was too mountainous and sparsely inhabited to make it attractive for extensive slaving, though eastern lowland settlements such as Mvumi had been burned down by Arab slavers and their Zigua allies. The last serious slaving in Ukaguru took place in the late 1860s, when Hehe repeatedly raided the southern mountain area; men were slain and women, children, and livestock seized, presumably for use in Uhehe and not exported (Last 1883b:584–586). The Kaguru highlands with their regular supply of water and relatively reliable supply of foodstuffs (at least when compared to areas between Ukaguru and the coast and the Marenga Mkali to the west) made Ukaguru the main resting spot and provision center before the next harrowing passage westward. Arabs even encouraged the planting of coastal crops such as fruits, palms, and sugar cane, though the major local crops were sorghum, maize, beans, yams, plantains, groundnuts, castor, tobacco, manioc, and tomatoes (Lambrecht 1903:393–394). Sorghum was the major crop, especially in the west, followed by maize. There was no dependable food surplus. Cultivation was by hoe or, where metal was scarce, by wooden digging stick (ibid.:395). Long before the caravan trade, Kaguru had a flourishing group of ironworkers who sold to their neighbors (Beidelman 1962b). Kaguru say that when they acquired firearms, local smiths were able to repair them and replace parts. Kaguru also sold tobacco, metal goods, beer, and salt to Baraguyu, Kamba, Maasai, and others (Kjekshus 1977a:87–89, 98).

Early written reports on Ukaguru do not convey a picture of a solidary ethnic group. Various writers describe them as Sagara, Gedja, Tumba, Megi, Sika, as well as Kaguru or Kagulu, though even Burton and Meyer who describe Kaguru as such (Meyer 1909:193; Burton 1860, I:168–169) note that they are often grouped with the Sagara.[5] It was Burton who first published the Chikaguru word Wakaguru (the plural form of Mkaguru, a Kaguru person), which means "mountain or hill people."

The earliest reports of Kaguru leadership describe a "sultanate" at Mamboya that forced nearby Kaguru leaders to acknowledge its paramountcy. These reports stress the lack of unity of Kaguru and note there were leaders north and east of Mamboya who claimed to have their own chiefships and rejected the claims of Mamboya (Schynse 1890:68; Last 1878:645; 1883b:585; A. N. Wood 1889b:24–28). Kamba, Nyamwezi, and Zigua had settlements in Ukaguru, and each tried to run village affairs independent of any Kaguru leaders (A.N. Wood 1889b:28).

Kaguru say a chief should display leadership (undewa), and indeed the Kaguru word for chief is mundewa. A leader should command respect or influence (chipeho), have strength (ludole) and ability (udaha), and be a fighter (chitang'ata, warrior). Some say a chief should have medicines (uganga) to combat the ill will of competitors. A chief's enemies may term this his witchcraft (uhai). A chief was entitled to a portion of the people's harvest and to some of their labor by right of his clan owning the land. He was said to have the stool (igoda), that is, to sit in judgment before those standing before him. He sometimes worked with a council (chalo) of elders (A. N. Wood 1890).

The leader of Mamboya who first took full advantage of the caravan trade was named Senyagwa Chimola (senyagwa, eloquent; chimola, forceful one). Dealing with Arabs and Islamicized Nyamwezi, he changed his name to Saidi Chimola, though he remained a pagan. Senyagwa descended from a matrilineal clan that claimed to own the area around Mamboya. The clan was originally called Tangwe (mediation) because they led others by moderating between contending groups. They later changed their name to Jumbe (the Swahili term for a headman or local official). This would make sense if they wanted to claim some sort of leadership that would appeal to the Swahili-speaking Arabs and Nyamwezi (Kilosa District Book; Price 1879a,b).

The Tangwe/Jumbe clan's legendary founder was named Chibawka (clever one, circumcisor, anointer) and was succeeded by his sister's son, Semwali, who in turn was succeeded by another sister's son, Chipala. Chipala's younger matrilineal kinsman was Masingisa (dominator) who became chief of Geiro, another key caravan stop lying eighteen miles west of Mamboya.[6] Masingisa made blood brotherhood (*umbuya*) with the Baraguyu who helped him raid caravans. While Masingisa's mother was a Kaguru of the Jumbe clan, his father was a Baraguyu.[7] One legend says that Senyagwa/Saidi was the younger brother of Masingisa. When Chipala of Mamboya died, he was succeeded by his younger brother, Chibanda, and when Chibanda died he was succeeded by a woman named Madalamengi. Kaguru say that some Kaguru scorned a woman leader (though Kaguru legends tell of women leaders). For this reason, she was deposed and replaced by Masingisa's younger brother Senyagwa/ Saidi Chimola, the first colonial chief of Ukaguru. These different legends are told by elders of the Jumbe clan, though disparaging countertales are told by elders of other, competing clans. The main opposition to the Jumbe clan was from the Gomba clan, who contested Jumbe ownership of both the Mamboya and Geiro areas. The Gomba are also traditional ritual joking relations (*watani*) to the Jumbe and therefore bound to criticize them.[8]

Saidi Chimola sold beer to the caravan porters and built a large palisaded house and beer club. He made friends with the leader of the Nyamwezi porters and traders based at Mamboya (Last 1880:742; Price 1879b). He also welcomed Kamba who served as enforcer-thugs for some of his orders. Even so, in 1888 Kamba and Kaguru raided and burned one another's villages northeast of Mamboya (Roscoe 1888a). When the British Church Missionary Society arrived at Mpwapwa in 1876 and at Mamboya in 1880, they found Senyagwa in charge. Both the missionaries and the Arabs before them considered Senyagwa the chief of the area. The missionaries even gave firearms to Senyagwa. In October 1880, under the advice of British Consul John Kirk, Sultan Bargash of Zanzibar built a fort at Mamboya, manned by two hundred African mercenaries, mostly Zulu, led by a British naval lieutenant, Lloyd Mathews (Lyne 1936:292–294, Last 1883b:541). This fort was established to safeguard the caravans sent out from Zanzibar in ever large numbers. Mathews's troops traveled as far as Ungulu, fifty miles to the northeast of Mamboya, in order to quell caravan raiders (Wissmann 1889:295). Senyagwa clearly thrived; Moloney reports that in 1893 when he passed through Mamboya, he found Senyagwa with ten wives, four sons, and six daughters (1893:41–42). Some claim Senyagwa made blood brotherhood with Sultan Kunambi of Morogoro; at the least he had some kind of political understanding with this more powerful chief (Stuhlmann 1885:223; Schneider 1877:232; Elton 1879:405). Others claim that the Mamboya and Morogoro leaders were joking partners (*watani*; ibid.).

In 1885 Senyagwa was the Kaguru leader who welcomed the notorious German adventurer Carl Peters when he toured the area asking Africans to sign over their allegiance to him.[9] Jumbe clan legends tell of Senyagwa protecting Kaguru from Peters, who was described as a man-eating leopard (a kind of witch). Near Mamboya the Germans tried to force local Kaguru to be porters without pay, and in the ensuing skirmish a Kaguru and a German were shot (Roscoe 1885). Senyagwa summoned eleven Kaguru elders and urged them to submit to Peters. Peters had one of these leaders, an elder from Kitange west of Mamboya, later executed for opposing him. To placate Peters, Senyagwa collected twenty cows and thirty goats from his followers. In turn, Peters awarded him with a cap (*kofia*) of office. Peters's purpose was to displace the Zanzibar Arabs from the region, though Senyagwa could hardly have realized this. It was likely Senyagwa saw Peters as yet another alien ally who could furnish him with goods in turn for protection and supplies. Peters's group built a small fort at Mpwapwa in 1887, but avoided contact with the Arab fort at Mamboya, presumably out of fear of Mathews's garrison.[10] Senyagwa had provided Kaguru to help the Germans rebuild the Mpwapwa fort and was paid in cloth, beads, guns, and ammunition (Last 1880:742; Falkenhorst 1890:47; Koponen 1995:115).

Senyagwa Chimola's ambitions were aided and challenged by the three different kinds of foreigners: Muslim Arabs, British Christian missionaries, and the Germans. The most familiar and easily understood were the Arabs, whose main aim was trade. Senyagwa found them useful allies who promoted his power. Besides, the Arabs all spoke Swahili and therefore easily communicated with at least some local Africans. Yet most Kaguru were hostile to Islam because they associated it with slavery. Ukaguru never became a target for Arab slaving, but the Kaguru's neighbors to the east, the Ngulu and Zigua, had converted to Islam in large numbers and obtained arms from Arabs, and earlier had raided Kaguru for slaves and livestock.

The British missionaries first reached Ukaguru in 1876 and established a station at Mpwapwa in 1878. Later, in 1880, they set up a station in central Ukaguru in Mamboya. Yet they had little success converting Kaguru during their first ten years in the area; their initial impact was economic and political.[11] They brought in cloth, beads, metal-goods, and even firearms to exchange for the labor they needed. They introduced European-style buildings and flew the British flag. During the unstable period before formal colonial rule, many Kaguru saw the British flag as symbolic protection against local abuses by Arabs and African caravaners. This was because the missionaries had firearms and political clout, since the British government had influence with the Zanzibar Arabs. While Kaguru were ignorant of the actual political situation in Zanzibar, they noticed that the British missionaries were unafraid of the Arabs and even, at times, behaved arrogantly toward them. They also saw that the Arabs were wary of offending the missionaries, despite the missionaries' difficult behavior. The missionaries repeatedly reported back to British Consul Kirk in Zanzibar when any local abuses occurred from Arab caravans (Baxter 1879:534; Rees 1900). The missionaries were even able to interfere at times with the slave caravans, and today a number of "Kaguru" in the Mamboya and Berega areas descend from alien slaves whom the missionaries took from the Arabs. In revenge the Arabs told the Kaguru that the missionaries were cannibals who ate the fugitive slaves whom they sheltered (Rees 1902).

When the Germans arrived, the British missionaries tried to make it clear to Kaguru that they were not related to the Germans (Price 1888). The Germans were the most volatile, arrogant, aggressive, and difficult of the foreigners. Their activities disrupted the economic and political arrangements carefully built up by the Arabs. Peters himself seems to have been a sociopath whose brutal and unpredictable behavior caused trouble wherever he went.[12] Those adventurers he brought with him were little better. For example, when an African speared a Swahili working for the Germans near Mpwapwa, the Germans shot the African and then burned his body in public, an act sure to horrify local Africans (Pruen 1888). The Germans were interested solely in quick profits and showed little political sense (Gwassa 1969:92–95). After Peters's disruptive visit, the Nyamwezi traders at the Ukaguru caravan stations became increasingly unruly (Last 1883a:293; Wood 1888). At this time, 1888, the Sultan of Zanzibar was forced (under pressure from the British) to grant trading rights in the area to Peters's private company. These growing disruptions in old trade and political arrangements led in this same year to a widespread Arab rebellion, which began east of Ukaguru but which eventually spread to Mamboya and Mpwapwa (Kieran 1970:169; Müller 1959:234–237, 269; W. Smith 1978:97). Throughout this time Kaguru increasingly viewed the British missionaries as more dependable allies than the Arabs or Germans.

All through the nineteenth century firearms trickled into East Africa, including Ukaguru. First there were muzzle-loader muskets, then breech-loaders, and finally repeater rifles. The technology of firearms developed rapidly during this period, and as each type of weapon was superannuated, Arabs and later Europeans took up the new and better form and sometimes sold the older models to Africans. Sometimes old and damaged weapons were even abandoned by caravans. Some German administrators illegally sold weapons to Africans. Charles Stokes, an Irishman thrown out of the Church Missionary Society for marrying a Nyamwezi, became an ivory trader and gunrunner with important affinal ties with the African traders and porters based at Mamboya (Beachey 1962:450; Kjekshus 1977a:144–145). The number of firearms increased steadily in Ukaguru (Last 1880, 1883a:25).[13] Eventually Germans began to realize the dangers of this and tried to suppress the arms trade. This was in large part due to their alarm at a nearly successful rebellion of coastal Africans led by an Arab, Bushiri, in 1888–89.

News of this unrest led to the recall of Mathews's Zanzibari troops at Mamboya on December 26, 1888, since the Arabs needed them to fight Bushiri on the coast (Roscoe 1888b). Bushiri was defeated by Zanzibar and some Germans, but only after he had destroyed much that the Germans had established on the central caravan route. Having been defeated near the coast, Bushiri and some of his men fled westward to

Mamboya and then to Mpwapwa. The Kaguru did not join him, but his main goal was not to recruit Kaguru but to seize more arms and to kill Europeans in the area. Bushiri burned the Mamboya Christian mission and the Arab fort, and then moved on to try to storm the German fort that Peters had established at Mpwapwa. The missionaries at Mamboya and Mpwapwa hid in the bush with the help of the Kaguru.[14] A Scandinavian who worked for the Germans at the fort at Mpwapwa was killed, and the sole German fled ignominiously to the coast, but the African mercenaries employed by the Germans held the damaged fort. During the unrest local Africans sought to profit; Chief Waziri of the Sagara burned Kaguru villages south of Mamboya and took some Kaguru as slaves (Müller 1959:237). After failing to take Mpwapwa, Bushiri retreated and was eventually captured near the coast and hanged. The German economic adventure and British mission work in Ukaguru had been seriously set back, and the Mpwapwa fort was soon abandoned and allowed to fall apart.

The German public was shocked by these events, and a small German force, headed by Hermann von Wissmann and made up mostly of African mercenaries, was sent in to restore order.[15] The region was officially declared the colony of German East Africa in 1891. Wissmann toured much of Ukaguru. He passed through Mamboya; there he was greeted by Senyagwa Chimola, who brought him livestock, flour, and maize much as he had done earlier for Peters. Wissmann moved on to Mpwapwa, where he rebuilt the fort. He asked a local Arab trader to secure Africans to work, and when none showed up, he shot three Arabs and hung their bodies up for public display (A. N. Wood 1889a). Six hundred Kaguru were conscripted to rebuild the fort. Wissmann left it manned by a German officer, three German NCOs, a trained Swahili soldier, and 75 Zulu and 15 Sudanese mercenaries (Admiralty 1916:32, 35–36; Price 1890; Behr 1891:100, 205, 207; Schmidt 1892:185).[16]

Following Wissmann's instructions, the Germans at Mpwapwa sought to intimidate local Africans so that no future rebellions would occur. They repeatedly allowed troops to invade Kaguru villages, beating people and seizing livestock and goods. They are said to have hanged a few uncooperative Kaguru as examples (see Stoecker 1977:105–106). In 1890 and again from 1895 to 1897 they made raids into outlying areas of Ukaguru and Ungulu to burn villages and subdue potential restlessness

(Briggs 1918:32; Price 1888, 1890, 1891; Stoecker 1977:102–106; Koponen 1995:101; Langheld 1909:39).[17] The notoriously cruel and ruthless German officer Tom von Prince described touring Ukaguru to intimidate the local people, whom he considered somewhat timid. He remarked on how a show of troops, a few corpses hung for display, and some burned houses and seized livestock quickly made Kaguru behave (1911:117–119). These were hard times, especially 1894, 1895, and 1896 because these were years of famine for Ukaguru, and even more so for people in the drier areas to the north and west (Baxter 1894; Cole 1895, 1896; Rees 1902). No wonder Kaguru resisted handing over food supplies to the German fort. By now the area was unquestionably going to be controlled by the Germans, and quick-witted, opportunistic Kaguru realized this. It was now also clear that Mamboya, and indeed all of central Ukaguru, would no longer be so important economically. Central Ukaguru was being displaced by Mpwapwa and even more by Kilosa and other areas further south along what would become the new German-built railroad (Schmidt 1892:130, 180). Central Ukaguru was destined to become a backwater, contradicting Roger Price's earlier 1877 enthusiasm for the area as an ideal spot for European settlement (E. Smith 1955:8), or Meyer, describing it as a "sanitorium" of "indescribable fertility" (1909, I:19).

Courting the Germans as he had earlier courted the Arabs, Senyagwa/Saidi Chimola hung on as purported chief of the Kaguru, yet his position was weakened. Wissmann favored Swahili and disliked Arabs and those known to have associated closely with them. He appointed coastal, Swahilicized Africans as officials in most upcountry areas (Gann and Duignan 1977:74; Beck 1977:8). These appointees were called *akidas*. At the start, Wissmann stationed one at Mpwapwa and another at Mamboya. The akida at Mamboya exerted more influence than Senyagwa, who was presumably kept on mainly because he had useful local connections and because he knew both Swahili and the local language. Senyagwa had a serious disadvantage; he was illiterate, whereas the akidas were chosen because they could read and write Swahili and thereby could receive and send messages to the Germans and make tax, census, and case records. Germans gave instructions to the akidas, who then relayed the orders to local African leaders such as Senyagwa. The introduction of the akidas was a constant source of concern for the missionaries, who equated coastal Swahili culture with Islam. It was now clear to the cleverest Kaguru that proficiency in Swahili would be essential for anyone seeking to gain political power from the Germans and that being able to read and write would be an immense advantage.

Senyagwa did not get on well with the Germans. In 1890 this was because he failed to provide sufficient supplies to the post at Mpwapwa; later it was because he failed to provide Kaguru labor to the German estates for cotton, sisal, and kapok production set up in the lowlands to the southeast (Kilosa District Book). At this time the Germans, who were trying to build roads and work newly established farms, suffered from acute labor shortages, since most Africans had few motives for engaging in steady work. Even those who would be employed were unwilling to work during the seasons of cultivation and harvest. To solve these labor problems Germans put severe pressure on akidas and other African leaders to recruit African laborers forcibly. We can therefore understand why Chief Senyagwa was briefly tied up and displayed in public by the Germans for his alleged uncooperativeness. He was released only after his son and CMS missionaries interceded. After this public humiliation, Senyagwa/Saileni became ill and urged his son to replace him. He died in 1897 and was succeeded by his son Saileni, who was also illiterate.[18] Saileni was of the Mjeja clan and had strong ties to Kaguru in the Berega area (Deekes 1896).

By now British missionary work in Ukaguru had expanded. By 1900 the Church Missionary Society had set up additional stations at Berega (about eight miles north of Mamboya) and at Itumba (Uponela, about six miles to the south). Kaguru who had previously resisted conversion now sought it in large numbers. They saw that those who became literate secured posts in the local German administration or with other European employers. These were new sources of cash and some local power. Besides, literate Africans were too valuable to be wasted on hard labor and would be immune from the resented forcible labor drafts set by the Germans and the akidas. In Ukaguru the only path to literacy was through the local mission schools, and only those committed to conversion were allowed to attend. Many Kaguru closely associated with the mission were usually protected by the missionaries and consequently escaped forced labor calls for porterage and other demands by the Germans and their African henchmen. Kaguru quickly realized that the Germans and the British missionaries were culturally different from one another, and consequently somewhat hostile, so Kaguru often tried to appeal to the missionaries against government interference. The Germans found the British missionaries tiresome but vital to their work, because they promoted education and provided medical facilities. They generally tried to avoid annoying them.

The missionaries still made frequent use of Consul Kirk in Zanzibar and were quick to criticize any alleged German brutality. The Germans in Ukaguru were either rather rough, even brutal planters or noncommissioned army officers, or else they were upper-class military officers. Lower-class German attitudes about social conduct, including drinking, gambling, cursing, sex, and violence, were strikingly different from those of the evangelical Protestant, lower-middle-class British missionaries. Even upper-class German officers, who usually drank and smoked, found little in common with the CMS. These Europeans, British and German, were usually forced to communicate with one another in Swahili since neither group was willing to learn the other's language. Finally, German formal etiquette, as evinced by the upper-class officers, made the missionaries uncomfortable, but then the CMS were never flexible cross-culturally, even with other whites.

German Rule Takes Hold

The main pattern for German colonial rule began with Wissmann; he was briefly military governor but was soon replaced by the civilian Julius von Soden, who set up fourteen districts, each headed by a German district officer (*Bezirksamtmann*) at a headquarters garrison and fort. Even the best of these officers had diminishing influence the further they moved out from this center. District officers made periodic forays, often punitive, into the outlying areas, but poor communications due to lack of adequate roads and lack of personnel drastically limited any official awareness of what actually occurred in the bush, especially since German administrative districts were extremely large and travel very difficult and dangerous (Koponen 1995:116, 202).

Wissmann returned briefly as governor in 1895 and was followed in 1896 by a series of governors of varying degrees of competence and harshness. It is striking that the colony had eight governors during the brief 25 years of German rule, too varied to allow any clear or sustained policies. The Germans were ill prepared and had no consistent ideas about how to run the colony (Beck 1977:57–58; Gann and Duignan 1977:68–71). German officials remained highly dependent upon local African underlings for local information. Most district officers were bound to their headquarters. District officers had between 100 and 200 troops, mostly Africans, hardly enough to be very effective since one could not safely take the full contingent a long way from headquarters and leave it unguarded. German officials lacked the tradition of colonial service that proved so valuable to their British successors. Many German colonial officers had little commitment and confidence in pursuing difficult policies and often did not want to remain long, given their unassured professional futures (Gann and Duignan 1977:88–89). Unlike the British, German officials and military did not see the colonies as a good arena for advancement.

The Germans never described their local rule in terms resembling those used by the British when they described Indirect Rule. Yet the Germans were forced to rule in similar ways, being dependent upon the information and cooperation of local chiefs and outsider Africans (akidas) even more than the British who succeeded them (Iliffe 1968:293–294; Koponen 1995:117, 281, 284; Gann and Duignan 1977:71, 79; Buell 1965, I:448). Over time, the number of akidas seems to have increased, but each akida still had to supervise at least 25 thousand local Africans, so that the two Swahili akidas in central Ukaguru, one in the eastern lowland border area of Mvumi and one in the heartland at Mamboya, had their hands full, especially since they probably could not speak the Kaguru language and during this time many Kaguru knew little or no Swahili (Gailey 1974:xv). Presumably the akida at Mpwapwa was no better off. Obviously the akidas were dependent upon local Kaguru collaborators. The akidas reported to the German headquarters at Mpwapwa and Morogoro, though just before the outbreak of World War I the eastern akida started to report to Kilosa (Kilosa District Book; Koponen 1995:115).[19] By that time, the progressive German officer at Mpwapwa, Sperling, was recruiting literate Kaguru Christians as future akidas and helpers (Iliffe 1969:185–186). The Germans at Kilosa saw their station as a bulwark against the continued threat of raids from the south, mainly fomented by Hehe (Temu 1980:103–104).

The Germans established their various headquarters as military garrisons. In looking at what structures have survived, one is still impressed, even today. When these stations were later staffed by German civilians, many of these were former military men and the prevailing tone of German administration remained martial (Koponen 1995:114; W. Smith 1978:99). Because of poor communications, the district officers were chiefly responsible only to the German governor in distant Dar es Salaam, which allowed them remarkable discretionary powers over huge areas (Austen 1968:83–84; Iliffe 1969:143).[20] This thinness on the ground of German administrators (and their consequent relatively autonomous individual power) can be best appreciated if we remember that even as late as 1914 there were only 48 Europeans of all types in the huge district of which most of Ukaguru was only a small part, and there were only 74 local German government administrators for the entire enormous colony, an area with a few poor roads and over twice the size of France (Meyer 1909, I:81; M. Bates 1957:23).[21] Furthermore, the Germans never had more than three thousand troops in this vast colony of six to seven million people (Iliffe 1968:392). It may be that much of the often-noted brutality and violence of German rule, the frequent floggings and hangings (Gann and Duignan 1977:154), were rooted in German uneasiness at trying to dominate such an enormous land with so many unwilling subjects (Koponen 1995:359–360; Henderson 1962:10).

As German rule stabilized and administrative boundaries were established, Ukaguru was divided between two administrative districts. At first, the bulk of Ukaguru became part of a huge Mpapua Bezirksamt (Mpwapwa District) including Ugogo, Kondoa, Singida, and much of Maasailand, with the big station at Mpwapwa. Later the district was considerably reduced in size and renamed Dodoma, with the main station at Dodoma town further west, leaving Mpwapwa as a minor post. The eastern borderlands of Ukaguru were then incorporated into Morogoro Bezirksamt with a big station at Morogoro town and a minor station at Kilosa. The British later changed boundaries and district affiliations, but these initial German boundaries set a continuing pattern of Ukaguru being divided into two different administrative units. Thus, while colonialism led to a local consolidation of a Kaguru sense of ethnicity, it also led to a continuing though varying political division of Kaguru lands that would forever inhibit Kaguru in the eastern and western regions from feeling fully part of one common group.[22]

A striking outcome of German colonial rule in Ukaguru was a great change in Kaguru demography. German military force made this clear when frequent raiding ended. Kaguru who had settled in the more inaccessible and precipitous mountain areas moved down to the warmer, more arable lands of the Kaguru plateau. This undermined the influence of mountain leaders and made those who could dominate the increasing populations of the lower plateau river valleys far more influential. While Kaguru were now nearly free of raiding, their new locations made them far more accessible to local officials seeking taxes, imposing forced labor, and seizing goods (Anonymous 1909:219; Tucker 1911:30; Briggs 1918:20–21, 23, 29).

Initially the Germans simply demanded or seized livestock and food to support their garrisons. When political order was achieved, they began to collect regular taxes. These early years were especially hard, because Ukaguru suffered severe food shortages in 1893–94 (Turshen 1984:102–105). A hut tax was introduced in 1897, levying 8 to 12 rupees in the towns and 2 to 3 rupees in the bush, which included all of Ukaguru.[23] At first Africans were told that if they lacked money they could pay in livestock and foodstuffs, but soon payment was demanded in cash. The aim of this was to force Africans to enter the colonial money economy. Africans would either have to produce an agricultural or livestock surplus that could be bought at low prices by the Germans or, better still, they would enter the labor market at low wages, thereby facilitating development of German estates and plantations (Koponen 1995:346–347). Even so, an acute shortage of willing and steady African labor continued (Sunseri 2002). In 1900 the hut tax was shifted to a head tax of 2 rupees (4 shillings) because the domestic arrangements in some African housing (such as the often extensive *tembe* structures in western Ukaguru, see Beidelman 1972) accommodated more than one adult, taxable male (Koponen 1995:382–386). Yet these laws were slow to take effect inland. The first really regular cash taxation in the Mpwapwa area did not occur until 1903 (Iliffe 1969:185).

The collection of taxes was pursued only selectively in the bush areas, since poor communications and lack of officials made it virtually impossible that every African man could be tracked down and made to pay. Taxes were keenly collected in those more accessible areas and at those times where and when labor was needed for government and commercial needs. At other times taxation was pursued less vigorously. In no way could taxes be efficiently and thoroughly collected in much of Ukaguru. When tax drives were called by the Germans, it was hoped that many Kaguru lacked the cash to pay, so that they could be taken as forced laborers to work off what they owed in taxes and tax delinquency fines through labor on the new estates that Germans and Greeks had established in the lowlands east of Ukaguru or by working on road or bridge projects. It was the Kaguru living near petty administrative centers such as Mamboya, Mvumi, Berega, and Geiro who were most likely to be nabbed. Those in mountainous areas could often elude officials. Kaguru were sometimes seized to work on government projects, though German officials did not need the excuse of tax collection to force Kaguru to work for a short time on roads, as porters, or as attendants to traveling dignitaries (Buell 1965, I:450).

A chronic labor shortage lay at the heart of German frustrations over the poor economic development of their colony (Kjekshus 1977a:154; Koponen 1995:321; W. Smith 1978:97–100; Sunseri 2002:53–71). This explained the persistence of slavery even after German rule (see Deutsch 2006). Coerced labor was a common feature of life in German East Africa (Koponen 1995:398; W. Smith 1978:102; Sunseri 2002). Workers constructing government buildings and roads and serving as porters were simply dragooned and never paid (ibid.:345). Since wages were poor and labor conditions harsh, there was little reason for Kaguru to seek wage labor other than to pay taxes (Koponen 1995:335).[24] Germans and British missionaries admitted that they benefitted from famine because it drove Africans into seeking work with them (Koponen 1995:346). There were no laws to protect workers from savage mistreatment and poor wages (M. Bates 1957:27). The usual local wages for casual and unskilled African laborers were 8 rupees a month, 16 pice a day. Even when workers were seized, many ran off, and almost every Kaguru resisted such coercion during the peak cultivating season when they needed to work their own fields (Rees 1902). Periodically German district officers ordered local akidas and chiefs to coerce local labor (ibid.:340). Each planter was allocated a local African agent to coerce labor for him, and these men received bounties based on how many workers they brought in when calls were made (Koponen 1995:369).[25]

A missionary in Ukaguru wrote: "Again the existence of some twenty cotton plantations within a short journey of Ukaguru, with the consequent levy of workmen for them, constituted a distracting element and the chief of Momboya (sic) in collusion with the Mohammedan steward of the district [the akida] took advantages of the opportunity to oppress the Christians" (Church Missionary Society, *Proceedings* 1913–14:60–61). The missionary alludes to the common belief that Germans tended to prefer Muslim foremen and labor agents to pagan or Christian African staff (Austen 1968:72–73). The labor levy at issue here refers to the many estates set up outside Ukaguru in the lowlands north, east, and south of Kilosa, which began to be cleared by Germans and Greeks in the early 1900s (ibid.). Cotton was developed by Hamburg-based German planters around Kilosa (Koponen 1995:292, 408). The Otto cotton plantation funded out of Stuttgart in 1887 was particularly vast, but it soon confronted serious financial difficulties due to labor problems (Sunseri 2002:15, 151–154). In 1902 sisal was introduced, and it soon became the major cash crop (Stoecker 1977:109). Besides planters with these large holdings there were also a few foreign settlers near Mpwapwa who also demanded workers (Koponen 1995:284; Kjekshus 1977a:155). There were also at least eight Indian traders in this larger Ukaguru area, presumably buying and selling at a more local level than the Germans (Meyer 1909, I:81; Fuchs 1907:19). For all these reasons we should not be surprised that while Germans banned the slave trade in 1890, they rejected outright abolition of slavery, which continued locally until it was banned by the British in 1922 (Sunseri 2002:27–30; Deutsch 2006:1–3, 97–98, 151–154, 217). Germans could not legally own slaves, but they could rent them from Arabs and Africans.

A free African cultivator in areas like Ukaguru, where there was ample land and usually sufficient rainfall, had little interest in working steady for others (Koponen 1995:326). This even posed a problem for the few enterprising Kaguru trying to enter the cash economy (and this is still a problem today), since chronic labor shortage impeded local Africans from developing gardens larger than what an extended family itself could tend. In one case a horrified missionary reported that an affluent Kaguru teacher at the mission employed 28 slaves (Parker

1904). A few Kaguru were able to sell foodstuffs to the estates (Iliffe 1979:314). Some even trekked east to the more developed areas nearer the coast to sell goods for better prices (Church Missionary Society, *Proceedings* 1911–12:50), but the majority had to make themselves scarce when officials came around or else bribe local officials. Otherwise, they risked recruitment for hard labor, especially if they lived near areas where chiefs or akidas were located. As the Church Missionary Society educated increasing numbers of Kaguru, these found jobs as petty clerks, teachers, and catechists and were exempted from forced labor. The Germans felt ambivalent about such educated Africans, recognizing that they were essential for building a lower-level cadre to support their colonial domination and commerce, yet they were anxious because such "trousered Negroes" disdained manual labor and demanded more social rights (Koponen 1995:356). Germans encouraged education in Swahili but were uneasy about educated Africans learning to read and speak German or English, though they recognized that this too could be valuable (Church Missionary Society, *Proceedings* 1912–13:51; Furley 1971:61). The missionaries in Ukaguru were hostile to all Muslim influence and promoted Christian education to prevent Muslim clerks from taking over locally (Rees 1913:154; Briggs 1918:41). Unlike the missionaries, the Germans showed no interest in educating African women (Koponen 1995:324; Hornsby 1964:8). Germans remained distrustful of mission education because they believed that it stressed loyalty to a mission rather than to government (Austen 1968:70). Yet one source records that "a considerable increase in the number of students took place in the autumn. It was due chiefly to the action of Captain Fonck, the German officer and a good friend of the missionaries, who continually impressed upon the Natives the advantage of being able to read and write, and urged them to attend the mission school. Moreover, he established a school at the fort [Mpwapwa], and compelled a certain number of youths to attend it daily" (Church Missionary Society, *Proceedings* 1903–04:98; see also the Church Missionary Executive Conference December 1903 for an account of the German governor's support of the Ukaguru mission). By 1910 mission schools were strongly endorsed by governments (Church Missionary Society, *Proceedings* 1910–11: 57; Oliver 1952:198). By 1913 the Germans had begun to pay subsidies to missions for running schools (Mbilinyi 1979:77). Despite their suspicions, Germans began to believe more in encouraging African education than did the British in neighboring Kenya during the same period (M. Wright 1968:627).

Many Germans believed that improved transportation would solve the acute labor problem, and therefore looked forward to building a railway across the center of the colony. The railway reached Kilosa in 1909 and Gulwe, eight miles south of Mpwapwa, in 1910. The Church Missionary Society also built a wagon track from the port of Sadani to Mpwapwa, and another road was built from Kilosa to Mpwapwa, but both were soon eroded because Africans were unwilling to maintain them (E. Smith 1955). The improved transportation, especially the railway, attracted even more German settlers to the Kilosa sisal and cotton estates (Koponen 1995:27), increasing the demand for labor but not appreciably changing the supply. When Germans tried to introduce machines in estates to compensate for the lack of labor, these machines quickly broke down and no skilled local artisans could be found to repair them (Sunseri 2002:151–154).

In 1905, four years before the railway reached Kilosa, a large rebellion broke out in southeastern German East Africa. Its roots were complex, but it is generally credited to African opposition to German exploitation and abuse of their labor, to disturbance of the local African economy, and to ensuing environmental collapse, as well as to general German brutality. One must remember that forced labor and German interference in African agricultural practices were especially severe in the southeast of the colony, where the rebellion first broke out. There Germans tried to force Africans into cash cropping cotton, even at the cost of endangering the production of local food supplies (Sunseri 2002:52, 76–103). The rebellion got its name, Maji-Maji (*maji* is Swahili for water) from the fact that many of its members believed they had medicines that would turn German bullets into harmless water. While Maji-Maji mainly affected the southeastern portion of the colony, it reached as far as the southern borders of Ukaguru. Fighting reached Kilosa. The Germans hired 300 local Baraguyu to augment their regular troops during the crisis (Fonck 1907:91, 118, 215; Rees 1905). Still, the Kilosa fort was considered especially strong because it had a machine gun (Rees 1905). The Kaguru did not take part in Maji-Maji, but some of the defeated Maji-Maji fled into the Kaguru mountains and were hunted down by African scouts of the Germans (Briggs 1918:35). Some Kaguru were coerced into being porters for the German troops. The mission stations in central Ukaguru were unharmed, but with all the rumors of danger and unrest the missionaries abandoned them and fled to Mpwapwa, the nearest German garrison (Church Missionary Intelligencer 1906:115; Proceedings of the Church Missionary Society 1906–07:74–75). The mission's work was consequently set back.

As a result of Maji-Maji, the German colonial government softened some of its policies (Gann and Duignan 1977:178–189), but this was counteracted by a deeper realization of how hostile many Africans were. The administrative districts were increased to 24 so that Africans could be more closely watched.[26] Germans tried to hire more local and sympathetic Africans as akidas (W. Smith 1978:103; Iliffe 1969:181–182). The German government belatedly began to provide some colonial training to officials before sending them overseas (Gann and Duignan 1977:44). During this more liberal period, settler activity was somewhat reined in by the colonial administration. Africans were encouraged as agricultural producers, and more Asians entered the local trading sector (Iliffe 1968:56; Hirji 1980:216). Most important of all, German administrators reconsidered their policies about labor. They abandoned their aggressive policy of forced labor and coerced cash cropping. Instead, they tried to encourage a more wage-competitive labor market. In the Kilosa area the arrival of the railway led to a dramatic increase in plantations. The resultant labor shortage led to laborers being "stolen" from one estate by another, with Africans wandering here and there seeking the best terms (Sunseri 2002:131–157). Demand for labor became especially intense in eastern Ukaguru and Kilosa once the railway reached this area (Sunseri 2002:167–168). By 1911 the Germans were even trying to tax local African beer production, a major interference in one of the key areas where Kaguru women gained some access to a cash economy (J. Willis 2002:123).

All these changes were short-lived, because World World I soon broke out and German East Africa was attacked by British, South African, and Belgian forces operating out of neighboring Kenya and the Belgian Congo. By 1915 the countryside was so disrupted that there were shortages of nearly everything (Henderson 1962:91). The British second division took Mpwapwa on August 12, 1916. The Germans retreated down the Mukondokwa River Valley to Kilosa, which fell on August 22. They then retreated to Morogoro and continued fighting in the far south even after the 1918 Armistice (Hordern 1941:350–354; no one could get word to the German army, which had retreated to the Mozambique borderlands). What remained striking about the German African army was the deep loyalty evinced by many African troops toward their officers. When the remarkable German general of the campaign, Paul von Lettow-Vorbeck, later returned to visit British Tanganyika, he was greeted with euphoria by many African veterans.

The war had a horrendous impact on Ukaguru. The British missionaries were removed and interned by the Germans. The Germans especially persecuted African converts of the CMS British and the Roman Catholic French missionaries, which included the Kaguru and their neighbors, singling them out for porterage, looting their homes for supplies, and destroying property (Iliffe 1979:255). Many mission station buildings were destroyed, and German and later British troops stripped food from Kaguru land and seized those able-bodied men they could catch to force them to be porters (Kjekshus 1977a:153; Miller 1974:182; Briggs 1918:25).[27] Retreating from the British, the Germans destroyed their own buildings and official records (explaining the present dearth of historical information for this area) as well as wrecking bridges and sections of the railway. Morogoro, east of Ukaguru, saw especially fierce and prolonged fighting (Miller 1974:187–188, 222–232).

After the war Ukaguru, like much of the rest of Tanganyika, was hit by a terrible famine caused by drought, but because the Germans had seized local Africans to be army porters, they had prevented many men from cultivating either because they were taken away or because they had fled to the hills. This famine was followed by the great worldwide influenza epidemic, in which half the African population was affected (Beck 1977:40–41). These disasters were made worse because the local mission medical facilities had been destroyed. (One should remember that the Germans had not developed much medical care outside the larger towns; the mission dispensaries in Ukaguru at Mamboya and Mpwapwa were among the few bush medical facilities in prewar German East Africa [Koponen 1995:467].[28]) Furthermore, food and other supplies were difficult to receive because the transportation system had been deliberately wrecked by the Germans. The arriving British found a disabled and suffering area, which was difficult to help since a worldwide economic depression followed shortly after they were given official custodianship of the colony through the League of Nations. This limited government funds and dried up mission resources.

Scholars are divided regarding the contributions of the Germans during their relatively brief rule. Germans promoted the use of Swahili, which now serves as a unifying language for the country (Morrison 1976:62–63). They made significant contributions to the colonial infrastructure in education, urban health, tropical medical and plant research, and the railway (Koponen 1995:25; Dundas 1955:106–107; former Governor Schnee's views about Germany's great contribution are probably too positive (1926:62–73, 101–128), but Eberlie's study seems fair and balanced (1960). I encountered the same view among Kaguru and Baraguyu that Listowel describes as typical of Tanganyikans, namely that many Africans preferred the direct harshness of the Germans to the allegedly ambiguous and concealed ways of the British (see Listowel 1965:74; Liebenow 1971:85). In contrast, British and even some recent German writers are harshly negative, stressing German brutality and exploitation of Africans (Listowel 1965:51; Moffett 1958:70–71; W. Smith 1978:77; Bald 1970:135–171; M. Wright 1968:621–623). Gann and Duignan go so far as to characterize the German colonial civil service as "morally unsavory" (1977:90–91).

The British Takeover

British military rule was soon replaced by formal British mandated League of Nations control of most of German East Africa, though the rich and populous far west, what is now Rwanda and Burundi, went to the Belgians. All these areas were officially held in trust as mandates first for the League of Nations (1922) and later, after World War II, as trust territories for the United Nations (1946). Despite their special status, for most intents and purposes these lands became British and Belgian colonies much like any others, though their status discouraged white settlement and encouraged a policy of considering Tanganyika to be reserved for eventual African self-government (Iliffe 1979:162).[29] The British, short of staff and funds, continued the 22 districts that constituted the part of German East Africa they had gained, now called Tanganyika. They kept the akidas[30] and the centralized administrative system whereby district officers reported directly to Dar es Salaam, probably because the new governor, Horace Byatt, was a cautious leader and disliked delegating authority (Iliffe 1979:318–331; Austen 1968:149; Liebenow 1971:88). About 1920, Kaguru Chief Saileni died and was succeeded by his son, Saidi Methusaleh, of the Ponela clan. The British made him an akida. He deeply antagonized the mission as soon as he took office by running off with a married Christian woman. Like all Kaguru chiefs, he mingled with missionaries and other Christians but remained a pagan (Report of the Tanganyika Mission of the C.M.S for 1925).

The early postwar years saw further famine (Listowel 1965:69–70; Turshen 1984 102–106). The German estates and town properties were confiscated and sold, mostly to Greeks (Cypriot British subjects) and Asians, for a quarter or less of their real values (Listowel 1965:68; P. Mitchell 1954:92), though Dumbuya claims some were sold for only 5 percent (1995:107), drastically lowering land values and antagonizing the settler community. These included the large sisal estates in lowland eastern Ukaguru. On account of the mandate, Tanganyika was declared an area to be kept African (Iliffe 1979:262) with African interests paramount (Chidzero 1961:14; Gailey 1974:40), though the British at times tried to convert the territory into a state where Africans would have weakened powers, shared with Asians and whites. They even tried to incorporate it into some kind of union with Uganda and Kenya that would have disadvantaged Tanganyikans. Before 1923 no further lands were alienated from Africans, and subsequently only limited areas were taken, mainly for sisal estates in such districts as Kilosa and Morogoro (Mair 1938:140–142). Africans were protected in 1923 by a new ordinance preventing European and Asian shopkeepers from prosecuting Africans for debt (Listowel 1965:70). This was ostensibly to protect Africans from going into serious debt, but McCarthy argues that this actually prevented Africans from entering business except at the lowest level and that the passage was due to local Asians wanting to prevent Africans from competing with them (1982:37–49). These were austere, unconstructive years representative of a long, lean future where "continuing poverty was Tanganyika's leading characteristic" (Iliffe 1979:261).

The new British governor, Sir Horace Byatt, hired many demobilized British military men to work in his new administration (Sperber 1970:30). At the onset of British rule these new administrators were nearly as brutal as the Germans (G. Alexander 1936:194). They were sorely overworked

(Allen 1979:71), partly because Byatt himself was a poor and unimaginative administrator who perforce left many decisions to local district officers (Gailey 1974:38). Still, Byatt's administration nearly doubled the European staff, which was a mere 108 for the entire territory when he began (Dumbuya 1995:107).[31] In 1921 and 1923 Byatt issued ordinances legalizing local African chiefs as petty administrators (Gailey 1974:38; Dumbuya 1995:109). Local district officers were told to find the traditional chiefs (Austen 1968:165). Chiefs were no longer to receive Africans' tribute in goods or labor but instead were put on government payrolls and employed to collect local taxes (Austen 1967:582). Their help was needed because African taxes were increased in 1923, and such taxes seemed the only dependable government income. In fact, the ordinary African bore the greatest financial burden to support his own subjugation by the British.

A formal policy of Indirect Rule and local African Native Authorities is generally credited to the next governor, Sir Donald Cameron, but it is clear that both the Germans and Governor Byatt had already set the stage for a system of rule by local African chiefs that fostered the tribalism characterizing Tanganyika's grassroots colonial rule, and which is a central theme of this monograph. For his efforts to improve the system for Africans, Byatt was disliked by the white settlers and considered a negrophile (Dumbuya 1995:102–110). It was he who began building an administration where the governor and related secretariat in Dar es Salaam held so much power (McCarthy 1982:87). In 1924 he left to become governor of Trinidad.

Cameron, Tribalism, and the Ideology of Indirect Rule

When Sir Donald Cameron arrived as governor of Tanganyika in 1925, he had already achieved a reputation as a liberal working in the secretariat of Nigeria under Lord Lugard, the supposed inventor of African Indirect Rule. Ironically, though Cameron has invariably been pictured as an advocate of African self-rule and a protector of Africans against European exploitation, he himself, always a central authority bureaucrat, had almost no firsthand experience with everyday African life and the thinking of ordinary Africans (P. Mitchell 1954:105; Austen 1967:585; Gailey 1974:79–80). Those who worked under him, such as Charles Dundas, had far more firsthand knowledge and were critical of Cameron's views about African rule and tribalism (Graham 1976:5). Certainly the early district officer at Kilosa was skeptical about his orders from Cameron to rule through local chiefs (Kilosa District Book), though he had little difficulty locating the Kaguru leaders at Mamboya and elsewhere. Like other district officers, he was expected to find distinct "tribes" with rulers for each (Graham 1976:4–7), because "tribes" were essential to Cameron's vision of Indirect Rule (Iliffe 1979:323–324). Ironically, Cameron's supposedly innovative efforts to foster local African government increased the power and work of the white district and provincial officers who had to supervise them (Dumbuya 1995:147).

As soon as Cameron arrived, he established a secretary of native affairs (Charles Dundas) and ordered local district officers to seek out local African traditional leaders who could be put in charge of local government. In 1926 Cameron issued the Native Authority Ordinance, a more detailed and extensive version of Byatt's 1921 edict. Cameron's ordinance is generally seen as the key foundation of Indirect Rule in Tanganyika, and Byatt is given little credit. It is also important to remember that it was the white secretary of native affairs, and not any African, who reported for Africans in making policies. Local Africans, not even chiefs, were consulted about any high level policy even when it involved their own affairs (Dumbuya 1995:135). Cameron named his new creations "Native Authorities" and assumed that they usually reflected clear-cut tribal entities (Gailey 1974:49). While this plan has often been termed Indirect Rule, Cameron preferred the term "Local African Administration" or simply "Native Administration" (D. Cameron 1939:75). He described East Africans as "primitive" and "ignorant" (ibid.:77), needing a local government founded on surviving indigenous systems of rule (ibid.:79), which would provide them with training for eventual self-government (ibid.:87; see Buell 1965, I:451–455). Cameron distrusted educated Africans and envisioned a system of chiefs supporting colonial government and opposed to "political agitation" (Graham 1976:3). The more one reads about Cameron's policies, the more one wonders why earlier colonial historians ever thought of him as liberal, progressive, or even well informed.

Cameron considered his creation of local African Native Authorities his greatest political achievement (D. Cameron 1939:257). Yet he conceded that such rule was greatly due to the lack of British staff and funds, that it was based on "expediency" as much as on any high-minded political vision (1970:124; 1939:81). Cameron admitted that in many cases the local officials he created could be "almost as ignorant as the people they are to serve" (1939:99), but admonished potential critics who might "look for too high a standard in the uneducated Native Chief" (ibid.:101). While Cameron warned that British might wrongly assume a legitimacy in local African rule that was not there (1970:7), he contradicted this by repeatedly urging local district officers to find local African rulers.[32] Given the pressure from those above that such officials succeed in fulfilling this order, local, ambitious colonial administrators felt compelled to find and recognize such so-called traditional leaders, whatever their misgivings were to the contrary. Where such chosen leaders were clearly ignorant and inept (as in Ukagru), "it is the primary duty and obligation of the Administrative Officers with tact and patience to educate the Native Authority in their duties to their people according to civilized standards" (1939:98). These are pronouncements by a governor with almost no first-hand dealings with ordinary Africans.

Cameron's central assumptions involved a simplistic, tribalistic view of local African life that was paternalistic, naive, ignorant, self righteous, and reactionary. Cameron repeatedly asserted that local Africans saw the leaders of local Native Authorities as legitimate (1970:128), something British officials on the spot often found it difficult to swallow as they encountered frequent local quarrels over who had rights to such leadership. "The allegiance of a people to a tribal head freely and spontaneously accorded without external cause, is the very essence of true indirect administration" (1939:95). Such accepted leaders would supposedly not be particularly corrupt (ibid.:183) and would be locally unquestioned (ibid.:176). Cameron even thought that by making local chiefs collect government taxes he could deflect hostility from the British administration onto the chiefs (ibid.:176–177), though he must then surely have realized that this would have led Africans to see the chiefs as mere British stooges. Native Authorities became the mouthpieces by which the British issued any unpleasant local orders (Buell 1965:I, 455).

Cameron decided that the key to providing local chiefs with power and authority was through the local courts. This was because Cameron believed that African chiefs traditionally were both executive and judi-

ciary (Gailey 1974:79–90), just as colonial district officers also turned out
to be. To insure this, he removed the Native Authority courts from the
jurisdiction of the high courts overseen by European judges and instead,
by the Native Courts Ordinance of 1929, transferred control of Native
Authority courts to the provincial commissioners and through them
to local district officers (Gailey 1974:80; M. Bates 1957:129, 134; Austen
1968:154). One must remember that these local British officers rarely had
much or any legal training but were expected to study up on this, or else
just use Solomonic common sense.

Cameron was intent on creating Native Authorities, no matter how
weak or questionable. This vastly increased the paperwork and supervisory time of district officers, who had to prepare all the Native Authority
materials themselves to make it seem they had been successful in applying Cameron's misguided recommendations. After all, these junior
administrators wanted promotions. While creating more work for local
administrators, Indirect Rule did increase the actual power of district officers, especially in areas with weak and uneducated chiefs such as those
in Ukaguru (Gailey 1974:84). These Native Authority courts were soon
organized to form an extensive system. In Ukaguru this was because
the area was too large in size and population to be run through a single
court and chief. Several courts and levels of authority were created, a
paramount chief's court and several subordinate subchiefs' courts as
well as many headmen, a vast change from the initial version of the
system with one chief at Mamboya and two akidas.

Cameron's vision produced a complex and cumbrous Kaguru Native Authority hierarchy and a mass of local, poorly educated, and inept
African officials consuming taxes with their wages and expenses drawn
from the Native Authority treasury. Whether more direct rule would
have been more efficient, and whether younger, better educated, untraditional African staff should have been employed, are ifs and maybes
we must wonder about. The district officer at Kilosa toured Ukaguru
and held meetings where Kaguru elders argued their cases for selection
to office. The Kilosa District Book contained various accounts of the
traditions and legends related to the Mamboya chiefship, including one
detailed genealogy of over 130 names apparently constructed to benefit
those members of the Jumbe clan who had submitted it; that branch was
presented as senior to that of the present paramount chief and therefore

more deserving of his office. Inevitably, the accounts provided by local Kaguru represented biased and calculated reports, each promoting some group over others. Yet the eventual location of courts and their chiefs was never based on strict adherence to Kaguru traditions but rather on the British Administration's needs. Who got to be a subchief and head-man and who did not was as much based on geography, demography, and roads as on any tradition. The chain of authority had to be spread evenly and conveniently over the landscape. Cameron put chiefs on a Native Authority payroll and banned chiefly demands for tribute (Gailey 1974:67). The main sources of revenue were hut and poll taxes, which chiefs were now to collect (Gailey 1974:67; Sayers 1930:44). The Native Authorities were to be paid out of rebates from these poll and hut taxes, and therefore much tax money went for salaries rather than for local development and local services (Gailey 1974:67). Before Cameron, local fines and fees went to the district office; now they went to the Native Authority (ibid.:73).

The contradictions and paternalistic unrealism of Cameron's argu-ments created a political system that made much work for local British officers, who were usually the only officials present who could read, write reports, draw up budgets, or understand bureaucratic procedures (Aus-ten 1967:589). Many district officials shared the early Kilosa district of-ficer's annoyance that the Native Authorities were inefficient and created far more problems than they solved (Graham 1976:6–8) and that chiefs were hard to supervise and yet corrupt and dangerous if left on their own. In 1930 Cameron further undermined district officers' capacities by instituting a policy of rotating local administrators from district to district from tour to tour, supposedly to broaden their political perspec-tive but probably more to serve as a reward and punishment system by posting men to "better" or "worse" districts after their current tour's achievements had been evaluated (Austen 1967:594). Such a policy hardly allowed any administrators to know well the local ins-and-outs of any particular African political system or society, much less learn any local language or build up really useful personal ties with influential local Africans. It was one of Cameron's worst ideas.

Cameron's new local administration was not practical under the old administrative units established by the Germans. Consequently, from 1925 onward the British began revising the boundaries of local districts, increasing the original 22 German districts to more and smaller units. Cameron first increased them to 37 in 1926, to 46 in 1928, and in 1930, the year before he left, they numbered 44. Much of the rationale behind this political tinkering was supposedly to create districts reflecting ethnic groups or bundles of related ethnic groups rather than areas based on geographic realities. Other things, such as the establishment of mines or the creation of a large development project, might lead to a new district, just as migration of population or introduction of new roads might lead to amalgamation. In subsequent years districts further increased, decreased, or otherwise changed as the central administration continued to fiddle with the system. Cameron also eliminated the old German arrangement by which district officers reported directly to the central government in Dar es Salaam. Instead, in 1927 he created a tier system by making 11 provinces, and nine years later reducing these, to be in effect the year after he left, 1932 (L. Berry 1971:108–109; Gailey 1974:73–75; Austen 1968:154).

Cameron was a keen bureaucrat and by these measures increased the paperwork and decisionmaking of both provincial commissioners and district officers, as well as that of the secretariat in the capital. For better or worse, this led to more regional diversity in how policies were carried out and inhibited any territorial-wide common and consistent working policies. In the case of Ukaguru, the area was split with the eastern two-thirds assigned to a redrawn Kilosa district now a part of Eastern Province with Morogoro as provincial capital.[33] The western third of Ukaguru at first became part of Dodoma district which was part of Central Province with Dodoma town as its provincial capital. Later, long after Cameron left, western Ukaguru became the major part of a new Mpwapwa district, though still a part of Central Province. Thus, despite Cameron's so-called policy reflecting tribal integrity, the British administration had divided Kaguru even more than the Germans, who had kept all but the eastern borderlands under one administration. These new boundaries dividing Ukaguru remained until 1967, long after Tanganyikan national independence. Kaguru were consequently rarely allowed to think of themselves as an entirely integrated ethnic and political entity, even though the British colonial administration repeatedly seemed to preach and even invent such ethnicity. The eastern Kaguru were thrown into a province dominated by other matrilineal peoples with cultures similar to theirs, while western Kaguru were placed in a province dominated by the patrilineal Gogo rather different from them culturally.[34]

Cameron made other changes as well, most intended to better Africans' lot. He tried to cut down on flogging (Gailey 1974:46) and set a policy of discouraging European settlement in the territory, repeatedly citing the League of Nations Mandate (Gailey 1974:45, 54).

Historians have probably been kinder to Cameron than he merits, judging from the long-term negative impact of his policies of Indirect Rule and tiered administration. Given the lack of funds and European staff, some form of Indirect Rule was probably inevitable, but the forms Cameron endorsed inhibited modern political development (Stephens 1968:53–54). The Native Authorities were so self-contradictory that it confused everyone; Indirect Rule did foster "tribal consciousness," but that is now seen as undermining future national unity (Graham 1976:9). Iliffe equates Cameron's governorship with a "creation of tribes" (1979:323–324), probably an overstatement, but Cameron certainly fostered ethnic divisions. In Cameron's defense, one could make a case for preserving local perspectives on rule and development rather than adhering exclusively to a Tanganyikan territorial perspective. While Cameron thought he was avoiding the roughshod imposition of Indirect Rule that marred Lugard's policies of expediency in Nigeria (Gailey 1974:278), Cameron's attempt to weave a myth of African tradition and participation did another form of harm. It fetishized Native Administration as a sacred cow. "Once this expediency became an ideology and an accepted institution of local native administration, it actually worked against the development of political institutions along representative and elective lines" (Chidzero 1961:16–17). It discouraged the best-educated, progressive, and more ambitious African youth from entering tribal politics, and where they did, given how the system was set up, they were bound to fail.

Indirect Rule was certainly not democratic as Mitchell, Cameron's aide, argued (P. Mitchell 1954:126–129).[35] Jingoist colonialists and advocates of Empire such as Sayers praised Indirect Rule, claiming that it would be able "to maintain and develop all that is best in tribal custom and institutions, and to avoid, as far as possible, everything that has a detribalizing tendency" (1930:126). In contrast, Dundas, Cameron's first secretary of Native Affairs, saw Native Authorities as neither innovative nor traditional: "Always we controlled subject races—unholy word in these days—through their indigenous authorities. So indispensable had they seemed to us that where we did not find such authorities we created them. In tribal areas in which there were no conspicuous leaders almost any man who brought himself to notice or made himself useful might become a chief" (1955:133). Dundas goes on to charge, witheringly: "Bogus or genuine, the native authorities we recognized were expected to carry out our behests and be our general agents. But we had not put them in a position to maintain their authority nor equipped them to cope with new conditions resulting from our intrusion in their communities" (ibid.:134). Dundas knew a great deal about what went on at the African grassroots. He was a former district officer with an outstanding record of insight and achievement. He seemed to suspect that Cameron was a humbug, despite all the praise accorded to him. No wonder Dundas did not last long in his job.

African Education and American Racism

Probably the factor that most harmed economic and social development in Ukaguru and in Tanganyika in general was the lack of education among Africans. This was related to the general poverty of the area and the inadequate level of education promoted by the conservative Christian missionaries, but it also reflected government policies strongly reinforced by the arrival in 1923–24 of representatives of the American Phelps-Stokes Fund, an educational policy group that influenced British colonial government educational policies and hence Christian missions, which were subsidized educationally by that government. This group had been deeply influenced by the prevailing racist policies in the United States, which emphasized training blacks in agriculture and trades along with Christianity rather than in higher education in the liberal arts and sciences (Furley and Watson 1966:473). It was everything that W. E. B. Du Bois was not. Many of the British were racists, but Americans had a long record of far more pervasive and virulent racial prejudice, which was expressed even in supposedly liberal bodies such as the Phelps-Stokes Fund. The baneful effects of the Phelps-Stokes reports did lasting harm to education in the territory encouraging an educational philosophy that long doomed most Africans to being, at best, literate farmers (Thompson 1968:17–24). Cameron supported such policies (Furley 1971:62–63).

The Tanganyikan educational system had been the target for criticism, with its over-emphasis on agriculture and simple skills (Furley and Watson 1966:474). Africans themselves were keen for a more Western education than what either government or mission schools offered (ibid.:485). The Phelps-Stokes group visited CMS schools in Kilosa and Morogoro districts, and even they found the existing system conservative (Jones 1970:xvii–xxiii, 14–43; Furley 1971:64–65); in 1924 no English whatsoever was taught in Ukaguru (ibid.:184). These early schools all emphasized agriculture and simple trades, much as what many schools in the southern United States then offered blacks (Mbilinyi 1979:81–84; Beidelman 1982a:112–116, 120–123, 231 n. 62). Such schools' staffs trained Africans to be peasants, or at best petty clerks (Mbilinyi 1980:242–250). Southern racist attitudes entered Africa under the alarming assumption that such Christians in the United States had long experience in producing the "right kind" of blacks. Tanganyikan Christian missions had long resisted any development of higher education (ibid.:254–264). The CMS in Ukaguru were especially conservative (Beidelman 1982a:112–123). The earlier German educational system actually provided a potentially better and more progressive plan (Morrison 1976:56–59). The African demand for education vastly increased with every year of colonial rule, and even more after World War II, as schooling was seen as the key to any and every economic and political advantage. Cameron had encouraged territorial government funding of mission education as a cheaper alternative than if that government itself embarked on running schools. Given the conservative nature of CMS missionary attitudes toward society and education in Ukaguru, we can see how and why the educational sector suffered and why local government in Ukaguru remained so backward and poorly trained. The racist, reactionary influence that the U.S. educator Jesse Jones and the Phelps-Stokes mission presented with a "philosophy of adaptation" in education supported the inadequate education that the CMS in Ukaguru already favored (Thompson 1968:17–34). Cameron left Tanganyika in 1931, reassigned to a more prestigious post in Nigeria. He was succeeded by Sir Stuart Symes (1934–46). These were cheerless and depressing years with little innovation (Lohrmann 2007:263–264). Ralph Austen describes them as a time of "political darkness" (1968:202).

The post-Cameron years were a time of stagnation all over Tanganyika, and especially in Ukaguru. Roads were poor, and the major concern of local government was a shortage of food and income, sometimes to the point of local taxes having to be paid in produce for lack of any available cash (P. Mitchell 1954:135; Fuggles-Couchman 1964:419–421; Beidelman 1982a:95–96, 112–116, 120–123, 169–170).

In these early years of British rule the district administration relied on compulsory African labor for most of its local projects. In 1924 the Kilosa district administration extracted an incredible 400,000 workdays of toil from local Africans. Once such a system had fallen into place, it seems to have become addictive to administrators facing any problem; it provided an unimaginative and feudal alternate to developing wage labor, even though this undoubtedly went against the terms of the territory's League of Nations mandate status (Buell 1965, I:463–468). So too, later, was the territory's Masters and Servant Ordinance, which allowed whites to imprison or flog employees who broke their labor contracts (it later was employed to discourage unionization and demands for better wages and working conditions (ibid.:500–501; see Bujra 2000:67–71, 78–85).

The Native Authority treasuries had little cash, which in turn sorely limited development (Stephens 1968:55–56. During this time Kaguru Chief Saidi Methusaleh died (I could not secure an exact date) and was replaced as paramount chief by Yustino, Saidi's younger brother and therefore another member of the Ponela clan. Yustino was both ambitious and literate. Local affairs were otherwise uneventful, since this was a "bureaucracy without popular representation" (Dundas 1955:148). Local policies were "contradictory" (ibid.:137) and not well run. "It could be said of administrative officers that they were amateurs, in as much as they had no definable qualifications for their jobs" (ibid.). "Indirect Rule became a means of social control rather than social progress" (Iliffe 1979:226).[36]

World War II and After

World War II was a difficult time for Ukaguru. Africans were urged to produce more, despite the fact that there was such a severe famine in 1943 that the Kaguru Native Authority had to distribute free food (Turshen 1984:105). There were even problems staffing the British administration, because men were drafted into more essential government services and into the military. Many of the 92,000 Tanganyikans who joined the King's African Rifles had life-transforming experiences overseas (Listowel 1965:120–123). The African archdeacon of the CMS in Ukaguru served in Palestine and elsewhere, and a man subsequently appointed headman of Mamboya gained skills as a mechanic, acquired literacy, and developed many abilities in leadership. Seeing whites and blacks shoot Germans and Italians and seeing how the British tried to dominate other peoples in the Near East and South Asia created a few more perceptive and questioning Kaguru leaders.

During this time, Kilosa district had its most anthropologically oriented district commissioner. C. M. Coke compiled a modest ethnography of the local peoples, as well as a history of the chiefship of Ukaguru. His researches did not, however, convert him to Indirect Rule. Instead, he wrote of the Kaguru chiefship that despite the promotion of Native Authorities by the provincial administration, it "was merely due to historical accident and political unconscience [sic] that this family [the Jumbe clan] had been established by the British government in a position of chiefship that never previously existed in Kaguru tradition" (Kilosa District Book). Shortly before completing his tour of duty, Coke had a serious run-in with Chief Yustino. The most reliable sources suggest that this had to do with Yustino resisting Coke's demands for drafts of Kaguru forced labor for Kilosa district projects. Revealingly, Kaguru provided me with a wide range of other reasons. Whether or not any of these were accurate, they reveal the wide range of ill feelings that Kaguru harbored toward both the chiefship and colonial rule. For example, some Kaguru said that a notorious white Rhodesian farmer, Baines (see later), living reclusively in the Itumba Mountains above Geiro, had wanted permission to divert four streams from Kaguru lands to his farm, and that Chief Yustino had refused. (Chief Malanda, Yustino's successor, later agreed to Baines's proposal and was, according to some Kaguru, bribed to do this.) Chief Yustino's refusal to divert the water supposedly angered the Kilosa administration. This seems implausible, because most Tanganyikan district British administrators I met were usually more protective of African interests than of those of local white farmers or estate owners, especially farmers like Baines, who had been rumored by most of the European Kilosa community to be a difficult, unsociable, and even very strange person. (Baines was a legendary eccentric that few whites in Kilosa district had even met, though most knew rumors about him.)

Other Kaguru said that Chief Yustino was taking bribes from Baraguyu for settling homicides through blood money rather than reporting such crimes to Kilosa headquarters. This was potentially a serious offence, but even if it had occurred, I doubt it would have led to Yustino's dismissal; I witnessed comparable corruption when I lived in Ukaguru and this never led to any Kaguru official losing his post, even when it was officially reported. Still other Kaguru claimed that Chief Yustino had ordered one of his messengers to beat a dissident Kaguru (one of his own affines), who later died. Yet this did not fit other reports by Kaguru of related events. Obviously Chief Yustino was pictured sometimes as a defender of Kaguru against the high-handed British, sometimes as a clever manipulator using everyone for his own advantage, and sometimes as a cruel despot. The assertion that the dismissal was over Yustino not supplying forced labor to the district administration fits best with other reports and experiences I have had, though all of the tales could have held some measure of truth.

In any case, Chief Yustino was deposed in 1945 and was briefly imprisoned. The succeeding district commissioner had to spend many weeks trying to find a suitable successor to Yustino. Yustino's son wanted the job and was literate, and therefore well qualified, but conservative Kaguru elders at Mamboya cited the official ethos that Indirect Rule should employ traditional customs and noted that not one Kaguru paramount chief since Senyagwa/Saidi Chimola had been a member of the Jumbe clan, even though that was what was supposedly required. Several candidates refused the office when it was offered, and finally, for lack of any suitable contenders, the post went to Daudi Malanda, an elder of the Jumbe clan who was illiterate and had the reputation of being a drunk and dissolute. He was an unattractive person who had failed at most things he had tried to do. Malanda claimed to be the great-great maternal nephew of Senyagwa/Saidi Chimola and consequently a truly traditional matrilineal clan heir to the office. It is said that the British administration reluctantly accepted this outcome of the murky machinations of the Mamboya elders and seemed resigned to put up with a weak, ignorant, corrupt, incompetent, and unpleasant local ruler. I personally think they found the choice of such a weak man convenient.

In 1946, after World War II ended, Tanganyika became a United Nations Trusteeship subject to the new and liberal concerns of that body, an institution far more likely to question colonial rule than the preceding League of Nations. Subsequently, annual investigations and visits of commissioners from the United Nations became more intrusive. The British were told they had to present some kind of timetable for future African independence. The full implications of this annoying change only slowly dawned on the British administration. For the time being the same old ways and abuses remained, but these same old abuses were now to vex the new Trustee Inspectors and prompt some international debate. These United Nations reports forced successive Tanganyikan administrations to defend and reexamine these actions and lose some confidence in their policies. The economic disarray due to the postwar shortage of funds for development meant that this land, which was not even a proper British colony, continued in penury. These economic difficulties were intensified by the fact that 1943, 1949, 1952, 1953, and 1954 were years of drought and poor harvests (M. Bates 1957:249; Turshen 1984:102–106).

The British issued repeated statements about possible changes in their administrative policies, but affairs at the grassroots, especially for a backwater such as Ukaguru, remained much as before. Despite Indirect Rule, which was increasingly discredited within the more intellectual and liberal circles of colonial government, the paternalistic powers of the provincial commissioners and especially the district administrators remained unchanged (Chidzero 1961:131). Perhaps the most important change at the grassroots level was the establishment by 1948 of a wide range of specialized government departments providing technical services in such areas as labor, agriculture, livestock, and education (Dryden 1968:2). Of course, colonial governments had always expressed interest in such problems as far back as German times, but now more properly trained men, such as a local veterinary officer, labor officer, and agricultural officer, were actually available at the Kilosa district level. Such officers frequently visited bush areas and met regularly with local, trained African employees who were permanently stationed in Ukaguru. Unfortunately, very few of these trained Africans were Kaguru, probably because of the poor level of local Kaguru education. The veterinary officer especially took on added importance; local taxes on livestock were instituted in 1945, making the roles of cattle-rich Baraguyu and Kamba minorities in Ukaguru especially important to the Kaguru Native Authority Treasury (M. Bates 1957:251). Even so, the local treasury remained poor in areas such as Ukaguru, and consequently the Kaguru Native Authority continued to rely on the forced labor of those who could not pay taxes (African Studies Branch 1951:34). All unsalaried African men under 45 continued to face this threat.

The growing prominence of technical services undermined the already weak authority of the local Native Authority, because Kaguru officials were too uneducated to understand the issues involved. Instead, outsider African specialists attached to Tanganyika territorial services such as health, forestry, agriculture, and livestock took over and acted independently of local Kaguru. The uneducated Native Authority's ineptitude in technical decisionmaking led local British administrators to issue directives to Kaguru on their own or under pressure from department specialists in medicine, labor, livestock, etc., ordering local leaders to implement such departmental policies (Pratt 1982:265–266). A "local government phase" was set up in 1947 supposedly to interest and train educated Africans in local government and to bypass Native Authorities. Yet such local bodies, at least in Kilosa district, were mere puppets for the British administration. As Chidzero aptly states, British policies mouthed the highest principles while actually resorting to sordid expediency (Chidzero 1961:11), and did little to foster any broader nationalist awareness.

In 1948 the British considered various ways to modernize Native Authorities themselves, such as a council of chiefs (M. Bates 1957:252), which, in the case of Ukaguru, merged into a Kilosa district council on which the chiefs and other officials sat, but which was dominated by British administrators. No matter; any measure to attempt political reforms made little sense when lack of education and widespread poverty were not properly addressed first (Stephens 1968:91–92). In any case, it would be vexing for college-educated administrators to discuss policy planning with a chief who was illiterate, arrogant, and often drunk.

The postwar era saw a new and naive confidence in quick, economic development (Stephens 1968:83). One last burst of ill-conceived economic change drew worldwide public attention to Tanganyika and had a brief but striking ripple effect on Ukaguru. In 1947 the British Labour government was encouraged to spend stupendous amounts of money developing vast but grossly misconceived groundnut projects in southern Tanganyika and in far western Ukaguru and neighboring eastern Ugogo. The Labour government was looking for some "quick fix" to bring needed funds into their grasp and make their new administration look good. They sought some spectacular project and settled on a groundnut scheme for producing cheap vegetable oil in Tanganyika. They scouted the area, and among the "experts" they found was the recluse of Ukaguru, the Rhodesian farmer Baines, who figured earlier in Kaguru gossip about how Chief Yustino lost his post. Baines caught the attention of development officers, who in turn persuaded the British Colonial Office to embark on a gigantic groundnut project at Kongwa northwest of Mpwapwa[37] Baines gave bad advice on soil, climate, and rainfall. Local Kaguru and Gogo scoffed, but they were continually ignored in favor of the "pushy" white man. Eventually those who had listened to Baines and, more important, their British government converts persuaded pundits such as Colonial Under-Secretary A. Creech Jones and Frank Samuels, the head of Unilever, to sink hundreds of millions of pounds into this fiasco.[38] The project grew to be so vast that Mpwapwa District was divided in half, with the northern portion temporarily becoming Kongwa District from 1948–51, servicing the thousands of Europeans and Africans employed on the project. How much if any personal profit Baines made out of this venture is not known. He seems to have disappeared from the historical record.

The Groundnut Scheme got underway in 1947, but within a year it was clearly doomed, at least to anyone knowing the area. Even so, vast amounts of money continued to pour in. Local Kaguru and Gogo flocked to the area, because even unskilled laborers were paid wages over five times higher than what the Kaguru Native Authority Treasury could pay, plus free food and lodgings (Wood 1950:76). Considerable cash from Kongwa drifted back to nearby Ukaguru, and some Kaguru developed trade or craft skills at the Scheme that they would never have otherwise gained. When I visited Kongwa in 1957–58, long after the project had failed, it was still filled with European homes, more numerous and better than those at Kilosa town. Out in a semi-desert plain I found a luxurious swimming pool, tennis courts, a fancy European club, paved roads, numerous electric generators, an abandoned airstrip, and an improbable railway station manned by a uniformed attendant but without a working traintrack. It was a monument to the folly of mismanaged colonial development, administrative arrogance, and ignorance, and a source of bemused wonder to local Kaguru and Gogo. As Noël Coward perceptively wrote, "the natives grieve when the white men leave their huts, because they're obviously definitely nuts" (1995:122).

In 1949 a new governor, Sir Edward Twining, arrived, supposedly instructed to help the territory face the postwar era (D. Bates 1972). He arrived the same year that a highly critical United Nations report was published, a report condemning the British failure to develop modern self-government at all levels of the Mandate (Twining 1959:16). Twining was socially privileged and, at heart, a political reactionary. He saw the Africans fit for agriculture and needing to value the dignity of manual labor (Morrison 1976:57). His views did not encourage advanced education for Africans. Even as late as 1957, Tanganyikan educational policies still stressed supposed communal values and developing petty agriculture, and restricted education in English (Pratt 1976:180; Symonds 1968:188). At the time adult literacy was 5–10 percent (ibid.:23), and in 1956 only 29 percent of the children in Eastern Province attended school at all (Morrison 1976:55). The British record on higher education and training of future African leaders and administrators was probably the worst mark against their record in Tanganyika (see Kirk-Greene 1986:xviii–xix; cf. Kenya, Berman 1996:281). In part, this may have been because they utterly failed to grasp how soon African independence would come (Allen 1986:159–163). Governor Twining resisted the idea of an all-African state and characterized Africans as having a "peasant mentality" best suited to continuing the tribal Native Authorities. Twining strongly supported local chiefs as having "undefinable powers and influences" (ibid.:21–23). Spouting this kind of rhetorical claptrap, Twining argued as late as 1953 that "it is the intention of the Government of Tanganyika to maintain the tribal system." (Chidzero 1961:151). This seemed anachronistic even then, since by 1952 the Colonial Office in London had rejected the older idea of a paramountcy of native law and custom and advocated a multiracial state. This hardly fit well with tribalism and Indirect Rule, but it also negated the very concept of a representative African democracy advocated by the United Nations Trusteeship (Chidzero 1961:186–188).[39] Matters were worsened by a growing policy of using Native Authorities to compel Africans to participate in deeply unpopular forestry, agricultural, and livestock schemes said to be for the local Africans' own good. One deeply unpopular forestry scheme generated violent Kaguru hostility (see chapter 5). This high-handed colonial paternalism further eroded the authority of the already unpopular Native Authority leaders and correspondingly elevated African support of nationalist politicians who criticized these hated policies (Pratt 1982:276–278). I have never learned why the Colonial Office made such an appalling appointment as Twining, but then they had already made many earlier really bad decisions, such as going along with the Groundnut Scheme.

Twining remained fixated on a vision of an interracial state with equal voices for the white, Asian, and African segments of the population and called for near parity of racial representation in Tanganyika Territory, where there were over 400 Africans to one European and over ten Africans to every Asian. Such representation would undermine African sovereignty in their own land, going against both the United Nations Charter and terms of the Trusteeship, as well as the promises by earlier colonial administrators. Twining promoted the multiracial United Tanganyika Party (UTP) as a foil against the nationalist Tanganyika African National Union (TANU). He encouraged local Native Authorities to support the UTP (Chidzero 1961:201). During Twining's rule, Kaguru chiefs and headmen were encouraged to harass any African nationalists who ventured into the chiefdom. In 1953 Twining banned government employees and schoolteachers from joining TANU (Maguire 1969:14). Even so, many Kaguru teachers and clerks clandestinely paid the 2 shillings needed to join TANU, and after 1955 TANU radically accelerated registration, though its membership still was represented mainly by townspeople and estate workers and not the impoverished and uneducated rural masses such as those in Ukaguru (Stephens 1968:129, 150).

Throughout this period, Twining's conduct toward African intellectuals was crude and ill-considered, even resulting in the arrest of Julius Nyerere, the leader of TANU. Political parties were successfully replacing the ethnic divisions exemplified in the "temporary tutelage" of Indirect Rule (Mair 1938:150). At this time hot verbal debates and fiery denunciations were common in newspapers such as the government-funded *Mambo Leo,* the African radical journal *Mwafrika,* and TANU's *Sauti ya Afrika,* as well as the conservative English language *Tanganyika*

Standard (Stephens 1968:110, 144). Since so few adult Africans were literate, this published controversy mattered less than it seemed, though it clearly deeply troubled and preoccupied many British government administrators and white settlers. Only a handful of Kaguru teachers and clerks had access to such publications, but they avidly read them. Throughout his tenure Governor Twining obstructed or over-controlled United Nations Commission visits to Tanganyika and repeatedly tried to prevent Nyerere and his fellow nationalists from speaking to them (Dumbuya 1995:105–113). Twining described the United Nations visits as an "inquisition" (Lohrmann 2007:55–62, 113). Unfortunately for Twining, TANU, the nationalist party, had encouraged Africans to petition the United Nations about some especially outrageous British seizures of land (ibid.:262–348). Nyerere visited the United Nations in New York three times between 1955 and 1957. He spoke about his difficulties with the British, prompting vengeful threats from Twining (ibid.:69). British abuses about forestry projects and labor at sisal estates prompted local African protests and led the United Nations Commission to visit Kilosa and Morogoro districts in 1954 (ibid.:165). By then almost anything Twining's administration proposed was opposed by the African nationalists (Mueller 1981:477). The collapse of the Groundnut Scheme coincided with an end to Twining's term, and he left in 1958.

That year saw the arrival of Governor Sir Richard Turnbull, who apparently was on orders to reverse Twining's disastrous policies and dispose of Tanganyika as a British Mandate as quickly and cheaply as possible. Turnbull was a model of tact, patience, and cordiality (Pratt 1982:262). Twining's opposition party (UTP) collapsed. TANU prevailed, and the days of the Native Authorities were numbered. The colonial government and TANU began to cooperate. In September 1960 TANU leaders assumed key ministerial posts in a provisional African national government (Tordoff 1965:65). Many chiefs and Native Authority officials understandably felt uneasy about their futures, yet even as late as April 1961 the African minister of the interior declined to indicate what the new government would do (Taylor 1963:20). On December 9, 1961, Tanganyika gained its national independence. Yet, because there were very few Africans sufficiently experienced or educated to manage anything, many British colonial administrators remained for a year or two to run things locally. Even by 1960 only 478 Africans were enrolled in Standard

XII classes. By 1961 the African literacy rate was only 16 percent (Stephens 1968:108), and there was an even greater shortage of highly educated Africans (Symonds 1966:175). Consequently, the end of actual colonialism, a time without British running the administration or keeping accounts and records, came several years after national independence. In 1963 all Native Authorities were dissolved, and with that the history of the chiefdom of Ukaguru ended. Soon after, the area's administrative center was moved from Mamboya to Geiro, now called Gairo, almost a century after Mamboya had first laid claim to being Ukaguru's ethnic and political heart. The national state did not recognize or condone "tribalism" or even ethnicity, though it mouthed sanctimonious but vacuous praise of African traditions and ways of life. The "traditional" leaders, and even Ukaguru, itself were gone long before many European administrators and technocrats had left. Even I had outlasted it.

PART TWO

Colonial Life

TWO

Ukaguru 1957–58

This volume is an account of political life in Ukaguru, Kilosa district, during the years prior to the end of British colonial rule. To make this political account convincing I preface it with information on the general social and economic life within. In this chapter I briefly describe local African settlement and social organization and the ways Africans made a living, the markets, roads, climate, and terrain. I also briefly describe Kaguru beliefs and values, and the Christian mission and government schools, which changed traditional thinking. My study mainly involves the Kaguru, but it also involves the Baraguyu, Kamba, and Ngulu ethnic minorities; African outsiders working for the Native Authority, for the mission, and in the Asian shops; and the few Asian and Somali merchants and white missionaries. I therefore briefly remark on them as well.

The Lay of the Land: Getting Around the Chiefdom and Learning What's What

The main east-west road of central Tanganyika ran through the center of Ukaguru. At the time of my major fieldwork even this road was unpaved and consequently sometimes difficult during the peak of the rains, when upgrades were very difficult to climb even for vehicles with four-wheel drive or tire-chains. I often saw vehicles bogged down for many hours or even days, even though drivers had come with shovels and ropes. This main road passed by only one important Kaguru settlement, the subchief headquarters at Geiro on the western border of Eastern Province. To reach other Kaguru settlements one had to travel three to fifteen miles over minor, more difficult roads leading off from the main road. The roads to these more distant sites were sometimes very difficult during the height of the rains, so sometimes messages and packets had to be sent out on foot. Sometimes rivers crossing the roads were not fordable for several days, even by trucks. (There were no bridges in the upland area of the chiefdom.) There were small African and sometimes Asian shops at these sites. Native Authority trucks brought supplies and carried messages every week or so to many of these areas. Africans sometimes paid money to hitch rides on these vehicles. Asian-owned trucks, usually driven by Africans, brought in merchandise to many of these shops about once a month. Missionaries and some European administrators visited these areas, though often only once or twice a year. Only settlements such as Berega (because of the mission and its middle school and small hospital), Chakwale (because of the cattle market), and Geiro (being on the main road and with a petrol station) were visited more often. The Protestant CMS Mission ran the only postal service in the chiefdom. Native Authority trucks brought mail in and out of this area almost every week. Anyone wanting to send or receive mail had to hike or bike to Berega, often a day's round trip from much of the chiefdom even for a strong biker, since the chiefdom was so hilly. Traffic greatly increased after the rainy season ended, both because then roads were more traversable and because that was the time when crops were harvested and taxes due, so that markets and courthouses had to be visited. It was then too that Kaguru and other Africans had plentiful grain for beer to celebrate marriages and initiations. Then Asian trucks came weekly to government-run markets to purchase produce, tax-collectors came to collect from Africans attending markets, and sales at the cattle market increased on account of the need to pay taxes. Many Kaguru and Ngulu sold metal goods, tobacco, mats, beads, and pottery to Baraguyu flush with ready cash from livestock sales. The rainy season was the time for intensive agricultural labor and little travel in Ukaguru, and the dry season the time for travel, when cultivation tapered off and visiting, marketing, and celebration of initiation and marriages led to a stream of Africans trekking and bicycling over the roads and paths. It was also the time for Kaguru to do road work in lieu of paying cash for taxes.

To appreciate how poor roads hindered the movement of the British administrators, one must remember that none of the British administrators owned four-wheel drive vehicles. They mostly relied on their personal automobiles, for which they received government loans and travel allowances. This meant that administrators found travel difficult in the bush during the heavy rains. The Kilosa district headquarters itself had a few four-wheel-drive Land Rovers, but these were available mainly provided to the district commissioner, district officers or police for urgent, special official trips. Land Rovers were too expensive and consumed too much petrol to be privately affordable to ordinary administrators or for most ordinary journeys. The CMS at Mgugu-Berega also owned a Land Rover, but that too was used very sparingly by the frugal missionaries. Only a few Kaguru villages were actually on the roads. Most lay more distant, though easily visible and reachable by paths traversable by adept cyclists. Kaguru felt uneasy living very close to the alien traffic on the roads. Besides, the main concern of most villagers was establishing a homestead near fields or ready supplies of water, not near transport, for which they had no everyday use.

In upland Ukaguru, Kilosa district, there were only seven settlements. These were Geiro, Mgugu-Berega, Idibo, Chakwale, Mamboya, Iyogwe, and Nong'we. Each contained a few mud-brick or cement-block buildings with metal roofs, and many outlying African wattle and thatch houses. Each had its own character. Geiro, by the main east-west road, had the largest and most numerous shops (both Indian and African), a subchief courthouse, government dispensary, government school, CMS church, and buildings for African staff. It was the only settlement in the chiefdom where one could purchase petrol, a pump being there on account of the main highway traffic. (All vehicles based elsewhere traveled with petrol stored in drums and put in back during long trips. Otherwise, those needing fuel had to journey to Kilosa or Kimamba towns many hours away.) Geiro had the rough and busy character of a small settlement in the old American West.

Mgugu-Berega was the only settlement with permanent white residents, four to six Australian Protestant missionaries. It was about three miles from the main road and was at times cut off by a stream that flooded during heavy rains. The settlement was in three parts: about two miles from the main road were several African shops, and a market, at Mgugu, where crops could be sold under government supervision. About half a mile further, separated by another stream, was the only middle school in the chiefdom. It was run by the local CMS mission. There were cement and iron-roofed classrooms, dormitories, houses for staff, workshops, and a playing field. It was landscaped in a European manner, with blossoming bushes and small flowerbeds. Separated by another stream and up a very steep hill another half mile beyond was the actual CMS Station at Berega, with European residences, a mission primary school, a CMS church, a mission-run shop, a mission-run hospital and clinic, African staff residences, and a large, surrounding cluster of African houses. The hospital was the only medical facility in the chiefdom where surgery could be performed and in-bed patients properly quartered. One room in the main mission residence served as the chiefdom's only postal station. This area was landscaped in a European manner. The Berega-Mgugu settlement was enclosed by hills and gave the most European, salubrious, and sophisticated impression of all these places.

The road leading to the mission continued on past it for another 15 miles leading to Iyogwe and Idibo. Iyogwe was a very small station with a CMS church, a CMS school with staff housing, and an African settlement with a few small African shops. It was near the only Roman Catholic church in the chiefdom, a church bitterly contested by the CMS, which sought a religious monopoly in the area. (Roman Catholics were not allowed to proselytize in the chiefdom, so it was built just a few yards across the Kilosa district/Eastern Provincial border.) Iyogwe, sitting at the foot of the massive Talagwe Mountain, was pretty—green and well watered. Idibo had a market where much produce was sold, a Somali and several African shops, a government dispensary, a subchief courthouse, a CMS school, a CMS church, and many African houses. Idibo was on a hill overlooking an expanse of low hill settlements and the lone, towering Idibo Mountain. Chakwale contained a large cattle market, a small veterinary office, Arab and African shops, a CMS church, a market, a CMS school, and staff housing. It was a small, sleepy settlement that burst into frantic life once a month when several thousand people arrived for the cattle market and its accompanying petty trading and beer parties. During the market there was much drinking, and many Africans wandered about with considerable cash. Arab cattle dealers with very large amounts of cash attended. The cattle market was consequently the only time when police regularly sent a Land Rover to the chiefdom with armed officers to insure order.

Mamboya was quite small considering that it was the location of the paramount chief's courthouse and home. It had a small Arab shop, a few African shops, a CMS church, and a CMS school and staff housing. Located on a mountainside, it was lush with vegetation and was the most beautiful of the settlements, affecting a seedy and rundown charm. Nong'we, high in the Itumba Mountains, was the smallest and remotest station. Set on a high hill and surrounded by soaring peaks and plunging valleys, often engulfed in morning mists and fogs and sometimes even experiencing frosts, tiny Nong'we was the most dramatic settlement. Aside from a subchief courthouse, a tiny market, a government school, and a CMS church, there was little there, not even any proper shops. The view, however, was spectacular. Very few outsiders reached Nong'we other than some Native Authority trucks, since the road through the precipitous mountains was very difficult. No one could drive in during the worst of the rains, when government messengers came by foot or on bicycle.

I do not discuss settlements in the lowlands, since they were filled with a very ethnically mixed population and had no Kaguru character at all. These settlements served the traffic going between Kilosa and Morogoro and the capital city of Dar es Salaam, as well as the needs of the thousands of Africans working on the nearby sisal estates. Each of the stations I have just described, even the smallest, was a magnet for nearby Africans, who visited for litigation, paying taxes and fees, attending church services and school, and buying goods and selling produce when the markets were open. During the busy days at the markets and courts, several local beer clubs could be found on the edges of these settlements where Kaguru could exchange news, gossip, and pick up women. There were radios at Berega, Geiro, and Chakwale (owned by shopkeepers, schoolteachers, and missionaries), but aside from the news carried by African truck-drivers, recent news about the outside world was hard to come by. Old Swahili newspapers drifted into settlements and were kept and passed around to the few who were literate. Not many, not even most missionaries and Asian merchants, seemed very interested in events in the outside world or even what was happening in the district, provincial, or territorial capitals. Without the gossipy truck drivers employed by the Native Authority and by Asian shops, the area would have been shut out from most outside news. Each settlement was a world of its own, extending its influence little beyond the African villages near it. Yet Africans from all over the chiefdom did come to Berega on account of its hospital and its postal office, which included a postal savings service. Berega was the only place where one could always purchase a few books, papers and envelopes, and pens and pencils, though few outside those at the schools and courthouses had need for writing anything.

The Rural Landscape

I found most of Ukaguru beautiful, which was one of the reasons I worked there. The upland landscape of Ukaguru was scrub and woodland cut by river valleys that held the farmlands. In east and central Ukaguru small clusters of two or three to as many as ten houses formed hamlets, usually separated from one another by as little as a thousand yards or less. These houses, round or square, were made of earth and wattle and covered with thatch roofs. Only at the large settlements did one see sturdier construction, a more prosperous Kaguru's metal roof, or even more rarely a house made from cement or adobe bricks. As one moved out from the river valleys the distribution of hamlets became increasingly thinner. A lacework of footpaths connected these sites. Standing on any hillside overlooking a valley one could always see a dozen or more tiny villages, whereas one could go miles in the hilly uplands and find only seemingly uninhabited scrub and forest. There in those uplands was where Baraguyu built their cattle camps, several miles from most Kaguru villages, and usually difficult for any outsider to find. In the far west of Ukaguru, in areas such as Geiro and in the Itumba Mountains, Kaguru valley settlements were increasingly replaced with long, low dwellings of earth with flat wood and earth roofs (called *tembe*), often L- or U-shaped to accommodate a large livestock enclosure (Beidelman 1972). They looked like low, straggling forts. These settlements were small and more often atop hills for defense. Kaguru trekked far down from these hilly sites to fetch water every day. Here one still felt a sense of the old days, when raids by Baraguyu, Maasai, Kamba, and others made Kaguru defense a paramount concern. Most of this high area had been deforested due to cultivation during the era of raiding when more Kaguru had lived there, having fled their attackers. At the very highest areas of the mountains there were still thick forests. In the north-central hilly area of the chiefdom, mainly in Idibo subchiefdom, Kamba villages were apart from Kaguru but nearby and undistinguishable in appearance.

Everyday Kaguru life took place in small villages, and most everyday encounters between Kaguru of different villages involved people meeting at watering points, sharing work clearing land, harvesting crops, or building houses. In the dry season when agricultural work ceased, there were frequent gathering by men at village beer clubs, where as many as fifty or sixty people might drink and gossip; such partying often included Baraguyu and Kamba as well as Kaguru. It was only for court cases, paying taxes, selling produce or livestock, or buying cloth, metal tools, kerosene, hoes, sugar, salt, or other goods that most ordinary country folk visited the larger settlements. Many rural Kaguru only visited such places five or six times a year, and most had never visited a town such as Kilosa or Morogoro. Almost no one in the chiefdom outside a few clerks, teachers, and merchants had ever visited Dar es Salaam. The most likely rural Kaguru to travel daily from villages to any settlements were children, especially boys, who increasingly attended local primary schools.

Making a Living and Getting an Education

The major source of livelihood for most Kaguru was agriculture. In east and central Ukaguru the staple crop was maize; in the mountains and west this was often replaced or supplemented by millet and sorghum. In addition, Kaguru grew yams, cassava, sugarcane, peas, onions, plantains, groundnuts, sesame, and beans. A few grew tobacco, which they cured and sold to other Kaguru or more often to Baraguyu. This required much work and skill in cultivation and processing, so only a few attempted it. In the 1950s castor beans were a popular cash crop because the oil was then used for machine lubricants, but it required much work hulling. In 1958 the price of castor in Idibo plunged from 1 shilling per kilo to 65 pence. (There are 100 East African pence to an East African shilling. I am told there is no longer any market for castor.) Both men and women worked in the fields, usually together. Kaguru employed steel hoes and cleared land with machetes and axes. Cultivation and clearing were hard labor. Entire families worked from dawn to dusk during critical times such as planting, early weeding, and harvesting.

Some Kaguru throughout the chiefdom had small herds of goats and sheep. In the west (around Geiro), in the Itumba Mountains, and in the north (around Idibo), some Kaguru had many cattle. Herds were kept mainly for milk, or for sale or slaughter during special occasions such as initiations, marriage celebrations, and funerals, or for paying bridewealth or medical bills or court fines. Herding was usually done by boys, who were kept out of school for this. The largest Kaguru holdings of cattle were in northern and western Ukaguru, where herds competed with those of the Baraguyu (in the north and west) and those of the Kamba (in the north). Kaguru held sheep and goats throughout the chiefdom. Overgrazing had been a concern of the British administrators for decades. This was mainly blamed on the Baraguyu, who had large herds and, because they themselves did not cultivate, were not concerned with any damage livestock might do to agricultural land. Actually, overgrazing was probably due as much to Kaguru and Kamba, since the greater damage was said to be done by goats, which graze close to ground-cover. Kaguru holdings in sheep and goats far exceeded those of Baraguyu. Most Kaguru owned small small flocks of chickens and a few had ducks. These were the main sources of food for minor celebrations and for entertaining important guests or paying petty fines, costing only two or three shillings. Kaguru never ate eggs.

The major source of Kaguru petty cash was in women's brewing and selling beer, made from maize, sugar, millet, or rarely honey. Repeatedly, the British urged the Kaguru Native Authority to curtail brewing during the time of cultivation, wrongly claiming that Kaguru would otherwise drink rather than work. In fact, brewing provided beer to encourage and reward work-parties (see J. Willis 2002:116–117; Beidelman 1961b; 1971a:25–27). Although the Native Authority required a relatively small payment for a brewing license (30 shillings, about two dollars), most individual Kaguru could not afford it and pooled their resources to purchase one license for many brewers, or else sold illegally. British colonial authorities never appreciated Kaguru's profound and continuous need for petty cash, which brewing met when other resources were low, such as before harvests. Kaguru households always needed some cash to purchase salt, sugar, kerosene, matches, soap, and other foreign items, which they now considered essentials. Any Kaguru woman needing ready cash could purchase one or two shillings worth of sugar and turn it into seven or eight shillings by brewing, provided she avoided buying any brewing permit.

Local Baraguyu elders were the wealthiest inhabitants of the chiefdom; because of their large herds, they had a steady potential source of cash independent of the harvest season. Baraguyu elders consumed large quantities of beer and tobacco yet disdained agriculture. Consequently, Kaguru secured much of their ordinary cash by selling such goods to Baraguyu. Kaguru and Baraguyu remained familiar but wary enemies. Kaguru beer clubs were regularly attended by Baraguyu, but these sometimes became scenes of violence when too much had been drunk (Beidelman 1961b). Baraguyu disdained any labor other than livestock husbandry, so they purchased gourds, tobacco, pottery, and metal goods from Kaguru. Baraguyu also consumed considerable flour, which they purchased or traded with their neighbors. In the Idibo area, where I did much of my fieldwork, Kamba held far more livestock than Kaguru. Their relations to Kaguru were only slightly less problematical than those of the Baraguyu (Beidelman 1961c; see appendices on livestock holdings and ethnicity). Kamba lived near Kaguru but always in separate settlements.

The Kaguru and Kamba work-year was determined by the rains. There was frantic and ceaseless labor in late October and November when the rains were near, clearing fields, hoeing, and planting. The rains began sometime in December, commencing with spectacular violence and intensity. Only at first did rains fall all day. Later, some rains fell intensely for only a few hours and then gave way to clear weather. As the season progressed the rains gradually diminished, and then ended entirely sometime in June. Unexpected flooding might cause wash-outs and even force Kaguru to make a second emergency planting. Most of eastern and central Ukaguru usually got the thirty inches of rain needed for crops, but every third or fourth year might be lean, and famine from drought occurred at least once every decade. Only the very high, sparsely populated, and rugged Itumba Mountains of central Ukaguru had sufficient rain every year, and that area was too cold, bleak, and precipitous to encourage much population once raiding had ended with German rule. Rains in the western part of Ukaguru, beyond Kilosa district, could be more chancy. Sometimes Kaguru from that area (Mpwapwa district) bought or begged food from the Kaguru of Kilosa district. Harvests were in July or August, and by late June cultivation was nearly impossible because of the hardness of the ground. In the dry season, time not spent visiting or organizing ceremonies such as initiation was devoted to house building and repair (especially roof thatching), tool making, mat and basket weaving, path clearing, and other less urgent chores.

The Kaguru economic and social year was divided into two halves. First there was an intensive period of cultivation beginning in November and tapering off as the rains diminished, the ground hardened, and harvest approached. Then there was a dry season marked by harvest and a consequent peak in social life, beer drinking, travel, visiting, and ceremonial activities. This was also a time for required road work and clearing village paths. In contrast, the Baraguyu work-year was determined entirely by their herds. They moved camps when grass gave out and trekked ever further from camp with herds during the dry season, but generally their work patterns changed little with the seasons. Baraguyu were never called to do Native Authority labor. Forcing them would have been difficult, even dangerous, and Baraguyu were willing to pay small bribes to Kaguru headmen to escape such (in their eyes) humiliating labor.

Kaguru and Kamba secured land for cultivation by gaining permission from the local headman, who allowed access for a household (a person, his or her spouse and children) for his or her lifetime or until the person moved away or gave up regular cultivation (see next chapter). Most land was cultivated by families who had lived in a locale for generations, but newcomers, at least Kaguru and some Kamba, were usually given land because headmen wanted a following. Persons working for the Native Authority or CMS mission were also usually given some small plots of land. The most valuable land was near the streams and rivers, where annual overflow deposited fertile silt and where the water level was high. Land got less and less valuable as one moved further from the river bottoms. Riverine land would be cultivated for many years. Upland, drier areas were cultivated less easily because they were less well watered and fertile and required greater efforts to clear. Non-riverine land could be cultivated for three to five years with decreasing yields.

Such land should then be left fallow for about ten years, though with a growing local population it was increasingly given less time to recover. Most households had small garden patches adjoining the house where vegetables, peppers, and fruits might be grown. Most households owned a combination of riverine, medium, and poor land. Fields varied from tiny patches of about ten square yards to plots of about three acres. Most households possessed between three and four acres. Holdings were scattered because they were hard to get and had been acquired over some time under varied circumstances, but also because Kaguru wanted a wide variety of plots because any one plot might wash out, or be ruined by wild animals or insect pests, or other calamities. One did not want all of the same type of land in the same place. Variety also allowed a diversity of crops. Consequently, many Kaguru spent many hours traveling to reach their scattered fields.

The major problem limiting any household's agricultural resources was lack of labor. During the critical times of clearing, planting, weeding, and harvesting everyone was busy working at the same time. Few were willing to help neighbors, except briefly, since each had his or her own critical demands at the same time. Even if someone had extra cash (and few did), labor would not have been readily purchasable.

Kaguru households were poor. It was difficult to measure their actual wealth, since much was in livestock and stored food rather than cash. Besides, Kaguru were extremely keen to conceal their wealth from their neighbors so that they need not share it or be envied and consequently bewitched. It was clear that most households made far less than 500 shillings (70 dollars) a year in cash.[1] Fewer than two hundred persons in Ukaguru, Kilosa district, were regular wage-earners. Most of those worked for the government Native Authority, the CMS mission, or the few Asian and Somali merchants. Less than half of these two hundred wage-earners received more than 100 shillings (15 dollars) a month. Kaguru men could earn about 35 shillings (5 dollars) a month doing road work for the Native Authority in the dry season, but few did so unless they had no other means of securing cash for paying taxes. Kaguru cultivators were estimated in 1958 to produce between 300 and 600 shillings, 28–85 dollars) worth of crops in a good year. This amount included what they had to keep to feed themselves, so one could see how poor they were in actual cash.

Ukaguru was not the poorest area in Tanganyika—there were neighboring areas to the west and south that were even poorer—but poverty characterized much of the chiefdom and limited social development. No cash crop or other resource provided any good means for cash. Kaguru farmers led a difficult life dominated by constant pressure to survive, and they followed a monotonous cultivating schedule. Their world was the grubby world of the desperately rural poor everywhere (see Berger 1979:196, 207).

Kaguru had considerable difficulty bringing crops to market. Most men and women carried loads of grain, vegetables, tobacco, or whatever on their heads in baskets, pots, or cloths; a few men had bicycles and could carry larger loads further. No one could or would transport all his or her marketable goods at one time. Market prices varied from week to week, and people were cautious about parting with much food at one time. The coming year could be a bad one and then there would not be enough if one had sold too much. Besides, if there was a food shortage, one would have to buy food back for a far higher price than that for which it had originally been sold.

The hardest time for Kaguru households was before harvest, when food supplies were at their lowest and the cost of buying flour at a shop was high. Kaguru storage of food had always been bad. Grain was stored in either large roof-bins or cribs located next to a house, or more often in bins and lofts within a house itself. Rats and insects ate into this. Poor storage facilities led Africans to see little point in hoarding up more than they would need; Asians were better equipped for this (Fuggles-Couchman 1964:56).

Kaguru saw only two sure means to any permanent increase in wealth, and these were through education or setting up a small shop. All wealthy Kaguru (except a few chiefs or headmen who were actually not truly wealthy when compared to the highest ranking school teachers, clerks, or technicians) had educations. Cash wages allowed Kaguru to secure education and thus opportunities for their children. Cash wages bought material benefits in housing, clothing, better and more food, medical care, and even some luxuries. Some educated Kaguru invested money in small shops. Store ownership by salaried employees was not allowed by either the government or mission, but restrictions against employees could be circumvented by registering a shop in the name of a spouse or relative. Even so, no Kaguru shop owner had the wealth to compete with the Asian merchants. Government officials seemed to think that by charging Africans low licensing fees to run a shop (30 shillings, 3 dollars) annually, they evened the playing field with Asians. Unfortunately, the dire poverty of Kaguru still made this low fee far more of a burden to Kaguru than the far higher fee charged to Asians. Furthermore, local Africans were generally ignorant of what food prices were in town, though they knew that these were higher. Agricultural officers did not provide such information readily to those in the bush (Fuggles-Couchman 1964:51). For example, in 1958 maize was selling in Idibo market at 16 pence per kilo but at 22 pence 60 miles south in Kilosa. In any case, Kaguru had no means of getting there. At best Africans were restricted to selling in bush areas where they did not compete with Asians or, a dangerous option, selling goods to local Africans on credit, a practice forbidden to Asians. The danger in selling to one's fellow Africans was that one's kin and neighbors often argued that communal ties should weaken any obligations to repay such help. A few Kaguru used cash savings to purchase a sewing machine with which to make clothing on order for neighbors, but this meant someone had to know how to tailor clothing and repair the machines. Other Kaguru purchased bicycles and made money transporting goods for others, but these provided small and unsteady profits. Even owning a bicycle posed problems if one could not repair it oneself. Finally, unlike Asians or whites, Africans found it nearly impossible to get large loans or credit, which consequently locked out any serious business venture.

Every Kaguru settlement had a primary school. Most were controlled by the Protestant CMS, but the ones at Magubike (not a proper settlement, west of Mgugu-Berega), Geiro, and Nong'we in the upland Ukaguru area were run by the Kaguru Native Authority. Only CMS converts in good standing could teach at CMS schools. All primary schools, both mission and government, were poorly furnished and dilapidated. Such schools had between 100 and 150 students. Students in the first three grades of primary school went half a day in shifts, either in the morning or afternoon. Only those in the fourth grade sometimes attended all day. Most such schools had two to four teachers, usually two. Classes were taught by local Africans who sometimes had little if any training beyond tenth grade, though they were supposed to have had two years of teachers' training. Most such teachers could speak only a little English. These four years of primary school cost 10 shillings a year for boys; in the CMS schools girls paid only 5 shillings. Girls attended government schools free of charge. Even with this encouragement to girls, two-thirds of the primary school student population remained male. Sending a child to primary school was an immense economic burden for Kaguru households. Children in school could not help with household chores at home, and we have seen how very poor most households were. Such students had to wear school uniforms, which had to be purchased. Even buying pencils and paper was a burden for parents. Despite these sacrifices, primary school education provided insufficient training for any decent job.[2] There was a middle school for fifth to eighth grade at Mgugu-Berega. Run by the CMS, it was exclusively for boys and was the only such school available to Kaguru. Those very few Kaguru girls who sought a middle school had to journey at least a hundred miles away. Most Kaguru thought it a waste of time to educate girls; many explained that they did not want to lose money on a girl who would be someone else's wife and move away. To enter a middle school, a student needed to pass a written examination and submit teachers' recommendations to a committee selected and headed by the provincial educational officer (George 1960:46).

Middle schools provided initial learning in English as well as mathematics, advanced Swahili, general knowledge, history, and religion (George 1960). Much time, probably far too much, was consumed in agricultural labor and handicrafts. Only with education beyond middle school, standards IX through XII, was there real hope for serious economic advancement. (The headmaster of the middle school at Mgugu-Berega and a few of the local African technicians in the medical and veterinary services were the only local Africans with standard XII educations, and none of these was Kaguru.) Middle schools were boarding schools. Murray describes such schools as combinations of a native village and an English public school (1967:105). J. Cameron and Dodd describe such a school as an "education station," a little world of its own (1970:71–72). The boys lived in a dormitory and worked on the local school gardens to help pay for their education. They also did all of the other chores that maintained the school. Beside that, they paid over 250 shillings yearly in tuition, plus they had to purchase several school uniforms, books, paper, and other supplies. Very few local Africans were either clever enough or wealthy enough to get this far.

There were about 140 boys in the middle school at Mgugu-Berega, taught by six teachers. By European or American standards this was still low-level education, but it represented the very elite of Ukaguru.[3] Outside a few seeking advancement in the CMS clergy, no Kaguru had ever reached much beyond middle school at the time I was in the field. Boarding at middle school, away from home, profoundly affected all such students. They would have spent most of their time, for several years, in an environment of European-type dormitories that required daily cleanliness and proper grooming and neatness, and eating meals at tables following European etiquette. All would have lived far differently from how they lived at home. Few would have then been content with the daily life they had previously known, whatever their subsequent incomes. For the vast number of middle school graduates who did not go on, their social world was now one of considerable economic and social frustration and discontent. Many years after I left Ukaguru, I met Kaguru who had graduated from university, but such persons were no part of the Kaguru world I knew in 1957–58. To have been sent to a university a Kaguru would have had to pass the Cambridge Overseas School Certificate, and that would have required far more education than middle school (George 1960:46). It is important to note that no Baraguyu attended any school at any level, and that very few Kamba attended primary schools. Education was embraced only by Kaguru and Ngulu in the area.

The Native Authority and the CMS mission were the two major employers in the chiefdom. Neither allowed workers to engage in any active commitment to politics or trade. Those working for the Native Authority were afraid to be openly critical of local politics, although the more educated technicians working for the veterinary or medical services were free of such constraint, since no African official was over them. Those technical jobs, with their possibilities of favoritism in providing medicines and health care, provided many opportunities for extra money. Here the term "bribe" would be somewhat misleading. Except for the most highly educated Africans, who had absorbed some British attitudes about social rights to government services, most Kaguru believed that all services merited some payments, however small. I recognized this when many Kaguru told me they preferred paying something for medical services even when these were supposed to be free, because otherwise they saw no reason why a fellow African who was not kin should be bound to provide proper services at all. In contrast, Kaguru recognized that whites could not be paid in cash by Africans, though many Africans did think that any long-term relationship of work for whites automatically obliged white employers to treat them with gifts, old clothing, extra food, loans, and other benefits. One of the strains CMS missionaries experienced with Africans was that though the missionaries were poor and underpaid by European standards, they were still expected to be generous. Most missionaries I knew were willing to help when they could but were too poor to meet these expectations by employees. Kaguru and other Africans contrasted the frugal and seemingly stingy missionaries with the more easy-going British administrators.

For Africans, the ideal European employer was a bachelor. Bachelors were seen as less demanding and cost-conscious than married men, especially those with children, who had to stretch money further. When white men were married, dealings with domestic servants became the sphere of their wives, and most Africans thought white women fussier and more demanding about household routines and costs. Kaguru and many other Africans told me European wives, *mem-sahibs,* were always a burden to servants. Kaguru considered fellow Africans and Asians to be the least desirable employers of all. Those were seen as the least likely to provide extra benefits and to have the least wealth available for Africans to siphon off. They certainly had tougher ideas about local food and servant costs than did Europeans. For local Kaguru, all these views about the economic advantages of servanthood involved only a few Africans, who were generally viewed by other Africans as lucky to have an inside-track on cash and social connections.

In 1957–58 few Africans in Ukaguru employed other Africans for wages. Those few who did were unmarried teachers or clerks stationed away from their home villages. Such men sometimes employed a part-time woman or boy to fetch water or firewood or to wash, clean, and cook. The few Asians and Somalis in the upland area of the chiefdom employed boys to do household chores or menial tasks in shops as a "gofer" or as a turn-boy on trucks (a boy who turned the cranks on motors or did dirty or menial work, such as washing or cleaning cars, carrying messages, or digging cars out of the mud). The best job for Africans in such shops was as a sewing machine operator/tailor.

The CMS was the most demanding and culturally intrusive employer. All Africans working for them were expected to be loyal members of the church. Employees who were caught drinking, smoking, or attending traditional dances, or were thought to be fornicating, lost their jobs. Only abject apologies coupled with testifying at an evangelical revival service might save such lapsed workers. Nor would the vindictive CMS allow a morally fallen teacher to receive an alternate job in a government school. To my surprise, the Native Authority went along with supporting the CMS in blacklisting such errant workers, even though there was a shortage of teachers. Such supposed sinners were doomed to seek work somewhere in the distant towns and estates. The only exception were a few who became chiefs or headmen, but such posts owed everything to local clan politics and were therefore not likely to fall to younger men. Yet even those senior Native Authority jobs were poorly paid when compared to the high-level jobs of teachers.

The poverty of Kaguru allowed few to get sufficient education to secure very good jobs, while the poverty of the chiefdom itself restricted the opportunities for those with education, so that any truly well-educated Kaguru would have left. Kaguru teachers and clerks got on economically because they had local kin to support them if they ran short, yet these same kin consequently pestered them for economic aid in return. Ukaguru, unlike richer areas of Tanganyika such as Morogoro, Kilimanjaro, Iringa, or Buhaya, offered no bright future for those who might triumph over the bitter odds against economic/educational success. That few Kaguru left the chiefdom was due to two facts: almost no Kaguru had the educational skills to succeed outside; and, though poor, Ukaguru still provided better low-level opportunities for survival than being a poorly paid worker in a sisal estate, or a desperately poor road worker or porter in some town, a dangerous world that few Kaguru knew.[4] Even if one were foolish enough to move away from the chiefdom, one could not afford to take one's family. It would have been easier to survive together cultivating back in Ukaguru, despite all the difficulties.

Religion and Domestic Social Organization

The CMS was a major economic and cultural force in the chiefdom, controlling most of the primary schools and the single middle school. The mission bitterly fought every effort by other groups, government, or other churches, to establish alternate social services in the area. The lone Roman Catholic church on the northeastern border of the chiefdom near Iyogwe (at Ijafa and therefore technically outside the district and province) was a source of endless complaints by the CMS to the British district administration. It was ironic that the Roman Catholic church was better built and more physically attractive than any of the CMS buildings in Ukaguru. It was also true that the lone African priest serving the few Roman Catholic converts in the area was more sophisticated, more suave, and better educated than any of the Australian missionaries in Berega, having attended ecclesiastical college in Rome and knowing French, Italian, English, Greek, and Latin. Educated Kaguru were quick to point out these contrasts to me. The CMS and Roman Catholics had fought bitterly in the decades before the British came, beating up one another's converts and burning down one another's buildings. To prevent such conflicts it became colonial government policy to set up "comity" in different rural areas, each restricted to one Christian group. It was only in the towns that different churches could openly compete. Strictly speaking, the Roman Catholic church near Iyogwe was just across the district border (at Ijafa) and therefore technically located within a zone relegated to Roman Catholic comity; even so, the CMS saw that church as a bridgehead built by the Catholics to poach converts from them.

I never met a Kaguru Muslim;[5] Islam was at first disliked by Kaguru because it was associated with the slave trade and with the Arab-led caravans that raided Kaguru. Later some of the Kaguru's neighbors to the east, the Ngulu, Zigua, and Luguru, converted to Islam and used their Arab connections to secure arms to raid Kaguru. Still later, the Germans employed Muslim Swahili akidas to administer their harsh rule. Kaguru never had good associations with Muslims. (The few Arab and Somali merchants in the chiefdom showed no interest in converting anyone nor in associating socially with Kaguru.) Kaguru saw that power was held by Europeans, who were not Muslims, and that access to a European language (in the past almost never known by Muslims) was through Christian or secular, not Muslim, connections. (I had to speak in Swahili to the Arab and Somali traders in the area, even though some of the Arab cattle traders were rich and sophisticated.)

Kaguru were known as a matrilineal people. Traditionally this was so, yet for over a century Kaguru had been exposed to aggressive, intolerant Christian missionaries committed to patriarchal values. Muslim Swahili and Arabs whom Kaguru encountered also emphasized patriarchy. Neither the missionaries nor the Muslim Asian and coastal peoples considered matriliny a proper, moral mode of social organization. Christians and Muslims thought that men who headed households were entitled to hold their authority uncontended by other men, such as mothers' brothers, who headed clans and matrilineages and who always saw their power to control their heirs, their sisters' children, as depending upon undermining the authority of their sisters' and nieces' husbands. Only by such means could matrilineal elders draw junior matrilineal kinsmen (their matrilineal heirs) into their control. Kaguru courts often supported the claims of matrilineal kin, especially regarding political claims for leadership within a matrilineal clan. That made sense, since court elders held their appointments because British administrators had been told to respect and support Kaguru matriliny as far as that supported the supposed traditional chiefship integral to Indirect Rule and the Native Authority. Yet the power and authority of matrilineal kin were gradually being eroded. This was because matrilineal kinship had been supported traditionally by the need for lineal cohesion, for cohesion of groups larger than households, which could provide political and economic support, especially during the tumultuous earlier era of raiding.

With the political stability of colonial life, the smaller household became the most important social unit. Broader, protective groups were losing importance. As church and state encouraged patriarchy, women's powers decreased, while powers increased for educated men. Women were rarely educated, because this was thought only to help the men they married. Wealthier, educated men almost always claimed to be Christians; consequently, they were unwilling to divorce, thereby depriving women of a key traditional power employed against abusive men. In the past, recalcitrant, abusive husbands could be threatened with divorce and return of bridewealth. Since Kaguru were traditionally polygynous, such women could easily secure new husbands, and women's matrilineal kin gained further bridewealth when such women remarried. Women who left their husbands even increased the power of their matrilineal kinsmen over those women's offspring, especially if they took those children with them. Despite the claims of many Christian missionaries that they were fighting to increase the dignity and security of women, the mission's hostility to polygyny, divorce, and matriliny weakened Kaguru women's domestic positions. They could no longer so easily pit their husbands against their mothers' brothers or brothers, and without polygyny they could not pit their own children against those of a disloyal husband's other wives.

By 1957–58 Kaguru remained nostalgic about their past, about their ethnicity, which embodied matriliny, even though some, especially Christians, saw matriliny as backward. Kaguru courts partially enforced matrilineal order but also subverted it. Even the oldest court officials, however much they valued tradition, saw courts as means to support the power of men and crush insubordinate women. In doing so, they subverted matrilineal values that depended on marital instability, divorce, and women's ties to their children. Subtly, Kaguru men, through the courts, slowly undermined the domestic traditions at the core of the beliefs and values that were repeatedly, and at times hypocritically, claimed to be at the heart of the Native Authority system.

Kaguru society was not an easy-going assembly of kin and neighbors. Kaguru remained intensely suspicious and envious of one another. Impoverished and often faced with food shortages, Kaguru professed two contradictory values about their social life. Neighbors, especially kin, should support one another when in need. At the same time, the difficulties of modern life, the mercurial and unpredictable vagaries of a cash economy, frequent droughts, demands for taxes, needs for educational or medical fees, led to frequent crises where needs of a household trumped needs of distant kin and neighbors. At those times, other Kaguru social values took precedence, and needs of one's own household were the most important of all. On account of these conflicting demands, Kaguru were wary of letting other Kaguru know their true resources. While Kaguru, like many other people, took pleasure in showing hospitality to others, wearing nice clothing on special occasions, and educating their children, most remained cautious about displaying how prosperous they might be. Any economic windfall would prompt others' demands for loans and help or, worse yet, might incite witchcraft and sorcery by jealous kin or neighbors who had been refused help that they thought should have been given. For most Kaguru, anyone who got ahead, especially local political leaders and shop owners, was suspected of witchcraft, the underlying assumption being that such success was inevitably secured by "eating" others, by keeping resources to oneself and not sharing them. Kaguru believed in witches. Even the most sophisticated and educated Kaguru I met expressed concern that there were people with strange and unaccountable powers to succeed. Kaguru were troubled by the fact that unscrupulous and reprehensible people often succeeded, whereas worthier people seemed unrewarded. Kaguru saw social fate in personal terms and repeatedly interpreted the failure of social justice in malevolently personal terms (Beidelman 1963a, 1986 ch. 6). Rumors from Morogoro and Dar es Salaam suggested that thinking about witches persisted even among the most sophisticated African elite.

Kaguru believed in the powers of the dead. They repeatedly performed ceremonies honoring dead ancestors or, at least, ceremonies intended to keep the disturbing dead assuaged and distant. For Kaguru, riled and annoyed dead were sources of illness, infertility, and other misfortunes. If misfortune was not caused by witches, then it was caused by the dead who had been disturbed by the misconduct of the living or by the living having too long neglected to offer beer, flour, or a slain animal's blood to their ancestors. Any serious antisocial behavior such as incest, cursing of relatives, shedding of blood, or disrespect to elders might have caused misfortune and required the propitiation of the dead. Persistent illness or repeated accidents led Kaguru to consult diviners who could tell whether these difficulties were due to people's own failings, and hence the anger of the ancestral dead, or were due to the envy of neighbors or kin who were using witchcraft or sorcery against them. Consultations with diviners were almost always taken over by elder kin, so that judgments about misfortune supported the authority and influence of elders and voiced concerns about disobedience from the young. Taking on the power to consult the diviners oneself was a rebellious act of self-assertion by any young person, who thereby had skirted the authority of his male elders. The Christian mission condemned such beliefs and activities, yet by promoting the notions of life after death and the idea that there were prevalent supernatural evil forces in the world, they provided no real challenge to belief in such powers. Indeed, they unintentionally supported them. For many missionaries I met, it was not that witchcraft and evil magic did not exist, but rather that these had to be combated by Christian prayer and rituals. The mission sought to promote its owns rites of curing, purification, exorcism, or even rainmaking, but was adamantly against having its powers challenged by competing Kaguru beliefs about witch-finders, diviners, and magicians. Many Kaguru Christians played it safe and employed both pagan and Christian rites.

Kaguru society emphasized the importance of kin, and this remained the crucial measure of most values. Arguments, self-justifications, and pleas to any greater good inevitably involved reference to membership in a family, lineage, clan, or, rarely, one's ethnic group. In 1957–58, I rarely heard any Kaguru speak of national, broader values. What kinship meant was changing, and for more and more it meant the household, because education, religion, and emerging class consciousness tended to emphasize household and immediate kin rather than broader ties.

Personal Appearance

The appearance of the people of the chiefdom contrasted sharply in terms of ethnicity, education and gender (see Beidelman 1980). Even the most unobservant outsider could immediately recognize Baraguyu and Maasai from all other local Africans. These people prided themselves in not changing greatly from tradition. The garb and grooming of males distinguished uncircumcised youths, initiated warriors, and elder men. The Baraguyu warriors were especially striking with their long braids, red-painted hair and bodies, their revealing blue or red togas, striking beaded and metal jewelry, stretched ear lobes, and the spears, swords, and clubs they always carried. They looked like they had stepped out of exotic travel posters and postcards. They were elegant and arrogant and, at least to many Europeans, utterly beguiling, though not to Kaguru. Their many weapons made them potentially dangerous. The youths and elders dressed less spectacularly, but all Baraguyu men looked like the European stereotypes of primitive Africans. The Baraguyu women also dressed strikingly, usually preferring beaded leather and avoiding cloth.

They wore large quantities of metal and beaded jewelry. Kaguru and Ngulu viewed Baraguyu as backward, as savages unworthy of respect. Yet Kaguru knew Baraguyu were rich in livestock, rarely short of cash, and that they were proud and aggressive when encountering any insult or abuse. Ironically, early pictures of Kaguru before World War I show men dressed as poor imitations of Baraguyu and Maasai, and women with bare breasts and much jewelry. Even in 1957–58 some Kaguru to the west, in Geiro and in Mpwapwa district, still decorated themselves with red ochre, wore braided hair, wore much jewelry, stretched their ear lobes, and knocked out their lower incisors. Christian Kaguru in most of Kilosa district were embarrassed by this "backward" appearance of their less sophisticated ethnic "cousins."

The Kamba dressed much like Kaguru but often had a distinctive shaved hair style, knocked out their lower incisors and often stretched their ear lobes. For Kaguru, even more disturbingly many Kamba filed their two front upper teeth into points. In sharp contrast to the conservative, pagan Baraguyu, ordinary Kaguru women wore the typical black or patterned two-piece cotton *kangas*, which were something like national dress in Tanganyika at that time. Kaguru women kept their hair short and braided and wore only the most modest bits of jewelry. On special occasions—dances, weddings, and other such events—Kaguru women brought out new, unfaded kangas or even European-type dresses, and sometimes even wore shoes. Most Kaguru men wore shorts and old tattered shirts, though most had some special wear for important occasions, including trousers, long-sleeved shirts, and shoes. Kaguru schoolteachers and government clerks and technicians always wore shoes. Kaguru men all kept their hair short and almost never wore beards. The only exceptions were a few young, educated political leaders who sometimes wore long Afros and wispy beards in imitation of radical black U.S. politicians whose photos they had seen in magazines. Educated, salaried Kaguru and Ngulu usually wore white or tan clothing, which they were careful to have laundered regularly. Older educated Kaguru men often wore trousers. Younger men, especially those in government service and teachers, tended to wear white shorts, white shirts, and long white socks up to the knees, imitating the standard working garb of British administrators. They could never be found barefoot. A few older Kaguru headmen and chiefs wore a combination of European and Arab garb, such as trousers and sandals with a white Arab-type *kanzu* on top, a white or red Muslim skull cap, and often jackets or vests. This was part of the tradition brought down from the early era of the Arab-influenced chiefship and the political domination of the early coastal Muslim akidas. Wives and children of government employees and teachers wore what ordinary Kaguru women would wear, but they all had extra, European-type clothing they could don for church and special occasions.

Given the relative poverty of Kaguru, outlays of clothing represented considerable expense and sacrifice. Good clothing was stored away in boxes under beds and brought out rarely. For example, I sometimes volunteered to take family photo portraits. Then Kaguru always excused themselves and dashed into their houses to emerge decked out in their special clothing, which I had never seen before. Ever since the missionaries and Arabs had arrived in Ukaguru, more educated and ambitious Kaguru and Ngulu set great value on presenting themselves in clothing so as to distinguished themselves from pagan, unworthy "bush" savages, people whom they said would resemble Baraguyu.

Kaguru quickly discovered the value of soap, which was considered essential to every Kaguru household. Soap was vital to keep special clothing clean as well as to wash bodies for church, school, and special festivities. Soap, too, for the impoverished Kaguru, was a considerable expense. None of this Kaguru grooming or garb remotely resembled what Kaguru were traditionally like before Europeans arrived. Early explorers describe Kaguru in red ochre, animal fat, long hair, dressed in animal skins, grass skirts, or bark cloth and wearing much metal, bead, and shell jewelry. Then Kaguru men walked about frequently revealing their genitals and Kaguru women were often bare-breasted. By 1957–58, partly clothed Baraguyu remained a common sight, but I never saw a Kaguru woman bare-breasted and even Kaguru men only rarely removed their shirts, even when working in fields in midday heat. Arabs and Christian missionaries had radically changed Kaguru into a people deeply concerned about hiding their bodies and appearing civilized by means of cotton cloth. Cloth and soap were as important to Kaguru as food itself, and far more money was expended on them than many could easily afford. Clothing and grooming were essential marks of modernity that most Kaguru sought, the single most obvious and important signs available to Kaguru by which they could express their desire for respect and dignity as people resembling those who had subjugated and dominated them. The most admired token of that, worn only by the most sophisticated Kaguru (but certainly no chief or headman) was a wristwatch. I knew some Kaguru who yearned for one even if they could not tell time, simply because it indicated sophistication.

House Furnishings and Other Goods

Kaguru generally did not want their neighbors to know how prosperous they were and tried to conceal the furnishings of their houses. They feared the envy and consequent witchcraft and sorcery of their neighbors and kin. They were torn between this need for secrecy and a desire to show others their success, especially since success could be a source of pride and esteem, albeit shadowed by ill-will. Neighbors could claim that another's prosperity was not due to hard work and frugality or even to the mystical benevolence of ancestors, but due instead to powers that harmed others.

Some household possessions were signs of modernity. At festive occasions and at visits by prominent people Kaguru would entertain in the space outside their house. Wealthy Kaguru with more modern houses entertained in a front room just inside the front door, where curious neighbors could peek in on what was going on. Modern and successful Kaguru would own a table, chairs, imported china, a metal teapot, and table utensils. Serving tea, with sugar and condensed milk and imported biscuits, was a sign of true modernized life and represented a large outlay of cash. Only really important visitors merited such hospitality. Yet even poorer Kaguru often owned at least one folding chair that could be brought outside for a distinguished person. Many Kaguru households had traditional African furniture—stools and beds with stringed frames. Some still used a traditional sleeping-shelf with mats. Kaguru cooked much food in traditional clay pots and used gourds, woven mats, baskets, mortars and pestles, and wooden spoons. African-forged metal goods were still common, and such tools had home-carved handles. Yet even the poorest household had some imported metal goods such as a fork, spoon, or some plates and bowls. Every household had metal tools such as a *panga* (machete) and hoes. Some also had weapons, such as bows with a quiver of poison-tipped arrows, and a very few even had shotguns, which were expensive not just because of their price but on account of the license required. Owners of imported weapons proudly toted them about on many occasions. Some householders visited and chatted at night using a paraffin (kerosene) lantern. Richer Kaguru such as clerks and schoolteachers had paraffin pressure lamps, which were far more expensive, and a few had flashlights. Imported soap and matches were no longer considered luxury goods but necessities. All metal and glass was prized, so that any containers I threw away were pounced on by anyone handy. Few Kaguru owned bicycles, and a Kaguru who owned one could consider it an asset that could be rented or used to carry loads to market for himself or others.

When I lived in Ukaguru, everyone had a hand-carved wooden comb or one of plastic, and almost every home had a small hand-mirror. Each home had a wooden box or perhaps a discarded biscuit tin, kept under a bed or sleeping shelf, where precious, fragile objects such as photographs, tax records, school receipts, and licenses were preserved. Papers were important even to illiterate Kaguru. Very few Kaguru owned any books, even Bibles, but any booklet or magazine, especially those with illustrations, were treasured, and bits sometimes were attached to walls, though these lasted only a short time. Yet even schoolteachers and clerks had surprisingly little paper. It was never wasted. For almost anyone to receive a letter was still a notable event.

Despite their poverty, it would be difficult to find any Kaguru who did not possess material tokens of the outside, modern world. Material goods, clothing, and literacy were the surest signs of personal modernity, and even small details of a person's appearance, grooming and accouterments mattered greatly in affecting how people were treated. All this took cash, so even a Kaguru who considered himself or herself highly traditional needed to purchase many things to appear respectable. Rumor and gossip put some damper on appearances, but how people appeared was always something to speak about.

This brief description of Ukaguru in 1957–58 describes a remote and poor area of a poor British colonial territory. Ukaguru had a long and more complex multiethnic history than one might expect from what appeared as a seemingly isolated and neglected area. Ukaguru was a chiefdom run according to the prevailing British colonial policy of Indirect

Rule. Most studies of Indirect Rule have dealt with far more prosperous, accessible, and well documented African chiefdoms and kingdoms. The Kaguru example may add a new perspective regarding how colonial life in Africa worked on the ground. Actually, less glamorous and more undeveloped areas such as Ukaguru were more typical of African colonial life. In any event, Ukaguru was a case that, as my earlier confrontation with Dame Margery Perham highlighted, contradicted some of the misleading, common stereotypes about Indirect Rule in Africa and the life associated with it.

THREE

The Kaguru Native Authority

The Kaguru Native Authority is the official governing body of Ukaguru. It was the outcome of British policy to rule their African possessions through Indirect Rule, allowing the British to govern with minimal staff and funds while claiming to encourage natives both to oversee themselves and to gain experience in modernization at a slow pace that would supposedly accommodate local African values and needs. I have already discussed the pros and cons of Indirect Rule as well as the ways that policy was initiated and pursued in Tanganyika. I sketched out the ties between the local British administration and the Native Authority. Here I describe the organization and general workings of the Native Authority itself. In the next chapter, I discuss how the Native Authority worked in Kaguru courts, the most prominent and significant feature of this system.

European Administration and the Native Authority

To understand political affairs in Ukaguru, one must remember a few basic facts about the British administration of this area. Ukaguru was an administrative unit within a much larger system. It was the largest and most important Native Authority within Kilosa district, which had three other smaller Native Authorities to the south as well as large areas of ethnically mixed peoples in the huge lowland sisal estates on lands alienated from African ownership.[1] There were also the towns of Kilosa (the district headquarters) and Kimamba (a smaller town serving the estates). These estates and towns were not subjected to any Native Authority. Kilosa district was the most westerly of eight districts in the Eastern Province, about two hours drive from the provincial headquarters at Morogoro and about four hours drive (in the same direction) from the territorial capital of Dar es Salaam. The Kilosa district administration was responsible to the provincial administration, but local district officers were given great leeway in making on-the-spot decisions, so long as they justified such decisions in their written reports to the provincial commissioner. The Kilosa district administration had many responsibilities besides overseeing Native Authorities, and we must keep this in mind to understand why the Kaguru Native Authority was not as closely supervised as one might expect. The power of the Kaguru Native Authority in influencing social life in Ukaguru rested on the fact that it was so poorly supervised, allowing Kaguru chiefs and headmen to take a free hand in how they enforced law and order.

The difficulties that the British had overseeing this area should be clear if we remember that Kilosa district was about 6,000 square miles in size (about the size of Massachusetts) and that the Kaguru Native Authority had jurisdiction over an area of about 1,500 square miles (about the size of Rhode Island). It is also important to remember that communication within the district, especially during the rainy season, was difficult. Kilosa District contained over 150,000 Africans, 50,000 residing in Ukaguru. The European administrative staff numbered two to five (usually two or three), along with six or seven other officers and assistants attached to specialist departments. All these men knew Swahili, but not one spoke any local language such as Kaguru, Kamba, or Baraguyu. None had the slightest understanding of the traditional social systems of the local inhabitants. Travel was difficult because of poor roads and bridges, especially during the rains, but also because there were only three government rest houses in Ukaguru, and few British were willing to spend a night in a tent or auto. In 1957–58 no district administrator resided in the chiefdom for more than a few days to a week and never more than one night in any one spot. Many months passed between visits. During my twelve months in Idibo (in 1957 and 1962) there was only one day-long visit by a district administrator.

In addition to the district administrators, there were specialist officers stationed in Kilosa town. These were sometimes described as part of the district administration, but they were not responsible to the district administration but to the provincial officers of their respective departments. For example, there was a medical officer posted in Kilosa, and while he frequently consulted with the Kilosa administration, he received instructions from the provincial medical officer at Morogoro or from even higher officers in Dar es Salaam. These various district departmental officers supervised African specialists working in Ukaguru. For example, the Kaguru Native Authority employed a staff at eight local dispensaries. Their work was overseen by the medical officer, who was responsible for their conduct, issuing their salaries, dispensing supplies, and checking records. The same held true, *mutatis mutandis,* for agriculture, forestry, labor, education, and veterinary services. In this way the Kaguru Native Authority was actually subject to influence by a whole range of outside British officers. These specialist officers were spread even thinner than the administrative officers, so that their regular contact with Ukaguru was limited. For example, during my first fieldwork the medical officer was directly concerned with Ukaguru only once in 1958, when there was a false scare of a possible smallpox case that had to be investigated. Similarly, in that same year I accompanied the veterinary officer to a Baraguyu camp in northern Ukaguru to investigate the sudden death of livestock, which might have signaled the outbreak of a livestock epidemic (it did not). The veterinary officer also visited the local livestock market each month at Chakwale in northern Ukaguru, since this provided a good means for learning news about livestock and herding in the area.

For the most part, local Africans employed in health, livestock, and other services did their duties on their own and contacted their superiors only through monthly written reports or in a rare emergency. These specialists were tied to both the Native Authority and district administration only by funding. The Native Authority treasury contributed part of the money for these services, the amount determined by the Kilosa district administrators who supervised the Native Treasury. None of these specialist services was funded entirely by local moneys. It was unofficial strategy of each of these government departments—medical, agriculture, forestry, veterinary, education, police, labor—to try to preserve their own power, so that there was often poor cooperation and poor flow of information between them (McCarthy 1982:9).

The British district administrators exercised considerable control over the policy and staffing of the Kaguru Native Authority. Although various African headmen and chiefs were chosen by their fellow Kaguru, no appointment could be confirmed without the approval of the district administrator in charge of the Native Authority. That administrator could remove any Kaguru Native Authority official. He might do this summarily, without providing any explanation. An official might be sacked for embezzlement or extortion but also simply because it was "in the public interest," grounds that provided a carte blanche for dismissal. Shortage of British staff, overloading of administrative duties, and poor communication limited the power of the British administrators to control the officials of the Kaguru Native Authority. Theoretically these administrators had power over them, and the vague threat of their disapproval inhibited such officials from grossly abusing their powers. Given the lack of education and the conservative disposition of most Kaguru Native Authority officials, most legislation by the Kaguru Native Authority was actually conceived and drafted by British administrators. The Kaguru Native Authority was described by some modern, educated Africans as a mere rubber stamp for what the British wanted. This was probably typical for Native Authorities over much of the territory. Lord Hailey notes: "All [Native Authorities] have been able to render assistance in such matters as the maintenance of order or the collection of tax but their lack of education or initiative makes them ineffective as agencies for the provision of the services that minister to the general welfare of the community. To that extent, their employment may be said to frustrate one of the purposes of the present system, since in the face of apathy, or incapacity on the part of the Native Authorities, the only course open to the Administrative Officer is to take the conduct of local affairs entirely in his own hands" (Hailey 1950:17). Administrators in Kilosa district appeared eager to do this, claiming this was easier than correcting the botched rulings of incompetent native officials or spending long hours trying to explain something to a chief who could not write up such a ruling himself. Posts in the Native Authority offered little attraction to educated Africans (Gann and Duignan 1967:223–224). Hailey considered the Native Authorities in Kilosa district among the most inept and unsuitable in the Tanganyika Territory (1950:313–322, 352–353).

British district administrators might make rulings for the public good and not even frame them in terms of their being rulings by the Native Authority. Any rulings had to be enforced by local Kaguru officials. The British district administrators were a politically supreme group dominating the Kaguru Native Authority. They combined legislative, administrative, and judicial powers that could not be challenged by Kaguru. The Kaguru Native Authority's legislation was a facade for British policies. Most Kaguru saw it that way.

Kaguru Native Authority Membership

The Kaguru Native Authority was staffed with two very different kinds of persons. (1) Kaguru chiefs, counselors, and headmen held their posts because they had been chosen by influential men in their local areas. The right to make such selections, as well as the right to be selected, were related to these men's kinship in matrilineal clans associated with particular Kaguru areas; these men were traditionally thought to own these areas. Officials were chosen because they appealed to tradition-minded elders, not for any education or sophistication, although even the most traditional Kaguru conceded that such qualities might prove useful. This was in accord with the spirit of Indirect Rule. Yet all Kaguru knew that any choices they made could be vetoed by the British administration without even having to explain why. (2) Many Africans, a few not even Kaguru, were employed by the Native Authority to serve as clerks, guards, and messengers to local courts, while other more skilled Africans served as school teachers, health workers, and veterinary or agricultural aides. Such workers might have been hired by local leaders, in the case of court employees, or they might have been appointed on the recommendations of British administrators involved in district government or connected to the various specialized services such as education, veterinary services, agriculture, and forestry.

What made these workers part of the Native Authority was that their salaries came mainly or partially from the Native Authority treasury. Their being part of the Native Authority was a facade encouraged by the British to make the Native Authority look more impressive than it actually was. In the case of workers who had education and special skills, they were not even responsible to local chiefs or headmen but to the local district or provincial British administrators and to the special administrators connected to other government departments. Many, especially those with higher education, might not even have been Kaguru. In general, only the lower level Native Authority employees, local Kaguru who lived in Kaguru villages, felt the direct influence of chiefs and headmen. In contrast, more educated employees filling jobs as teachers, dispensers, and such were often not even Kaguru and were, even if Kaguru, not from the locality where they served. Such skilled employees resided in Native Authority housing, setting them apart from Kaguru villagers and hence from the pressures exerted by local people. In areas where comparable staff were employed by the Church Missionary Society rather than the Native Authority, they also often had special housing, lived apart from local Africans, and were rarely from the local area, even when they were Kaguru. Some mission employees had part of their salary indirectly provided through government subsidies to the mission, but they remained free of all direct government connections. Still, these mission workers closely resembled government workers in Ukaguru, because they were educated and prosperous people less easily intimidated and affected by the Kaguru Native Authority leaders than were ordinary Kaguru.

The Amalgamation of Native Authorities

The Kilosa district administration supervised three Native Authorities in addition to Ukaguru: Usagara North, Usagara South, and Uvidunda. For convenience the district administration had amalgamated the four Native Authority treasuries, because none provided sufficient funds for efficient planning from year to year and because separate treasuries would have involved reduplication of bookkeeping by the overworked district officers who checked the accounts and drew up the budgets. While Native Authorities in some other districts of Tanganyika managed much of their own financial affairs (e.g., the rich and sophisticated areas around Moshi and Bukoba), the low level of education and so-

Table 1

AREA	POPULATION	AREA IN SQUARE MILES
Ukaguru	66,720 (48,249 Kaguru)	1,500
Usagara North	59,3641 (12,033 Sagara)[1]	1,400
Usagara South	7,528 (4,875 Sagara)	1,000
Uvidunda	13,233 (7,366 Vidunda)[1]	950

THE KILOSA NATIVE AUTHORITY TREASURY FUNDS
FOR 1956 ARE INDICATED:[2]

Native Authority share of personal taxes (some of this tax went directly to the District Administration)	£12,751
Court Revenues	£1,329
Liquor Licenses	£6,229
Market Receipts	£5,014
Produce Cesses	£3,046
Cattle Rates	£1,515
Sundries	£2,292
Total	£32,276

Notes:
1. A large number of the inhabitants in these chiefdoms were migrant workers temporarily employed on sisal estates. These were excluded from all Native Authority affairs and were mainly under the supervision of the managers of the estates.
2. I could not obtain figures for Ukaguru alone, but I estimate that about 70% of the income probably comes from Ukaguru. The personal taxes paid by the sisal workers were transferred to the home districts from which they came.

phistication of African officials in Kilosa district necessitated constant and intense monitoring. For convenience, the district administration formed a district council comprised of the paramount chiefs and sub-chiefs of the four Native Authorities, along with African officials in the two towns.[2] The council met monthly to discuss and judge the few cases appealed from the courts of the various chiefdoms and from the African town courts. The district commissioner and/or district officers sat on the council and used it to initiate and formulate policies. There were no chiefs in the district with sufficient education or sophistication to stand up to the British administrators on the council.[3] The figures in table 1 give some idea of the magnitude of the groups represented in the district council in 1956.

The Organization of the Kaguru Native Authority

Before discussing the various offices and activities within the Native Authority, I present an outline of the organization and its functions. There were 53 Kaguru headmen in the Kaguru Native Authority, each with several unofficial deputies.[4] Headmen had jurisdiction over areas varying in size from about 12 to about 80 square miles and varying in population from under 200 to over 4,000 people. Most headmen supervised about 1,200 people. Headmen were expected to enforce Native Authority and Tanganyika territorial laws, reporting offenses to their local chief or subchief. Headmen might collect personal taxes from all men eighteen years or over, though most men paid directly to the clerk of the local court. That made more sense, since few headmen were literate and could write receipts. Headmen might mediate between quarreling residents within their respective areas, but they were not empowered to enforce any decisions without bringing such disputes to the local court. Still, headmen sometimes persuaded locals to settle minor differences without going to court. They expected a minor payment for their time and trouble, some beer, flour, or a fowl. Most Kaguru encountered their Native Authority almost entirely through their headman. While local chiefs had considerable contact with headmen, British administrators rarely met them. Headmen were under one of five courts that served as both administrative and judicial centers. Four of these courts (Idibo, Geiro, Nong'we, and Msowero) were headed by subchiefs and one (Mamboya) by the paramount chief.[5] Within his own court area the paramount chief had duties and powers identical with those of the subchiefs. The paramount chief's court heard appeals from subchiefs' courts, though complaints could also be sent directly to the district administration, which might or might not choose to entertain such end-runs around the paramount chief's authority. Each court and its chief were relatively independent, and the post of paramount chief was actually more titular than truly authoritative, though he did have better pay and the use of a Land Rover. These five courts were empowered to hear cases, levy fines, and impose corporal punishment or imprisonment. They provided harsher legal sanctions behind the headmen's authority. They enforced the rulings of the Native Authority and the laws of the territory.[6]

I now indicate the powers and activities of these various Kaguru officials.

HEADMEN[7]

The grassroots officials within the Kaguru Native Authority were the 53 headmen (*jumbe*). These were selected by older, established men of the designated traditional dominant or owner clan within each headmanship. This choice was determined largely by the previous headman (unless he had been deposed at the request of his own people). Two cases of such official selection came to my attention while I was in Ukaguru. Both occurred before I had arrived in the chiefdom:

(1) The first case involved the selection of the present subchief of Idibo, but the method of selection was the same as for a headman. The previous subchief, Jenga, was a close matrilineal kinsman of the senior elder of the dominant Ganasa clan. It was said he had been deposed by the district commissioner for his insulting and arrogant behavior, and also that he owed his position to having gradually usurped power from his predecessor, Muhoni, who had got old and very deaf and was forced to depend on Jenga. The deposed subchief selected two kinsmen as candidates to replace him, to be voted on by his matrikin. The first candidate, Godwin, was a member of the matriclan. He was barely literate and was a former truck driver at the nearby defunct Groundnut Scheme. This candidate gained some prominence when he had served a prison term of several years. His truck had crashed into an auto occupied by a British official and his wife. When that official berated Godwin after the accident, he slugged the man with a wrench. This made him a hero to local Kaguru but doomed him as a choice that would be approved by the British administration. The other candidate, Yehudi, was the son of a man of the dominant or owner matriclan, and therefore not a clan member himself. He was a former mission school teacher who had been fired for fornication. He had then taken a job as a market master but had been fired because he was involved in black-marketing produce from the market during World War II when food prices were high. For that he had served a short prison sentence. At the time he was nominated, he had no regular employment, even though he was literate. Both candidates were assumed likely to remain dependent on the previous subchief for advice.

The overwhelming favorite was Godwin, who twice refused a crowd's demand that he serve. The second candidate, Yehudi, was reluctantly chosen by the matriclan and later approved by the district commissioner. He became subchief of Idibo and was my neighbor and landlord in 1958. The former subchief, Jenga, was often present at Yehudi's court and conferred frequently with him. Godwin steered clear, and local Kaguru said he was probably afraid of Yehudi's witchcraft. Godwin was a modest and unassertive man, quite different from Yehudi who was forceful, arrogant, and known to be dishonest.

(2) A headmen died, but before his death he had stated he would like either his son or his sister's son to succeed him. Both these potential successors lived in the headman's village. The sister's son was illiterate and very quarrelsome, while the headmen's son was literate and adept at dealing with people. Although it was said that any member of the dominant clan could be selected, it was clear that in practice this choice often depended on social skills and other leadership qualities. The son had considerable experience watching his father settle minor disputes, check boundaries of contested fields and gardens, collect fees, and attend court. He became the obvious choice even though he was a son of the matriclan rather than an actual member.

Education could be a factor in choosing a headman, but the most important factor was his reputation among local elders as a cooperative and helpful leader. Choices were usually of men who had stayed on in their local area and not men who had gone elsewhere, even if they had jobs due to their education. The educated Kaguru likely still to reside in his local area was one who had not been able to hold down good jobs elsewhere. All jobs held by well-educated Kaguru paid better than the wage for any headman and probably the wage of a subchief. Consequently, while education was desirable, local ties were crucial—not just because a candidate had to get on with local leaders but because the only educated Kaguru likely to be interested in a job as a Native Authority official was one who had failed in the larger educated world and whose options were therefore limited. Kaguru described the two examples I give as representative. Local people were usually confronted with two apparent candidates, but the choice was skewed because one was almost always preferable. The choices tended to contrast different competing values. For example, if a son of the clan was preferred, a clan member was often also proposed, though one who was less desirable on other grounds. In the first case I provide, the two candidates both had criminal records, but the one with a record that Kaguru would admire was not a realistic choice because he had violently challenged the British, whereas the candidate who had misbehaved according to Kaguru standards, and had even harmed other Kaguru, was. The nominators appeared to be giving people a choice and presented a range of contrasting Kaguru values about leadership, even while actually stacking the deck on the choice likely to be made.

The district administrators were not directly concerned with the selection of officials in the Kaguru Native Authority, especially headmen. They only knew that some local Kaguru candidate was nominated and then sent down to the district headquarters in Kilosa to pick up a tax book and a badge of office. A district officer would automatically approve such a candidate when he presented himself, unless the officer had earlier noticed him in some negative way, as in the case of the Kaguru who slugged a British official. I often heard district administrators complain that Kaguru headmen seemed to be inefficient and conservative. I could never figure out on what specific grounds these judgments were based. It was probably true that such Kaguru were inept by British standards, but the district administrators had few occasions to learn much about headmen to make a fair appraisal.

A headman was either a member of the owner matriclan (maternal nephew of a male clan member) or the son of a male clan member; no son of a son of a clan member should be considered. While many said it was good to select a member of the matriclan, others remarked that sons of the clan were also good choices. Such men would feel especially responsive to the wishes of clan elders because they were potentially more vulnerable to criticism, being less closely bound into clan/kin networks. I cannot judge the merit of these two views, but clan members and sons of members were both selected frequently. In both cases, the ethos of Indirect Rule was maintained, since the key factor for making a choice was close affiliation with the traditional owner clan of an area. The members of the owner clan were his kin, and he owed his office to them. They could even take his office away. Yet most Kaguru in a headman's area were not members of this clan and were not the headman's kin. Feeling they had been cheated out of local influence by the way the Native Authority was set up, some of these people were even members of clans who considered themselves his enemies. They considered themselves members of owner clans not recognized by the system of Indirect Rule; therefore they resented the local headman and wanted him to fail or at least have a hard time. A headman's task was consequently sometimes not easy, because he needed cooperation from these people if he wanted a good record.

Members of dissident clans sometimes created difficulties. They made visits to their subchief, the paramount chief, and the district officer, describing the failings of their current headman and citing earlier traditions that legitimated their own claims to political recognition. No petition for a change in the Native Authority had ever been effective, but from time to time Kaguru tried. Despite this, even in 1957 members of some dissident factions continued to claim autonomy. For example, the Mgugu headmanship was officially held by the Songo Duma clan, but the unrecognized Nhembo clan claimed the northern portion of the area (Inhembo). Similarly, in Chinyilisi the Gweno clan claimed to own the area that is now part of the Makuyu headmanship run by the Songo Ng'ombe clan. Even earlier, Chinyilisi was said to be in the Talagwe headmanship and under the Mukema clan. The Gweno clan demanded that Chinyilisi have its own headmanship, which they would head. The Semwa clan claimed the Simba clan had stolen control of the Kitete headmanship from them. The Ng'oma clan claimed the Ponela clan had stolen part of the Njong'we headmanship from them. The Nyandandwa clan claimed that the Chishomba headmanship was stolen from them by the Shomi clan. The Chayungu clan claimed the Ganasa clan had stolen control of the western part of Idibo headmanship from them—and so on. Because of such clan conflict and competition, Kaguru headmen had difficult times controlling their subjects. Such dissension was especially common in the mountain headmanships, because communications were difficult in the precipitous mountain areas. It was also because the physical fragmentation of the mountains created many different clans, each claiming a small valley or hill. Such tiny units were considered impractical under Indirect Rule, so the British amalgamated these mountain areas into larger political units. As a result, each mountain headmanship held many resentful clans that had lost paramountcy even though, by tradition, they could claim a headmanship.

A headman must be good at manipulating the various factions within his area, at retaining the cooperation of enough people that he could meet his government assignments and keep from being deposed. In more remote areas all kinds of things could happen without outsiders knowing, because local people conspired to keep matters secret. As an example of a headman's need to secure cooperation, consider the headman at Mgugu (near the Berega CMS mission), who had to moderate between the Kaguru Christians (many were employed at the mission and therefore lived nearby) and Kaguru pagans. Such Kaguru often quarreled about drinking, dances, and sexual behavior, since the standards held by Christians and pagans sharply differed, at least in public.[8] The Christians and pagans, often interrelated by kinship, were adept at concealing what they actually did, both from one another and from the missionaries. Similarly, Headman Tutilo at Idibo stood between the local rainmaker (who was his elder brother and still influential, though he kept a low public profile), the senior matrilineal elder, who had very traditional views, and members of the nearby subchief's court who were committed to enforcing more modern policies. The Idibo headman had close kin ties with all these who were tied in turn to the dominant clan, the very people who elected him. Similarly, Headman Dani Mlama at Mgugu, near the Berega CMS mission, had married his daughter to a son of the CMS African Archdeacon. That tie led the Mgugu dominant Songo Duma clan to cede 104 acres to the mission for the middle school. Headman Dani's drinking and adultery ran counter to mission doctrine, but he remained influential with both Christians and pagans on account of his kinship and helpfulness to both groups.

The wages of headmen provided only a slim advantage, since many of their subjects earned far more than they did. A headman's wage depended on the population of the area he oversaw. The average headmanship had about 1,200 inhabitants, and the headman of such an area received 30 shillings monthly (about $4.50). A few headmanships had only a few hundred residents, and their headmen received far less. Since the official minimum wage for an unskilled Native Authority laborer was one and a half shillings per day, some headmen were paid less than road workers. Of course, being a headman did not require manual labor, and a headman did not work daily at his job. Furthermore, a headman could make extra income illegally in bribes and gifts. The low wages of headmen explained why few educated Kaguru would take such jobs unless they had lost their regular ones. Poor wages also explained why headmen were not as respected as they might be, especially by educated, salaried Kaguru. Poor wages also explained why all headmen were said to take bribes and solicit money or gifts. Headmen rationalized this as morally justified because they were paid so little. For the most part, uneducated Kaguru did not seem to resent small payments to headmen, such as a fowl, some beer, or a few shillings for a favor. The headman of Idibo was paid 31 shillings a month and had authority over 1,500 people. He told me it was unfair that schoolteachers in his area were paid seven to ten times more, even though he officially had authority over them. He asked me rhetorically how he could be respected by such people unless he could get at least a bit more income one way or another.

Headmen's Duties and Powers

A headman was obliged to enforce all laws and regulations of the territory, the district, and the Kaguru Native Authority. A headman had to report infractions of these rules and either bring such rule-breakers to the local court for judgment or inform the court office so that a court messenger could bring them in. A headman himself could not use physical force, but a court messenger could and was armed with a club, stick, or whip with which he often beat those who resisted him. (Court messengers were chosen because they were young, big, and strong—whereas headmen were often elderly.) A headman could appoint an assistant or deputy, usually one for about every hundred of his subjects. Such a deputy was called a *chijiji* (a Kaguru diminutive term derived from the Swahili word *mji*, meaning hamlet, village, town). Such men received no official wages but were expected to accompany a headman when there was a difficult problem, providing backup. Such deputies also carried messages. A headman shared some of the gifts and bribes he received with his deputies. A headman could appoint or dismiss a deputy as he pleased, since such persons were not part of the official system. In 1957 I witnessed the sudden verbal dismissal of such a deputy at a beer party. The headman of Mgugu fired his deputy for several reasons. One was that the deputy's wife was committing adultery with several local men. It was said that if the deputy could not control his wife, then he could not be respected. Another reason was that the deputy had complained about local unlicensed brewers and had tried to extract bribes from them. This might have been acceptable had the deputy first consulted the headman for permission. If he had asked, he would have learned that the headman had already received bribes from these brewers. Finally, the headman had recently quarreled with the paramount chief, and the deputy was a matrilineal relative of the chief. The headman feared his deputy might try to undermine him for that reason, perhaps to get his job with the connivance of the paramount chief.

Uneducated Kaguru were eager to secure posts as deputies. Such posts were usually given to prominent elders in the various areas, men with many kin. A headman would also consider a kinsman or crony, someone who lived nearby with whom he drank beer. Some said that it was best for a headman to hire someone younger than he. Some Kaguru said that if a headman was illiterate he might want a deputy who could read and write, because such a deputy could help fill out receipts and forms. Others told me that an illiterate headman would not want a literate deputy because a literate man would always resent someone illiterate who had power over him. Such a person might take over a headman's job. How to choose a deputy depended on different strategies of power upon which few agreed. Using various deputies and threatening to dismiss them, a clever headman might manage a band of helpers, so long as he kept his eyes on them.

A headman exercised considerable power through arbitrary inter-pretation and enforcement of the laws and regulations he was supposed to enforce. Theoretically, a headman enforced all laws and regulations as best he could, with no bias or discrimination. Yet these regulations were not formulated in any detail. Besides, most Kaguru were illiterate and therefore unfamiliar with the exact nature of laws. A headman who knew all the ins and outs of an area was better equipped than anyone else to decide just how rules should or could be interpreted locally. This was the essence of what Indirect Rule was said to be about. Through his wide discretionary powers in interpreting and enforcing the law, a headman could reward his supporters and punish those troublesome subjects who opposed him.

In the eyes of the district administration, a headman's most important duty was collecting taxes, school tuitions, and brewing and shop license fees. This provided a headman with a powerful lever against his subjects. British district administrators had only a rough idea of the number of taxpayers in any area.[9] They only estimated the population of any headmanship and chiefship, and even after the 1957 census no figures were available breaking down populations below the district level. All of those in charge of Ukaguru, British and Kaguru alike, depended on headmen for knowing exactly how much was due in taxes from any headmanship and hence cumulatively from any chiefship. This gave considerable arbitrary power to headmen. A clever headman could under-report the number of taxpayers in his area. He could allow a person to escape taxes entirely. He could allow a person to be unreported and demand a bribe. Of course, he could not report too low a number of people owing money, since his pay depended on credible tax returns being collected. The British administration depended upon headmen to see that all the Kaguru who should have paid taxes did. The British themselves had only rough estimates based on outdated, unreliable census figures. They also guessed, based on previous outdated tax returns. The much-desired 1957 Tanganyika Territory census was taken while I was in the field. Many considered this only a rough account of how many lived in the country, and certainly an even rougher account for a bush area like Ukaguru, where information was poorly collected. What I saw of local census-taking and the filled-out forms did not give me great confidence in the figures. (I later was given access to much original census data stored in Nairobi.)

In recent years the British district administration sought to stem local corruption in the Kaguru Native Authority by sending special tax collectors from Kilosa up to the court areas and encouraging people to make payments there rather than to headmen. Even so, in 1957–58 the majority of Kaguru paid their taxes and license fees through their headmen. Kaguru felt more understanding with their local headmen rather than these outsiders. Besides, they were loath to trek five to ten miles each way to a court. The special tax collectors were on duty only a few days in the month. Since the total personal tax (territorial and Native

Authority) amounted to 30 shillings per adult man, each embezzled payment represented about a month's wages (or more) to a headman.[10] It was not difficult, and indeed was well worth it, for a headman to skim off a few payments unnoticed. There was still another way headmen might make illegal profits through taxation. The government recognized that some Africans were unable to pay taxes because they were sick or old, or because they had recently lost their homes and property through fire or theft. Such exemption required verification by the headman. Such an endorsement was not free. It had to be purchased. In some cases taxes were collected, but then it was claimed that such a person had been exempted on account of ill health or penury. Here is an example of such cheating. The bitter enmity between the paramount chief and Headman Yubi was due to Yubi's attempt to secure a bribe for a tax exemption. Before his appointment to office, the present paramount chief was an elderly, sickly man who was poor and not, at that time, imagined ever likely to succeed to his present post. He sought Headman Yubi for an exemption from taxes. Yubi is said to have demanded a calabash of beer and some shillings. The old man refused (or lacked the resources to pay) and was fined as a tax defaulter. He spent a short time in the local court lockup until his kin paid.

Even if a headman honestly collected taxes from all his subjects (most unlikely), he could still exert pressures on them through the tempo by which he sought collection. Some subjects were pressed early for tax payment, sometimes before harvest, while others were allowed to postpone payment until the deadline. A headman also had some hold over any man who had not paid taxes for some time. He could threaten to turn such a person in. Tax delinquents were often ignorant of the law and believed they were required to pay all of their back taxes, which could amount to a huge sum. In fact, they were only required to pay a small part of these. Kaguru told me of several corrupt headmen who had deceived tax delinquents into thinking they owed huge sums and who then let them off by making them do chores for them. Many Kaguru claimed that headmen and subchiefs had larger fields than ordinary Kaguru because of such coerced labor. (Shortage of labor limited the amount of land cultivated.)

While taxation provided the widest scope for headmen's corruption, collection of school fees followed a similar pattern. A child could attend school so long as his or her parents had a receipt of payment. There was no easy way for local authorities to pinpoint any investigation of discrepancies between school attendance and shortage of contributed funds. Only case by case questioning of students in classes might reveal this, and then this would only show whose parents had receipts and not necessarily whose had actually paid.

Beer licensing also provided profits for headmen. For Kaguru, brewing was an important sources of cash, especially during lean times before harvests. No individual Kaguru petty brewer could afford the 16 shillings a day license fee for selling beer. Even when Kaguru joined together, as they often did, such a fee cut deeply into profits. In 1957–58 the Kaguru district administration forbade all weekday brewing during the cultivation season (December 1 to June 1), supposedly to keep Kaguru sober for work. Yet it was at this time that Kaguru were most short of cash. Furthermore, many Kaguru brewed beer for work parties that cleared and cultivated land. In chapter 2 I showed why rules banning brewing ran against Kaguru economic welfare. Kaguru headmen allowed brewers to operate without licenses and during forbidden times. This was very popular with all Kaguru, and the shillings headmen gleaned for closing their eyes over this were not often begrudged. Headmen were seen as defenders of Kaguru traditions and needs against the stupid and unjust laws of ignorant and callous British outsiders. Periodically, British administrators showed an unreasonable contempt for African drinking. This seemed hypocritical considering the heavy drinking by many British officials. It is true, however, that a large number of Kaguru chiefs and headmen drank excessively. Holtzman perceptively points out that the high incidence of drunken behavior by East African chiefs and headmen may be an expression of power and success (2009:216–221). In Ukaguru, this was a trait especially found among Baraguyu and Kamba elders (ibid.).

Sometimes an audacious headman invented fake regulations to cheat his gullible subjects. During the 1957 national census one headman followed the African census enumerator from village to village. After the enumerator had left, the headman collected ten pence from each household, claiming this was the enumerator's fee. Another crafty headman visited people with a ticket book for a government-sponsored lottery, which had already been concluded several weeks before. He persuaded some of his illiterate subjects to buy tickets, saying that this was required by the government.

A headman collected labor for government projects in an arbitrary manner. He chose Kaguru who were his opponents and let go those who supported him. Some headmen took bribes for not choosing a man for work. In chapter 5 I discuss how labor selection was especially abused during a 1957 government reforestation scheme. More ordinarily, during every dry season Kaguru headmen selected men to clear paths linking settlements with one another and with water points. Headmen also reported men who had not paid taxes so these could be drafted for work on local roads. The low pay for such work was seen as a substitute for taxes. Of course, not all local delinquents were selected. This was work deeply disliked by Kaguru, even though it was vital for keeping up local back roads, which many Kaguru recognized as useful. Headmen also asked local Kaguru to carry goods, clean quarters, and provide water, firewood, and sometimes food for visiting government officials. These occasions provided dramatic means for headmen to single out opponents and earn credit with the British, since this was one of the few occasions where a local headman could show a supposedly efficient and helpful side to the ordinarily distant British administrators from district headquarters.[11]

Headmen and Courts

A headman relied upon the local chief's court to enforce his orders, and, as we shall see in chapter 4, the Kaguru court system could not function without headmen anymore than headmen could function without a court. Yet headmen tended to see the courts as a last resort. A headman's real skill and popularity were measured by the disputes and difficulties he could settle without going to court. A headman's support was important in any dispute that one Kaguru had with another, whether this was settled in or out of court. A court usually favored the opinion of a headman in any case. Sometimes just threatening to take a case to court, involving the loss of time, court fees, and traveling many miles from home, encouraged people to settle matters. If one Kaguru took another to court, the headman's testimony was sought because the one with his support had an advantage. In some cases a headman never testified at all.

Kaguru did not consider a headman obligated to testify in every case involving his people. When a headman did testify, a subject would usually make him a gift for the inconvenience of traveling to court. It was usually in a headman's interest to persuade Kaguru to settle petty quarrels out of court. Most Kaguru were keen to circumvent court whenever possible.

Every plaintiff paid a court fee of three shillings to initiate a case. If he won his case, the losing party paid this and the plaintiff's money was refunded. Three shillings might have seemed a trivial sum to the British, but to the poor Kaguru it was a lot. It could purchase six calabashes of beer, or over two days' supply of grain for a family. Litigation meant people had to trek many miles to and from court and lose time from work. If a case was complex, this might involve several trips, because court usually met only one day a week. Finally, since courts were open to all, some Kaguru wanted to avoid having their disputes, especially those involving sexual matters, aired in public. A headman was more familiar with local affairs and therefore more likely to render a workable solution to a dispute than was a chief, who usually did not live near the disputants. For these reasons, and because he had to live in the neighborhood of the litigants, a headman was more eager to find a judgment that would end dissension. A headman should receive some beer, a fowl, some shillings, or other payment for his efforts. I even heard of a headman sleeping with a woman disputant as recompense.

A headman could not force disputants to accept his judgments, but he could pressure them to see him and air their grievances. Here is a fragment from an Idibo court case:

HEADMAN WILSON: "One day I asked Mganga to visit my hearing (baraza), but he did not."

MGANGA: "I admit that I did not go there that day, and I was wrong to do that."

COURT CHIEF: "The court levies a fine of five shillings for Mganga's scorning the authority of his headman. A person should pay attention to the headman of his country."

Although a headman could not legally collect fines, beat or imprison a person, nor enforce any of his judgments, the Kaguru Native Authority recognized his value as a mediator and usually backed up his dignity and respect. In Ukaguru many minor cases of assault, insult, and debts were quietly settled by headmen out of court. Where the headman was likely to be called as the main witness in any case, many Kaguru were likely to settle with him rather than bothering with the court. Here are two examples of how headmen settled cases that might otherwise have gone to court:

(1) Dickson of Mgugu paid over 500 shillings bridewealth for his wife. She bore him two sons, both of whom died, apparently from poor care by the mother. (I took one of the sons to the hospital for diagnosis shortly before he died; the doctor said the child was severely malnourished.) Dickson decided to divorce her. He took his case to the local headman, who told him he had to deduct 60 shillings for each child, even though they were dead. He was also told that 100 shillings more had to remain with the wife's father's uncle. Consequently, Dickson received back only 280 shillings. With this he had little hope of remarrying, yet he preferred dealing with the headman to going to court. He probably would not have done any better there and was eager to rid himself of a bad woman as soon as he could,

(2) Antoni of Idibo had a hot temper, was often drunk, and was deeply jealous of his wife. Drunk, he accused my cook of sleeping with her and demanded she strip so he could see whether there was any sign of sexual contact. Had he not been drunk, he probably would not have dared to say such a crude thing in public. Kaguru onlookers were disgusted. That same day the couple fought at the river, where the wife had gone to fetch water. Antoni accused her of planning to meet a lover there. They hit one another, but the wife got the better of the fight because she was sober, while he was very drunk. The couple's kin (they were cross-cousins) lived in the neighborhood and persuaded the wife to give Antoni a half-shilling calabash of beer as a gesture of amity, though it seemed to me that Antoni should not drink more. A day or two later Antoni again quarreled with his wife. This was at a beer party that Antoni himself had sponsored at which his wife was selling beer. Antoni again accused the same man of trying to seduce his wife and his wife of encouraging this. This time the couple was sent to the Idibo headman who said that if a man had a beer club and let his wife sell beer at it, then he had to expect men to flirt with her. The Idibo subchief, who was the paternal uncle of the wife and the maternal uncle of the husband, lived in the neighborhood. He was keen that the fighting not reach his court, because

he found it shameful and thought it reflected poorly on him and his kin. The subchief and other kin saw the Idibo headman, to whom the couple were also both related, as a good arbiter. Relatives did all they could to force them to settle matters in a less public manner. Antoni, a horrid man, remained a constant source of strife and humiliation to his kin.

Kaguru chiefs tried to support headmen beneath them. They realized that the income and prestige of the court depended on the support and goodwill of the headmen. Headmen were responsible for many cases reaching the court. Chiefs saw the prestige of headmen connected to their own, since they all represented the Kaguru Native Authority. For the goodwill of their headmen, court chiefs sometimes went beyond their legal authority. Here are four examples:

(1) A Kaguru flouted the authority of a headman by beating his wife to try to settle a marital dispute rather than asking the headman to step in. Some wife beating was taken for granted by most Kaguru men, but severe and repeated beatings were not. The woman came to the Idibo court to accuse her husband of beating her on two occasions, once at home and once in public in sight of the headman. The wife had refused to prepare food for her husband and his visitors, and later that night she had refused to sleep with him. Traditionally, for Kaguru men, these were good reasons for beating a wife. The wife was angry with her husband because he had announced he was planning to take a second wife, something Kaguru men would consider reasonable. The Idibo court levied an outrageously heavy fine against the man, 100 shillings. This was only partly because he had committed a criminal act (wife beating); it was mainly because the man had beaten his wife in the presence of the headman. The court saw this as a serious offense. The man did not have 100 shillings and had no kin willing to help him with such an amount. The court was not interested in seeing the man in jail, so it reduced the fine to 30 shillings, which the man paid. The man was also given six strokes with a thick stick. There was no offense committed warranting a flogging. Furthermore, the man was flogged in the presence of the entire court, the attending public (including me), and, worst of all, his own wife. This was against Tanganyika law, which stated that flogging should be administered in private with only an officer of the court and a medical aide present, and no medical aide was present (Tanganyika 1957a:104–105). As I and a hundred others watched the flogging, Kaguru

remarked that flogging was not a bad thing, but being beaten in public, and especially being beaten in front of one's own wife, was a terrible punishment. The court acted in a high-handed manner and was incensed at someone showing disrespect for the headman. It was not especially bothered by wife beating.

(2) A man accused his headman of taking his tax money and not giving him a receipt. The headman was required to give the man his receipt. While the Idibo court admonished the headman for improper procedure, it did not punish him or ask him for the money, which he had probably stolen from the court; at least the court made no such comment during the hearing.

(3) The Idibo court supported a headman by levying a fine upon the headman's enemy in an indirect way. Chiduo accused Headman Amosi of making his life unbearable through constant harassment so that Chiduo would leave the headman's area. Amosi had announced to the neighborhood that he was banishing Chiduo. Chiduo countered that he had a right to live on the land, and that his house and gardens were there, and he could not and would not go. Amosi brought seven witnesses to support his defense. Each witness stated that Chiduo was an undesirable, quarrelsome neighbor who became especially pugnacious when he got drunk, which was often. These witnesses gave garbled and contradictory statements. The Idibo court chief concluded that Chiduo had no proper case against Amosi. It avoided addressing the issue of Chiduo's banishment, simply telling him to go home. Because Chiduo was judged to have no case, he forfeited the three shillings he had paid to the Idibo court for lodging the case. Chiduo was told to pay the costs of the seven witnesses who had traveled to court at Amosi's request. Their cost in terms of food and lost time and inconvenience was judged by the court to total 24 shillings. This was tantamount to Chiduo paying a 27-shilling non-fine for making a case against his headman. The Idibo court and Headman Amosi had apparently conspired to punish Chiduo for being a difficult neighbor and challenging his headman. Since Amosi had no legal grounds to force Chiduo to leave, everyone agreed that Chiduo was never in danger of being evicted.

(4) In this next case, evidence against a headman was overwhelming, yet the Idibo court limited the fine against him to a small amount, far less than many would consider just.

Chifuka accused Headman Yustino of ordering his three deputies to beat him. Chifuka was hospitalized and had papers from the local dispensary listing his injuries. When he had recovered and lodged a case against the headman, his house mysteriously burned down before he got to court. Headman Yustino claimed that he could not discover who the arsonist was. Refusing to bring his three deputies to court, Headman Yustino came to court alone. Only he stood accused, and only he would be liable for a fine. He knew the court would be more lenient toward him than toward his underlings. Knowing that one accused person would provide far less of a fine than four, he thereby indirectly robbed Chifuka of some compensation. Still, Yustino had a subject beaten, and no one but the court had the right to do that. None of the court officials followed up on the insinuation of arson. Yustino was fined 60 shillings, 20 to the court and 40 to Chifuka. The Idibo subchief was annoyed that his authority had been compromised by a headman. Still, Yustino was a headman whom the court subchief considered usually loyal, so he had levied a ridiculously small fine. Other men who had beaten people had been fined several hundred shillings by the same court that year. As word about such court cases spread in Ukaguru, the strength of local headmen was shored up. (Later my cook seduced the subchief's wife, and subsequently my cook's house, miles away in another subchiefdom, also mysteriously burned down. My cook thought it was the subchief's witchcraft, but I suspected he had employed an arsonist.)

There were occasions when charges against a headman were especially clear-cut and damning. These were especially telling if the plaintiff had close ties with the court chief or if the headman was on especially bad terms with a court, an unusual but difficult situation for a headman to be in. Here is such a case from Mamboya: Headman Robert and the paramount chief had bad relations. As a result, Robert was in an especially weak position in any case he brought to the chief's court. Robert made sure his cases were settled out of court if possible. Robert seriously overstepped himself once: Dansoni was a member of the paramount chief's matrilineage. One day Dansoni saw Chibaibai (Headman Robert's father's sister's son) leaving Dansoni's house. Both Headman Robert and Chibaibai were notorious womanizers. Dansoni criticized both Headman Robert and Chibaibai (Robert's deputy), telling Chibaibai that he would not tolerate the presence of either of them in or near his home.

Chibaibai reported this threat to Headman Robert who came to Dansoni and ordered him to leave the area. Dansoni refused and reported this illegal threat to the paramount chief, who summoned Headman Robert. The paramount chief threatened to dismiss Headman Robert if he did not back down and pay a fine. The chief was alleged to have said, "If a headman can tell one of his people to leave his land, can't a chief tell a headman to leave his as well?"

I know of no case where a chief, even the paramount chief, made good such a threat to evict someone. Yet the paramount chief's power to harass Headman Robert in future court cases was such a serious threat that Robert capitulated. Headman Robert paid a fine of one goat and 80 shillings, which were taken by the paramount chief and Dansoni. As a result, Headman Robert was sneered at by Dansoni and lost considerable local prestige. It was likely that Headman Robert was drunk when he threatened Dansoni (Robert drank a lot); this would explain such reckless behavior that cost Robert so much.

A headman might be dismissed by a subchief or the paramount chief, but this was considered unlikely. I heard of no cases of this ever happening, though I witnessed a case where it was attempted. Such an extreme measure was probably unnecessary, since other punishments were available. Besides, the approval of the Kilosa administration was required for any dismissal. The British administrators were hesitant to see members of the Kaguru Native Authority dismissed, unless they challenged the British themselves. One district officer told me it was better to have in office an inept man whom one knew and whose actions were predictable than to replace him with a tricky, clever fellow. I pointed out that the paramount chief was a drunk, corrupt, illiterate, a philanderer, unpleasant, senile, and unpopular with many Kaguru. The British officer smiled and said that such a man was easier to control than someone who was literate, steadfast, honest, young, and popular.

One rare attempt by Kaguru to depose a headman did take place during my fieldwork in 1958. Some members of the dominant Ganasa clan of Idibo resented Headman Tutiyo. One faction supported Tutiyo, while the other demanded his replacement by their favorite. Each faction insisted that its rivals were not actually members of the dominant clan but merely former slaves usurping clan rights. The issue had come to a head over the slaughter of a cow to celebrate the opening of a new mission school at Idibo. Tutiyo had provided a cow and had then requested contributions from the members of his clan to recompense him for this. His supporters contributed, but the other faction refused. The dissident faction sought the support of the local Idibo subchief, but the subchief supported Tutiyo. This was hardly surprising since the subchief and Tutiyo had cooperated together amicably in court cases for many years. This dispute was brought to the court of the Idibo subchief and was decided in favor of Tutiyo. The other faction contested this decision and appealed to the paramount chief's court. The paramount chief had quarreled violently with the Idibo subchief over the issue of forced labor on a government reforestation scheme (see chapter 5). The paramount chief was invited to Idibo and was entertained by the dissident faction, which was alleged to have bribed him. The subchief's judgment was reversed by the paramount chief when the case was appealed to his court. Tutiyo and the Idibo subchief then appealed the case to the district administration in Kilosa. The British supported Tutiyo, saying they disliked petty bickering in the Kaguru Native Authority. They did not want posts in the chiefdom to be used as pawns in local Kaguru clan politics. The British noted that Tutiyo himself had an acceptable record as a headman. The case was then appealed by the paramount chief to the provincial commissioner, who supported the judgment of the Kilosa district commissioner. Readers may recall that the Idibo subchief had criticized the controversial government forestry scheme. That apparently did not bother the British, since Idibo was far from that project and the paramount chief continued to support drafting labor from his own area, which was closer. The British discouraged quarrels between all local chiefs.

The British administration's pontification over keeping the Native Authority free of local plots seemed disingenuous. The very nature of Indirect Rule and the means of recruitment into the Kaguru Native Authority inevitably made local posts the stakes in clan politics. Why would this not be so when the system, after all, was lauded for epitomizing traditional clan and ethnic values? The case was a huge defeat for the paramount chief. It did show how loath the British were to let Kaguru politics interfere with their British stereotypes about a workable local government order.

Headmen and the Land

A Kaguru headman was considered the custodian of the land within his headmanship. This included land held traditionally by the officially dominant clan and lands of other clans that formed the modern amalgamated headmanship. A headman controlled the distribution and use of land as well as the right to settle on it. A headman had the right to refuse any African permission to settle in his area. I know of no instance of a headman denying such permission. Kaguru said that even in the past such permission would be given as a matter of course. They said, "Every Kaguru leader wanted as many followers as possible so he could ensure his power and wealth. Who would refuse someone who added to one's fighting force and to the goods produced by his country?" Today, once a man settled in a headman's area, a headman could no longer expel him as a clan elder supposedly could in traditional times. As we have already seen, even when Kaguru tried to do this, they got nowhere.

With modern communications and safe political conditions, Africans easily traveled within Ukaguru, especially along the main east-west road cutting through the center of the chiefdom. Transient Africans were often found in the houses built by enterprising Kaguru in the settlements along these routes. Such persons might temporarily use the facilities belonging to kinsmen or friends, and this required no permission from headmen. If these transients later settled apart from their hosts and built houses for themselves, they then had to seek permission from the local headman. Every new house built in a headman's area required permission by the headman, who received a small gift in return, usually a fowl, a few shillings, labor, or some beer as a "key" (*funguo*) for the site. Traditionally, a headman or his deputy should have ceremonially driven the first stake for such a house, but this did not seem to be necessary anymore. Once a house was built, the headman was obligated to provide the householder with some land for cultivation. He was no longer able to revoke his acceptance once that person had become a recognized resident. Yet the amount and quality of the lands a new resident might be given and the way he would be treated when and if disputes occurred depended on how well the new man continued to court favor with the headman and other elders. During his term of office, a headman usually allocated only a fraction of the land cultivated in his area. Once someone had been given land, he held it until crops were poor, and then the land lay fallow, unused, usually for at least three years, sometimes for longer. Most good land was continuously cultivated according to this cycle. (With the land shortage today, due to increased population, land is probably more overused.) Unused land devolved to the common holdings in custody of the dominant clan and supervised by the headman. This rule held even in unusual cases, such as this Idibo court case:

> HEADMAN SIPRIANO: Alinathani has cultivated a field in my country. Why has he done this? He did not receive my permission and does not live in my country.
>
> ALINATHANI (A MATRILINEAL KINSMAN OF THE SUBCHIEF OF THE IDIBO COURT): Yes, I have cultivated that field because it has been mine for a long time, ever since the rule of Headman Chilongola, who gave the field to me. Now I wonder why this man here says that the field is his. Could he tell me how it was that I took a farm that he says is his?
>
> HEADMAN SIPRIANO: That field was given to me as part of my country. Now the field is cultivated by someone of Headman Yubi's country. Why?
>
> WILLIAM: Yes, the field is cultivated by a person who is originally from Headman Yubi's country. But the boundaries between the countries of Yubi and Sipriano were redrawn and this field was put into the land of Sipriano. [Sipriano was then told by the court that he should look after the people and fields which had newly come under his control.]
>
> Those people should be allowed to continue cultivating their fields. But if he is supposed to look after these people, why does he now want to take this field away from a person who had it even before when the land was Yubi's?
>
> IDIBO COURT: The court has seen that the accuser has failed in his case because the field is Alinathani's and has been his for many years, ever since he first started to use it during the rule of the late Headman Chilongola. Even after the land was given to a different headmanship, Alinathani continued to use the field. Why didn't the headman complain then? It is wrong to take away people's land which has been given to them even if you do have the authority to rule a country and its people.

In the past a local Kaguru leader might have displaced a landholder if he had the support of many of his followers. In those times a man residing in one clan area did not usually cultivate fields in another, since each clan area was politically independent. With modern political security, it was fairly common for Kaguru to cultivate fields in more than one headmanship. On account of marriage or fear of witchcraft, a Kaguru sometimes moved from one headmanship to another, but so long as he continued to cultivate a field it could not be taken from him. The British would not allow this. This new spatial mobility of Kaguru greatly undermined any power Kaguru leaders had previously held in allocating lands. Now that they no longer led politically independent areas, they had little power to take land away from anyone.

Most Kaguru thought that they did not have as much prized river-valley land as they could profitably use. Of course, there was little turnover of such valuable land. Theoretically such land could not be inherited; it could be used by a widow but not by a dead person's children or nieces and nephews. Yet headmen were under great moral pressure to allow children and sisters' children to gain such land. Headmen had the ultimate right to bestow such land, but they needed to remain popular in their communities and consequently had only limited leeway in distributing the best land that became available. Some Kaguru tried to "soften" headmen by giving them gifts and labor. A headman was faced with a steady line of prospective clients seeking more land. While there was always a shortage of the best lands, less valuable scrub land was always available. A Kaguru must always secure permission for clearing and cultivating any land, however undesirable, but I never heard of a headman refusing permission for a local resident to use less desirable land. By clever distribution of local fields, a shrewd headman built up a group of loyal adherents. He even supplemented his small salary with gifts he received for allocating land. Rights to graze livestock were also supposedly conferred by a headman. The Kaguru Native Authority court-warrants issued by the district administration specifically mentioned this, but this was a law that did not seem to be followed. Kaguru and Kamba residing in any area automatically seemed to have the right to graze their stock. No one ever asked. Baraguyu moved from headmanship to headmanship and always built their camps in wooded areas far from any Kaguru settlements. They never requested permission to graze their stock. They assumed god gave all grass to them for their herds. It would probably have required armed police action to prevent Baraguyu from grazing their stock, and since their stock contributed considerably to taxes in the chiefdom, the district administration never would have supported this.

The Kilosa headquarters assumed a contradictory position regarding the Baraguyu. These people had been in the area since long before the British. While the British system of Indirect Rule assumed that Ukaguru belonged to the Kaguru and should be ruled by them, the British and the Germans before them had always tacitly acknowledged the rights of other ethnic groups—the Kamba, Ngulu, and Baraguyu—to reside in the chiefdom. Kaguru officials invariably assumed an ethnocentric posture against non-Kaguru, especially Baraguyu, but the Kaguru Native Authority gained so much financially from the Baraguyu through the sales at the Chakwale cattle market that no realistic person would have removed the Baraguyu. Furthermore, many Kaguru profited from the sale of beer and other goods to Baraguyu (see Beidelman 1961b and chapter 5). Some Kaguru headmen were said to have clandestine arrangements with Baraguyu. I saw Kaguru headmen feasting and drinking at Baraguyu camps during special celebrations such as initiations and marriages. Kaguru officials were savvy about where wealth could be gained, and Baraguyu were the wealthiest ethnic group in the chiefdom, despite their outward deceptive appearance of seeming primitive and backward. Comparable data from Uganda report how Indirect Rule provided dominant ethnic groups opportunities to usurp power by exploiting their ethnic neighbors (see Winter 1955:12–38; Roberts 1962).

Headmen: Evaluation

Although a Kaguru headman's powers were in part formulated in traditional Kaguru terms, they rested primarily on his official role as intermediary between the ordinary inhabitants of his area, the officials of the Kaguru Native Authority courts, and the British district administration. A headman's official duties such as law enforcement, recruitment of labor, collection of taxes, were ultimately supported by the threat of force. Yet actual use of political force was remarkably rare in Ukaguru. Still, the threat of court messengers with clubs and whips, the possibility of armed territorial police descending on an area, were possibilities that all Kaguru were aware of. All young Kaguru were told by their elders about terrible shows of force by the Germans who burned villages, hanged leaders, and seized livestock. Each month a troop of police with guns was seen at Chakwale cattle-market so we must assume that Kaguru remained aware that the Kaguru Native Authority and British colonial rule could have been backed by force if necessary.[12]

A headman was useful to the colonial administration only if he could enforce its rules and this required far more than force. The British colonial government was notoriously understaffed and underfinanced. It was not organized to exert constant force from the top to achieve its goals. In Ukaguru the goals of the colonial administration were to preserve peace and order and to secure enough wealth to let local colonial rule pay for itself. Ukaguru did not have any resources meriting great attention by the British.

To secure local cooperation, a headman had to offer something to his subjects while, however, not appearing a stooge of colonial rule. He offered advantages in two ways. First, he was his subjects' link with higher levels of political authority. In this role a headman could modify rulings in order to aid his subjects, or at least mitigate the effects of unpopular rulings by enforcing them in a lax or selective manner; he could do this because his British superiors were ignorant of local affairs. Second, a headman was the only local leader who could settle disputes and difficulties out of court. Local Kaguru saw a headman as a shield against officials from outside. A headman's followers controlled him by threatening to ignore him as a mediator and by forcing him to press hard and long for diminished taxes and fees and less of the labor his superiors asked him to supply. Local obstruction could wear a headman down and makes him look inept to his superiors. A successful headman met the demands of the majority of his subjects, but also satisfied his superiors. A headman was far nearer to his subjects in income, education, and values than were his superiors. He was linked by kinship to many of his people (see Gluckman et al. 1983; cf. Fallers 2955, 1956). A successful Kaguru headman was a juggler of motives and results, of pledges and appearances. His office and power rested on contradictory aims and values. Local Kaguru lacked the ability to translate and communicate their aims and values into forms acceptable or meaningful to a headman's superiors. In contrast, his distant superiors, the British, lacked the understanding and means, even the actual language, to communicate with those they sought to govern. They were too culturally distant and busy to care about any but the worst abuses by Africans against one another.

A headman attempted to justify his actions to his people by presenting himself as an unwilling pawn in a system imposed from above. He was the reluctant enforcer of unpopular measures who would try his best to cushion the harshness of alien rules and demands. Headmen never tried to argue about the need for taxes or the value of conscripted labor for public works. A headman presented these as inevitable evils. He claimed he was just doing his job, and doing it in a way that was more sympathetic than if the British or African outsiders did it. In contrast, when a headman reported to his superiors, he emphasized the conservative, ignorant, and stubborn nature of his subjects, stressing how hard he had to work to get his job done.

KAGURU CHIEFS

There were five Kaguru Native Authority courts in the chiefdom. Four of these, Nong'we, Idibo, Geiro, and Msowero, were presided over by subchiefs; a fifth, Mamboya, was headed by the paramount chief.[13] The paramount chief's court operated on two levels. It was a court for the Mamboya area in the same way that the four subchiefs' courts served theirs. This court also served as an appellate court to the other four. It was in their roles as heads of courts that Kaguru chiefs held most of their power. As Dougherty observes: "The primary purpose of the Native Courts was to bestow authority on the native chief" (1966:214). I discuss some of this here but provide more about Kaguru courts in the next chapter.

All Kaguru courts and the chiefly offices associated with them were creations of the British colonial administration (see chapter 1). Consequently, these chiefs emphasized the importance and value of the modern Kaguru Native Authority far more than the traditional political system from which it supposedly derived. The four Kaguru subchiefs and paramount chief were selected in the same manner as were the headmen of the areas where these chiefs' courts were located. The qualifications of clan membership for such selection were identical with those qualifications for choosing headmen. The members of the dominant or owner clan where a court was located selected two officials, a headman for that area and the chief of the court. Ordinary Kaguru repeatedly remarked how lucky (or opportunistic) such clans had been in securing such un-deserved political advantage.

While selection by local Kaguru was the same for headmen, sub-chiefs, and the paramount chief, there were other factors considered in choosing chiefs. Although some chiefs were illiterate, it was clear even to most Kaguru that literacy would have been a vast asset (see Furley 1971). It was to the advantage of Kaguru of a dominant clan to have a strong and effective chief who could control the various headmen from other areas in the chiefdom. One means of control depended on written reports about taxation and court cases and upon clever interpretation of typed government directives. In some courts illiterate chiefs were vulnerable to the machinations of their clerks. Nonetheless, half the sub-chiefs and the paramount chief were illiterate, even though they were chosen in recent years. This was due to the machinations, intrigues, and divisiveness of Kaguru clan politics, and because qualified people would do better financially outside such posts.

Kaguru had less leeway in their choices of chiefs than in their choice of headmen. I know of no chosen headman having been rejected by the district administration, though the Kilosa headquarters could do so. There were several instances of rejection of chiefs. Administrators inter-viewed all such chiefly candidates at the district headquarters and some-times rejected a nominee. In such cases, local members of a dominant clan had to find a new candidate. The few posts of chief required more abilities and involved monthly contact with the British administrators, something very rare between headmen and British officials. District ad-ministrators claimed that with a few well-chosen officials at the highest level, they could direct the political activities of a chiefdom. The local British administrators themselves had provincial superiors who were as uninformed about events at the district level as district administra-tors were ignorant of what went on at the grassroots. Much that passed for the reality of efficient governance in Ukaguru actually amounted to mere assertions in written reports. The census, tax registers, market reports, medical reports, accounts of court cases, constituted the paper reality to be measured in judging administrative effectiveness. As with so many bureaucracies, written records increasingly dominated how co-lonial policies were formulated and evaluated. Everyone involved in this system was protective of such records. Illiterate chiefs probably made it easier for the British district administration to orchestrate the image and reporting of what supposedly went on in the district and what would be learned at the provincial level. In the next two chapters we shall see how widely reality diverged from these written reports.[14] McCarthy points out how Tanganyikan colonial reports were widely presented more as "mere public relations statements than reality" (1982:12).

Although chiefs were selected by the same small groups of matrikin who selected headmen, their respective courts had jurisdiction over 5 to 19 different headmanships from different clans. A subchiefdom involved an area and population too large for any subchief to oversee without constant support by his subordinate headmen. A headman could make a day's round-trip journey on foot to any part of his headmanship, but no chief could ever hope to reach all of his area in a day, even with a bicycle or auto. Chiefs were consequently faced with far greater challenges to their control than were headmen. Chiefs could not even make much use of kin connections once they were outside their central court area claimed by their clan. A chief should have heeded the wants of the matriclan that selected him, but what that clan wanted might be different from what other clans in a chiefdom desired. A chief's manipulative politics could not hinge solely on clan politics but had to make use of the multiple loyalties of headmen and ordinary Kaguru in many outlying headmanships. A successful chief had to foster the limitations and divisions of his headmen in order to appear as the key mediator between these groups.

Salaries of Chiefs

Kaguru chiefs gained relatively little power or respect through their official earnings. Like headmen, chiefs had varying salaries depending upon the number of subjects under them. The most important subchief (at Idibo) received 120 shillings a month ($17.00), but some of the other subchiefs received about half this amount (120 shillings was far less than I paid my illiterate Kaguru cook, who had never even cooked until I trained him). The paramount chief received about 250 shillings a month ($35.50) as well as relatively lavish benefits in expenses for his journeys in the chiefdom and other parts of the territory. (He had a Land Rover.) The court elders or assessors who assisted the chiefs received very little by comparison, 16 shillings a month ($2.25).

In the eyes of most of their subjects Kaguru chiefs received comfortable incomes, far beyond the resources of most industrious and frugal Kaguru cultivators. Yet these chiefs considered themselves poorly paid. The subchief of Idibo reminded others that over 14 thousand people lived within his chiefdom and asked whether 120 shillings a month was fitting pay for a person with such responsibilities. Kaguru chiefs knew about the wealth enjoyed by Chagga and Haya chiefs; but those had advanced education and lived in areas rich in coffee and other crops.[15] Kaguru chiefs were not realistic; they complained that teachers, medical dispensers, veterinary assistants, truck drivers, and even clerks in their own courts made as much or more money than they did. A Kaguru chief applied the traditional values of his society (the very values repeatedly cited in establishing Indirect Rule). One chief asked me, "How can the leader of a country be poorer than one of his subjects?" In terms of how traditional Kaguru thought, this made sense. The Kaguru Native Authority competed with other government agencies and businesses to hire truck drivers and clerks. The very matrilineal clan-based nature of the post of Kaguru chief made it noncompetitive in the modern market world that dictated salaries. If the Kaguru Native Authority treasury had been controlled by chiefs, they would have received handsome salaries, but the Native Treasury and its budget were run by the British administration in Kilosa and only rubber-stamped by the chiefs.

There were two important upshots of the low salaries of Kaguru chiefs. First, low chiefly salaries related to the low educational level of chiefs. Only an illiterate, or a literate who has lost his proper job through wrongdoing or ineptitude, would see a chiefship as a lucrative post. Even young Kaguru, who sometimes demanded that more educated Kaguru be appointed chiefs, always assumed that such new chiefs would receive far better salaries than what were given in 1957–58. No local school teacher or clerk to whom I spoke ever said being chief was a job he would want. The salary system guaranteed that the Kaguru Native Authority got only poorly trained and unreliable recruits, illiterates, and/or crooks. Second, low chiefly salaries accounted for the corruption of Kaguru chiefs. Corruption was defined in terms set by the British district administration and was punishable by heavy fines and/or imprisonment. Yet many corrupt practices were not considered dishonest in the eyes of many Kaguru. A Kaguru who lost a case because the opponent paid a bribe might complain about the dishonesty of a court official, but on another occasion that same Kaguru would have offered a bribe if he could have afforded one. Most Kaguru, except for the most sophisticated, idealistic, and educated, did not expect any African official to mete out justice without some reward. The alien British concept of official honesty had little meaning to Kaguru.[16] The British often told me how corrupt Kaguru officials were; yet they never saw these examples as reflections of some failure in the British policy of Indirect Rule. Instead, British administrators argued that the corruption of Kaguru officials demonstrated how Africans remained unfit to govern themselves without British supervision.[17] Kaguru chiefs needed the extra money they took to sustain a prosperous and magnanimous image consistent with the supposed dignity of their office (Tignor 1971:349–351).

Powers and Duties of Chiefs

Every Kaguru chief headed a *baraza*, a Swahili word I translate as "court." The term refers to the court building and the office in it that recorded tax collection, fines, and licenses and received orders from the district administration and issued administrative orders to headmen and others. Baraza also refers to the actual procedure and hearing of a court case, and even of a case of mediation. The word refers to both the administrative and judicial aspects of Kaguru chieftaincy (indeed, these functions were never separated for chiefs). It also refers to any large political meeting, and therefore also means any assembly called by a headman or district administrator or even an African nationalist group.

A subchief's court office was the focal point for taxation in his chiefdom. Headmen turned in taxes and secured receipt forms through this office. These accounts were managed by a special African tax clerk sent to the subchiefdom from Kilosa district headquarters. This special clerk was present only during the last weeks of tax collection at the end of the tax year, so many tax payments were made earlier to headmen or the local court clerk, who were supposed to turn these over to the tax clerk. Many Kaguru paid their taxes after the deadline date and as a result were fined three shillings. A list of taxpayers was compiled and kept at the court office. Each subchief had to provide some explanation to the district administration if the annual payments received did not correspond to the amount expected as calculated from the tax rolls. The subchief would have to explain whether this was due to the slackness of the headmen or whether the records were faulty. In early 1957 the Kilosa administration did not have a clear idea of the number of taxpayers in any headmanship because no census had been taken for nine years. The district administration did not even have an accurate idea of how many people lived in the district. The court also kept a list of persons exempted from taxation on account of age, illness, or poverty. The subchief's office was also the collection point for local education fees, which headmen or their subjects themselves turned in for receipt. The court also issued permits and collected fees for brewing and selling beer and for bicycles, radios, and shotguns. Accounting for these various funds was the responsibility of the court clerk or the special visiting tax clerk, who sent these funds and receipts to the district headquarters at Kilosa.[18]

A subchief supervised how the headmen enforced the rules and regulations of the territory, district, and Native Authority. A headman was obliged to report any infraction of these regulations to his subchief and should have tried to bring offenders to the subchief's court for judgment. The district administration expected a subchief to be informed on local difficulties—e.g., grass fires, forest fires, livestock and human epidemics, floods, serious crimes—and for this information the subchief relied on his headmen. A subchief was empowered to give orders to implement various rulings within the chiefdom. It was the subchief more than the headmen who was held responsible by the district administration for seeing that the law was enforced in the bush.

A subchief was responsible for his headmen collecting labor for government needs. One of the most important needs for labor involved work in the vicinity of the subchief's court, where most local Native Authority installations were located. This involved the construction and repair of the court building, dispensary, market, houses of higher-level Native Authority employees, government schools, and resthouses. It involved the collection of labor for local road maintenance. The supervisor of road work assembled his laborers from the subchief's court, making use of trucks sent from Kilosa. A subchief or his representative was present at the organization of work parties. Court personnel would not direct such work. That was done by court messengers or deputies who had been instructed by representatives from the Public Works Department. Which headmen should be called upon to select laborers and how many each headman should provide were decided by the subchief. Chiefs' courts had rest houses located nearby, and these were bases from which touring British administrators inspected an area. This meant that chiefs had control over what affairs in their areas came to the attention of visiting British administrators. A British official usually met with people at the courthouse, telling them his plans and interests, and he then got orchestrated feedback.

A chief attempted to control his headmen (and thus his subjects) by taking skillful advantage of the generality of the laws and rules he was expected to enforce, interpreting them in a somewhat arbitrary manner. Such rules bore most heavily on those headmen most troublesome to the chief. For example, Headman Robert had offended the paramount chief (as I noted earlier in this chapter), so he was required to furnish more men for forced labor than many of his fellow headmen. This was well known and put a strain on Robert's standing with his subjects. Conversely, Headman Patrick, who had supported the paramount chief in disputes about the chief's lax sexual morality, was not required to provide so many persons. Headman Robert was often treated impolitely when he brought cases to the paramount chief's court, whereas Headman Patrick often sat near the paramount chief and his councilors (headmen usually had to stand) and was asked at court sessions for his opinion in cases not even related to him. Chiefs could treat headmen in very different manners before those assembled at a court. Flattering or insulting behavior was noted by the crowd and word spread around a chiefdom as to who had influence and who did not. Cases I report in the next chapter illustrate this.

By demanding that a particular headman enforce rules to the hilt, a chief could lead a headman into difficulties with his subjects. A headman, in turn, could withhold information and help from his chief. A few chiefs and headmen were in continual guerrilla warfare over such matters. A chief had the authority to appoint three counselors or assessors to his court. He often kept those already selected by his predecessor, merely replacing their number as they died or retired. Just like a headman, a chief might also choose unofficial deputies or messengers to help him, but the court had two or three officially paid messengers as well. Unofficial help were often paid out of court receipts. Theoretically, a chief had authority to dismiss any counselor, deputy, or headman in his chiefdom. As we saw earlier in this chapter, a chief's decision could be appealed to the British at Kilosa headquarters, but they were likely to reject most changes that seemed merely due to local Kaguru plots. A chief who tried to dismiss someone and failed would be publicly humiliated, so a chief had to think hard before trying such a tactic. As I showed earlier, no chief had succeeded in doing this in many years; so most Kaguru realized that a chief's blustering and threatening were often empty words, with none of the crushing force of even the briefest orders by a British administrator.

A chief's court counselors were the only Kaguru Native Authority officials appointed and dismissed by chiefs without interference by British administrators. This made them especially responsive to the wants of a chief. While their 15 shillings a month salary might seem like nothing to a European, this meant much to these elders. They were old, illiterate men who had no sources of cash other than the sale of livestock or produce. These 15 shillings were valuable beer and snuff money, since cash employment of old men in Ukaguru was otherwise unheard of. No counselor was likely to cross a chief and forfeit this income. Chiefs, like headmen, took advantage of the vagueness of rules and regulations to use them to single out difficult subjects for harassment or to gain some personal advantage. The law was often vague everywhere but could appear especially murky to illiterate Kaguru. Here are three contrasting examples of how a subchief tried to bend his authority, one where he succeeded and two where he met his match.

(1) In the view of Kaguru chiefs, the tour of inspection by a district commissioner required that he be provided with services and entertainment in order to show that he was welcome. British administrators like to speak of such favors as signs of their popularity. They rarely if ever acknowledged that such benefits were coerced. Chiefs saw such a show as demonstration of both their effectiveness and people's loyalty. In 1958 the district commissioner made an overnight stop at the Idibo subchiefdom court. A large barrel of water was filled by lines of women with tins and calabashes; fowl and fruit were provided. Local Kaguru were told to turn out to dance and drum for the official the next noon. Some local Kaguru were ordered to provide beer for the dancers. A few Kaguru were singled

out for these tasks. Some refused and were punished by being fined and/ or beaten by the subchief's messengers. In this way the subchief could harass those local Kaguru who had earlier given him trouble.

(2) The Idibo subchief announced that the Idibo Native Authority road should be widened. It led from his court past the mission school and teachers' houses and off to the vicinity of the hamlet where the subchief lived. Many thought the widening was mainly to help traffic passing to the subchief's house, to enhance his prestige. The subchief said that due to the road-widening, any cultivator with fields abutting the road should resign himself to losing some of his lands and crops. Some of the fields were being used by a mission schoolteacher and by a retired schoolteacher. These two stormed into the subchief's settlement, protested loudly, and threatened to file complaints with the administrators in Kilosa. Both teachers were literate and spoke and wrote English fluently (which the subchief did not). The subchief backed down, the letters were never sent, and the fields remained untouched. When I returned to Idibo to live several years later, the road was still as it had been before.

(3) The Idibo Subchief was foolhardy enough to ask for a bribe from a local mission schoolteacher, saying that for a consideration he would try to get a case heard without delay. (Postponing court cases was one way chiefs tried to put pressure on litigants, either to punish them or to seek bribes.) The teacher was furious, told all his neighbors and me about what had happened, and wrote a letter in English to the district commissioner. No one learned whether the subchief was ever criticized or punished by the district administration, but the case was quickly heard and a judgment satisfactory to the teacher provided.

THE PARAMOUNT CHIEF

The office of paramount chief (*mundewa*, herder, controller, manager) occupied a contradictory position within the Kaguru Native Authority. It was supposed to epitomize Kaguru ethnic tradition, to unify Kaguru, and provide a means for slow modernization of local government. Many Kaguru had strong feelings about the paramount chiefship. They spoke of Kaguru as having a common government with the chief as a focal point, and directed their agitation for change and modernization toward the chiefship (see chapter 5). Consequently, the chiefship served as a negatively charged lightning rod for Kaguru dissatisfaction about how they were treated and manipulated as an ethnic group. The paramount chiefship was "more traditional" than the offices of subchief or headman, since there had been someone at Mamboya claiming to be "the chief" as early as Arab times, even before German or British rule (see chapter 1). Yet such claims related to the influence of outsiders, to disruptive economic forces that had undermined the older order of local society. The further one went from Mamboya, the site of the chief's court, the more resistance to the paramount chief was expressed among ordinary Kaguru. If the paramount chiefship represented some kind of unifying factor, then this process of unification was itself fairly untraditional. Since it began, the paramount chiefship had always been contended by Kaguru, and I mean the office itself, not just who held it (Beidelman 1978).[19] The dubious nature of the claim that the paramount chiefship related to traditional Kaguru matrilineal values should be clear, because only the most recent Kaguru paramount chief owed his position to being a member of the supposed owner clan of the capital area of the chiefdom (see chapter 1). That was due to the British colonialists' attempt to demonstrate this supposed matrilineal base. The matrikin of the paramount chief held their claim to chiefship through membership in the Jumbe clan, which was the clan said to own the land around Mamboya. Even the Swahili term *Jumbe* suggested an alien, more recent, non-Kaguru concept. Furthermore, other clans contended that they and not the Jumbe actually owned this land. One can therefore see that the very paramountcy of the chiefly office was a shakier tradition than its proponents claimed.

For most purposes the paramount chief's duties were the same as those of a subchief. The British needed a figurehead to embody what the Kaguru Native Authority represented, a solidary ethnic and political entity. Having one chief over all of Ukaguru (at least all of Ukaguru in Kilosa district) provided a public symbol of this supposed ethnic integrity. Such a chief supplied a single face to confront and command, a single voice to be cited as representing Kaguru, even though not all Kaguru took this to heart. The administrative powers of the paramount chief were vague. Theoretically, he was empowered to make rulings for the chiefdom, preferably in consultation with his fellow chiefs, and more recently even with chiefs from other areas of Kilosa district since he began to sit on a district council, which met monthly in Kilosa. In 1957–58 the paramount chief accepted suggestions from the district commissioner about what rules to promulgate but showed little signs of making any policy himself. Kaguru pointed out that his main concern seemed to be finding personal advantages for himself. For example, during my time in Ukaguru, he obtained approximately 12 thousand shillings for a proposed trip to Britain, which was never taken. He also got a long-term, low-interest 7-thousand-shilling loan for a used Land Rover with which he could tour the countryside. That the present paramount chief was cautious about expressing any ideas might be explained by the fact that two of the past four chiefs were deposed by a district commissioner for voicing complaints about British policies. Yet the main explanations for the paramount chief's lack of leadership were his alcoholism (he was often drunk at meetings), that he was illiterate, and that he took office very late in life (in his sixties) with no previous experience leading anyone. Kaguru were also appalled when the paramount chief's maternal nephew died and he took the man's widow as his wife, a union that for Kaguru approached incest and suggested witchcraft.

The Kaguru Native Authority managed without a paramount chief assuming constructive duties. Over recent years, both the British administration and the subchiefs and headmen expanded their own activities to fill the vacuum left by such an inept and unpopular paramount chief. This seemed to be a situation the British administration liked. It allowed the British to make rulings in the name of the paramount chief and for the supposed good of Ukaguru rather than in their own name. For example, in 1958 various modern political parties had their rallies broken up by the paramount chief's messengers and thugs, even though the British district commissioner had issued permits for these meetings. It seemed unlikely to most Kaguru that these scuffles were the idea of the chief. Kaguru noted that just days before these meetings were scheduled, the district commissioner visited the paramount chief. Similarly, the deeply unpopular forced labor for a reforestation scheme was commanded by the paramount chief, not by the district commissioner, even though the forestry officer's local administrative ties were to the district commissioner. The incompetence and weakness of the paramount chief allowed the British to use him as a cat's paw, a ventriloquist's dummy for colonialism. For some Kaguru this made the chief more unpopular than the British. This was not difficult, since the chief was a miserably unappealing person.

OTHER GOVERNMENT EMPLOYEES IN UKAGURU

In the post–World War II decades, the British territorial government expanded the local special services in medicine, veterinary work, education, forestry, and agriculture. African specialists in these fields were then sent into bush areas of Ukaguru. In 1957–58 most of these were not Kaguru, because such workers needed fairly high-level educations. In Idibo, where I resided longest, there were only market and medical staffs, though elsewhere I met full or part-time workers in forestry, agriculture, and the veterinary services. None of these was Kaguru. Such special service workers lived as outsiders in settlements like Idibo, Mamboya, Geiro, and Chakwale. The Native Authority provided them with housing as good as or better than that of chiefs. Local headmen had to provide them with garden land and labor to keep up installations such as the dispensary and market area. Specialists' incomes were relatively high and many bought food and services from Kaguru.

These specialists complained about living in a place as remote and backward as Ukaguru, where so many people were illiterate and "primitive" (they called Kaguru "bush" and sometimes used the very insulting Swahili word *shenzi,* barbarous), because few Kaguru could speak English or good Swahili. Despite their complaints about staying in Ukaguru, these workers' housing was probably better than what they had at home, and they saved money because they were not tempted by modern entertainment or by shops where so little was available. Besides, there were no kin about demanding handouts. Such workers tended to be involved in their own affairs and were immune from pressures from local headmen and even chiefs. None thought of settling in Ukaguru. Most saved their money to take back to their homelands for securing wives, for children's education, or to set themselves up in petty trade. They did not socialize much with Kaguru, although the men who were unmarried sometimes got into trouble with local Kaguru women. Most specialists had no local supervisors. Their superiors were British specialists stationed at the district or provincial headquarters. Complaints about local African specialists were not common. After all, few Kaguru ever saw the British officers who had authority over these specialists, and even fewer had the education or inclination to write complaints, much less travel to a distant headquarters just to agitate and get nowhere. Specialists seemed fairly honest and conscientious by colonial standards, but they could also be high-handed and arrogant at times. They were the freest and most independent educated Africans at any settlement.

The wealthiest and best educated Africans in Ukaguru were school-teachers. The cash income of every teacher exceeded that of all Kaguru Native Authority officials except the paramount chief himself, and some teachers' salaries exceeded even his. Most teachers were Kaguru, though few were stationed near their home areas, so they often had to buy food locally because their wives were given few fields to cultivate. Most teachers were employees of the Church Missionary Society and worked in mission schools, and therefore were not under the control of the Native Authority or even subject to much pressure by headmen. This was because the local missionaries defended all their employees against interference by Native Authority officials, provided these African employees observed Christian conduct, meaning not drinking, smoking, dancing, or carrying on with women. In 1957–58 there were very few Native Authority schools in Ukaguru, but even that staff was responsible to the inspectors from the department of education and not to the Native Authority. Kaguru teachers were the elite of the chiefdom, but they were limited in the ways that they could help their fellow tribes-men develop. They were not allowed to engage in any political activities, however mild.

The lowest-level veterinary and agricultural specialists were termed aides and had little education and simple duties: enumerating livestock, providing basic information about livestock diseases and watering prob-lems, teaching elementary skills in animal husbandry and cultivation, inspecting and reporting offences in antifamine or antierosion regula-tions. These men were lightly supervised and spent much time cultivat-ing their own fields, since they were local Kaguru. They might take a few small bribes for not reporting local infractions, but they enjoyed little leverage, because Kaguru Native Authority officials were themselves unenthusiastic about supporting any government rulings on crops and livestock, and ordinary Kaguru knew this.

One important specialist was the high-level, well-educated African veterinary specialist at Chakwale. He was fluent in English, could administer medicines to livestock and diagnose basic animal ills, and had a sophisticated understanding of animal husbandry. He came from far outside Ukaguru and viewed his assignment at Chakwale, the site of the large monthly cattle market, as a post he would eventually leave for better training and promotion. He was distant from local people. Given his control of crucial livestock medicines, I assumed he occasionally took bribes. The Baraguyu cattle owners whom I knew said that he did. Most of these Baraguyu would have offered payment even without being asked. Other important specialists were market masters; they supervised the sale of African agricultural produce to Asian middlemen who trucked these products to towns. A market master collected government cesses on sales, supervised weighing goods, and preserved order at sales. Market masters worked hard during the harvest season but far less steadily the rest of the year. They had to keep careful records, since they were dealing with sales and government income in fees. I cannot prove it, but it seemed likely that such specialists took bribes, because they supervised sales to Indians, Arabs, and Somalis, and merchants from these ethnic groups tended to assume that some bribery to Africans was an essential part of any business deal. (They were right.)

Medical dispensers and/or nurses were the African governmental employees most closely involved with officials, far more than teachers or veterinary and agricultural specialists. This was because they were supposed to record every patient they saw, indicating the ailment and noting what if any medicines were dispensed. They received a supply of medical goods from Kilosa medical headquarters every month. Their reports were examined by the district British medical officer or his assistants. These were probably the most corrupt of all the specialists. This was because everyone (even the visiting anthropologist) was likely to need some medical help eventually, and when that was needed, the consumer wanted to please the dispenser and did not refuse if a bribe was suggested. A sick person would feel uneasy if a medical aide seemed annoyed while he or she was giving treatment. Dispensers were paid as well as many schoolteachers, but they had far greater temptation and opportunity to collect bribes. Dispensers disproved the British official claim that better-paid Africans would be honest. The problem was that better-paid Africans were better-educated Africans, and better education meant higher aspirations about material consumption. Besides, even the best-paid African considered himself poorly rewarded. Though British medical staff supervised local Kaguru medical records, this hardly prevented bribes or theft. We shall see in the next chapter that court records were dishonestly kept, so why would we expect medical records to be any better? There was no way for British in distant Kilosa to know what actually happened in the bush. Africans (and many other people) believed that one received better treatment and better medicine if one paid. I did.[20] Many dispensers asked for payments when they were engaged in long weeks of injections or medication, as when they treated yaws, leprosy, bilharzia, worms, and venereal diseases. Such payments were supposed to be for the extra work involved. No one would want to antagonize any dispenser by reporting him for fear he would give one bad or no treatment in the future. No one would expect a dispenser to lose his post simply for taking a bribe. He might be admonished, but he would still be there at the same post. Such men were hard to replace and hard for locals to challenge.

Court clerks were the least independent of the various specialists. They were stuck in a local chief's courthouse and under the chief's gaze. The written records were the responsibility of clerks (many chiefs were illiterate). It was a clerk, not a chief, who was first challenged when records did not make sense, and court records were carefully scrutinized. The most studied reports were the tax records, which were also filed by court clerks. One of the supposed aims of the Native Authority was to have clerks supervise or countercheck chiefs. As things went, clerks had little influence on how a court case was judged. Still, they appear to have been cut in on any illegal payments given to the court. There was no good reason why underpaid clerks would not go along with such an easy and convenient arrangement.

This is a long, descriptive chapter. Even so, I did not cover an important side of the Kaguru Native Authority, the courts themselves. Courts were crucial because they were the only arenas in which the authority and power of the Kaguru chiefs and headmen were formally demonstrated to ordinary Kaguru. They also provided the main written accounts available to British officials for checking how skillful the Native

Authority officials were in doing what Indirect Rule was said to be all about, controlling local Africans in the bush. I therefore postpone my evaluation and analysis of the Kaguru Native Authority until the end of the next chapter, when I can take into consideration the ways the court system related to other sides of Kaguru government.

FOUR

Court Cases:
Order and Disorder

A Kaguru Court

A Kaguru chief's court was ordinarily held every Saturday at the Native Authority courthouse, usually starting about nine or ten in the morning and continuing nonstop until about four or five in the afternoon. Occasionally court was held on additional days as well. Very rarely a chief might hold an open-air court in an outlying area if he thought the cases and people involved merited this.[1] Applicants with cases registered their suits a few days to several weeks ahead, paying three shillings registration fee (*uda*) in civil cases, a fee later paid by the defendant if he was found liable. Criminal cases did not require a fee.[2] The length of time taken for a case to reach a hearing and settlement after its registration depended on many factors. Weeks might be lost trying to trace an unwilling defendant or witness who had fled, or in seeking someone living in another court district. Sometimes delays were made by the court itself in order to increase chances of securing a particular judgment or to avoid hearing a case at all. Sometimes an accused, especially if he was a Baraguyu or Maasai who would be hard to recapture, was kept in the lockup for many days.[3]

The court clerk registered all cases and sent litigants a notice of when the case would be heard, usually through a court messenger or headman. The court decided whether a case was criminal or civil. If it was criminal, fines, flogging, or imprisonment were possible. In civil cases there were no punishments. Debts and damages were paid and social relations resolved. Often a court could not decide how to categorize a case until it had been heard, which was a good excuse for writing up many cases only after the trial was over.[4] For that reason, most illiterate Kaguru were told to pay a court fee regardless of whether or not their case was civil or criminal. I never saw the court clerk writing up any hearing. He relied on later accounts of the court officials to learn what was said and done.

Court records were divided into criminal cases (*mashtaka*) and civil cases (*madai*). Each consisted of a two-page booklet. The outside page of each booklet, whether criminal or civil, listed the name of the court, the number of the case in the yearly court file, the date the case was entered, the accuser, the accused, the offense or dispute at issue, the date the hearings began, the date they were concluded, the judgment of the court, the date any fines or compensations were paid, and whether the case was appealed. On the inside of the booklet was a list of the witnesses and digests of their testimony, along with a few sentences indicating the nature and reasons for the court's judgment. Below this were the names of those who sat in judgment, usually the chief and two to four court elders. Below these were the names of the contending parties with their signatures, or far more often their thumbprints, and the dates of payments and acknowledgments of the judgments. Almost always only two sides of the four available page-sides were used.

The most common civil cases heard by Kaguru chiefs' courts were: disputes over payments of bridewealth, divorce and return of bridewealth, accusations of adultery, disputes over loans of wealth, disputes over inheritance of property, and disputes over boundaries between cultivated fields. The most common criminal cases were: wife-beating, assault and verbal abuse, theft of property, and destructive trespass by livestock on cultivated fields.

A Kaguru court was empowered to use the following sanctions depending on the severity of the offense. It could imprison a man for up to one year at hard labor in the district jail at Kilosa. (Women could not be imprisoned by any Native Authority court, nor could women be flogged.)[5] A native court could fine up to 1,000 shillings (143 dollars) or its equivalent in goods, usually livestock. In addition to fining a guilty person, a court could confiscate property in lieu of cash. Finally, a native court could administer flogging, up to eight strokes with a whip (*kiboko*) or stick.[6]

I visited all of the upland Kaguru courts. A typical courthouse was not much different from other structures built for the Native Authority, except that the sides of the courtroom itself were open. The courthouse was a cement building with a sheet-metal roof. The main room was about thirty feet by twenty. There was a slightly raised area at the front, with a large table and chairs where the chief and three assessors sat. The sides of the courtroom allowed a crowd to sit and watch the show. Other attendees sat on the floor of the courtroom. Usually about eighty to a hundred people attended. One of my more sophisticated Kaguru friends described it as "the Kaguru local cinema with a show once a week." The persons involved in the cases stood at the front of the courtroom before the chief and assessors. The court clerk sometimes sat near the chief and assessors, but he was often absent when cases were heard, even though he wrote the court record.[7] At the end of a case, the subchief of the court (if he was literate) or the clerk was supposed to read the court's judgment so all could hear the case's outcome (Tanganyika 1957a:52).

At the back of the courthouse were two smaller rooms. One was the court clerk's office, where money and records were kept for the past three years.[8] There were boxes and shelves for files, and a table and chair where the clerk worked. The other, even smaller room was the lockup. It had no furniture and only a small, barred, shuttered window. Any prisoners kept there had to sleep on the floor or get their kin to bring them bedding.

The courthouse was the largest building in Idibo settlement. Near it were the dispensary and Native Authority–owned houses for the local dispenser, a nurse, and the market master. Farther away were a CMS school and houses for the two teachers, and even farther away were a mission church and a pastor's house. Near the court was also an African *hoteli* selling beer, tea, and snacks and occasionally putting up visitors. It was usually full of patrons during court days. Even farther away were a Somali and several African shops, the local Native Authority market, and a few African houses. This congeries of structures was typical for all the chiefly court headquarters. There were fewer than a hundred people in the settlement, though many Kaguru hamlets were visible from the hill where the Native Authority headquarters was located. During court and market days, several hundred people might be found in the settlement. (In Ukaguru and in most other parts of Tanganyika, government and mission headquarters were usually located on hills. Natives were accustomed to ascend toward authority.) As Noël Coward wrote, "The sun never sets on Government House because English might selected the site" (1955:124).

The Laws, Enforced and Not

While the British continually described their policy of Indirect Rule as one allowing Africans to rule themselves according to their own customs, they actually made Africans obey and enforce a wide range of alien laws. They also forbade Africans from following some of their own traditions. Sometimes these changes were introduced as inevitable aspects of colonialism, such as paying taxes, buying licenses and permits, or banning certain weapons such as rifles. Other rules were introduced to accommodate colonial racism, for example, not allowing African courts jurisdiction over cases involving non-Africans.[9] The British banned African courts from dealing with all serious criminal cases where a death sentence or a long prison term were involved. In 1957–58 a Kaguru court could hear civil cases involving property only up to 3,000 shillings in value (about 438 dollars). Furthermore, Kaguru could not deal with cases that involved Christian religion. No Kaguru court could terminate a Kaguru marriage that had been performed by a Christian pastor or priest yet, oddly, such a court could deal with bridewealth payments related to such a marriage (Tanganyika 1957a:24–25). Finally, all kinds of laws were introduced that were said to be for the good of Africans but which Africans themselves often did not view as sensible.

In short, the British allowed Africans to rule their local areas but not control everyone found in those areas. They assumed that Africans were neither competent nor reliable enough to deal with really serious legal matters. (To be realistic, very serious crimes were rare in Ukaguru, and likelihood of Africans wanting to litigate with non-Africans was slight.) Some laws were dictated to local Kaguru by the British, so that these Kaguru officials had to proclaim, wrongly, that the Native Authority and not the British were making these laws. This explains the universal unpopularity of local laws about agriculture, brewing, deforestation, hunting, and animal husbandry, all of which were flagrantly disobeyed and slackly enforced, if at all.

Some Kaguru customary practices were even made into crimes. For example, killing twins and other "abnormal" babies (Beidelman 1963b: 53–57) was judged to be murder, a capital crime tried by British officials, even though such killing was viewed by most Kaguru as necessary for the safety of others. In contrast, some practices that Kaguru viewed as wrong were still not viewed as wrong in the way that the British saw them. Witchcraft, for Kaguru perhaps the most dangerous of all offenses, was not even viewed as an actuality by the British. Yet it was listed as a crime to be tried only by the British unless special permission was given. For the British, the crime of witchcraft existed in someone claiming to be a witch or claiming to detect witches, or in persecuting an alleged witch, but not in actually being one. The punishments involving witchcraft were too fearsome for Kaguru to be allowed to adjudicate—seven years in prison and/or 4,000 shillings fine, and/or possible forced relocation outside the local area (Tanganyika 1947:231–232).[10] For Kaguru, traditionally witches were often killed (Beidelman 1963a). Finally, Tanganyikan territorial law listed bestiality as a serious crime consequently subject to British and not African trial (Tanganyika 1947:159). In contrast, Kaguru saw bestiality as shameful but not as a terrible offense (Beidelman 1961a). Rape was the only serious crime allowed in African courts (a life sentence was possible), but even there, such a sentence needed to be approved by a British official and, in any case, no Kaguru court would have viewed rape in the serious way the British might (Tanganyika 1957a:24). In contrast, Kaguru saw rapes as minor offenses punishable by fines and appropriately handled by local courts, if they were handled at all.

In the following two cases I show how in 1958 the Idibo subchief's court dealt with both bestiality and rape in ways that seemed just to most Kaguru.[11] I show how Kaguru courts tried to make sense of offenses that potentially could be considered serious crimes by the alien reasoning of Tanganyika territorial law.[12] These first two cases illustrate a more central issue: how Kaguru (and indeed most traditional Africans) viewed law. Kaguru failed to make a clear distinction between civil and criminal cases, and they favored judgments that involved fines and compensation, rather than imprisonment or flogging. The first two cases involved bestiality and rape, both very serious crimes according to Tanganyikan territorial law, and both demanded very harsh punishment, imprisonment. Both cases were converted into civil cases where fines and compensation were given the injured parties and no jail time was considered. These were judgments more in restorative, rather than punitive, law. As Lonsdale perceptively notes:

> Customary law, the main field in which the British sought to hitch local culture to ruling hegemony, rested on a legal delusion, DC's and senior African men together tried to limit the new liberties with allegedly "customary" rules that were equally novel. Chiefly influence in the African courts made the position worse. Repeatedly efforts failed to separate "custom" from the corruption of office. The state could not disengage from the partiality of its African agents; these in turn were trapped between colonial coercion and moral community (2000:200).

CASE 1

Mbaluka and another, older man appeared in Idibo court.[13] Mbaluka accused the older man over the actions of his son, a youth in his twenties who was not in court. Mbaluka said that the youth had sexual relations with one of his (Mbaluka's) sheep. Mbaluka claimed the youth had bathed in a stream near where Mbaluka's son was herding a flock of sheep and goats. He said that after the youth had bathed, he asked the herdboy to watch his clothes until he returned. Then the youth went off naked into the bush. This was very unusual behavior for Kaguru, who were extremely shy about appearing naked. The boy was suspicious and followed him. He found him mounted on a sheep having sexual intercourse. The boy reported this to his father. Mbaluka asked the youth's father to pay a fine, but the father refused. Then Mbaluka confronted the youth himself and asked him to pay a fine, and he too refused.

Mbaluka repeatedly complained to the court that the youth had no right to have sexual relations with a sheep that did not belong to him: "It was my sheep, not his," and "How can I eat that sheep after he had sex with it?"

Mbaluka did not bring his son to court with him, saying that the boy was too young to appear in court. Mbaluka said, however, that the accused had admitted his offense in front of several others. Mbaluka had not brought these people to court either. The youth's father had not brought his son to court because his son denied doing anything wrong.

The elders of the court said that the disputants should return to the next session (the following week) and bring the sheep in the dispute with them. They said that Mbaluka's son and the accused should also appear. If the sheep had been a woman, she would have had to appear along with her kin or husband as well as the offender and perhaps his kin. By making the request for the sheep to be brought, the court had implicitly compared the case to an ordinary case of sexual trespass in which a man had sex with a woman over whom he had no rights, in violation of the rights of the man who did, such as a husband or father. The court elders added that the boy and other witnesses would have to appear and testify. The court added that Mbaluka's son was not a good witness, since a small boy might not recognize a sexual act.[14]

On the next session of the court, the sheep was brought, as well as the herdboy and the accused. The sheep had to stand between the accused and accuser, just where an adulterous woman would stand in a case between her husband and lover. The subchief asked, "Is this the sheep in question?" The various persons in the case all agreed that it was, and even the sheep made a noise. The Kaguru spectators all snickered. The accused youth looked extremely embarrassed. The youth admitted his guilt. He was fined one goat and one kid, a fine amounting to about 60 shillings, an appropriate fine for adultery. Both the accuser and accused accepted the court's judgment without argument.

Kaguru regard bestiality as unnatural and ridiculous, but not as an object of horror. The Kaguru audience sitting around the court were vastly amused at what the youth had done. I asked older Kaguru what would have been done in the past. Some said that the sheep should have been killed and then thrown away because it was now unclean. They said it was spoiled and good for nothing. A few Kaguru in the audience wondered whether Mbaluka was really a Kaguru, because he had still kept the sheep in his herd and not disposed of it. Mbaluka apparently considered the sheep too valuable to destroy. Today bestiality might require some sacrifices and prayers of cleansing by some elders, but those would not be court matters. To make a case in the Kaguru Native Authority court, Mbaluka had to stress that his property rights had been violated. The youth had enjoyed Mbaluka's sheep without Mbaluka's permission. One judge even asked rhetorically why the youth had not had intercourse with his own sheep instead of Mbaluka's. The court elder remarked, "Who would have brought a case like this to court if the sheep was the youth's own?" The court treated the case like any other adultery case and even referred to the fine as *ugoni* (sleep), the term for an adultery payment.

Neither the accuser nor accused seemed aware that bestiality was actually a serious crime according to Tanganyika territorial law and that such a case could have been sent to a British-run hearing. The punishment for bestiality according to Territorial law was up to 14 years imprisonment, a severe punishment that shocked me, and that I discovered only when I got to Dar es Salaam to secure a copy of the law (Tanganyika 1947:159). During the trial, when I mentioned that I thought bestiality was probably an imprisonable offense, Kaguru expressed disbelief. Some remarked that putting someone like that in prison would have helped no one, certainly not the man whose sheep had been violated. The court had made a judgment far more acceptable to all Kaguru. The case was not recorded. Some Kaguru told me that this was because Kaguru would not want non-Kaguru to learn about such an offense because the British would laugh at them for being primitive (Swahili, *shenzi*).

CASE 2

Mamjumbe and Semundo were both old women, each over 55 years old. Mamjumbe was married to an affine of the subchief of Idibo court where the case was heard. Semundo was a clan sister of the same subchief. Semundo was not married and made her living partly by selling beer and partly by some prostitution.

One night Mamjumbe and Semundo went to a dance and got very drunk. On their way home, the two old women met a youth named Saidi walking along the path near their village. People in the village heard a great commotion and found Saidi, Semundo, and Mamjumbe yelling and quarreling at the side of the path. The women claimed the youth had raped them both. Saidi was very drunk and belligerent and could not speak coherently. When he was accused by the women, despite the difficulty of seeing the three clearly in the dark, witnesses thought that the three's clothing seemed disarrayed, possibly from sexual relations. Some of the Kaguru spectators at the court suggested that perhaps the two women had seduced the youth and that, when they noticed people approaching, the women screamed and struggled in order to defend their reputations. (Kaguru considered sexual relations outside a house, in the bush, shameless, though, of course, it was sometimes done.)

The youth, Saidi, was seized and given over to the Idibo court messengers, who took him to the Idibo subchief, who suggested that he be locked up overnight. A friend of Saidi, Eliazir, intervened and said he would be responsible for Saidi coming to court when he was called. Eliazir was a distant relative of the subchief. Saidi had no close kin living nearby. In court, Saidi was accused by the husband of Mamjumbe and by Semundo. They both said that Saidi had sexual relations with the two women, over whom he had no rights. Mamjumbe's husband stood in the place of the accuser and the two women stood between the accuser and the accused. Although Semundo was also an accuser, she had brought no male relative with her to accuse Saidi.

Saidi denied remembering anything about what happened. He said he did not even remember being arrested. This could not have been an attempt to escape responsibility, because Kaguru do not recognize drunkenness as an excuse for any offense. This denial was probably used as an excuse by Saidi for not testifying about what happened. He might even have been trying to avoid admitting he had sexual dealings with women old enough to be his mother.

The court was not concerned about whether Saidi had used force. This eliminated any charge of rape. It sought only to determine whether or not Saidi had or tried to have sexual relations with the women. The testimony about grabbing body parts was heard with ribald amusement by the court officials and onlookers. Two witnesses testified that they had seen Saidi struggling with the women and saw him throw first one and then the other to the ground. The court asked Saidi how he could have had the strength and skill to master two struggling women if he was so drunk that he could remember nothing. The court said Saidi must have been more or less sober to have that much control over two women, so he must remember. In defense, Saidi pleaded, "How could I run about with these two? They are too old to run at all!"

The witnesses and the two women added more and more lurid details. Then Saidi admitted that he had fondled the women. The court asked why he had fondled them, and he said it was because he was drunk.

The two women insisted he had done more than fondle them, that he had sexual intercourse with both of them by force. Saidi admitted embracing them. He said, "I only hugged them. They did not see my penis." Mamjumbe angrily denied this and said, "First he had this other woman [Semundo] and then he had me. First he enjoyed her and then he pushed her away and grabbed me. He took his penis and pushed it into my vagina. He had orgasm with me three times and I saw his seed all over my body." The court seemed very amused. The women in the audience tittered and covered their faces in gestures of modesty. The men in the audience laughed loudly and said that Mamjumbe and Semundo truly had no shame to say such things in public. Then Saidi said that the two women had forced him to have intercourse with them. He said that Mamjumbe had grabbed his penis and demanded that he have intercourse with her. The two women angrily denied this and the other witnesses supported their story. After nearly two hours of further argument, Saidi admitted the charges.[15] When the court gave its judgment, it phrased the offense as one much like any case of adultery, one requiring a fine for sexual trespass (*ugoni*). No mention was made about force. Saidi was told he had to pay the customary adultery fine of 60 shillings to each accuser. In the case of Mamjumbe this was a simple procedure, for the husband was there in court ready to receive the fine. Semundo had no husband and presented no man in charge of her. She was an older woman living alone. The court awarded the second fine to her, so she really had appeared in court as a quasi-male.

The striking aspect of this case, to me, was that it opened with an account of sexual intercourse by force, which would have made this a serious criminal case. Some of the Kaguru present knew that British law punished rape with a long prison sentence, but no one knew how long. In fact, territorial law provided for imprisonment up to life. Yet I never heard of any Africans in the territory receiving such a sentence for forcibly having sex with another African. I am pretty sure that this territorial law was viewed mainly as a deterrent to Africans thinking of raping white women; this would explain why the British never minded Africans trying alleged rape cases among themselves, as though this were not serious.

During the case, both the judges and the audience stated that women do not refuse sexual favors. "What woman would refuse what man?"

Kaguru custom did not usually grant consideration to women regarding whether they did or did not want to have sexual relations. If a woman had been given for bridewealth, then she should accept sexual advances from the man who had paid. She should be beaten if she refused for no good reason. Yet in this case we find that the women emphasized their unwillingness to have sex. I think that this was because Mamjumbe wanted to defend herself against any accusations by her husband, and Semundo had to find some explanation why she, a well known easy woman, should be compensated for sexual relations. Assault was a convenient argument. Everyone agreed that it was not clear whether the women had done anything to encourage Saidi. He had not paid for sexual relations, and that was enough.

The Courts and Ethnicity

The British conceived of Indirect Rule working in ethnically homogeneous areas. The Native Authority officials and the courts were assumed to be homologous with the local population. Such assumptions made poor sense for Ukaguru, which was one of the most ethnically diverse areas in Tanganyika Territory. The Kaguru Native Authority courts were exclusively run by Kaguru.[16] This meant that Kaguru officials were able to use the courts to dominate the ethnic minorities who resided in the chiefdom, especially the Baraguyu and Kamba. In the following cases from Idibo we can see how this was done.[17]

CASE 3

A Kamba appeared at the Idibo subchief's court complaining that she had lost two teeth during a quarrel with her husband, another Kamba. She claimed that her husband had borrowed one of her large baskets and when he was done with it, left it in the sun where it might warp. She criticized him about this and he beat her. She presented the teeth to the court as evidence. Her husband defended himself by saying that he had found his wife eating with another man within her house, and that this showed that she was committing adultery. He said he therefore had a right to beat her. The court fined the husband 110 shillings, 60 to the woman and 50 to the court.

On the surface this might seem straightforward, but it was not. A few weeks earlier the same court had fined a Kaguru husband a total of only 50 shillings for beating his seven-months-pregnant wife for refusing to have sex with him, a far graver offense, since by Kaguru custom women near childbirth were allowed to refuse having sex with their husbands. By both Kaguru and Kamba custom, a woman sharing food with a nonkinsman inside her house could be considered adulterous and deserved to be beaten, though perhaps not to have her teeth knocked out. In Idibo subchiefdom Kamba had more livestock per capita than Kaguru, and Kaguru often got on poorly with their Kamba neighbors, whom they envied. In general, Kaguru fined Kamba and Baraguyu more harshly than Kaguru, arguing that, being richer, they needed to pay more to be punished on the same level as Kaguru. This was a biased practice going against Tanganyika territorial policies for courts.[18] Such practices allowed local Kaguru to extract wealth from Kamba and keep them in their place. The case was not recorded, so it seemed likely that the court pocketed the fine.

The next two interrelated cases contrast sharply with this.

CASES 4 AND 5

Nzangu lived in Nguyami in the Idibo subchiefdom. He had a Kamba father and a Gogo mother. His family members were notorious for their tempestuous relations. His mother accused him of beating her. Although this was a terrible offense in any African ethnic group, Nzangu was fined only 15 shillings to the court and a goat to compensate his mother. At first, I was surprised at this.

Shortly after the preceding case, Nzangu and his mother accused Nzangu's younger brother (by the same mother) of beating them both. The brother was also accused of threatening Nzangu with a knife. He in turn accused Nzangu of trying to raise cash by pawning their sister, and claimed that to prevent this he had planned to carry his sister off. (Such pawning was customary in the past but was now illegal.) Nzangu wanted to pawn the woman to raise funds to pay for other court fines, whereas his brother wanted the sister to be married so he could use the bridewealth for his own marriage. Before running off, the youth got drunk and beat Nzangu and one of his friends. He denied attacking his mother, and he denied using a knife. The court pointed out that the youth already had a very unpleasant previous criminal record, which it was taking into account.

The father of the two men testified that the youth had only used a club, not a knife, but the court said that his testimony was useless, though it did not explain why. The mother was then asked to testify, and she stated that the youth had beaten them and that he had a knife, though she never said he had tried to stab anyone. At first the youth denied this and only admitted threatening people with a club, but after much questioning he admitted brandishing a knife; however, he continued to claim he had never tried to stab anyone. The youth was returned to the lockup, where he was kept for another week before the final hearing. He was fined 200 shillings, and he paid another 50 shillings compensation to Nzangu and 50 shillings to his mother.

Before one can understand the two preceding cases, one must know relations between Nzangu and the subchief of Idibo. Nzangu was a well known trader in livestock. He was on good terms with many people from all ethnic groups in the Idibo area. For that reason, he was a useful ally. Before these two cases were heard, Nzangu lodged with the subchief, to whom he had brought a goat and for whom he did chores. Nzangu assured me that he would win the case because he had the friendship of the Idibo subchief. (I rented a house from the Idibo subchief, who lived next to me, so I saw all the comings and goings to the subchief's compound.) We can now better understand the subchief's persistent questioning of Nzangu's brother, his impatience with the testimony of Nzangu's father, and his jailing of Nzangu's brother in order to wear him down into accepting a heavy fine. The court was not treating Nzangu or his mother badly in the way it would many other Kamba, because Nzangu was a crony of the subchief. Yet the fine and compensation exacted by the court were far higher than those usually asked of Kaguru. For example, shortly earlier the same court tried a Kaguru for beating and trying to stab another Kaguru whom he suspected of adultery (unproved) with his wife. The Kaguru was fined only 20 shillings and had to pay only 10 shillings compensation. This alerted me to the other, earlier case, made against Nzangu by his mother. There, too, a relatively low fine was exacted considering the offense. Yet the mother was also placated with the added gift of a goat. It now appeared that this was so she would cooperate in testifying for Nzangu in the other, bigger case against his brother. These cases with Nzangu were the most blatant instances of bribery that I witnessed. Before the trial I saw a goat delivered to the subchief, and I saw Nzangu herding livestock and repairing tools for the subchief. There were many other cases where it seemed almost certain that a court was bribed or pocketed a fine, but no one ever made successful accusations about this while I was in Ukaguru, at least not any that led to punishment of any Kaguru official. Giving or receiving a bribe were serious offenses that would cost an official his post and could lead to two years in prison and/or 2,000 shillings fine (Tanganyika 1957a:93). Local Africans making such an accusation would get in deep trouble if they could not conclusively prove such a case, for they would have to live under the power of officials they had accused.

CASE 6

A Kamba was apprehended after having stolen two donkeys from a Kaguru. He was caught by the Idibo court messengers with the stolen animals in his possession. The Idibo court ordered the Kamba to return the donkeys to their owner, compensate the owner with a calf (50 shillings) and pay a fine of 100 shillings to the court.

Here the Kamba paid a stiff fine, but it was far less than what a Baraguyu would have paid for a comparable offense. This was because the Kamba were judged poorer than the Baraguyu. As I already noted, such variance in fines depending upon wealth of an accused was common, though condemned by the British.

CASE 7

An old woman of mixed Kamba and Gogo descent complained that the headman of Idibo had sent his messengers to beat her until she bled.[19] She said that she and other women were summoned to draw water for the district commissioner and his entourage (he was making his first visit to Idibo). She fetched one jar of water and so did the other women (Kaguru). The others were then allowed to leave, but when she tried to leave, she was told she must continue to draw more water. She claimed this was unfair and again tried to leave. She said she was discriminated against because she was a Kamba. The court admitted that the headman's deputies had usurped one of the court's basic powers by beating someone. (In fact, it was illegal for any court to order a woman to be beaten.) The court fined the messengers a total of 5 shillings, a ludicrously small fine. Then, before the payment, the subchief told the old woman that she herself would be accused by the deputies whom she had accused of beating her. The subchief said that this was because she had disobeyed an order of the Idibo headman. The Idibo subchief said that this offense by the old woman would involve a heavy fine. Then the subchief added that if she would withdraw her own case, the court would forget about the entire matter. The old woman left. The affair was not entered in the court record.

This case involved serious abuse of authority by the Idibo headman and intimidation by the Idibo court itself. It illustrated how a court supported a headman whom it favored. (The Idibo headman and the Idibo subchief were affiliated to the same owner clan and worked well together.) Kaguru officials often picked on ethnic minorities, and the Kamba were fair game in Idibo.

CASE 8

A man of mixed Kamba and Gogo descent had been asked by the Idibo headman, along with many Kaguru, to dance for the district commissioner, who was making his first visit to Idibo in 1958. The man refused, as did many Kaguru. The Idibo headman did not lodge a case against his fellow Kaguru, but he made one against the ethnic outsider. The man refused to pay a fine and was publicly flogged six strokes for his disobedience. This same man had earlier led a group of Kamba complaining to the Idibo subchief about anti-Kamba behavior by the Idibo headman. The case was not recorded.

CASE 9

A Kaguru elder brought his daughter and a Kamba youth to Idibo court, asking the court to settle a dispute between them. He did not charge the Kamba with any specific offense. He simply stated that his daughter had eloped with the Kamba and had borne a child. The Kamba had already paid an adultery fine and returned the daughter to the elder. The girl continued to sleep with the Kamba whenever she could, even though she had returned to her village, where people objected to this liaison. Later the baby died, and the Kamba brought a kinsman to have sexual relations with the girl, saying Kamba custom required a mother to have purificatory sexual relations after a child's death. It was not made clear why he brought his brother and did not himself have sex with the mother.[20]

The girl's parents refused to allow this. The father said he knew the Kamba wanted to adhere to their customs, but both parents expressed utter dislike of both Kamba and their customs.[21] The girl said she would gladly leave her kin for the Kamba and adhere to Kamba customs. She and her Kamba lover pleaded that they be allowed to marry and that the bridewealth the Kamba offered be accepted. Yet when the Kamba youth's parents were asked to testify, they disapproved of the match as strongly as the girl's Kaguru parents.

Some court members spoke heatedly against interethnic unions. The court ruled that despite the desires of the couple, the marriage could not take place. The youth was told that if he visited the girl, he would be fined. The case was not recorded.

CASE 10

Kamba (A) accused Kamba (B) in Idibo court. Two donkeys had been stolen from a Ngulu. When the Ngulu came to the Kamba area searching for the donkeys, he found them owned by others who said they had bought the donkeys from Kamba (A). The Ngulu accused Kamba (A) of theft. Kamba (A) said he had bought the donkeys from someone else but for three days refused to say that it was Kamba (B). When accused, Kamba (B) at first said Kamba (A) was lying, but later the two Kamba agreed to go with the Ngulu to the local Kaguru headman. The court said the Kamba were complicating the story in order to cover up matters and that the two Kamba were probably both guilty. Then Kamba (B) said they had found the donkeys wandering in the bush but had not stolen them. Instead of turning the lost animals over to the headman as they should have, the two Kamba sold them, splitting the cash. Kamba (A) denied this.

Kamba (A) brought two Kamba witnesses who swore that Kamba (B) alone had sold the donkeys to Kamba (A). This was damaging to Kamba

(B), because the witnesses were Kamba (B)'s own uncle and affine. The court argued that Kamba (B)'s kin would not testify against their own kin if he were not guilty (an odd conclusion, considering the many cases the court heard of embittered kin testifying against one another).

What emerged after several hours testimony was that the donkeys belonged to the Ngulu, and the court even cut the Ngulu short when he offered to bring witnesses to prove that the donkeys were his. The Idibo court suggested that the donkeys be returned to the Ngulu along with a cow as compensation. The Ngulu refused, arguing that the two donkeys had been pregnant. He had learned that one of the donkey foals had died but that the other still lived. He demanded two young donkeys as well as the two mature donkeys and the cow. The court agreed, but Kamba (B) refused to speak, and Kamba (A) sat down with the spectators, thereby signaling that he considered himself out of the dispute. Kamba (B) was put in the lockup, and Kamba (A) and the Ngulu left. It was decided that on the following Wednesday, court would have a special session and Kamba (A), Kamba (B), the Ngulu, the donkeys, and their current owners would attend.

As the preceding hearing progressed, Elder Nzangu (a former Kamba assessor at the Idibo court who had earlier resigned) interfered more and more from the sidelines, mainly in Kamba. While all the Kamba present could speak Swahili and Chikaguru, no Kaguru present understood Kamba. The Kamba spoken in court increased as the case went worse for the Kamba. None of the Kaguru officials understood what was being said.

At the next session of court, Kamba (B), who had been in the lockup for three days, changed his story and admitted being the lone thief. The two buyers of the donkeys, Kamba (A) and the Ngulu, returned them to the rightful owner. Kamba (B) was fined only 100 shillings (a relatively small sum for major theft) and paid 60 shillings compensation (equivalent to a cow), all from his elder kin who were at the court. They also paid the two buyers. Why the Ngulu no longer wanted the two donkey foals was never made clear.

The case illustrated two key points. (1) Holding someone in the lockup could force confession and flush out kin to pay fines. This tactic was common if the accused was an ethnic outsider not vulnerable to the usual kin and neighborhood pressures exerted by Kaguru headmen. (2) The language and social gaps between the Kaguru, Kamba, and Ngulu involved kept many relevant details and motives veiled from the Kaguru running the court. There were a few Gogo as an ethnic minority in western Ukaguru. They often did not fare well in Kaguru courts,[22] as the next case illustrates.

CASE 11

A Gogo living near Chakwale accused three Kaguru Native Authority messengers of having beaten him up. According to the Gogo, he had been accused of damaging a bicycle belonging to a Kaguru, but when he appeared at Chakwale to confront his accuser, the latter was absent. The Gogo tried to leave, but the Native Authority messengers insisted that he remain until his accuser appeared. When he refused, he was beaten. Later, when his accuser still did not turn up, the Gogo was let go, but before then he was beaten again. The Gogo said he waited around until a British administrator drove through the area and he told him his troubles. He claimed that the British told him to make a case. The Gogo came to the Idibo court with one witness and a letter from a second witness, a Native Authority messenger employed at the subchief's court at Geiro. The Gogo was illiterate and did not know what was in the letter. The Idibo subchief began to berate the Gogo for bringing only one witness and said the Gogo was likely to lose because he was so ill prepared. He then said the messengers might accuse him for running away from Chakwale before matters had been settled. I interrupted the hearing and asked that the letter from Geiro be read in court.[23] The letter supported the accuser and was countersigned by the Geiro subchief himself. The court postponed the case until the witness from Geiro could be brought. I left Ukaguru before the case was settled, but the court seemed to be following its usual tactics of trying to intimidate or mislead witnesses who undermined the authority of Idibo Native Authority officials.

CASE 12

In 1962 a Gogo was accused by a headman of seducing the headman's wife. The headman's children had reported this to him. The Gogo had been taken in by the headman during the serious famine in Ugogo in 1961. The Gogo worked for the headman and had saved some wealth. All of his savings were demanded by the headman in compensation, three goats, 61 shillings, two gardens of unharvested maize, and a box of cloth. This was an extraordinarily harsh punishment for the Idibo court to allow, since it usually punished adultery by a 10 shilling fine and 60 shillings compensation. The Gogo had appealed the case to the district headquarters in Kilosa but was sent back to Idibo. The Gogo had admitted committing adultery, and local Kaguru said he deserved harsh punishment because he had betrayed the man who had helped him during his need.

The Baraguyu were the ethnic group most disliked by Kaguru. They were culturally profoundly different from Kaguru and had a long tradition of ambivalent relations with them, raiding but also trade. An incident in another case in the Idibo court underscored this hostility. During a case where a Baraguyu was being tried for an alleged offense against a Kaguru, a Baraguyu in the audience tried to introject a useful comment (something Kaguru sometimes did). The Idibo subchief shouted at him, "This is a Kaguru court, not yours!" Baraguyu and Maasai, from whom Baraguyu derived, had more livestock than Kaguru and therefore were fined far more than Kaguru for similar offenses. Kaguru argued that Baraguyu had to be fined more to be punished comparably.[24]

CASE 13

A Kaguru court messenger brought a Baraguyu to Idibo court in handcuffs. The Baraguyu had got drunk at a Kaguru house where beer was sold . He quarreled with the homeowners, slapping the wife, and in turn was beaten by her husband. The Baraguyu ran off but returned with a bow and arrow to attack the Kaguru. Other Kaguru seized him and he was taken to the local headman. The Baraguyu argued with the court but eventually admitted his offense; however, he refused to explain where he got the weapons. (Bows and arrows were Kaguru and Kamba weapons, not weapons a Baraguyu would ordinarily employ.) The Idibo court had him flogged, but he would not tell. Then the accusing Kaguru said that a Kamba had earlier offered a bribe to him if he would not make a case. The Baraguyu was accompanied by several Kamba. Previously the Kamba suspected of providing the Baraguyu with weapons was called to appear in court but instead sent his kinsmen. The Idibo court reprimanded them for coming in his stead and then locked some of them up. Once the missing Kamba appeared, they were quickly released. When the court reconvened, the accused Baraguyu was fined 100 shillings or six months in jail. He mustered 50 shillings and was told he would spend three months in jail. He asked for a delay until he could find more money. While the court waited, the accused stayed at Idibo but was no longer locked up. The accused Kamba and his father were fined for furnishing weapons to a drunken man. The outstanding fines, amounting to 150 shillings, were paid by several Baraguyu and Kamba, including the Kamba elder Nzangu, who had formerly been a member of the court.

CASE 14

A Baraguyu accused two Maasai of stealing two calves. He tracked the stolen animals to the camp of the accused and found a local court messenger to verify his case. The two Maasai confessed and each was fined 300 shillings and three cows. They were told they would be jailed for five months and some livestock confiscated if they did not agree. They did.

Where local Baraguyu could not enforce order upon other pastoralists (they lacked kin or political ties with Maasai), they could sometimes rely on a Kaguru court. This was because the court would make a considerable profit in fees and fines and not inconvenience any Kaguru. Baraguyu would not, however, succeed against Kaguru in a Kaguru court.

CASE 15

A Baraguyu appeared in Idibo court claiming a Kaguru had stolen a cow. He said he was taking his livestock to Chakwale market when one cow got lame and he left it in a nearby Kaguru hamlet. After market, the Baraguyu returned to the Kaguru hamlet, but the Kaguru disclaimed any knowledge of the cow. The Baraguyu brought two other Baraguyu as witnesses. The Idibo court said there was insufficient evidence and rejected the case. Nothing further came of the case and it was not recorded.

CASE 16

A Baraguyu accused another of beating him. He brought a Kaguru head-man as witness to the Idibo court. The Baraguyu paid a fine of 200 shil-lings and compensation of 200 shillings, about eight times what a Kaguru would pay for a comparable offense.

CASE 17

Five Baraguyu were accused of beating a Kaguru. A Kaguru headman supported this story. Each Baraguyu was fined 100 shillings and com-pensation of 200 shillings. This surpassed any punishment the Idibo court gave to Kaguru for a similar offense.

CASE 18

A Kaguru messenger from the Idibo court accused a Baraguyu of defying him. The messenger had gone to fetch the Baraguyu to court over debt to Nzangu, the Idibo subchief's Kamba crony. The Baraguyu refused to come and told the messenger that if he came back, he would stab him. The Baraguyu admitted his offense and was to pay 100 shillings fine. He was told he would go to jail for three months if he did not. He paid.

CASE 19

A Baraguyu accused a Kaguru of stealing a cow. The Baraguyu claimed his wife was tending their herd (most unusual) and a cow strayed into the field of a Kaguru. The Kaguru seized the cow, and when the Bara-guyu woman protested, he beat her. The Idibo court rejected the claims. The Baraguyu went to Kilosa headquarters to complain but was sent back to Idibo.

CASE 20

A Kaguru claimed two Maasai had stolen three of his cows. He brought two Kaguru witnesses. The Maasai denied the theft but another Maasai testified against them. They were each fined 200 shillings and were to return the stolen cows plus two more each as compensation for a total of seven cows. This would have been an extraordinary payment for a Kaguru.

CASE 21

While I and my field assistant were hiking, we stopped a Baraguyu from spearing a Kaguru bicyclist.[25] The Kaguru was bruised and bleeding. I turned the Baraguyu over to the Mgugu headman. The Baraguyu was later jailed at Mamboya. He was fined only 30 shillings plus 20 shillings compensation to the Kaguru. This was unusually light punishment, which puzzled me until I learned that the accused had also given a cow to the paramount chief before the trial. My clerk and I were later given a beer party and a chicken by the accuser. The case was not recorded in the Mamboya court where it was heard.

CASE 22

A Ngulu trader accused a Baraguyu of theft. The Ngulu claimed that the Baraguyu had stolen his tobacco at Chakwale market. When he tried to stop him, the accused and another Baraguyu beat him and ran off. The two Baraguyu were caught and the Idibo court judged each had to pay 100 shillings fine and 50 shillings compensation. They were told they would be jailed for three months if they did not pay. They paid these large amounts, far larger than any Kaguru would pay for such an offense.

Courts and Local Kaguru Politics

Kaguru courts could be arenas where chiefs and headmen supported or undermined one another:

CASE 23

This is a case I mentioned in the preceding chapter. In 1957 Headman Dani Mlama of Mgugu was fined one goat and 80 shillings by the paramount chief. The headman was accused by Evarasto, who lived in the market settlement at Mgugu. Evarasto saw Mugwa, the headman's cross-

cousin, leaving Evarasto's house. He accused him of having sexual relations with his wife. Both Mugwa and Dani were notorious womanizers.
Evarasto verbally abused Mugwa harshly. Mugwa reported this to Dani,
who went to Evarasto and told him to leave Mgugu because he had
insulted him and his clan, the owners of Mgugu. Evarasto responded
by going to his kinsman, the paramount chief. Dani, the headman, and
Daudi, the paramount chief, were bitter enemies ever since Dani had put
Daudi in the Mamboya lockup many years before when he was a poor
nobody who could not pay his head tax. In those days Dani had verbally
abused Daudi and even tried to extract a bribe. Daudi sought revenge for
this past humiliation. Kaguru said he told Dani, "I have a list of headmen whom I'd like to see quit working in my country. If you don't pay
the fine, it will be a good reason for me to dismiss you. After all, if you,
a headman, can tell someone to leave your country, can't I as chief tell a
headman to leave mine?" Dani paid.

The animus between the two officials was known by many Kaguru.
What perplexed Kaguru was why Dani had risked Daudi's wrath by such
high-handed behavior. Both Dani and Daudi had bad tempers and were
often drunk, so the rash talk might be explained by intoxication. Neither
had the right to banish anyone, but it was dangerous for someone from
Mgugu to insult Paramount Chief Daudi, because Mgugu residents had
to bring cases to his court.

CASE 24

The headman of Chakwale was an overbearing Kaguru who was often
brought to court by his subjects. He was accused in Idibo court of beating a man unjustly. The accuser told the court that the headman had
sent two men to beat him. An elderly witness said he tried to stop the
fighting and one of the messengers had hit him on the head. (He wore
a head bandage.) The Idibo subchief said he would make a judgment at
a later session, but in the meantime the Chakwale headman should kill
a sheep for the men to feast on since he had shed blood. The court appeared annoyed that the headman had taken punishment into his own
hands. No one mentioned why the first man had been beaten. I did not
hear how the case ended, but the headman was punished for usurping
the court's powers, something he had often tried to do.

CASE 25

The headman of Chakwale brought seven men to the Idibo court. The headman had built a new homestead and demanded that these men build a road from the house to the main road. They had already cleared a path, but the headman said that a proper, wide road was needed because, if the Arab buyers at the Chakwale cattle market had problems, they would need to drive to him. The court tried to support the headman, but all of the people at the court opposed him. The headman exclaimed, "Who is your headman? Who owns the land?" In return they acknowledged that he was a Muhako (the owner clan). The headman shouted, "If you refuse, you must leave my country." They answered, "No, why should we leave our own homes? It is you who had better give up being headman." The court tried to back off making any judgment. Then the headman shouted, "I shall accuse you all again next week." The accused replied, "We have feet [to walk to court to confront him]."

The Chakwale headman was a very aggressive and quarrelsome man. He often accused others of offenses and was in turn accused by his subjects. Many accused him of being a witch, for they asked how otherwise such a horrible person could continue in office despite so many complaints. There was so much public outrage against him that even the Idibo court seemed uneasy about supporting him. The case was postponed and eventually petered out. Everyone knew that a headman could not evict people from his land.

Kaguru Courts and Domestic and Village Strife

Most cases in Kaguru courts involved domestic disputes, quarrels over debts and bridewealth, or brawls. Here is a representative selection, from major cases to ones that do not seem worth the time and money spent. They represent a fair cross-section of the ordinary litigation between Kaguru, most of it rather humdrum.

CASE 26

The headman of Chakwale accused Muganasa of having purchased a beer license for one day and selling beer for two. After many angry words, the man admitted this and paid a fine. Such a simple case should not have gone to Idibo court, but it was clear that the headman and Muganasa so hated one another that only the court could end the matter. Perhaps Muganasa enjoyed the opportunity of denouncing his enemy at length before a large audience.

CASE 27

Edmalek accused Henri, the Idibo subchief's maternal nephew, of allowing his herd of cattle to spoil Edmalek's field of beans. Henri was a very unpleasant and quarrelsome man. During the court hearing, both the headman from Nguyami, where Edmalek lived, and Jenga, the former subchief of Idibo, interrupted proceedings to say what a bad neighbor and quarrelsome person Henri was. He was also often drunk, violent, and abusive. Henri lived in the Idibo subchief's neighborhood and repeatedly visited him. The subchief said that without any witnesses, Edmalek had no case. I heard the subchief support cases with far less evidence. The subchief never recused himself from any case involving his own kin.

A headman's testimony was often crucial backup for some cases.

CASE 28

Majele accused Frederik of not repaying all his bridewealth after he sent Frederik's sister back. He had paid four cows in bridewealth but claimed Frederik had returned only three. Frederik claimed he had paid back all and brought his headman as a witness. The Idibo headman confirmed Frederik's claim. The Idibo court rejected Majele's claim and told him he had lost his court fee.

CASE 29

A mother took her eldest daughter to the Idibo court for using obscene abuse (*maligo*) to her own mother. The mother brought a letter from her younger daughter which stated: "This woman accuses her daughter of abuse. You who are here to listen to the case should think whether a mother would accuse a daughter of something like this if it were not so." The mother and daughter had quarreled over firewood. The younger sister was ill and each day expected a fire near her bed to combat her chills. The elder sister complained because the younger sister did little to collect the wood she consumed. When the daughters began to fight, the mother had tried to separate them and angrily asked her elder daughter why she wanted to stay with them when she did not like them. She brought up the fact that the elder daughter was having a long-term affair with an ethnic outsider, a Zaramo tailor in a local Somali shop, and although she had two children by him she was still not married. The mother called the daughter a slut. Angrily, the daughter said that her mother was also a slut because she was regularly seeing a lover, not her husband. In doing so she used words about sexual intercourse and the genitals that were utterly forbidden between parents and children. This was actionable verbal abuse. The Idibo court officials were extremely critical of the daughter, especially regarding her referring to male and female genitals in front of her mother and now even in court. Some of the elders wanted the daughter flogged immediately. To call one's mother, even if she was a morally loose woman, by such disrespectful terms was a terrible offense. At first the court condemned the daughter to being flogged six strokes (an illegal judgment), but the daughter claimed she was sick and should not be hurt. The court then fined her 25 shillings, a relatively small amount that she could easily get from her lover. Despite the verdict, many in court also expressed deep disapproval of the mother. They said that such verbal abuse between parent and child was so shameful that truly decent people would have kept matters quiet and never allowed the public to hear about them.

CASE 30

Ndagila had been accused by his son's father-in-law of not completing paying bridewealth for his son's wife. He owed payments totaling two cows. The Idibo court told Ndagila to pay his debt with 120 shillings. Ndagila appealed to the Mamboya court, which judged he owed only 60 shillings. This was contrary to Kaguru custom, which rated cows as equivalent to 60 shillings each. Ndagila had taken advantage of the animosity between the Idibo subchief and the paramount chief at Mamboya to get the judgment mitigated.

CASE 31

Musele's mother was accused by Musele's father of not giving him his share of his daughter's bridewealth. The father had originally asked for bridewealth of 300 shillings for his daughter. He told his wife the girl's matrilineage should get 100 shillings of this. His wife refused and said the matrilineage should get 200 shillings. (Kaguru fathers expected two-thirds.) She added that these days bridewealth should be 500 shillings and that he had not asked enough, and that in terms of the bridewealth she deemed proper, her matrilineage deserved 300 shillings. The husband got angry and called off his daughter's marriage. Then his wife, who was very aggressive, gave over her daughter for only 300 shillings bridewealth but kept 230 shillings for her matrilineage, giving only 70 shillings to the son in lieu of his father. The son maintained that this was fair because his father had not helped him get bridewealth to marry. The father demanded that the Idibo court give him the 70 shillings that his son had taken. The court agreed and judged that the wife must also give back 130 shillings more to her husband. Musele and his mother agreed but remained on bad terms with the father. This is a good illustration of how a mother might try to turn her son against his father when they had a falling out, using the claims of matrilineality and need for bridewealth as ploys.

CASE 32

Mamiwa, an elderly woman, took her husband Jenga to court for verbally abusing her. She said while they both were drinking beer, he tried to have sexual intercourse with her, but she had refused. Then they quarreled and hit one another. Jenga told her that she was older that he. She said that he told her, "You are an old woman while I am younger. Your body is finished. You are skin and bones. I cannot enjoy eating your cooking [i.e., having sex] because your vagina smells bad." He then said he wanted to divorce her. She agreed and later they went to her brother to get back the bridewealth. The brother said he was willing, but that it was a matter for the Idibo court.

In court, Jenga agreed to all that Mamiwa and her brother said. He admitted that he should not have abused his wife with obscene language.

He kept repeating, "But she is my wife, after all." He said he would pay a fine and compensation to show how sorry he was, but he did not want a divorce. Mamiwa said she wanted a divorce. She said he had wanted a divorce earlier, so why should he change his mind? The court repeatedly asked the woman if she had a better reason for a divorce than the fact that her husband had asked for one when they were drunk and quarreled. She said, "He says I am old and finished, so let's be finished." The court said that was not a good enough reason. The court had the man pay her 25 shillings for his abuse and 10 shillings fine to the court. The couple left the court with him looking pleased and the wife still muttering angrily.

CASE 33

Madikunde accused her husband Mikaeli of refusing to pay her medical bills at Berega mission hospital. Madikunde disliked living at Talagwe with her husband Mikaeli. She told him there was witchcraft in the area, and she wanted to move. Mikaeli had spent all his life in Talagwe and refused. Then their daughter married a man from Mwandi and soon after burned her leg in the hearth. The burn became infected, and she was in and out of Berega mission hospital for nearly a year. Madikunde went to Mwandi to tend her daughter. Mikaeli repeatedly asked her to come home. He told her that the daughter's illness was her new husband's problem, not theirs. Even after the daughter recovered, Madikunde refused to return to Talagwe. Still the couple did not get divorced. While living at Mwandi, Madikunde developed a severe skin infection and ran up bills at the Berega hospital. Mikaeli refused to pay them. He said Madikunde was no longer his real wife because she had left him for over two years. Furthermore, Talagwe had a free government dispensary, so Madikunde would not have had to run up such bills if she had stayed home. The court rejected Madikunde's claim.

CASE 34

George accused Muhando of not paying blood-pollution wealth (*idosi*). He told the Idibo court that Muhando had got drunk and beaten him at a beer club. (It was a serious offense to beat a Kaguru until he bled.) It had been judged by the headman that Muhando should pay a goat for a feast, which both would share with their kin to settle the bad feelings. Muhando failed to do this. The court judged that Muhando would have to pay the goat, but it would no longer represent a reconciliation for all concerned; instead, it would stand as compensation to George.

CASE 35

John accused Yered of disposing of his red fez. John had pawned his cap to Yered in return for two shillings worth of beer. Yered had sold the cap to another man claiming that the pawning time had elapsed. The court summoned the man who had purchased the fez and had it returned to John, who in turn paid Yered his two shillings. This case involved the least wealth of any case I heard in Idibo court, with the value of the disputed object being less than the court fee for lodging the case. Public venting of personal ill-will was an important aim here.

CASE 38

A pregnant wife took her husband to Idibo court. The husband had sent her back to her father saying he could not get along with her, though he refused to explain why. The wife's father refused to give back the husband's bridewealth. He rightly said that this was because Kaguru custom forbade a husband divorcing his wife while she was pregnant by him. This was thought to endanger the unborn child. The court defended the father. The husband then said that if he could not get back his bridewealth, then he wanted his wife back. The court reminded him that he was the one who had sent his wife away in the first place. The wife said, "Was I pregnant only today? Who took care of me all the months of my pregnancy? Why should I go back now? You are deceiving the court. You do not want me. If I go back, you will mistreat me because I took you to court." The court did not force her to go back. It gave up on the case. It asked the husband to pay the expenses of the woman's father for journeying to court, but he refused. Since no one had broken any law, the court could not force anyone to do anything. Kaguru said the case would probably be resumed after the woman gave birth.

CASE 37

John accused Omari of sleeping with his sister's feeble-minded daughter. The sister was divorced and dependent on her brother to litigate. The feeble-minded girl had several children by various local men. Omari denied everything, but the girl said he was the father, and the Idibo court asserted that she was too simple-minded to lie. Omari continued to deny everything and was locked up. After only half an hour, his kin paid the compensation of 60 shillings to the uncle and 10 shillings fine to the court, and a shilling to the court messenger. Later Omari admitted to sleeping with the girl but insisted that the pregnancy was not his.

CASE 38

In 1958 two women, Maria and Maminyau, brought Joseph to the Idibo court. Maria and Maminyau were friends who made cash brewing beer and in prostitution. Maria lived in the Idibo subchief's village and was his kin. She and her mother regularly brewed beer and sold it in their house without buying a license, counting on the fact that they were related to the Idibo subchief. Joseph, a matrilineal cousin of Maria, came to drink. After consuming three calabashes of beer, he was drunk but refused to pay the one and a half shillings he owed. The women demanded that he pay. Maria's mother began to make sarcastic remarks about their kin ties, and Joseph struck her. Then Maria and Maminyau began fighting with him. Maminyau encouraged the two other women to go to the Idibo court. This made things difficult for the subchief, because the brawl reflected badly on affairs in his hamlet and both Joseph and Maria were his kin. The women charged that Joseph hit them. They would not explain why, because they did not want to mention brewing beer without a license. Joseph, who was drunk in court, admitted to fighting over paying for beer. The subchief repeatedly tried to get the two sides to stop quarreling, since they were indirectly humiliating him. Joseph began to weep drunkenly in court, lamenting that his kin were taking sides with Maminyau against him. The subchief criticized Maminyau as a troublemaker and told her that she should stay out of his hamlet. He avoided making any judgment in the case and said matters should have been settled by an elder or the headman without ever reaching the court. He would not allow the case to be judged and was determined that eventually the ill-will would dissipate. To the public, it looked as though the subchief could not control his own subordinate kin, and that really annoyed him.

CASE 39

A Kaguru and his daughter appeared in Idibo court. There was no case. He said that his daughter had been beaten by her husband and that she had fled to his house. He said he did not want to pay any fine for wrongly harboring his daughter, and that he was waiting for his son-in-law to come and explain the problem. The father wanted to present himself favorably to the Idibo court before his son-in-law made the inevitable case about wife desertion. The father-in-law could expect either to collect money eventually on account of his daughter being beaten for no good reason or, at the least, some favorable consideration by the court in any looming litigation. He was showing forethought and prudence and currying favor ahead of time for a case he saw looming ahead.

Kaguru Court Records

There was considerable discrepancy between what was in court records and what actually happened. To underscore this, I provide some examples of how brief court records may be. Here are some verbatim English translations of three cases heard at Mamboya court.

First, here is an average-length entry (still absurdly short when compared to Western court records).

CASE 40

MAMBOYA 15-9-56 ACCUSER: Mgutu Chadibwa
DEFENDER: Salimu Mbili
CASE: Mgutu asks why his daughter has been married without any bridewealth being paid.
MGUTU: I accuse Salimu because he took my daughter. I charged him one goat and 70/- and I told him, "If you are late in paying the rest, all this money will be considered an adultery fine." After he agreed, time passed and I still received no money. I went to take my daughter. Then this man's

son came and took my daughter back again. I do not dislike this man, but he himself had failed in paying the bridewealth.

SALIMU: Yes, my son took Mgutu's daughter. Then when Mgutu came and wanted money I gave him 70/-. Then we made agreements that I should find the bridewealth. But before I got the money, he came and took back his daughter. Then my son, the husband of this man's daughter, went and took her back again.

WITNESS, SENYAGWA: Mgutu ordered me to go and fetch the girl, but before fetching her to him, I was supposed to beat her three blows. I refused. The reason for the beating was that she wants to be married to a boy who is poor.

SETTLEMENT: The Court has decided that the defendant should prepare the bridewealth. If he does not pay this money, the money already paid will be lost. The case ended before the chief and court.

Here is a long case entry:

CASE 41

MAMBOYA 19-1-57 ACCUSER: Mohamad Hasan (Tuliani)

DEFENDER: J. Selema Kilongola (Maguha, Nyangala)

CASE: Mohamad Hasan asks why his daughter has been sent to him, her father, without any reason.

MOHAMAD: I accuse J. Selema because he has sent back his wife to me while I still have the bridewealth. When I gave him the bridewealth, he refused it. What does he want? I have come with the bridewealth and now he must take it.

SELEMA: Yes, I wrote a letter for the purpose of getting back the bridewealth. The wife said, "Let us go to my father and get back your bridewealth." That is why I wrote the letter in order to get the money. My wife said arrogantly, "You may take the bridewealth." For that reason I wrote a letter to him and the subchief said there was no justice in it, and that I could not get the money. The father of my wife refused to pay the money. Now he wants to give me money. What kind of money is it?

MARIA HASAN [SELEMA'S WIFE]: My mother said to my husband, "Why do you treat your wife like this? If you do not like her, send her away." Simply because the house [where she was staying] had no door [nothing was barring the way out] and my husband was away in Mguha, that is why I went to my mother.

MOHAMAD: This man was forced to give bridewealth. He is not good. He did not give food to his wife for two days.

SELEMA: This wife stays at her mother's and her mother says, "My daughter, go to your husband for I have no food to feed you. Now you should go back to your husband."

SAID SEFU [PRESUMABLY A WITNESS]: We saw the letter from Selema and we wondered when he wanted us to pay the bridewealth quickly. We went to him and we asked him why. He said, "Your daughter is a witch. She wants to kill her husband."

HAMIS ATHMAN [SELEMA'S FATHER]: This wife went to these people's house in order to get money. That is the reason for the letter. The reason for their quarrel is that during the night when they were sleeping the wife said, "I have no magic. I should give you some so that you may die."

JUDGMENT: The court judged that Athman has no case and his faults are: (a) he prevented his son's wife from going out and did not give her food for two days. (b) He wanted the bridewealth from the girl's father and when he was given the money, he rejected it. He himself has admitted that he was wrong. He must pay a fee of 4/-. Also the wife must go back with her husband and cannot leave him without a divorce certificate.

Without having been in court or knowing the protagonists, no one could be sure exactly what was going on here.

Finally, here is an example of a short entry:

CASE 42

MAMBOYA 22-2-57 ACCUSER: Jumbe William Mug'ong'ose

DEFENDER: Micka Mtitu

CASE: Jumbe wants one cow worth 30/-.

JUMBE: I accuse this man because he refuses to pay the bridewealth for my daughter.

MICKA: I took him 10/- and I promised to pay another 15/-.

WITNESS, MBELESELO SENG'HOME: I saw this man taking the 10/- and making agreements that he will pay 10/- more and also he will pay another 10/-, making 30/-.

JUDGMENT: The court has forced the defendant to pay what he agreed to pay. He has promised to pay it on 25-4-57.

It seems unlikely that the examining British administrators could be sure what really happened in any of these cases. They would only assume (or hope) nothing significant was left out. I provide these examples to underscore how useless court records often were in determining what was actually involved in the cases. I have already noted that many cases were not ever recorded at all.

The Kaguru Native Authority court system provided the only legal means available in the chiefdom by which people at odds with one another could sometimes be compelled to settle disputes. Of course, the old common needs and pressures of kinship and neighborhood compelled cooperation and conformity without litigation (see Tanner 1955), but these traditional bonds were steadily eroded by new economic and political forces. For the Kaguru, many of the demands of colonial life would have been ignored or even defied without the legal threat of force implicit in the courts (McCarthy 1979:10–18). It was through the local Native Authority courts that most ordinary Kaguru encountered the alien frictions of colonial life and continued to appreciate the power, veiled but real, lying behind colonial order (Hailey 1950:222).

The British fantasy about the value of Indirect Rule should be scrutinized through the realities of local rule seen in the activities at the Native Authority courts. Ironically, the British often saw the Native Authority as a mainly executive body, whereas rural Africans saw it as mainly adjudicative (M. Bates 1957:127). On the positive side, we can see that the courts provided some order and stability at little financial cost. A few British had co-opted a handful of local Africans who could and did help maintain order in a large area. Indirect Rule could here be seen as oppressive rule by a minority of chosen Kaguru over many Africans. It also facilitated oppression by many Kaguru over the ethnic minorities in their midst. Kaguru courts provided some order for both the British and Africans, but at the price of producing a lumpen-elite of chiefs, headmen, clerks, and specialists who dominated and sometimes oppressed their fellows. Once chosen and lodged in place, the officials of the Kaguru Native Authority were hard to oust. "The primary purpose of the Native Courts was to bestow authority on the native chief" (Dougherty 1966:214).

For many Kaguru, these officials represented Kaguru hegemony in a country where local ethnic identity was increasingly at risk. They represented a chosen political group, one the British found difficult later to abandon or disclaim without discrediting all their past bad decisions about colonial rule. The British had an interest in protecting and crediting the misconceived local system they had created.[26] These forms of local oppression were repeatedly limited by the ultimate vulnerability of Kaguru leaders to local sabotage from below. Kaguru courts were limited in how far they could run afoul of local popular opinion. The Native Authority's rule was fragile because it was so alien to actual tradition. The occasional upsurge of local protest, usually verbal, sometimes only withholding cooperation, rarely led anywhere. Kaguru seemed cautious about seizing upon any firm course for change. Even more striking, Indirect Rule created a subcolonialism in which the Kaguru were able to dominate or even mistreat other ethnic groups despite British colonial rhetoric about fair-mindedness and egalitarianism in their governing of Africans. While the colonial system exploited Africans, it also allowed some Africans to exploit one another. This was inevitable, not only because of the way Indirect Rule was set up but because of the way social change occurred, where some got educated or secured advantageous appointments while most did not.

Most disconcerting of all, the British themselves, despite their frequent mention of democracy and benevolent paternalism, cynically manipulated the local system and made use of illiterate and oppressive elements in the society, condoning some violence, exploitation, and corruption so long as a facade of local order was maintained. M. Bates rightly remarks on the extreme incompetence of many chiefs, even after the system was long in place (1957:250). This continued even when brave or angry local Africans called local abuses to British attention. In many cases, complainants were turned back to the oppressors, thereby harming the complainants. The British did little to correct a bad system. The Kaguru Native Authority supported colonial rule in a poor, backward, neglected area of a generally neglected semi-colony United Nations Trusteeship. Indirect Rule provided cheap and easy rule with little effort by and cost to the British themselves. The British created a flood of reports and records that masked the shabby details of how things actually happened. These reports did not show how little was being done to fulfill British obligations toward their stewardship for the international community. Without a serious gap between the realities of what occurred and what was reported and recorded on paper, the system could not have continued to present Indirect Rule as working because Africans supposedly liked it. That things did not become uglier and messier was probably due to the fact that so little wealth was at stake in Ukaguru, that there was not enough material incentive for anyone to fight violently for a bigger share. Besides, Kaguru themselves, for all the petty bickering and grudges revealed in my account, appear a relatively nonviolent and easy-going people, remarkably tolerant even of those who abused them and whom they disliked.

That the courts and other aspects of Indirect Rule were put up with for so long and with so little active opposition by local Africans may also have been because the system was so inefficient. Much could be settled through local African power relations, and so long as some taxes, fees, and information reached the British, they did not try, or even seem to want, to know the actualities of local African affairs in Ukaguru. The British did not meddle a lot with everyday life in Ukaguru, but the unreliability and inaccuracy of information flowing between grassroots Ukaguru and Kilosa district headquarters, and then further above, made things appear better than they were. The shoddiness of the Native Authority records, especially the court records, was an essential factor in explaining how Indirect Rule survived. It survived in spite of a shoestring budget, inadequate staff, and general neglect of Ukaguru. Government in Ukaguru bumbled along, at least for most. What the preceding two chapters should underscore is that the actual system was not the system that was officially reported. It was not even the system some historians and social scientists described, if they believed the written record. It was probably not even the system that many British colonial officials themselves honestly thought they had. Still, the British themselves were remarkable in swallowing so many of their own delusions and illusions. The next two chapters may help us appreciate this.

For now I note that the Kaguru court system was part of the broader landscape of colonial illusion and delusion. The validating district officer who read and signed the court reports had not even attended the cases. Many of the cases heard by local courts were not even recorded. Even a cursory reading of the court record made it clear that far more must have gone on than the terse reports related. Some of the cases did not even make much sense as they were recorded. Without knowing the facts, an outsider would have an unreal picture of how the court system actually worked. From what I knew of these aspects of the court system reports, I assumed that most other local administrators' reports from elsewhere were probably also comparably unreal. They were only approximations of reality on the ground. Given how very few British administrators there were in Kilosa district, given the large number of Africans they supposedly oversaw, given how few of these were very literate, given the huge areas under supervision, and given the problems of communication, no thoughtful person would reasonably assume that local reports could reveal very much. If something out of the ordinary took place, such as the rise of a Kaguru vigilante group (see my account of Umwano in the next chapter), some report would probably have been furnished, though hardly a full story, as we shall see. There was no way a researcher such as myself could ever have made a systematic study of the discrepancies between government reports and ordinary events, but it should be clear that there was a big discrepancy. Officers I asked told me that they reported as best they could. (This was hardly an issue I could comfortably pursue over drinks or dinner without "spooking" them.) Anyone who knew the system, who knew about its lack of staff and poor communication, would have expected no more. So long as there was general peace and order and local taxes arrived in amounts close to what were expected, reports were accepted at their face value.

FIVE

Subversions and Diversions:
1957–58

This chapter is about discontent, about Kaguru striving to change their social world. In 1957–58 Indirect Rule and the Kaguru Native Authority were presented by those in power as manifestations of a social order redolent of Kaguru tradition, an order legitimized by its supposed ties to the past and to Kaguru ethnic identity. These constructions were, at best, half-truths. At worst, the system was oppressive and frustrating, resented by many Africans who lived under it. For many decades the Kaguru colonial world continued against little opposition. Yet the foundation supporting this seeming stability was the fact that Africans knew the British would use force if necessary to impose their will, whatever Kaguru thought. In 1957–58 this ugly fact was recognized by all fifty thousand Africans living in the chiefdom, though the only times Kaguru were openly confronted with British armed might were during the monthly forays of Tanganyika territorial police who came up to maintain order at the Chakwale cattle market. Otherwise, a Kaguru had to venture to the lowland estates during a labor riot or perhaps to Dar es Salaam to see armed police or soldiers guarding important public buildings. Yet, as John Iliffe observes: "Behind the whole structure, latent and rarely visible, was the underlying violence of colonial government" (1979:326).

This is a chapter about discontent, but it is not about any violent protest directly against the British. Instead, these subversions involved violence by Africans against one another. Some Kaguru, long a peaceful people, sought to undermine the side of colonialism that most immediately annoyed them, the Native Authority. This discontent was reflected in three social movements in Ukaguru. Two exclusively involved groups of Kaguru, Umwano and USA, who were preoccupied with Kaguru issues; the third, TANU, the nationalist political party, involved a very few Kaguru and many outsiders inadvertently caught up in local Kaguru issues, which they did not clearly grasp. None of these three movements got very far during my initial stay in Ukaguru, but each promoted new views of ethnic identity and related strategies for social change. Of course, TANU eventually succeeded in throwing the British out and establishing a new, independent nation, but those events were far away from the Kaguru world of 1957–58.

Umwano

Umwano is a Chikaguru word for "war cry." It was the alarm blown by war horns when Kaguru were attacked by their traditional enemies. By 1956–57 interethnic skirmishes between Kaguru and Baraguyu/Maasai in the Idibo subchiefdom became very frequent. These involved brawls at beer clubs (see Beidelman 1961b), cattle rustling, and damaging trespass onto Kaguru fields by Baraguyu herds trampling crops. There were even some killings of Kaguru, probably by Baraguyu, though these were never witnessed and no one was ever prosecuted. Kaguru appealed to the Kilosa district headquarters to keep order. The district commissioner, a former army officer, was reported to have made the inflammatory suggestion to Kaguru to "defend yourselves like men." I could never verify whether this rumor was true. In any case, Kaguru at Idibo envisioned Umwano as a solution to this growing strife but also as a way to enhance their own influence.

The organization called Umwano originated in the northern Idibo subchiefdom where Kaguru and Kamba had herds of livestock larger than elsewhere in Ukaguru. No comparable organization was formed in any areas further south, although these areas also experienced sporadic interethnic friction. This may have been because only in the northern portion of Ukaguru did both Kaguru and Baraguyu own fairly large numbers of cattle in competition for the same grazing areas and watering points.[1] There too, Baraguyu and Kaguru livestock owners competed at sales in the same cattle market at Chakwale. There they also came into conflict when, drunk on alcohol bought with their new cash, they all frequented the same beer clubs, or quarreled over the sale of tobacco and metal goods. The Kaguru from Idibo's dominant chiefly clan, the Ganasa, were the brains behind Umwano. Much support and probably some funds for Umwano came from the previous Idibo subchief and from the current subchief who had replaced him. The new subchief was very responsive to his predecessor's advice, since it was to his predecessor that he owed his own nomination by the clan, a nomination confirmed by the Kilosa headquarters. Both these men, especially the elder, previous subchief, possessed considerable livestock. Umwano provided a new means by which the former could still exert power. The new subchief also benefited from Umwano because he could use a nonofficial new group to wield extra-legal power to support some of his goals, including extra-legal income.

To understand the complex relations between the former and present Idibo subchiefs, as well as both men's relations toward the paramount chief at Mamboya, one must know more from the past. When he was still a child, the elder subchief and his family lived at Mamboya. There his father was a crony of the previous paramount chief, the predecessor to the one in office when I did fieldwork. For reasons no one would reveal, ill feelings developed between the Ganasa clan people living at the subchief's settlement at Mamboya and the paramount chief and his entourage. It was rumored that this involved allegations of witchcraft. Among the Kaguru, suspicions of witchcraft reflect conflicts over power. In the view of the Mamboya paramount chief and his Jumbe clan, the Ganasa clan had probably become too powerful. Whatever the problem, it was serious, and the Ganasa fled to Idibo, the area they traditionally dominated and from which they originally came. Subsequently, after the boy (who would later become the elder, retired subchief) had grown up, his father sent him from Idibo to the mission at Berega, where he learned to read and write. He was obviously being groomed for leadership back in Idibo. Later, his family in Idibo summoned him to return to his fellow Ganasa, where he was taken under the care of the Ganasa clan leaders. Eventually those leaders selected him to replace the ruling subchief who was old and wanted to retire.

This is the story the former subchief of Idibo told about himself. It was a story that portrayed him as destined to be a leader. It was also a story that portrayed the leaders at Mamboya as sinister and questionable. The Idibo subchief was a forceful and educated leader who eventually clashed with the British at the district headquarters. The former Idibo subchief portrayed this conflict as being due to his own forcefulness and integrity, and he claimed to have resigned rather than to have been dismissed. Other Kaguru told me that he had been removed from office by the district commissioner because of his arrogance and alleged financial irregularities. I could find no written record in the district books of what had actually occurred, but that was not too surprising. The story that a man as ambitious as the former Idibo subchief would have resigned struck me as dubious. The possibility that such an aggressive and arrogant man was fired by a British official seemed likely. He also might have resigned rather than submit to being removed in order to save face.[2] Whatever the case, the elder, former subchief succeeded in choosing his own successor. I do not mean that he himself nominated his replacement to the district commissioner; rather, he persuaded local Ganasa clan elders to nominate the man of his choice to be presented to the district commissioner, who presumably approved with no knowledge that the man he had sacked chose his own successor.

The choice for a new Idibo subchief was a "son" of the Ganasa, not a proper clan member, but still a kinsman. That made the new subchief especially responsive to those clansmen who had chosen him.[3] The new Idibo subchief, the chief who ran the subchiefdom at Idibo when I did fieldwork, was a forceful personality, though not as forceful as his predecessor. What was especially striking for Ukaguru was that the new subchief was also literate, like his predecessor. The new subchief had been a schoolteacher who had worked for the CMS mission. I was told that he had lost his job due to fornication and theft of funds and that he had even briefly been jailed. He may have been dishonest, but he was literate, vigorous, and intelligent. This was especially striking, because the previous Kaguru paramount chief at Mamboya, the one who had clashed with the Ganasa, had himself been deposed and had been recently replaced by a senile, alcoholic, illiterate elder. The contrast between him and both the Idibo leaders was striking. Both the former and the new subchief at Idibo relied on their relative wealth, clan connections, and past and present associations with the Native Authority. They saw themselves as far fitter leaders of the Kaguru than the decrepit and ineffectual new paramount chief.

As a result of their envy and old resentments, the Idibo rulers avoided showing public deference toward the Mamboya paramount chiefs. The leaders of the Idibo area were notorious for their independence and arrogance, and this independence was reinforced by the poor communications within Ukaguru, which made contact between Mamboya and Idibo hard, especially during the rains. For the leaders of Idibo, Umwano provided a new organization, which might elude control of the paramount chief and thereby undermine his influence and augment their own. The new subchief ran the court, and shortly after he took office, he named his predecessor as a court elder. The new subchief could use the court to support Umwano, though as a Native Authority official, he could not be a formal member of it. In contrast, the older, former subchief, now being only an elder advisor on the court, could serve as a leader of Umwano while still having influence on the court as well.

Several literate men in or related to the Idibo Ganasa clan provided Umwano with financial backing. The former, elder subchief and an ex-schoolteacher drew up the necessary application papers for the organization's official permit. When this was secured through the government headquarters at Kilosa in March 1958, those in Umwano acted as though this permit conferred some kind of official, legal authority to Umwano, though, of course, it did not. I was therefore not surprised when Umwano's activities were reinforced by the Idibo court. The former subchief became Umwano's president, though a younger kinsman acted as general secretary, and another as treasurer, more public roles. Only the vice president appears to have been unrelated, and he was from the Limbo clan, joking-relations to the Ganasa. This former subchief was also one of the few elder Kaguru keenly interested in TANU, the nationalist party, but until the first general elections in 1958 he met with little support from other Idibo Kaguru (see Mlahagwa 1973). After national independence, when Nyerere promulgated the Arusha Declaration in 1967, this same opportunistic president of Umwano promoted an Umwano march from Idibo to Kilosa to celebrate this. This was long after the Kaguru Native Authority and the chiefships had been abolished, so it represented a last attempt by the elder to keep on the political bandwagon (Mlahagwa 1973:154).

Several reasons were promulgated by the Idibo Kaguru for founding Umwano. They told the district administrators in Kilosa that Umwano was "a mutual aid society" formed to protect cattle owners. They did not mention the bellicose Chikaguru meaning of the name. To Kaguru themselves the name Umwano clearly indicated that "mutual aid" consisted mainly of devising violent means to oppose and punish the Baraguyu and Maasai (and to a lesser extent the Kamba,) who were blamed for most of the cattle thefts and trespass by livestock in the Idibo area.

In the past the warlike Baraguyu, whose youth wandered about Ukaguru heavily armed with spears, swords, and clubs, intimidated many Kaguru. With Umwano, Kaguru thought they could turn the tables on the Baraguyu. In 1958 an issue of *Sauti ya Ukaguru* (Voice of Ukaguru), the mimeographed local Umwano newspaper, described Umwano as "the union that is busy taking care of livestock and stopping the bloodshed of Kaguru." Alongside this statement was a drawing of stick figures: two Kaguru armed with bows and arrows confronting attacking Baraguyu armed with spears. None of the formal Umwano speeches or writings mentioned Kamba as enemies to be attacked by Umwano, but Kaguru considered the Kamba as potential sympathizers with Baraguyu. Kamba owned almost as many livestock per capita as Baraguyu, and Kamba were known to trade often with Baraguyu and Maasai. Kamba lived in villages close by Kaguru and, unlike Baraguyu, Kamba were bilingual in their own language and Kaguru, not just in Swahili. Kamba, as a Bantu people, occupied an intermedial position of alien status between the Para-Nilotic Baraguyu and the Bantu Kaguru. They were always discerned as alien by Kaguru but appeared to many outsiders as being quite similar in appearance and comportment to Kaguru themselves. They were less easily portrayed as enemies than were Baraguyu. The Kaguru spoke of Umwano as an exclusively Kaguru organization. This did not exclude Ngulu, some of whom (the subchief of Idibo was half Ngulu, as were two of his councilors) played prominent parts in all of the Umwano meetings I attended. The matrilineal Ngulu were sometimes described as "like Kaguru." In contrast, Kaguru initially refused to admit any Kamba to Umwano, even those Kamba who had tried most to fit into the Kaguru Idibo community. One Kaguru told me, "No Kamba can be trusted, because some are secretly friends of the Baraguyu. Kamba buy stolen Kaguru livestock or secretly sell such livestock elsewhere for the thieves." This sometimes did happen. Shortly after Umwano was founded, Idibo Kaguru leaders tried to extort a fine from a local Kamba who had, they claimed, insulted a group of armed Kaguru Umwano members who had passed near a Kamba settlement. Such a charge had no legal grounds and was never in fact formally pressed. At the first general meeting of Umwano, held at Idibo, leaders reaffirmed that Umwano was strictly for Kaguru and that no Kamba could join. They were not even allowed near the open-air Umwano meetings.

The relations between the Kaguru and Kamba in Idibo were said to have been more amicable in the years just prior to my first field-work. Prior to 1957 a Kamba elder served as councilor on the Idibo sub-chief's court. Consequently, although Kamba had no official headman or chief, they had some voice in local Native Authority affairs. Later this Kamba councilor resigned from the court, demanding that he be made a subchief who could represent the Kamba separately. Clearly, in Kaguru eyes, any Kamba "given a break" by Kaguru would only ask for even more. The Idibo headmen and subchief, the same men who would later urge the establishment of Umwano, considered this new Kamba demand a serious threat to their own power. The Kaguru in the Idibo Native Authority and the British administration in Kilosa rejected the Kamba petition, presumably on the grounds that it would further divide an area that was already difficult to supervise because of its ethnic diversity and rifts.

The meetings of the newly formed Umwano reflected many cultural features reputedly derived from the Kaguru past, a past based on less Kaguru ethnic homogeneity and solidarity than was now claimed. It was said that Umwano members took an oath and drank a bark medicine (*mfulaita*) boiled with meat, which would give them courage in battle and which was often taken accompanied by an oath. These were practices that appalled some Kaguru Christians; indeed, they resembled something a Baraguyu might do. The Umwano meetings I witnessed were held in the bush, out of sight from any settlement and away from the eyes of ethnic outsiders. Only men attended. Kaguru elders came with staves and flywhisks and sat at the center of the gathering. They wore their best attire, white *kanzus* or white trousers with dark jackets or vests and white Swahili caps or red fezes. Younger men came with staves, but many others came with bows and quivers of poisoned arrows; a few brought shotguns. The younger men wore a wide range of clothing from trousers and shorts to sarongs and from tee-shirts to dress shirts and jackets. Many wore European hats. Everyone wore what would have been considered "formal attire." A few Kaguru brought traditional war trumpets made from kudu horns, the sources of the original Umwano war calls. After the first big Umwano meeting the men marched together back from the bush to the Idibo administrative and market area. To the sound of war horns they paraded about in the open space before the courthouse. Some Kaguru wistfully told me that this was "just like in the Kaguru past."

Membership in Umwano required payment of annual fees graduated according to a member's livestock holdings: a cattle owner paid 5 shillings, a Kaguru with only sheep and goats paid 2 shillings, and a Kaguru with no livestock at all paid only a shilling. This amounted annually to about 500 shillings, not including the fines from members who broke Umwano rules or the fines extorted from other ethnic groups who were brought to the Idibo subchief's court by Umwano. Any fines actually paid on the premises of the Native Authority court were supposed to go to the Native Authority treasury, but this did not usually happen. (I assert this because I could find no mention of such payments in the court records.) There was no indication in the Umwano charter as to who would manage this wealth or how it would be spent, though the ambitious elder, the former subchief, seemed to have taken charge. It was later claimed (by Umwano leaders) that over five hundred Kaguru and even some Kamba and an Arab had joined Umwano; I doubt this (see Mlahagwa 1973: 149–153).

I attended the first general meeting of Umwano celebrating and announcing the group's government permit. This was held near Idibo in April 1958.[4] About one hundred eighty able-bodied men and about thirty elders attended. The elders sat apart, the most distinguished on stools or camp chairs. The elder speakers rose one by one to address the group. The general secretary recited the rules of Umwano listed in its permit and noted that the British administration had recognized the organization— though exactly what this meant remained vague.[5] An elder instructed the young men, the warriors, on how to retrieve missing livestock and how to confront Baraguyu without prompting needless violence. The meeting concluded with a heated argument about what kind of relations should exist between the Idibo Kaguru and Kaguru from elsewhere and whether Umwano should continue to be controlled by the Idibo elders. The Idibo leaders pointed out that since they had initiated Umwano, drafted the charter, and successfully put their case for the organization before the colonial officers in Kilosa, it was theirs. They were challenged by leaders from Berega and Mamboya. Those leaders were from areas that tended to look down on Idibo Kaguru as "hillbillies." Mamboya was the long-time headquarters of the Kaguru Native Authority and the residence of the first foreign-recognized "chief." Nearby Berega was the locale with the richest, most educated and sophisticated Kaguru because of the location there of the CMS mission, hospital, bookstore, post office, and middle school. Both thought they should control the new organization. The Idibo Kaguru argued hotly that they were unwilling to have their brainchild plucked from their control.

After the meeting, the group paraded back to the Idibo Native Authority headquarters. Then many of the members of Umwano went to the nearby largest beer club in the area. The owner of the club was a patrilateral relative of the dominant Ganasa clan of Idibo and a strong supporter of and contributor to Umwano. He made a big profit after the meeting. I felt uneasy that so many armed Kaguru were getting drunk.

The Umwano permit authorized three general meetings a year, which had to be held at Idibo, not at other Native Authority centers. This made it difficult for many of the Kaguru from outlying areas such as Berega, Mamboya, and Geiro to journey there, since it would take over half a day each way by bicycle and would be even harder on foot. Besides indicating the general meetings at which major policy decisions would be decided, the permit provided for monthly local meetings at any outlying branches of Umwano at places such as Berega, Mamboya, Geiro, Iyogwe, Chakwale, and elsewhere. These branches were supposed to provide their own small, self-supporting defense groups. It soon became clear that these branch groups were too small and too poor to form effective posses for retrieving livestock. These branches had difficulty forming groups large enough to intimidate or attack cattle thieves. Nor could they easily pay for the costs in food and transport for any large group to track missing cattle long distances. For example, the main Idibo group had earlier financed a posse to track down stolen livestock far away in Monduli, in the heart of Maasailand, over two hundred miles north of Ukaguru. The large total body of Umwano could never be readily mustered at one time, and even small expeditions as far as Monduli were too costly to be undertaken often. Yet Kaguru had gained a sense of ethnic pride and confidence from striking back at Baraguyu, Maasai, and Kamba. Umwano's meetings and posturings at parades had given Kaguru men and spectators a new sense that Kaguru were strong and important.

The leaders of the dominant Ganasa clan at Idibo were clever to have thought up Umwano and shrewd to apply for a government permit. They were also lucky that the acting district commissioner was strongly inclined toward macho, bellicose behavior, something that appalled some of the later colonial officers. The Idibo leaders phrased their charter in terms of Kaguru ethnic solidarity. Yet by securing a permit endorsed by the district commissioner they locked themselves into a monopoly on local self-help power. As a result Kaguru from outlying areas were faced with the distasteful alternatives of not joining Umwano and appearing cowardly and ethnically divisive, or joining up and acknowledging Idibo's unorthodox paramountcy. The Kaguru Native Authority and Kaguru popular sentiment tended to recognize Mamboya, Berega, or even the western market center of Geiro as more important than Idibo. Yet everyone agreed that the colonial administration was not likely to issue additional charters to other self-help groups parallel to Umwano. Umwano was less lucky in the fact that the aggressive district commissioner went on leave four months after the society's permit was approved. The new district commissioner was a more moderate and thoughtful administrator, less willing to endorse any high-handed behavior, especially if it might lead to interethnic conflict.

Some Kaguru who resented Idibo's leadership told me that Umwano represented just another attempt by the Idibo Ganasa clan to dominate the outlying areas. Other Kaguru pointed out that the Idibo subchief was the best educated and consequently ablest of all the Kaguru chiefs. Umwano also epitomized the schemes and ambitions of the autocratic deposed subchief. To show their resentment against Idibo, the men from outlying areas did not always come when summoned by the Idibo leaders to join posses. According to the Umwano charter, uncooperative men were to be fined. The delinquents argued that the summonses were unjustified or that they had other pressing duties. If a local group had a delinquent member, that Kaguru was supposed to kill an animal, usually a goat or sheep, to provide a meat feast for the other local members. Even when this was done, it tended to take place only within local branches, and outsiders such as the Idibo were cut out from sharing in such feasts. The Idibo leaders of Umwano often failed to make their fines stick. They could have expelled such recalcitrant members, but that would have only made Umwano smaller. Besides, local branches would have continued to do what they wanted anyway.

Umwano, despite its rhetoric of ethnic solidarity, could not surmount the fierce local parochialism and jealousies of Kaguru. Kaguru of the various headmanships and subchiefdoms only grudgingly and partially placed themselves under the Idibo leaders. When they cooperated at all, it was because the Idibo Kaguru had control of an organization officially sanctioned by Kilosa headquarters and there seemed no other resort. Umwano's power rested mainly on the fact that at least within the Idibo subchiefdom its leaders did control local administration and courts.

Kaguru Native Authority officials had means of controlling their fellow Kaguru. It was over the Baraguyu and Kamba that Kaguru officials had far less power, and this was why Kaguru officials formed this vigilante group. Umwano's power to unite Kaguru and combat ethnic outsiders was not legally invested in its charter, which supposedly endorsed a strictly private and voluntary organization. It was the overlap between its leaders' roles as Native Authority officials and their roles as Umwano leaders, along with the questionable endorsement by the district commissioner that empowered them. Legally no Baraguyu, Maasai, or Kamba was required to submit to any Umwano rulings. Yet during Umwano's first year, its leaders led many uneducated local Africans to believe Umwano was legally able to control others and that they had government support for this. In a way this was true, since the local British administration was apparently willing to overlook many local abuses. This was not as disturbing to Baraguyu or Kamba as one might suppose. That was because Baraguyu and Kamba had long assumed that ever since the Kaguru Native Authority had been established, it was a vehicle designed for Kaguru to dominate and exploit ethnic outsiders.[6] With that in mind, Baraguyu and Kamba realized that the best way to combat Kaguru domination was to avoid Kaguru in everyday affairs and to provide as little information about themselves to Kaguru as possible. When all else failed, there was bribery. Yet both Baraguyu and Kamba remained necessarily involved with Kaguru at beer clubs and in trading goods.

In the first Umwano trial I witnessed at Idibo, I saw an illiterate Baraguyu brought before the Idibo subchief and his elders at the local court. The Baraguyu assumed he was being prosecuted for breaking some actual government law, even though he was being harassed for having flouted Umwano. His alleged offense was having spied on an Umwano meeting. He was fined 100 shillings. Since I found no entry of this case in the Idibo court records, I assumed the collected money was pocketed by the Umwano elders.[7] On another occasion, a Baraguyu was fined one cow (a stiff fine) and some cash for allegedly having driven his herd through a Kaguru field of crops. Another Baraguyu was fined a cow and about 70 shillings for allegedly having attacked a Kaguru woman (it was simply her word against his). Unlike the first case mentioned, the latter two cases actually did involve legal offenses, but the evidence presented was flimsy. Yet even in those two cases the court judgments were questionable or illegal, because the fines were excessive by local standards and because the cases were not registered in the court record. I assumed local Umwano leaders pocketed the wealth in these unregistered cases as well.

Toward the end of 1958 Umwano leaders at Idibo invited the paramount chief and headmen from other areas to visit Idibo, supposedly to learn more about Umwano. The paramount chief and some of his advisors arrived in the chief's Land Rover. Kaguru at Idibo told me they considered it a sign of their own new importance that the paramount chief came to them rather than asking them to visit him at Mamboya. They said they would not have gone to Mamboya even if they had been summoned. I wondered why they even cared about what the paramount chief thought or did, since they repeatedly denigrated his importance. Tables and chairs were brought out to a shady space in front of the Idibo courthouse. Two Maasai, alleged cattle thieves, had been in the jail attached to the courthouse and were marched out and displayed to the assembled Kaguru. These prisoners were forced to sit on the ground (demeaning for them) before the Kaguru as living proof of the power of Umwano. All this was illegal behavior. The Idibo leaders exhorted other Kaguru from outlying areas to follow Idibo's example. They implied that since they, the Idibo Ganasa clan, had a government permit, these late-joiners would be under Idibo's leadership. As a result several outlying Umwano groups were established.

Three cases heard at the Idibo court in 1958 illustrate how Kaguru Native Authority leaders used their power and local ignorance of the law to bolster Umwano.

Case 1: In August 1958 many Maasai gathered at the Chakwale area on account of the cattle market. Three Maasai were accused of stealing a Kaguru's bull, but they ran off. Umwano tracked down the father and elder brother of one of the suspects. The Idibo court put the father in the court lockup and told the son that he should track down the thieves and bring them to the court if he wanted his father set free. The son was very angry and went to Kilosa district headquarters to complain about this illegal behavior. He was sent back to Idibo. He then went several hundred miles north into Maasailand. He came back with two of the suspects, who were put in the lockup, and the innocent father was set free. One of the captured Maasai was the helpful Maasai's younger brother and the other was his cousin. One Maasai suspect accused the Idibo subchief of being a liar and insulted him in court. The subchief slapped him and had the court messenger flog him. (All this was illegal.) The Maasai was then put in the lockup with the other Maasai. The Umwano members and other Kaguru at the court cheered and wanted the Maasai to be beaten even more. The two captured Maasai rashly admitted the theft, boasting about it, and said they had eaten the animal. When they were asked for the hide, they said it was lost, but some weeks later Umwano recovered it and brought it to court. Since the third Maasai remained missing, settlement of the case was further postponed. The case dragged on for two months while the two Maasai remained in the lockup. At Umwano meetings they were repeatedly brought out in handcuffs and displayed. The innocent Maasai lingered around Idibo but was free to come and go. His father stayed briefly and then disappeared.

Umwano tracked the third Maasai thief to nearby Handeni district. The Maasai who had brought back the other thieves offered to go with the Kaguru court messengers to fetch the third thief. He was anxious to cooperate in order to get his two kinsmen released. The Maasai and the messengers went to Handeni, but on the way back the captured thief escaped. Alarmed, the helpful Maasai also vanished. The messengers returned and were harshly criticized by the court, especially when they asked for extra pay for their travel expenses. The two hostage Maasai now decided they would never be free until the case was settled, so they persuaded their kin who visited the lockup from time to time to pay all of the fines that the Idibo court sought, even those for the Maasai who was not apprehended. One Maasai agreed to pay four cows and 300 shillings. The other paid five cows. These were the highest fines I ever witnessed in a Kaguru court, beyond anything proper for such an offense. During the case the Idibo court had with impunity broken laws on detention, flogging, and degree of punishment and fines, possibly with the implicit permission of the British.

Case 2: A Kaguru was brought before the Idibo court. He had been summoned by Umwano to find a missing cow that was feared to have been eaten by lions. Several Kaguru searched the area at night and thought they heard an animal in the bush near the complainant's hamlet. The accused shot poisoned arrows at the sound but killed the missing cow. The shooter sold the dead cow's meat and hide and bought a calf to give to the dead cow's owner. The owner remained angry and took the other Kaguru to the Idibo court, maintaining he should be compensated with a full-grown cow, not a calf. The court was outraged, praising the accused Kaguru as a responsible and loyal member of Umwano who had behaved in exemplary fashion. The complaint was dismissed.

Case 3: A Baraguyu's herd of cattle were alleged to have trampled the crops of a Kaguru, who demanded compensation. The Baraguyu claimed he was innocent and that Kaguru in Umwano had threatened him with bows and arrows until he paid them 80 shillings. Two Kaguru and the headman from the area told the Idibo court that they supported the accuser's story even though they had not actually seen the Baraguyu's herd do any damage.

Much to my surprise, the Idibo court rejected the Kaguru's claims. I was puzzled until it was pointed out to me that the Umwano men and probably the headman as well had probably pocketed the money themselves without any consultation with the court. The Idibo subchief would never have tolerated fines being collected by anyone beneath him who had thereby circumvented the power of his court, not even by members of Umwano. The court supported Umwano, but never to the cost of its own powers and profit.

All these incidents involved illegal conflation of private and official roles and activities of court judges, court messengers, and others. Illegal treatment of Baraguyu continued until the end of 1958, when two such cases of ethnic abuse came to the official attention of the Kilosa district administration. (I assume the British administration already had some idea such persecutions were going on.) This denunciation of local policies was through the effort of the only highly literate Baraguyu in Ukaguru (a close friend of mine). The British administration could not easily turn a blind eye to his written complaints, since they also could have been sent to the provincial commissioner or to African nationalist politicians. The Idibo leaders of Umwano were reprimanded by the district officers, but Umwano did not lose its permit, nor were the Kaguru officials dismissed or fined. The district commissioner announced that in the future Umwano was to act "only under the authority of the Native Authority." Since some Umwano leaders were also leaders of the local Native Authority, the British statement can be seen for the hypocritical double-talk it was.

After I left Tanganyika I wrote to the district commissioner in Kilosa (unlike his predecessor, he got on well with me), who wrote me a long letter. In it he claimed: "The Umwano *wa Ukaguru* was not originally specifically intended to combat cattle thieves. It started as a kind of general mutual aid society but has crystallized into its present form. The society was registered under the Society Ordinance and is still so registered. There has been no change in its status. There was a tendency for this body to abrogate [sic] to itself powers which it does not possess. This was checked and the posses now go out in support or at the request of the Native Authority and all cases go through the courts" (Piper 1960). In my earlier letter, I had not mentioned to the district commissioner that Umwano meant war cry, hardly the name for a mutual aid society. When I returned to Ukaguru in 1962–63, I found that Umwano continued to overstep the law and that court records did not reflect what had actually occurred. When I asked the new district officer about Umwano, he said he had no record of its having any permit.

Neither the local British colonial administration nor the African nationalists would officially support the view of most Kaguru that Ukaguru was for Kaguru alone. The TANU nationalists could take this stand because they did not have to administer the area and because at that time their political support came almost entirely from ethnically mixed areas such as towns or rural estates. For TANU, tribalism ran counter to the trans-tribal nationalism they advocated. As early as 1954 TANU had declared that it would "fight against tribalism" (M. Bates 1957:337). TANU also declared its opposition to Native Authorities (ibid.:359). The British had established the Kaguru Native Authority, which implicitly excluded non-Kaguru from government but did provide local government without much effort or expense from the British.

Such an organization allowed Kaguru the means to persecute ethnic minorities, the Baraguyu and Kamba. Typically, the British took inconsistent and vaguely phrased positions, which allowed them to follow a policy of political contradiction and expediency. Even at this time the British administration was supposedly committed to a form of modernization that was potentially antithetical to "tribalism." It was becoming clear that Indirect Rule inhibited the development of modern local political institutions (Chidzero 1961:17–18; Dumbuya 1995:133; Lohrmann 2007:85). The British administration remained committed to governance on the cheap, which they thought in Ukaguru necessitated an ethnic Native Authority. In the ethnically mixed town areas of Kilosa and Kimamba and in the proletarian sisal estates in the lowlands of Kilosa district, the British administration had already abandoned Native Authorities. Unsurprisingly, these were the areas most strongly supporting TANU and African nationalism. Yet in most of Ukaguru the Native Authority remained, even where significant ethnic minorities resided. In such areas as Idibo, governance and order were not easy to maintain strictly according to the terms of the Native Authority as it had been defined. The British legal and moral compromises over Umwano reflected British perplexities as to how to make such a contradictory system work in an ethnically mixed area.

The aims of the Idibo leaders of Umwano were complicated. They wanted to control non-Kaguru living in their homeland, but they also wanted to establish some organization by which they could extend their domination over Kaguru groups outside the borders of the Idibo subchiefdom. Idibo, as the subchiefdom most distant from the paramount chief's headquarters at Mamboya, long resented the titular primacy of the paramount chief. The ambition of individual Idibo leaders had been refashioned to appeal to local Kaguru as a public-spirited defense of all

Kaguru against ethnic outsiders. However illegal such actions might be, they were considered morally justified by Kaguru. Those Kaguru with positions of authority in the local Native Authority and those not holding offices but with some cash and livestock formed an alliance to gain power. They played upon the ethnic sentiments of local Kaguru who resented the authority of the paramount chief. One trivial incident epitomized this infighting over local prestige. An Indian shopkeeper at Geiro donated money for an Ukaguru Knock-Out Cup, for which the champion Berega and Mamboya football teams were to play. Reasonably, the donor insisted that the game be held at Geiro and that he present the cup to the winners. The paramount chief objected, asking why he did not get to present the cup and why the game would not be held at Mamboya. He browbeat the Mamboya team into not going. The Berega team played the Geiro team at Geiro instead; Berega kept its local championship title.

Umwano leaders played upon a vague desire of less educated Kaguru to achieve security by regaining a supposed past ethnic glory. Their power to carry through such a movement derived from their own ingenuity and the force of their intense ambition, mainly from their ability to manipulate the Native Authority, especially the courts. Paradoxically, Umwano was a legal organization (i.e., licensed) devoted almost entirely to illegal activities. It was enabled because of the illegal use of power by legally constituted officials. This state of affairs was possible because local Kaguru administrative and judicial organizations were one and the same and were poorly supervised by the British administration.

USA

The abbreviation USA stands for the Ukaguru Students' Association. This name has parallels with TANU (Tanganyika African National Union), the African nationalist political party. Both are catchy terms that fit well into Swahili, though they are English acronyms. For Kaguru and many other Africans, such acronyms suggest a modern perspective. Kaguru also promoted other new organizations with English acronyms: UMT (Ukaguru Motor Transport), UTA (Ukaguru Teachers Association), UFU (Ukaguru Farmers Union), and UFA (Ukaguru Football Association). All these were founded by Kaguru with education, including some who spoke English and aspired to elite status. All these groups, to varying degrees, were ill-disposed toward the Kaguru Native Authority, which they saw as too conservative and closed to more progressive and educated Kaguru.[8]

One might have wrongly assumed that a student association was exclusively for school students, possibly even for persons who had not yet become adults. While most of USA's members had attended school, some were old, even gray-haired, and most were not now affiliated with any school. A few members were even illiterate. When I called this to the attention of an older leader of USA, he said, "We are all learning about the world until we die. We are all students." Yet the Kaguru Native Authority did not consider USA a mere student organization. To Kaguru officials USA was a political movement, and consequently employees of the Native Authority were discouraged from being members, just as the Native Authority had forbidden employees from joining TANU, the African nationalist party.[9] This simply confirmed USA members' assumption that their own progressive interests were inevitably opposed to the old-fashioned and backward aspects of the traditional Kaguru leaders in the Native Authority.

USA was founded in 1952 by a Kaguru attending a Church Missionary Society secondary school located at Dodoma, far to the west of Ukaguru. He was the son of a previous paramount chief who had been deposed from office by the British district commissioner. This young man had hoped to be chosen to be his deposed father's successor. Many Kaguru insisted that his deposed father had to be replaced by a sister's son, inheriting in the true matrilineal fashion of Kaguru, even though the chieftaincy was a recent cultural invention and many past paramount chiefs had been sons, not nephews. Some argued that although the chieftaincy was a relatively new post and though previous paramount chiefs' sons had sometimes inherited, the office really should follow proper Kaguru matrilineal tradition. The district commissioner agreed, because he was eager that the Native Authority conform to the basic assumptions behind tradition-grounded Indirect Rule. The frustrated heir saw himself needing some other kind of leadership to succeed in the manner he felt he deserved. The result was USA, for which he successfully proposed himself as president.

When USA was first formed, it was made up only of students and was concerned only with agitating for improved conditions at local mission schools. Soon USA broadened its aims and membership, and by 1958 it advocated all kinds of modern changes in Ukaguru. USA's members believed that educated Kaguru should cooperate to initiate modern improvements and that they were better qualified to lead Kaguru into modern life than were the tradition-bound and poorly educated Kaguru Native Authority officials.

USA advocated the "progress of Ukaguru." Its mimeographed publication *Sauti ya Ukaguru* (The voice of Ukaguru)[10] stated that "the aim is to improve the country and the time will come when Ukaguru will be improved by Kaguru. Amen." "You are enabled with USA to be able to improve your education or that of your child. Do you want to get a spokesman for your welfare? Do you want to be a member of USA, to sit on a chair?" (To sit on a chair meant to be prominent like a chief or elder.) To each question the answer given by the newspaper was for the reader to join USA.

Up until 1958 USA's efforts consisted almost entirely in exhorting Kaguru through speeches and student demonstrations, and especially in drafting and sending complaints to British government officials, something less-educated Kaguru would be reluctant to do out of fear that they did not write well or cleverly. The favorite places for USA to demonstrate were areas near schools. Consequently, Berega-Mgugu, where there were both a CMS primary and middle school, was the best of all. The USA newspaper declared, "Our aim is for members of USA to learn ways by which Ukaguru will no longer be criticized thus: 'The Kaguru are still sleepy.' When we are about such actions we [meaning USA] are Kaguru with songs, laughter, and play." The USA publication from which this quotation was taken had an accompanying drawing of dancing figures with songs in the Kaguru language placed over the figures' heads. In this passage USA leaders were alluding to their practice of entertaining their audiences with skits, songs, and anecdotes using references to traditional Kaguru culture, history, and language. USA newspapers and meetings mixed Swahili, English, and Chikaguru. USA leaders wanted to appear educated and progressive, but they also wanted Kaguru to know that their education had not made them disdainful and alienated toward Kaguru history or language. They wanted to appeal to both modernity and ethnicity. They wanted to displace the Kaguru Native Authority leaders, but they did not want to get rid of Kaguru tribalism in the way that TANU leaders did.

USA attempted to appeal to all Kaguru, but emphasized the features that would appeal especially to literate, dissatisfied young men who had found no satisfactory position in local Kaguru society. In 1958 most educated local Kaguru worked for the Native Authority or the Church Missionary Society, both organizations offering only a few jobs at fairly limited salaries. A better option for educated Kaguru was to leave their homeland and work elsewhere. Few educated Kaguru had enough savings to go into petty trade. Those who did work for the Native Authority or Church Missionary Society were expected to be restrained and uncritical of the political and economic *status quo*. They were also not expected to engage in business, though they could set up shops under the names of their wives or kin. Unhappy with this situation, USA members increasingly focused on possible opportunities in Ukaguru: petty trade, local government, and the mission.

No figures were available on USA's membership. When I attended USA's general meeting held at Berega in December 1957 there were about one hundred people present, about two-thirds men. Unlike Umwano, USA admitted women, though few spoke at the meetings, which were controlled by men. (Kaguru women traditionally found it very difficult to speak out in public, especially in front of men.) Earlier I attended USA meetings in the outlying northern areas of Idibo and Chibedya. At each of these, about fifty people were present, mostly young men under twenty years old. It was not possible to determine how many of these were actually enrolled in USA.

On the evening of its December 1957 general meetings, USA held a program in which songs and skits were performed by young people from the nearby mission middle school. These performances were mostly in Chikaguru, the Kaguru language, though mixed with some Swahili. Some were on comic subjects, but a few described the suffering of Kaguru whom the government had forcibly evicted from their lands or who were forced to work in the mountains, both results of a controversial government reforestation project.[11] The evictees had been paid a total of 1,000 pounds to leave within a year but remained unhappy. One of the songs criticized the forestry officer in charge of this project and described his alleged ferocity. In November 1958 the head of USA wrote a letter to the Kilosa district commissioner. It was garbled and not as bravely hostile as the author later claimed when describing it in his speeches to Kaguru. Most significantly, although it mentioned abuses, it never criticized the chiefs or the Native Authority. USA continued to hold sporadic meetings all over Ukaguru, with varying success. In June 1958 I came upon one at Chibedya, a remote area northeast of Geiro. About fifty people were there, including Baraguyu who seemed at a loss as to what it all meant. I was surprised to see a friend, a former clerk at the mission bookstore who had lost his job, now campaigning. (He later turned up working for "the enemy," the supposedly evil government forestry scheme.)

Admission to membership in USA cost 2 shillings. Annual dues were 5 shillings for non-students and half of that for students.[12] This meant that about 600–700 hundred shillings had probably been collected in membership fees. USA was trying to appeal to a more affluent Kaguru crowd than was Umwano. Most of USA's assets were not, it was said, from membership fees but from donations made by senior members rumored to be interested in the possibilities of some of the financial schemes USA advocated.

USA's meetings were held irregularly, since its leaders were employed outside the chiefdom and consequently could be in Ukaguru only a short time each year during leaves and vacations. Day-to-day management of USA was therefore divided, and many activities were actually carried out by those literate Kaguru who had free time because they were unemployed (often fired on account of unacceptable behavior or even dishonesty), so that divided, discontinuous, and unreliable leadership hindered USA's development. Meetings were advertised and information spread by mimeographed handouts, either circulated by hand or nailed to trees or walls. One handout urged: "After reading this, give this to your comrades to read so that this may be made known." This was more effective than outsiders might think. In 1957–58 any printed material was so rare and valued that it was kept or circulated. Magazines, newspapers, or spoiled paper I threw away were pounced upon. Here is an example of an USA notice on a tree announcing a meeting in Iyogwe northeast of Idibo in 1958: "Brothers in USA and Ukaguru, you are invited to a meeting which will be held at Iyogwe on the 8th of November. Come and hear so that you may get blessings from God. USA and your arrival [at the meetings] will be a way of making Ukaguru prosper. Amen. Justin Mwegoha, General Secretary."

USA exhibited an odd amalgam of Christianity, tribalism, and modernity. The Christian side of USA was not surprising, since all its members had passed through mission schools. The few lower-level local government–sponsored secular schools had been in operation only a few years and had yet to produce senior graduates. This was mainly because the mission had obstructed their establishment, even though this would have added to the opportunities for Kaguru to find education. For these reasons, Kaguru associated Christianity with literacy, European power, and efficiency—in short, with "progress." Only a few Kaguru were actually convinced that I had abandoned my Christian upbringing and was an atheist. They firmly associated conservative Christianity with all proper education. Kaguru would have been even more surprised how few of the local British administrators were churchgoers or even steadfast believers.

USA's publications made frequent references to Christian sentiments, and its newspaper and programs were formulated in a rather biblical style. Many USA messages ended with "amen" (*amina*). Here are some examples of USA's Christian statements, all taken from its newspaper: (a) "God is bringing blessings"; (b) "USA has no discrimination. Men and women take the USA card as a shield for God is watching over us"; (c) "God being the torch, the daily lamp"; (d) "Agree with the good for then God is [your] gift"; (e) "Let us glorify God"; (f) "Follow Almighty God's wishes for what is to be done in Ukaguru and in the whole world"; (g) "Union, love, peace and forgiveness"; (h) "Before going to the Sunday service, the new leaders of USA and the old will shake hands"; (i) "Almighty God who is in Heaven may enable us to do this [viz., solve the problems of the country] until the day comes. Amen"; (j) "Almighty God bless this groping toward progress. Almighty God be with you in your work of harvesting. Almighty God be glorified for now the Kaguru man is using the knowledge which He has given him . . . in any union"; (k) "Father Almighty God gave us Kaguru gifts in order to use them in a proper way. If we do not use these gifts, we shall be like [a foolish] baby . . . If we use them, God will drop us some more gifts from above"; (l) "Come and hear so that you may get blessings from God"; (m) "All Kaguru are of Almighty God who is above."[13]

The African Church Missionary Society archdeacon attended and blessed the general meeting of USA and secured the use of the mission school and its grounds as a place to meet at Berega. USA's subsequent general meetings were always held at Berega, the center of Christian mission work in Ukaguru. One sophisticated irreligious Kaguru referred to Berega as "the Vatican of Ukaguru," an ironic quip, since he knew how violently anti–Roman Catholic the Protestant mission was. (The use of the very central space of the mission for USA meetings contrasted with Umwano meetings, which were held in the bush and never at the courthouse or market area of Idibo; these were reserved for parading. USA never assembled secretly. It wanted to be seen in progressive surroundings.) This use of mission station space did not imply that the white missionaries approved of such meetings. In fact, missionaries were often not informed of such African affairs. The African mission staff strongly supported USA, but they had not shared their views with their white superiors. The African archdeacon and his two ambitious sons were eager to enter the business ventures USA promised, business ventures that would not have met with missionary approval. White ignorance and naivety were clear to all the Africans present when a missionary inadvertently walked into a USA meeting and briefly spoke approvingly. This seemed striking to me, because just before she spoke, the USA leaders had addressed the assembly to criticize the Native Authority and the Kilosa colonial administration harshly concerning forced labor and other matters, all in Chikaguru, something local missionaries did not know well if at all. Anticolonialism was anathema to the white missionaries.

USA made use of ethnic as well as Christian motifs. Its newspaper described various plans "to give freedom to all people who are of Ukaguru (Kaguru)." USA seemed to have felt it necessary to add the word "Kaguru" in parentheses just to make sure that no one assumed that they included Kamba or Baraguyu. At all USA meetings there seemed to be special efforts by the leaders to use some Chikaguru terms in place of Swahili just to emphasize that it was to Kaguru alone that the group referred.[14]

Even in 1958 pure Kaguru speech was unusual, and most Kaguru spoke mixing Chikaguru and Swahili. Since Swahili and English were the only languages taught (or even allowed to be spoken) in either mission or government schools, it might seem that educated Kaguru would be proud not to speak Chikaguru if they wanted to appear modern. Instead, USA leaders stressed their pride in local customs and language. A return to more use of Chikaguru was one of the goals of USA. One of the quandaries faced by educated Kaguru was the fact that they embraced education and keenly advocated more teaching of English, but at the same time they repeatedly spoke regretfully about the fact that their education in Swahili and English was leading them to forget their native tongue. The USA newspaper asked, "Do you want to get a newspaper in your own pure language?" It assured readers that USA would help people secure this blessing. USA's newspaper, *Sauti ya Ukaguru*, appeared irregularly, mimeographed off a mission-owned reproducer. During the eighteen months of 1957–58 when I was in Ukaguru, only three issues appeared. Inevitably, despite USA's frequent mention of promoting Chikaguru, the newspaper continued to appear mainly in Swahili, with Chikaguru phrases and words only salted in. This was because those literate Kaguru most likely to buy and read the newspaper were themselves more fluent in Swahili than Chikaguru, thanks to current government teaching policies, both secular and religious.

Sometimes USA leaders tried to strike a tone that blurred divisions between Christian and pagan, between the modern and the traditional. Members referred to their fellows as *ndugu katika USA* (kin in USA), an expression appropriate to both a Christian church or a pagan ceremonial gathering. A long USA song, which was generally Christian and god-fearing in sentiment, rather like a hymn, mentioned that "Our elders may accuse us if there is any bad feeling. Our USA is yours. Tomorrow it is [our] grandchildren's. USA is preparing for those who shall come. Those above will boast [of this] to us. This is our blessing." Kaguru said that "those above" referred to the ancestral dead. Traditionally the dead were thought to dwell on top of mountains and were thought to be aware of the good and bad deeds of their living kin and to reward and punish them. Kaguru Christians still believed that the dead influence the living but did not find their intense concern about the ancestral dead to be in any conflict with Christianity. Kaguru Christians avoided such comments when they were around white missionaries.

USA advocated modern improvements in Ukaguru, especially ones that would be dramatically striking and readily visible such as better roads, more and larger school buildings, and more lorries (trucks) to take Kaguru and their crops to market so Kaguru would not be at the mercy of the Asian and Somali traders. USA's leaders tried to conduct meetings in ways that would impress ordinary Kaguru that they were on top of the latest modern advances and were politically sophisticated. At meetings USA leaders made a point of exhibiting a typewriter even though no actual use was made of it at the meetings. They showed and discussed formal, typed letters that they planned to send to government officials or try to have published in newspapers. They always wore especially clean and natty European clothing. I never saw any Kaguru at USA meetings dressed in conservative *kanzus* and Swahili caps in the manner of those Kaguru at Umwano meetings. The president of USA at one point sported the only Afro hairdo I ever saw in Tanganyika, presumably because he had seen one in an American magazine where it was associated with black political radicals. Some Kaguru found this odd, because such long, seemingly unkempt hair was traditionally a sign of mourning, spirit-possession, or some other form of mental disturbance.

USA leaders hoped that their organization might be favorably compared with more famous East African modern groups. For example, the nationalist political party TANU had its newspaper, *Sauti ya TANU*, and USA had *Sauti ya Ukaguru*. USA had its first general election just a few months prior to the first general election for all of Tanganyika at a time when newspapers and radios were filled with discussion about the procedures and importance of voting and how the election would have an immense impact on the future and national consciousness. USA supported a Kaguru football tournament and wanted the USA team to play in UFA (Ukaguru Football Association), a team mainly from the Berega mission; this was at about the same time as the East African football tournaments were publicized and broadcast. USA said it would present the USA Cup to the winner. I never learned whether such a game took place, but I doubt it. USA promoted the USA Cup in imitation of the Gossage Cup, which was awarded to the winning football team in the East African British colonies. USA's headquarters, a metal-roofed market building owned by the local Church Missionary Society archdeacon, was furnished with a colored drawing showing a luxurious multistory building that members said would one day be the Ukaguru Community Center "after USA succeeded."[15] This drawing appeared to be a crude approximation of the famous Chagga center built at Moshi in northern Tanganyika, a symbol of wealth, education, power, and success for all of Tanganyika. The greatest symbol of all of USA's crusade for progress was a truck it helped purchase through another branch group, UMT (Ukaguru Motor Transport). This group was sponsored by USA and was composed of USA members, the most prominent being the two sons of the mission's African archdeacon. One of their handouts stated: "We members of UMT have as our goal to remove the difficulty of spending a long time by the roads waiting to go on a journey. UMT is ready for you and your crops, for members of UFU (Ukaguru Farmers Union) and all Kaguru to sell anything they like."

UMT failed less than a year after it was begun. Its truck broke down and there was no money to repair it and replace broken parts. Over 1,000 shillings were needed to repair it, and the truck languished at a garage in Morogoro many miles away. The staff of UMT quarreled and accused one another of inefficiency and stealing funds, apparently with some justification. Truck turn-boys, the driver, the clerk, and the two sons of the archdeacon were all said to have fought bitterly, sometimes in actual brawls. The Kaguru farmers who had turned over some of their harvests to the UMT truckers were never paid. Within a year of USA's first general meeting in December 1957 and less than six months after its various offspring unions and associations were named, all these new groups had either failed or were failing. This was not surprising, because those Kaguru involved, despite their education, had little or no practical experience in business or even in handling large sums of money, and because there had been no clear rules or contracts drawn up by which cooperation could be regulated, responsibilities allocated, or people held accountable. In 1958 it was alleged that over 1,000 shillings were missing from UMT alone.

The chief losers in all these failed ventures were said to be the mission schoolteachers, who had put some of their life savings in these groups. As government/mission employees, these teachers were officially forbidden from joining any business ventures and consequently feared to publicize their losses or make legal cases against those they suspected of having swindled them.[16] A few educated Kaguru might grudgingly admit that they lacked the technical competence or resources to compete effectively against Asian truckers and traders, but not one educated Kaguru would ever concede that they were less able than the present officials of the Kaguru Native Authority, most of whom were illiterate or with only primary school education, and who had in the past been given Native Authority funds that they had quickly squandered, without apparently being held accountable.

USA persisted in sending out letters to British officials, posting notices, and circulating newsletters, but its promises were eventually seen as unreliable. Many in USA may have meant well, but too many Kaguru were ill-trained and too poor to run any such movement. Furthermore, some of those involved had local reputations as scallywags even before USA was established. One incident illustrated how USA could make a generous gesture that could end with everyone annoyed. A student at the mission middle school quit for lack of tuition money. The headmaster, an USA supporter, received a letter from USA demanding that the student be taken back, promising to provide the school fees. These were never sent, and the frustrated student, his kin, and the schoolmaster were then even angrier than if nothing had been promised in the first place. They themselves now also looked undependable and stupid because they had believed that the support would come.

Young educated Kaguru advocated the introduction of modern qualifications for Native Authority officials. They contended that leaders of Ukaguru needed to be educated men if they were to serve the Kaguru people properly. Yet any policy of appointing Kaguru officials according to their educational attainments would cancel out the present terms of appointing officials because of their local clan affiliations and the support of tradition-bound elders of certain owner clans. Such appointments were unlikely to be made by the many Kaguru because most remained uneducated and still in favor of supposed Kaguru traditions. Apparently USA leaders would have liked political reforms to be imposed by the British district administration, though they seemed embarrassed about making any direct demand that this be done. This would have implied they were dependent upon the decisions of Europeans (as most Kaguru were at this point in their colonial history). USA leaders continued to declare that most Kaguru wanted to see more educated, younger leaders chosen, though the success of Umwano and the failure of all the schemes thought up by USA strongly suggested that USA might actually not well reflect ordinary Kaguru thinking.

In 1957–58 the angry young men of USA had much ammunition for attacking the Kaguru Native Authority. In these years the local Native Authority had taken part in measures that Kaguru deeply resented. Land in a remote mountain area northwest of Mamboya was expropriated for a government softwood reforestation scheme. The few Kaguru settled there were forced to leave, paid for their land, and resettled elsewhere. Some remained bitter, for this was ancestral land that Kaguru were loath to abandon, land where their dead ancestors were buried. Even with the contested land secured for the reforestation project, the scheme was stalled, because a road was needed to serve the forestry camp. Few Kaguru were willing to sign up for the road work even though they would be paid the going rate. Most Kaguru disliked work outside their local areas and were unwilling to leave home unless faced with famine or other dangers. The project was in the heart of the Itumba Mountains, some five thousand feet up. It was cold and damp, and the road work involved blasting, which deeply frightened Kaguru. The forestry officer was ordered to complete the project on a deadline. The district commissioner at Kilosa was put under pressure by the provincial commissioner to support this project.[17] These expectations were passed down to the Kaguru Native Authority and finally to local Kaguru headmen (see Native Authority as a cat's-paw (Ingle 1972:46–47; Pratt 1982:216–218; Mamdani 1996:52; McCarthy 1979:10).

While the Kaguru who had lost land appeared bitter but resigned to their removal, the forced recruitment of labor for the project rekindled everyone's resentment. Now many Kaguru said they never would have accepted the move if they had known it would lead to these other injustices (actually they had no choice). To solve the labor shortage Kaguru headmen were required to recruit local Kaguru men for a month's labor, by force if necessary. This recruitment was not supervised by the British and was extremely arbitrary. Some Kaguru were made to serve several times, while other did not go at all. Local headmen took bribes from some who did not want to go. Headmen threatened others with being sent if they did not help them with chores or errands. Headman profited and used recruitment policies to implement old grudges and reward old favors. They collected and pocketed fines from the relatives of men who had tried to avoid recruitment by running away but who were later caught by Native Authority messengers. Men who resisted were beaten, and sometimes also Kaguru bystanders, men and women alike, who complained or helped the resisters.

Kaguru resentment grew widespread, focusing not only on the British but also on the Native Authority. Kaguru saw the entire project as a scheme by which outsiders were exploiting them. No one thought that the project would ever provide any benefits to Kaguru themselves, despite the platitudinous comments by colonial officials that the scheme was being promoted to help the area economically and ecologically. It was just one more example of the alien colonial administration stupidly and arrogantly meddling in local life. Still, some Kaguru in the Native Authority, especially those near the project, probably thought they had no choice but to seize laborers, not to mention the fact that they could use the scheme for their own corrupt advantages. Yet it was clear to most Kaguru that local Native Authority officials, from headmen to messengers, and certainly the paramount chief himself, profited from recruiting such labor and had used their powers to get even with those who had opposed them over other issues.

Recruitment of unwilling Kaguru was impossible without intimidation and brutality. Some local British administrators remarked that "natives" were accustomed to rough tactics from one another, since it had been a tough world in Ukaguru even before European rule. I was unable to elicit any remorse or guilt from any of the British when I described the situation. It was true that, in the past, traditional Kaguru leaders had exerted force, but this was only possible within the bounds of some communal acceptance. What the Native Authority officials did crossed all popular opinion. In a Pollyanna way I pointed out to some Kaguru that by the time the trees in the reforestation project were fully grown, they would be a valuable asset for Kaguru in what would surely no longer be a colonial Tanganyika. Kaguru replied that this helped no one locally now, and besides they doubted that the forest would ever be directly used to help Kaguru, because any scheme thought up by outsiders, black or white, had never been cooked up to help Kaguru. They were proved right. Furnivall termed such totalitarian "benevolence" "compulsory welfare" (1956:430).

Kaguru in the Mamboya and Geiro chiefdoms were especially hostile toward the forestry project because they were the nearest to it, and so their chiefs and headmen were under the most pressure to provide workers. The Native Authority officials in more distant Idibo refused to cooperate in labor recruitment, and since the Geiro and Mamboya chiefdoms had provided sufficient workers, Idibo officials were not pushed to capitulate in their stand. This recalcitrant side of the Idibo subchiefship accounts for the support that Idibo leaders had from other Kaguru and their own air of presenting themselves in the guise of Umwano as the true defenders of Kaguru traditional rights.

The president of USA wrote letters to the British administration complaining about the expropriation of Kaguru land, forced labor, and the beatings of those who resisted, criticizing the Kaguru headmen and paramount chief. USA had copies of these letters circulated and posted throughout Ukaguru. USA held meetings at various market centers and threatened to bring the abuse to the attention of TANU (which would later, after independence, themselves be guilty of far worse local cruelties against ordinary Kaguru). A TANU representative visited the area of recruitment in 1957. By chance I was visiting with the TANU representative and took him for drinks at the local Kaguru beer club at Mgugu. There we encountered several Kaguru Native Authority messengers with whips, leading a group of Kaguru men who were roped together. Some had been beaten and were bruised and bleeding. We saw women related to the men trying to interfere and saw them struck by the Native Authority messengers. The messengers had a large collection of chickens, sheep, and goats that had been seized from the captured men's villages. The messengers described these as fines collected as punishment for these men trying to run off or resisting seizure. We got the court messengers to stop the beatings, but we could not get them to release their prisoners.

This incident later triggered local TANU attacks on the reforestation scheme, both at meetings and in letters to the British administration and the African press. Oddly, TANU only criticized the British for this, never the corrupt and brutal Native Authority. This led me to write a letter of complaint to the district commissioner. I threatened to write to the United Nations Mandate Commission about this obvious violation of the Mandate rules. As a result, my ties with the district government were severed (no cooperation and some frostiness when I visited Kilosa) until the district commissioner went on leave. The harassment of Kaguru, at least in the area where I lived, did end, but probably not elsewhere. I doubt my letter had really done much good, except that I had greatly

improved my popularity among radical young Kaguru. I certainly would
have looked bad if I had done nothing. Besides, I enjoyed writing a negative note to the macho, gruff district commissioner.

During this hectic period, USA was declared a political organization and its membership forbidden to all Native Authority employees
or anyone else receiving money from government subsidies (the mission). This made membership illegal for many Kaguru members who had
joined earlier. This was a hard blow to USA, since its most enthusiastic
members were the clerks, dispensary-dressers, veterinary aids, teachers,
and other educated elite of the area. This ban actually had far less effect
on USA membership than the Native Authority had probably hoped,
because many educated Kaguru could afford and did continue to pay
dues secretly to USA. What hurt USA more was that its new political
status required them to secure written police permission before every
meeting. Even when USA secured written permission from the district
administration, local Kaguru leaders sometimes claimed that they had
not been notified and encouraged their messengers and local thugs to
break up meetings anyway, probably under orders from the same British
officials who had signed the permits for the rallies. This fit in with British
policy to encourage Native Authority chiefs to intimidate any progressive (radical?) African activists in the area, a policy that destroyed all
hope that the Native Authority could ever survive after national independence. The necessity of police permission made it hard to schedule
meetings less than several weeks in advance, something difficult indeed
to manage in the African bush, even without getting permits. Ironically,
neither the Native Authority nor the British administration labeled Umwano a political organization, presumably because it did not question
the formal political, pseudo-traditionalist status quo. Yet members of
Umwano employed force and abused the very essence of the local court
system. As a result of being declared a political group, USA sometimes
held illicit meetings, a practice Africans copied from TANU, which had
long faced similar government obstruction. Harassment led USA leaders
to feel defensive. In their newspaper they wrote:

> MEMBERS OF USA ARE NOT ANGELS. USA members are only human be-
> ings like others. Members of USA make mistakes just as other people do;
> so I am asking you members and all Kaguru, "DO NOT MIX MATTERS."

USA is USA. USA decides things in meetings and then these matters are announced. Or if we are demanding things, then we send these things to the Government Officers if it is for the Progress of the Country of Kaguruland. So if some other members are doing things even though they are outside USA and if these members are not passing into the meetings of USA, you must understand that USA will not take the blame or even good recommendations for these things but these concern the doer himself. It is not anything to do with. USA. NOTHING AT ALL.

To me, such a letter seemed pretty weak-kneed. Despite their airs of radicalism, USA had yet to get much independent backbone. They had too long an association with the colonialist establishment, both the government and mission, albeit this had been of a servile nature one would have hoped would have conjured up more aggressive anger. USA's troubled relations with the district administration and the Kaguru Native Authority appeared to have improved somewhat after forced labor in the reforestation project was lessened. USA was aided in purchasing a truck for UMT, and its leaders praised the government for its assistance in this loan. However, when I had left Ukaguru in 1958, USA remained on hostile terms with Kaguru officials, who still regarded it as a group whose ultimate aim was to displace them as leaders of the chiefdom. They were right to feel distrustful.

USA may be described as a tribalistic counterpart to TANU, because the aims of both were unity and cooperation to achieve modern development. USA was an organization Liebenow would have called "tribal nationalists" (1971:233; see Ranger 1983:254; Maguire 1969:1–2). While USA was not militantly hostile to other ethnic groups in the manner of Umwano, it confined itself to Kaguru and excluded other Africans living in Ukaguru. USA's aim was for greater political representation by young and literate Kaguru in local affairs. Like TANU, USA faced its main opposition from the British administration and from the local Kaguru Native Authority, but its ultimate loyalties were too narrow to be considered really modern by my most radical local African friends. Despite its criticism of the Native Authority, USA's ethnic parochialism was ultimately a product of the cultural atmosphere produced by the very Indirect Rule that it criticized; USA could not rise above that same tribalism. As Dundas, a famous former secretary of native affairs under Cameron, wrote, "An ancient order had been sedulously resuscitated and it matched ill with the principles of the new order. For the essence of Indirect Rule was tribalism, and as such it was everything else but preparation for democracy, the very basis of which is national unity"(Dundas 1955:135). For many Kaguru, modernism was still linked to tribalism (see J. C. Mitchell 1960:15–20), even though it thwarted most forms of cooperation on a national level (ibid.:24; see Ranger 1982:136–137, 1983:254). Tribalism and traditionalism had attractions, especially as defenses against predator outsiders, but they were ultimately poor defenses against the future.

In later years, those who had been enthusiastic for USA and even for Umwano reconsidered TANU as their only hope for advancement. Unfortunately for them, this would mean that they would have to relinquish their commitment to Kaguru identity through ethnicity and culture, and perhaps even to some extent to their well-founded commitment to local control. In 1960, after I had left Tanganyika, TANU met opposition in Kilosa district when it promoted an ethnic outsider as a candidate for local election to the national assembly. Kilosa Africans, including many Kaguru, preferred a local Kaguru and formed a dissident group that questioned TANU policy. Their preferred candidate was a former officer of USA. He and his supporters, who were also local TANU members, were expelled from the party. Despite that, they continued to insist that their aims and those of TANU were the same.[18] TANU was never popular in Ukaguru, not even after independence. Later this former leader of USA was savagely persecuted by the African national government.

That a tribalistic but modern-oriented group such as USA flourished in 1957–58 in Ukaguru was mainly because Ukaguru was geographically and culturally still isolated from the nationalist movement and from the social and economic changes that had fostered it. Even the best educated and most ambitious Kaguru could see that their goals would not be met through any available nationalist group but only through local ones. They were later proved partly right. The particular and temporary difficulties of Ukaguru in 1957–58, forced labor, the reforestation scheme, the corruption and ineptness of local Kaguru officials, seemed to have little importance outside the narrow confines of Ukaguru itself. These were not even general knowledge or concerns in other parts of Kilosa district, much less elsewhere, even though they later could be seen as boding many ills on the horizon.

TANU

In 1957–59 the African nationalists party TANU (Tanganyika African National Union) embarked on a campaign to recruit members up-country. At that time TANU was expanding rapidly in power and reputation. Its candidates had done remarkably well in the first national election in 1958, and it felt a need to expand its influence beyond the towns and African unionized workers in the large agricultural estates. TANU opened a modest office at Berega in a building owned by the CMS African archdeacon. Later TANU opened a branch farther west, at Geiro, along the main east-west road. Yet the heart of Ukaguru where most people lived remained off the main road and relatively untouched by nationalist politics. Political recruiting in Kilosa district was far more successful in Kilosa town and among the unionizing workers on the huge sisal estates in the lowlands south and east of the chiefdom.

In September 1958 a TANU organizer, a young Luguru from Morogoro, a standard VIII graduate, visited Mamboya and Berega in the very heart of the chiefdom, areas several miles off the main road. He wore a green sash labeled TANU, gave out leaflets and tried to recruit members. The paramount chief at Mamboya had harassed the young organizer into leaving his area, sending his court messengers to make him stop speaking at a market. The chief pointed out that the young militant had no official permit for a political meeting, and he was not about to issue one. The impromptu speeches made by the organizer hardly qualified as a political rally. I met the organizer later at Berega; he was unsuccessfully trying to drum up interest at the local market and mission station where a few interested schoolboys, teachers and educated shopkeepers had gathered. The recruiter had again been discouraged from speaking by a headman. I took him to my house and gave him dinner and drinks and put him up for the night. We talked for many hours. The recruiter was glum and discouraged, though he said he had got fifty Kaguru to sign up. He had hiked on foot over much of central and northern Ukaguru, from Mamboya and Berega to Idibo, Chakwale, Talagwe, and Iyogwe. He spoke no Chikaguru. Educated Kaguru were sympathetic to TANU, but Tanganyika government policy had forbidden its employees from joining TANU.[19] Likewise the Church Missionary Society frowned on political involvement by its employees. This left only a few petty traders at the market and my field assistant as likely enrollees, and he was already a TANU member. The TANU recruiter hitched a ride back to the provincial capital at Morogoro the next day.

In the 1950s, Ukaguru presented unfriendly and conservative grounds for nationalist recruitment. Ordinary Kaguru were too parochial and uneducated to join TANU. Most were too poor to consider paying even a few shillings to join any political party. I recall a TANU rally at Idibo in June 1958 that was a total flop. This poor showing reflected the fact that few Kaguru had the sophistication to enthuse about national politics. Besides, like those in USA, TANU recruiters lacked the experience to make clever criticism that would touch on local issues. Most were very young, which did not impress Kaguru. TANU speakers in Ukaguru avoided direct criticism of the Native Authority, even though the British used the Kaguru chiefs to suppress and harass TANU activities. Elsewhere TANU leaders had repeatedly expressed hostility toward all chiefs and tribal authorities. The TANU organizer at Idibo, a friend, wrote me in 1959 after I had left Tanganyika:

> We know that in all countries under British rule, the main stooges are chiefs. TANU knew it, and we tried to avoid it. How did we avoid? We knew who [sic] we are after—we were after British Government. The chiefs were rude to us but we kept our pace after British. The DCs even refused to give us permit to convene meetings, without the consent of the chiefs but we tried our best to make them understand, but we did not criticize them in public meetings or in newspapers. Even now we leave the chiefs as they are.

Interestingly, the same TANU organizer had been somewhat effective in mediating conflicts between Kaguru and Kamba, entering the same arena of interethnic conflict that had attracted chiefs, headmen, Umwano, and USA as an avenue of influence.

The Kaguru most attracted to TANU and most likely to become valued members were the few who were educated and salaried and employed by the government or mission, and consequently the very targets for enrolling who were most inhibited about risking membership. While any African with six years of education could expect some salaried job, most aspired to posts far beyond their actual educational qualifications. An overproduction of semi-educated youth had created many discontented young men (Morrison 1976:61, 69). The colonial government wanted semi-educated Africans in low-paying Native Authorities, not highly educated ones in regular government where the actual power was (Pratt 1982:251). This political conservatism was to change radically by the time I returned to Ukaguru, the day after national independence in December 1961. By then many male Kaguru claimed they had supported TANU and national independence all along, no matter how awfully or indifferently they may have actually behaved.

In 1958 TANU represented the most radical alternative to the present political system. It was against chiefs (Liebenow 1956a:138–139). It seemed an alternative meaningful mainly to town people, to semiliterate younger men frustrated with their limited opportunities, and to those in the new labor unions. Ordinary Kaguru cultivators saw little in this for themselves, and Kaguru elders engaged in the local Native Authority rightly foresaw TANU as ultimately hostile to their own narrow ethnic loyalties and privileges. Until independence most Kaguru resisted or ignored efforts by TANU to subvert the local order, even though many were unhappy with that order.

Umwano and USA served as training grounds for Kaguru trying to learn ways to organize broader groups for community action. They represented real local attempts for government at the grassroots. Yet their intense commitment to Kaguru ethnicity ran counter to the growing nationalistic political trends steadily engulfing Tanganyika, forces that emphasized values and actions transcending ethnic boundaries. Umwano and USA showed how the tribalism or ethnicity encouraged by the British unexpectedly developed into groups critical of the colonial state that had spawned them: "tribe became a body of defense against and demand upon the state, a formerly unimagined role" (Lonsdale 1992:113). Umwano and USA would be considered backward and tribalistic by TANU politicians (if they considered them at all). Yet much earlier, African nationalists had taken advantage of local ethnic politics, which had provided training for future radical nationalism. By 1958 TANU opposed these same ethnic loyalties as undermining the future unity of a new African nation-state. Ethnic or tribal politics were associated by TANU with colonialism because of their long entanglement with Indirect Rule. Colonialism inevitably bred nationalism (Hobson 1967:11), though it had initially promoted tribalism. This explained the hostility many chiefs and headmen showed toward nationalist politics, and toward younger Africans who claimed leadership by right of education and militancy and not by right of membership in or respect toward any traditional lineage or clan. A few African chiefs and headmen in some parts of Tanganyika supported TANU, but many more were pressed by the colonial government to oppose it. Since all such leaders were replaced soon after Tanganyikan independence, those chiefs and leaders who had opposed the nationalists were more realistic about where their own self-interest lay than were those who had supported TANU. In 1957–58 Kaguru political thinking was backward and intensely parochial, even by the standards of Tanganyika, itself a comparatively unsophisticated colony. The Kaguru chiefdom was socially and politically backward, so Umwano's and USA's quixotic attempts at changing it meant little. Yet the fact that Kaguru had imaginatively, though ineptly, attempted change at all tells us that even in a place as insulated and benighted as Ukaguru, forces were afoot to attack Indirect Rule.

SIX

The World Beyond:
Kaguru Marginality in
a Plural World, 1957–61

Ukaguru is the main subject of this book, but it needs to be seen within the larger context of the colonial system in which it was set, however insignificantly. For this reason, I here consider the chiefdom within the broader context of Kilosa district and, to a lesser extent, Eastern Province. Broader concerns of the district and provincial administrations, the nature of the British colonial civil service, the everyday worlds of the Europeans, Asians, and non-Kaguru Africans who lived outside Ukaguru must be understood to grasp what went on in Ukaguru itself. I began this consideration earlier with a study of the CMS (Beidelman 1982a, 1982b, 1999), so I do not discuss here again the important aspect of outside Christian missionary influence upon Kaguru and their land. Ironically, while the concerns and attitudes of outsiders often determined how Ukaguru was treated politically and economically, most of the time these strangers thought little about Ukaguru and Kaguru.

Kilosa District and Eastern Province: Size,
Population and Relative Importance

In 1957–61 the Kaguru chiefdom occupied the northern portion of Kilosa district, the westernmost district in Eastern Province.[1] Eastern Province was about 40,000 square miles in size (like Ohio or a bit larger than Indiana) and had a population of slightly over a million people.[2] This population was overwhelmingly African, although a large number were transient, ethnic outsiders employed on the many Greek- and Indian-owned sisal estates scattered throughout the region. There were about 6,000 Europeans in Eastern Province, but over 4,500 of these resided in the territorial capital of Dar es Salaam.[3] The rest, most of them Greeks, were scattered thinly over the remaining area. The large Asian population, mainly Indians, Goans, and Pakistanis, numbered over 32,000, but over 27,000 of these resided in Dar es Salaam. The other 5,000 were scattered fairly evenly through the towns of Eastern Province as traders, shopkeepers, clerks, and artisans. In smaller trading centers they were replaced by Arab, Somali, or African merchants. The administrative headquarters for Eastern Province was Morogoro, an attractive town of over 14,000. It was a major transportation hub lying on the main east-west railway as well as at the intersection of major roads going north-south and east-west. The beautiful mountains south and west of the town were extremely densely populated.

Eastern Province was regarded as an important province.[4] An administrative posting there was seen as a sign of a colonial administrator's upward mobility in his career. The main administrative concerns in the province involved the large sisal estates, which brought in considerable revenue. In 1957–58 TANU-influenced union organizers began politicizing the large number of estate workers, so that conditions on the estates and the danger of labor unrest and town-centered protests became big worries of provincial colonial administrators. In 1958 the African Sisal Workers Union was officially established, and workers began to threaten strikes (Guillebaud 1958:70–81). Uluguru chiefdom, the major Native Authority in the vicinity of Morogoro, was being used as a major testground in forcibly introducing unpopular new policies of cultivation, crop management, and reforestation. These were promoted to halt continuing erosion in the intensely overcultivated mountain country above the capital. Provincial administrators tried to ram through these deeply resented policies by requiring officials in the Uluguru Native Authority to enforce and implement them. This led to riots, destruction of property, and some deaths. Some Luguru leaders were hated by their people for following such commands and were harshly criticized by TANU, the African nationalist political party, while other leaders resisted these orders and lent support to TANU and other African dissidents, thereby antagonizing their colonial masters (Young and Fosbrooke 1960, Fosbrooke 1959a,b; Maack 1996). Unrest in the nearby countryside was soon translated into action in town, because many ambitious Africans had ties to both areas and saw an opportunity for political advantage (see Vincent 1974:261–267). This difficult, volatile situation led provincial administrators in Morogoro to be concerned about comparable resistance by Kaguru against a smaller unpopular forestry project (see the preceding chapter). Morogoro town and surrounding Morogoro district were the first stops for visiting Europeans leaving Dar es Salaam for up-country. Consequently, colonial administrators were keen to present a picture of order and stability (the area was invariably visited by United Nations Trusteeship investigating teams and surveyors). TANU and the labor unions were aware of this and centered much agitation there, so that Morogoro sometimes seemed to figure more prominently in Tanganyika territorial news than perhaps was warranted (Lohrmann 2007:69).

In contrast, Kilosa district was regarded as a backwater. True, it was only a hard day's drive to Dar es Salaam (211 miles) and only 90 miles from Morogoro. It was on the main east-west railway connecting the coast with the rest of the territory all the way to the great inland lakes. Kilosa district was about 6,000 square miles in size (like Connecticut) with a population of over 150,000. There were only about 500 Europeans (mostly Greeks), 1,000 Indians and about 500 Arabs. Its capital, Kilosa town, had a population of 3,000, almost entirely African. A dozen miles east of Kilosa on the railway was the smaller town of Kimamba (1,000), dominated by Greek planters. It was the shipping point for the local sisal estates. Kilosa district was a shabbier, quieter version of Morogoro district and of Eastern Province as a whole. Kilosa district had several Native Authorities but was dominated by a large, restless, and varied transient alien African population on the huge estates. While administrators were concerned with local Africans, their first worry remained the stability of the huge Greek-run sisal estates during a time of growing labor and political unrest. For decades colonial officials equated "detribalization" with destabilization and consequently viewed the great number of migrant Africans on the estates as dangerous, like townspeople. Aliens who migrated to Kilosa district would gain legal rights if they accommodated themselves to local ethnic customs, but that rarely occurred (Molohan 1959:1, 92; Guillebaud 1958:64–81; Cooper 1989:752–760). Estate workers were not a coherent ethnic unit but part of the "sprawling migrated structures of colonialism" (Samuel-Mbaekwe 1986:93). TANU politicians and union organizers saw the estates and two towns as crucial arenas where political pressure could be put on Europeans.[5] The British administration, estate owners, and Asian merchants continually looked to Morogoro for signs of what was happening, convinced that whatever troubles might arise there would eventually be repeated in Kilosa.

THE KILOSA DISTRICT SCENE

Kilosa district encompassed great variety. Its western half was a series of precipitous mountains, the most spectacular being the Itumba of Ukaguru, which in some places reached six to eight thousand feet. The Mukundokwa River valley cut through the mountains south of Ukaguru, providing a route for the east-west railway. The areas immediately below and east of the mountains contained some African settlements, but much of this eastern area had been alienated from Africans and contained huge sisal estates, vast and seemingly endless rows of sisal plants occasionally dotted with a semi-industrial cluster of buildings—African migrant worker barracks, huge decorticating and flushing plants, some administrative buildings, and a few residences for the Greek and Indian managers and foremen and their families.

In the north of Kilosa district , the main central east-west road of Tanganyika Territory cut through Ukaguru. In the eastern lowlands the district was crossed by a north-south road connecting northern Tanganyika to Kilosa and lands farther south. Another road ran off from this to end at Kimamba. This north-south road was the communication spine of Kilosa district, just as the east-west road was the means (along with the railway) by which Kilosa was connected to the greater outer world, the provincial capitals of Morogoro and Dodoma, the territorial capital of Dar es Salaam, and the coast. A number of narrow, difficult, dead-end roads ran out from these two main routes. These led to Native Authority courts, markets, schools, and mission stations and were difficult to traverse during the rains. No road in the district was paved except for a few streets in Kilosa town. Though Kilosa district was relatively small, the difficult roads meant that the more remote areas, such as most of Ukaguru, sometimes could not be reached in less than a day; for this reason the government built simple rest houses for touring administrators. South of Kilosa town were more sisal estates edged by further mountains. These highland areas were populated by the Sagara and to the south of them, the Vidunda. Both were matrilineal people, less numerous than Kaguru but culturally resembling them. Each had its own Native Authority (see Beidelman 1967b).

KILOSA TOWN AND ITS POPULATION[6]

Colonial Africa was described as "a continent of outposts" (Frankel 1938:30). In many ways the various colonial stations in Tanganyika were all quite similar. Like most East African small towns Kilosa occupied a surprisingly large area, because its various ethnic quarters were so widely separated from one another. It was a socially segregated town (see Hammond and Jablow 1970:113; Kieran 1972:240; R. Kennedy 1945:308– 313, 321; King 1985:21–22, Balandier 1970:33–35). At the center were the railway station, post office, prison, and police station. These were the most imposing buildings in town, thick-walled and whitewashed, with red tile roofs. All colonial buildings and European residences, British and Greek, were landscaped with flowering plants and lawns, and a few educated Africans tried with fewer resources to do the same with their houses. Except for the Goans, few Asians were interested in such beauti-fication. Shaw sees such efforts as colonial attempts to imprint European culture on an alien environment (1995:181–182).

Facing these large government structures was a tree-shaded street lined by a Greek owned store, two small Greek hotels, a Goan photogra-phy shop, and an Agha Khan Muslim community center. Going north-west past these, out of town, one encountered a derelict German fort guarding the hilltop at the opening of the river valley through which the railway passed going west. There the tarmac paving ended. To the north of the hotels was a German cemetery for the dead of World War I. Northwest of the train station, the European quarter occupied the hilly high ground. Proceeding due north from the railway station one passed Protestant and Catholic churches (there were no permanent European clergy), then the police barracks, and then on a hill the district headquar-ters or *boma*. Farther on, just before the tarmac ended was the district hospital. In the hilly land northwest of these were the Kilosa European Club or gymkhana and a scattering of European houses, each widely separated from the other.[7]

Near the large colonial buildings, especially the *boma,* were "the lines" of housing for low-level African government employees. One called them "the lines"; for example, African police were quartered in "the police lines." On lower ground farther east of the train station was the Asian quarter. Here, around a large open space where there was a livestock butchery (run by Arabs), there were about twenty or more Asian shops with attached living quarters. Two large ones stocked a wide variety of European goods and even out-of-date European magazines and newspapers. Here too was an Asian-run cinema, which showed Indian and European films Friday, Saturday, and Sunday nights. Crossing an underpass leading south from the railway, one entered the large African quarter located on low ground, the unhealthiest section of the town, since it was sometimes subject to flooding. The raised railway grading and underpass made the African quarter almost invisible to those in the European and Asian quarters. There was little tarmac there. Houses were tightly packed together. There were small African shops, bars, teashop-hotels; artisan stores such as carpenters, sandalmakers, tailors; a school, TANU headquarters, and one large European-type structure, the Kilosa community center, where some meetings were held and where an African band played for dances on Saturday nights. Unlike the European and Asian quarters with their modern metal- or tile-roofed buildings, street lights, lawns, flower gardens, and trees, the African quarter was a wild mixture of buildings, some modern in cement, brick, or wood, but most in wattle with thatched roofs. Dwellings were mixed among shops and other buildings. While some of the European and Asian areas were served by privately owned electric generators, nearly all of the African quarter except the community center was lighted by kerosene lanterns or candles.[8]

The African quarter held a wide mixture of ethnic groups but surprisingly few Kaguru. Of the 3,209 Africans registered in 1958, only 16 percent belonged to ethnic groups from Kilosa district, and only 209 were Kaguru. There were Africans from many parts of Tanganyika and from Nyasaland (now Malawi), Kenya, and Zanzibar; I even attended a spirit-possession ceremony held by Sudanese.[9] Swahili was the *lingua franca* of this quarter, and other African languages were usually politely avoided in public. It was Swahili speakers who were seen as the social pacemakers (see Vincent 1974:269). I here often met with inmates from the prison, because many were loaned out to work during the day at Asian shops, cutting grass, or raking roads, and then spent brief times drinking beer at the local African clubs before going back to confinement. Most of the local Africans with jobs were employed in government or worked as clerks or servants for Europeans or Asians. Those who worked for Asians usually lived in the African quarter, but most house servants who worked for the British were given free housing in small buildings behind their employers' homes. These Africans often visited one another or sometimes trekked to the African quarter nearly two miles away. During the day the narrow earthen streets of the African quarter were filled with people, since much work, whether preparing food or making furniture, was done outdoors, at least during the dry season. The area was constantly abuzz with people visiting and gossiping. Most Africans made small purchases at tiny African shops in this quarter. Only important purchases, such as European shoes, European tools, bicycles, or books were made in the Asian market, which was over a mile away. Aside from going to work or visiting offices to cope with government regulations, most Africans showed little interest in the European or Asian quarters, except to go to the cinema or buy at the butchery, both luxuries only a few could afford. Unlike Europeans, Asians, and Arabs, very few Africans had autos, but many bicycled to work.

The Asian community (about 400) was sharply divided. The few Christian Goans had nothing to do with other Indians, and the Hindu and Muslim Indians had nothing to do with one another (Allen 1979:57). The few Arabs (about 50) also stuck to themselves, though one became my friend. In general African relations to Indians were strained, possibly because there was little contact outside exploitative trade relations (Goldthorpe 1958:273). Relations between Africans and Arabs were much freer.

The European community (under 50) was also divided. The few Greeks in the town socialized only with other Greeks. On weekends the Greek hotel bars were often scenes for dances and card-games with heavy stakes, though the Greeks in Kilosa also drove to Kimamba which had a far larger Greek community (nearly 500), a large Greek hotel and bar, and a Greek community center.[10] The British generally viewed the Greeks as barely European, even though some of the estate owners were probably richer than they. After all, the Greeks mostly came from Cyprus, a British colony. Otherwise they could not have got to East Africa so easily. British disapprovingly told me that many of the Greeks took "mail-order" brides (I knew and socialized with one such couple), and gambled so seriously that they sometimes shot one another over alleged cheating. It all seemed alluring to me, like the Wild West, and besides they had great food and terrific music.

The British in Kilosa were all government administrators at the District Headquarters or supervisors in the specialized services such as the police, hospital, post-office, public works (roads and bridges), agricultural, labor or veterinary branches. Less than half of these men were married and there were no children of school age since those were sent to school in Britain or South Africa (Allen 1979:110). British administrators almost always first came to the colonies as bachelors. Most waited until they received a more senior posting before marrying, both because pay and allowances were then better and because they then felt more obligations to entertain (see Strobel 1991:20). Unlike the African and Asian communities, the Europeans were nearly all between the ages of 25 and 55. The young were away at school and the old had gone home to retire. The British sank no permanent roots here.[11]

The British were what Weber terms a "status group," a group who tried to present a style of life that would be an influential model for other groups around them. They often assumed a premodern view of government by examples of good character, somewhat like that of the outdated English gentry (Turner 1988:6). It was clear that few British thought Africans or Asians would ever be their equals as rulers.[12] The British administrators kept themselves a close-knit group, restricting the benefits of their status to themselves (see Rex 1980:121). This was so even though many British in Kilosa were far from representing the class they tried to portray. All were in government employ and tended to regard most white people they encountered who were not employed by government, especially those in trade, as inferior (see Ranger 1983:218). Even within government, those in administration looked down on lower-class British employed in the public works department involved in constructing and maintaining roads, bridges, and government buildings. A few down-at-the-heels British also worked in hotels in nearby Morogoro. They too strove to assume middle-class airs.

Aside from interacting when required in commerce and government business, Asians and Europeans never socialized with one another, but both dealt constantly with Africans, because all Europeans and Asians had African servants. It was master-servant relations that provided the key model by which most European and Asian attitudes toward Africans gained their tone. These relations provided local administrators with the germ of their attitudes toward the Kaguru and other Africans whom they governed in the Kilosa area. My European friends "excused" my constant socializing and even living with Africans in town as part of my fieldwork. Few ever thought I preferred the company of Africans or that I had really close personal ties with some Africans and Arabs, which I did. I often stayed at one of the Greek hotels and occasionally with British administrators, though I did not want to inconvenience them or appear too close to the colonialists in African eyes. When I spent long periods in town, I stayed in the house of my African field assistant, a house I had helped him build. When I stayed in Dar es Salaam, I also divided my stay between hotels and the homes of colonial administrators and friends in the African quarter of the city. I often brought African friends to European hotel bars and to the homes of my British friends.

European Masters and African Servants

Every European in the district had at least one African servant, and some households had many.[13] Almost everyone complained about servants— their mistakes, ignorance, dishonesty, unreliability, dirtiness—yet many servants were also described as loyal, honest, and earnest. In the sense that Europeans almost never had to do tiresome or monotonous manual labor, they all had it better than they ever did back home (see Cannadine 2001:128–129; Crowder 1968; 399; Sofer and Ross 1951:315–319),[14] and keeping servants enforced the local Europeans' image of themselves as some kind of gentry. Missionaries with their lower incomes had fewer class pretensions, employed fewer servants, and paid lower wages, while government officials had the most social airs and servants, especially those who were married with children, since wives seemed especially keen to reinforce and promote their husbands' ranks and perquisites. I here only consider the behavior of the British—not Greeks, who were said to be less generous and harsher than most British, just as Asians were said to offer even less, presumably because they had less to provide and because servant-master relations in their culture were more demanding.[15] The few Greeks I knew well were hospitable and charming. No British in Kilosa came from households that, at home, had servants, a far different situation from earlier colonial times. Only rarely did I meet really upper-middle-class British administrators. For a time, one of the junior district officers in an area where I later worked (Ungulu) was married to the daughter of the head of my Oxford college. I even had the rare experience of dining with the head of my college and his wife while I was in Africa.

In the post–World War II era, many British colonials had learned how to treat and train servants. Some were not very good at this. One of the first litanies of instructions recited by old-timers to all newcomers to the territory was a set of warnings about how to treat or not to treat African servants. Most old-timers seemed especially concerned that newcomers would set a bad example by being too understanding and indulgent, or by paying unduly high wages. It was considered important that British administrators did not do manual labor, even when that would have been easier than waiting for an African to do it (D. Kennedy 1987:153). As an American I was seen as often likely to "let the side down" on that front.

The youngest and most junior British administrators were always unmarried and often employed only one servant or "boy," itself a revealingly demeaning term, since some servants were older than their employers. This servant was expected to cook, clean the house, wash and iron clothing, polish shoes, and keep track of household supplies. British bachelor administrators were not usually expected to entertain formally, only occasionally to provide drinks or a bed and bath for a visiting male coadministrator, so an accomplished servant was not essential.

Most masters would shop for supplies themselves, but some gave petty cash to a servant so he could hunt down local foodstuffs such as chickens, fruit, and vegetables. Scrounging for food could be time-consuming, since it involved haggling with widely scattered local Africans rather than purchases at a single Asian shop. It was usually assumed that a servant might skim off part of such money, just as it was assumed that he would steal from the household some supplies such as flour, sugar, salt, and kerosene. Liquor, beer, and wine were usually kept under lock and key and repeatedly checked for theft and to see if they had been watered down. So long as these tacitly accepted rights were not abused, casual tapping of supplies was often considered a servant's perquisite. In addition, servants often expected some hand-me-downs of used clothing or other objects and certainly had no scruples in appropriating any items thrown out by a master. A few especially indulgent masters advanced loans to servants, although nearly everyone warned me against this.

There was a hierarchy of servants in terms of respect, duties, and salary. The highest-ranked servants were cooks and drivers, though no official in Kilosa district , except the district commissioner, was senior enough to merit an African driver, and even he often preferred to drive himself (see Sofer and Ross 1951:321). Cooking European-type food in Kilosa took a lot of time. An African cook who could make good bread, pastries, cakes, pies, and some sophisticated sauces was highly valued and would have had no difficulty finding another job if he was unhappy.[16] Such cooks expected considerably higher wages than ordinary ones. The houses provided by the colonial government were all equipped with some form of stove, but these were often difficult to use. African cooks were expected to know how to cook on portable kerosene stoves, converted *debbies* (four gallon paraffin drums), or even on open fires when they accompanied officials on inspection tours into the countryside. Even a skilled cook faced serious challenges when trying to prepare a complicated meal under such conditions.

Servants were expected to know how to work and repair kerosene lanterns, pressure lamps, and water purifiers. Most European housekeeping habits and tools were vastly different not only from those of Africans but even from those of most Asians. Just learning how to set a table, open tins, and wash food, or wash, wax, and polish a wood floor or furniture, were skills no European could assume that an African automatically knew. Polishing shoes was not an "obvious" skill. Proper ironing of shirts, blouses, and dress clothing was a considerable accomplishment for anyone, given the primitive nature of the kinds of irons available. Proper washing of clothing had to be explained in detail; after all, some clothing had to be bleached, some had to be washed in cold water to prevent fading and shrinking, and some cloth was delicate and other cloth tough. Most Africans initially considered all cloth alike and thought it should simply be washed and beaten on flat rocks. Some time-consuming washing, ironing, or cooking requirements at first seemed odd to me but turned out to be essential. For example, kerosene (paraffin) lamps needed to be regularly cleaned and repaired, and the lighting bonnets required very skilled treatment. Charcoal fueled flatirons required special skills to avoid serious burn damage to clothing. Drinking water had to be properly boiled and filtered. All cloth, even sheets and blankets, had to be ironed, not for mere appearances but to kill parasites that deposited eggs on clothing drying outdoors, since otherwise these would cause horrifying sores. I learned this through great pain.

When a new European arrived at a station such as Kilosa, word would go out through the servant network and a string of aspiring African employees would come by the house seeking work. They would have letters from previous employers vouching for their capabilities and honesty. Some papers were obviously forged. It was difficult to determine whether such letters even referred to the persons bearing them, and in any case a newcomer rarely knew who the Europeans who wrote these letters actually were. A new British official would have to chance his luck with one of these applicants or, as I did, spend many days training a raw African in all the rudimentary techniques from how to make bread, make and operate a jerry-can stove or use a European one, iron clothing, make a bed, and set a table and serve a meal (see Bujra 1992:249–250; see D. Bates 1962:15–21). There was no reason to assume that servants were literate, so one could not assume that they could be given shopping lists, or read labels on tins or a note of instructions you might send when you were absent. (Every European told tales about personal difficulties in training African servants.) When a European was married, he delegated such training tasks to his wife. If he was lucky enough to have a seasoned servant of many years, he might entrust him with the task of training a new recruit. In general, each European household had its own rules and routines and therefore trained or retrained whatever servants came its way, even experienced ones.

A senior married British administrator would usually have a cook, a houseboy, and one or more garden boys to do yard work. If a European was unmarried, he probably was too junior to afford more than one servant, and that servant would probably take on cleaning and washing along with cooking. Some older cooks would consider some tasks beneath them, especially if they were highly skilled and capable of making sauces, cakes, pies, and other complex European dishes. In such cases, they in turn would hire other Africans whom they would expect the European to pay. No household servant would dream of doing yard work. Instead, he would interview younger men, even boys (*watoto*, children), who would be hired to cut grass, weed and water the garden, and perhaps do other rough jobs that the main servant saw as demeaning, such as feeding and tending a dog or carrying a message to another household. Some *watoto* were needed for trips, serving as "turn boys," who cranked recalcitrant engines, helped change tires, or did the dirtiest work in getting a vehicle out of the mud.[17] Every large European household had at least one such *mtoto* (child) acquired by senior servants. They were considered especially useful on stays in the bush where errands, guarding supplies, and other petty chores abounded. I asked some African servants whether they considered cooking a feminine task unbecoming men. I was told this would be so in an African household, but European food preparation and presentation were seen as so alien and complex that these were thought beyond the supposed limited capacity of African women and fit only for African men (see Bujra 1992:242–249).

Being a servant in a British colonial household often provided an African man with an opportunity to learn a wide range of new skills that were not only highly marketable but valued as tools for modern life and town living (see Hansen 1992:17; Bujra 1992:242, 248–249). This was especially the case for cooking, ironing, and acquiring skills with European utensils, bicycles, or even a motorcar. Working for British could also provide means for patronage by which a senior servant could find employment for other Africans and provide benefits to them from filched household goods and hand-me-downs. A servant might also provide temporary housing or secure official help from his seemingly influential master. The most skilled and senior servants in European households would expect to make more than most other Africans not employed by government, and the very top servants, such as cooks, might make more than some low-level schoolteachers. In the early 1950s the average African male wage earner made about 40 shillings per month ($5.50), whereas domestic servants, even the most disadvantaged, made 50 to 100 shillings ($8 to $14), not counting free lodging and perks (Bujra 1992:253). Servants of important Europeans were free from harassment by other Africans or even other Europeans. When I lived in Ukaguru, few African officials bothered my servants, though when my cook had a sexual affair with the wife of my landlord, the subchief, my life got complicated.

After an African had worked as a servant for many years, he inevitably developed new tastes and needs in food, clothing, and furnishings, the most obvious being a desire for tea, sugar, better soap, and nicer clothing. These new wants were now more realizable because, however low servants' wages might seem, such pay was higher than that given to some Kaguru headmen and subchiefs (Bujra 1992:253). Contact with whites and to a lesser extent with Asians, even just watching them, taught Africans to be different persons (see Abani 2000; Ferguson 2002:353–355). Such cultural intimacy with foreigners unsettled boundaries and created ambitious and restless Africans. If a British official was married and had young children, he might hire an *ayah*, a female nurse or baby tender, though many preferred to use men as babysitters.[18] Many British thought that African men were far more dependable and emotionally stable than women. Certainly most African men disapproved of Europeans hiring African women as servants (Bujra 1992:244–249; D. Bates 1962:72–84). Many British felt that having both male and female servants set up a potentially difficult situation in which sexual intrigues might develop, undermining household order. In a few cases I heard of European men having fleeting sexual affairs with African female and sometimes male servants; I never heard of any European women having affairs with any Africans. Nearly all Europeans assured me that Africans, both men and women, had a far higher sexual drive than Europeans. This seemed ironic to me, given the constant gossip about sex and adultery among colonial Europeans. In contrast, some of my African friends thought Europeans were far more obsessed with sex than were Africans. Each group entertained wistful illusions about the sexuality of the other.

If a European man was married, much of the everyday contact with his servants was through his wife. This could be difficult for several reasons. Some African men, especially older ones, resented being ordered about by women. Furthermore, while all British officials were required to pass an examination in Swahili within their first two years, British wives often never studied Swahili at all and picked up what was termed "kitchen Swahili," a crude caricature of the language that did not allow for subtle or tactful expression of orders (see Steward 1965; D. Kennedy 1987:156–157). The relations between male and female British masters and African servants were the subject of a huge body of folklore by both the British colonials and the Africans who worked for them (see Lewis and Foy 1971:162–167; Hansen 1989:47).[19] As Noël Coward wrote, "The Natives grieve when the White men leave their huts because they're obviously definitely nuts" (1995:122). Finally, most younger British women, especially by the 1950s, had little previous experience dealing with servants (see Tanner 1966:392). If one drank in African bars frequented by African servants (as I often did), one sometimes overheard outrageous gossip and complaints about British employers. Once an African told me that African servants had perjured themselves in testifying to cover up the murder of a wife by a colonial administrator in a famous local scandal. (The official version was that the husband had been cleaning his gun when it accidentally went off.) At any colonial station, gossip and rumor about British households circulated widely between African employees. African household servants almost never admitted to knowing any English, but it was clear that those who had worked for many years in British households understood a good deal that was said, including much that their masters thought to conceal. It would be difficult to have many secrets from people who witnessed all your meals, cleaned your house, washed your intimate garments, and entered your bedroom in the morning even when you were still asleep in bed with someone.[20] As Trollope wisely observed about English servants a century earlier: "Servants are wonderful actors, looking often as though they knew nothing when they knew everything—as though they understood nothing when they had understood all" (1964:515).

British masters were keen to keep the same servants over many tours of duty, but this posed a problem since the British went on periodic home leave. A few British simply paid their most valued servants their wages even while they themselves were away. This was not really very extravagant since the salaries were so low. Others tried to pass their servants off to friends and colleagues who in turn passed their servants back to them. For many British, each tour of duty posed the challenge of setting up a new African staff. This was especially difficult for those posted to remote and difficult stations, where more sophisticated African servants might not want to go and where new, trained servants might be hard to find. British said it was worth it to pay their servants salaries while they were on leave in Britain, because it was good to have familiar servants waiting at the docks or airport when one got back.

Most British masters expected their African servants to live in the small houses that were provided at the back of the European government-provided dwelling. The servants were expected to sleep and cook their meals there. Most servants lived alone but some stayed with women—rarely their actual wives, more often local women. Most servants came from areas far from where they worked and left a wife or wives and children back home. It was often said that one should not hire local Africans as servants because such people would be too distracted by nearby kin (see Hansen 1989:40). They would always be inviting their relatives around or going off to see them, or stealing food for them (see Hansen 1989:90). In Kilosa district few local Africans, especially Kaguru, had the skills for servant work. If they did, they were probably clerks or schoolteachers who would disdain being household servants.[21]

Because African servants lived on their master's premises, it was assumed that a servant could be awakened and called to work at any hour. Most servants were up before six in the morning preparing food since Europeans were at work by eight. Lunch was served around one. Servants served dinner at seven or eight, so few were done with their tasks before ten or eleven at night. Many Africans told me that they preferred working for unmarried men who were away most of the day at work and who gave them more free time. Because British men did not know much about cooking and housekeeping, they were said to be less fussy and demanding than British wives.

Africans could be given time off for church, special occasions, and emergencies, or even relaxation, but servants were rarely given entire days off, and so slack periods during the day when masters were away at work were important to them. Servants worked especially hard when they were expected to go on safari with their masters, cooking and washing under difficult conditions, often in surroundings that they themselves, as town Africans, considered "bush" and difficult, even if they may have originally come from such areas. They all expressed contempt for "bush" Africans, whom they described as barbaric (*shenzi*). Servants were generally seen as tools that could be loaned; for example, a European would not hesitate to order a servant to carry some other European's luggage, help another with a stuck auto, or run someone else's errands (see Ranger 1983:223). In short, servanthood was what Coser terms "a greedy institution" (1974:69–75).

Masters had strong ideas about how servants should appear. Most did not want servants to wear shoes while they worked indoors. If a servant had a wristwatch or other "luxury" goods, he was not expected to flaunt it at work. Servants were expected never to wear "primitive" items such as earrings, necklaces, or charms. When masters entertained guests, which could be quite often, the servants who brought food and drinks were expected to wear a neat and clean white *kanzu* (Arab-type gown) or else a neat white shirt and shorts, along with a white cap or a red fez. They were expected to look "African" (see J. C. Mitchell 1960:181; Fanon 1965:35–47). Whites wanted their house servants to look like "authentic" Africans, never like black Europeans. Educated Africans who sported European dress and manners disturbed all but the most assured and high-ranked whites, who were not threatened by such behavior (see Kirk-Greene 1986b:xiv). (I recall once talking to the employees at a major hotel in Dar es Salaam while they were in the back getting dressed for work. They pointed out how they had to give up their European shoes and trousers and wristwatches to go barefoot, don *kanzus* and sometimes even fezes just to please the Europeans. They hoped such demands would end after independence.) Many Africans expected a master to provide them with such special servant garb. If there were houseguests, a servant expected a modest tip from visitors, especially if he had done extra laundry or other chores for them. Most British liked their servants to dress like coastal Swahili Muslims, even if they were actually pagans or Christians. In general, Muslim servants were preferred. British said that Christian converts tended to be "cheeky," "uppity," and aspiring to imitate Europeans, something Muslims or pagans would not do. I was advised not to hire a Christian. Muslims were seen as the best servants of all, because it was assumed that they would not get drunk or steal the valuable and vital liquor supply which was usually kept locked up.

African servants rarely made suggestions about their duties, even when they knew their masters' instructions were inept. They obeyed but did not approach work as something they had any personally creative stake in doing. While masters expected servants to be at their beck and call much of the time, few British would have thought of actually visiting the servants' living quarters, even though these were usually only forty or fifty feet from the main residence. African servants were summoned by voice or bell, almost never personally fetched. Proper bathing facilities were never provided for servants, so there were many jokes about how servants smelled. African servants were often described as people totally apart from the British, and in their own domestic affairs lived utterly apart from their masters, yet at the same time African servants moved quietly, freely, and without any seeming notice by the British in every domestic and personal space, even bedrooms and bathrooms.

The British in Kilosa

In Kilosa district I never encountered any social life shared between British and educated Africans. This did rarely occur in Dar es Salaam, but there one could find some few Africans with equal or higher education than some British. British in Kilosa district resided almost entirely in Kilosa town, colonial staff renting government houses that were provided with government-owned furniture. The quality of housing depended on seniority, but I found houses pretty much the same, except that some had far nicer locations and views than others. Furnishings seemed drearily the same. Shipping costs were high, so most large pieces of furniture were rented, ugly standard government-issued items, though everyone tried to bring out a few things to mark off a house as distinctive and nostalgic for home and to give some signal about taste and class. A few more senior staff actually brought a few valuable pieces, in one case a piano, to "make a difference" (see Tanner 1966:276–277; Kirk-Greene 2006:296). Good furniture, rugs, pictures, and china presented a problem because of the high costs of shipment, risks in storage (staff went on leave about every three years), and danger of damage and loss from inexperienced African servants, humidity, theft, and insects. Consequently, even senior officers had homes little better than the most junior. I never saw a really elegant European home in East Africa. This was probably hard for some British, because most keenly entertained a romantic nostalgia about "civilized" life back home, even if it may not have been that way in reality (Turner 1987:153–154). It would be a rare person like Karen Blixen (Isak Dinesen) who would bring antique furniture, fine art, Oriental rugs, crystal, and silver to a colonial bungalow. (When I lived in Ukaguru,

I tacked postcards of paintings by Matisse and Cranach on my walls to remind me of the world I had left.) When I visited some European friends in Dar es Salaam, especially those who had lived there for some time, I did find some homes furnished with good Oriental rugs, Arab antiques from Zanzibar, and some good European silver and china, but this was not usual.

Besides housing and access to cheap government furniture, administrators needed at least one automobile. Life was considered impossible without one (during my first field trip, British friends were amazed that I had only a bicycle and relied on hitchhiking). Government advanced loans to officials for the purchase of an auto and provided allowances for expenses where the use of an auto was directly related to one's duties. The use of an auto often took on dimensions rarely considered back in Britain. At times people drove hundreds of miles just to shop or even to attend a much anticipated party, even though travel was always full of risks and surprises (K. Cameron 1990). I did learn that one should never drive anywhere alone, at least not up-country. Amazing problems sometimes arose that one could not manage alone, such as running into a large animal, losing a wheel on a hillside, or dropping an axle. There were no handy tow services or garages.

Aside from those in the colonial administration, in Kilosa district the only persons vaguely qualifying as "British" were one old, lone, eccentric recluse Rhodesian farmer, who lived in the Itumba Mountains of Ukaguru and saw almost no other Europeans (see my account of the Groundnut Scheme in the epilogue), and the Australian CMS missionaries, who rarely visited Kilosa and who had no social life with the British, whose drinking, smoking, dancing, and card playing were judged sinful. (During my stay, I knew no British administrators involved in any church matters. One of my closest friends was expelled for a week from Kongwa club for pissing on the leg of a teetotaling Protestant bishop who had dared to enter the bar. That, of course, was extreme but did not make my friend a social pariah.) In Kilosa district the label "British" was generously applied to any white, English-speaking subjects of the empire. For example, one district commissioner was a New Zealander with very un-British habits and speech. On my second field trip to Kilosa district, after I had degrees from Oxford and wore English clothing, I was considered practically British. This would never have happened back in Britain, however long I lived there, but in Kilosa district white speakers of good English and reasonable dress and manners were in short supply. (By then I had a perverted British accent, which friends told me sounded like I came from Belfast. Luckily, I lost the accent.)

Social life for the British centered around the Kilosa Gymkhana Club, whose membership was by election and payment of annual dues (see Tanner 1966:297; Kirk-Greene 1986a:280, 283; Allen 1979:60–61). Non-British were never members, though outsiders such as myself could be admitted as guests of members. No cash ever openly changed hands at the club. Bills were put on account and usually settled after paydays or, at the worst, before one left one's tour. The club had a small library, but its main attractions were its bar, lounge, verandah, and tennis courts. Most local British met there every day from late afternoon until into the evening. The club was staffed by Africans. Occasionally the club launched special affairs such as a lawn party (sundowner) or a dance, sometimes with a phonograph, though an African or Asian band could be hired. (The word "sundowner" related to the belief that one should not drink alcohol, at least not in public, on weekday evenings until it got dark. Otherwise it might look like you had a drinking problem.) Even less often a football match was held between the British civil servants and local African and Asian teams. Card games (bridge) were also a pastime. British also invited one another for drinks and/or dinner at home and put up visiting colonial officials. Such invitations and contacts were usually initiated at the club. There was no other respectable social life, so that by the end of a three-year tour of duty everyone knew everyone else very well, sometimes too well, given that there were only about thirty people in the group and often even less. There were many informal rituals of male bonding in sports and parties (R. Willis 1981; Tanner 1966:290).

Kilosa society was rife with gossip and rumor, as is any small, closed society where maintaining a facade is essential. Everyone wanted to learn what actually lay behind some public statement, promotion, or visit (West 1965:42–43). Rumors became even more widespread after independence, when almost no one officially said what was really taking place. Of course, salary, past official postings, education, and other such matters were regularly published in the *Colonial Gazette* (Kirk-Greene 2006:198; Tanner 1966:291; Allen 1979:52, 1986:62), which was readily available and was studied to determine colleagues' records. At any new posting, one rushed to read up on those at the site. Older officials turned to the annual royal New Year's honors list to see who got an award, just to track careers. This, however important, was always described with some deprecatory irony; for example, the OBE (Order of the British Empire) was often described as "Other Bodies' Efforts." The "real" information about people, the gossip, required more investigation, and there were consequently speculations about one another, especially about sex.

Station life was always concerned with rules, garb, etiquette, and "what was and was not done." Noël Coward wrote, "In a jungle town where the sun beats down to the rage of man and beast, the English garb of the English Sahib merely gets a bit more crease" (1995:123). The higher an officer's rank, the more fuss was made about rituals and precedent (D. Kirkwood 1984:154–155; Callaway 1987:13, 173; Allen 1979:10–11, 62–63, 86–87, 158–165; Ranger 1980:350–351; Hobson 1967:198–215; Gann and Duignan 1978b:84; Sofer and Ross 1951:323–324; Kirk-Greene 2006:8–12; 1978:217; Gartrell 1984:170).

The administrators at Kilosa headquarters and at the special services such as the hospital, train station, post office, and police station spent Mondays through Fridays at work by about eight, lunch about one, and a short afternoon ending about four. Saturdays were half-days of work, and Sundays were free unless there was some local crisis. After work and on Sundays most officials drifted off to the club until dinner time. Everyone retired fairly early, except perhaps on Saturday nights, to be ready for another grueling routine at dawn the next day. Those junior officers working for departments such as veterinary services, agriculture, labor, and forestry spent a great deal of time making site visits and consequently had far more varied days, with much time outside the town.

Administrators were expected to make field tours every year, during which they inspected local courts, markets, dispensaries, and other facilities. Yet as the administration demanded an ever-increasing number of reports and records, many spent much more time in their offices in Kilosa than they desired (see Liebenow 1971:150; Allen 1979:71; Kirk-Greene 2006:89–101; Gann and Duignan 1967:211). The younger men especially enjoyed time in the countryside, which they still saw as an adventure (Allen 1979:79). Older, senior administrators were more likely to be married, and while some of their wives liked roughing it in the field at a rest house, other wives disliked this and would not go. Whether the men liked being with their wives or away from them, most officials viewed these tours (safaris) into the "bush" with emotions varying from anticipation to annoyance, depending on the dynamics of their marriage. In the past, before World War II, safaris had been seen as essential for learning about the district and its people. Safaris were still considered by most officials as obligatory demonstrations of one's authority and prestige, providing local Africans with an opportunity to demonstrate their loyalty. Given the location of rest houses, usually on a hill far from any African settlement, the tours were more removed from African everyday life than one might suppose (see Schumaker 1999:330), even though they were always dramatic departures from the limited but very real amenities of the station. Unlike Asians and highly educated Africans, the British of all ranks were ready to muck about outdoors even in bad weather. "Mad dogs and Englishmen go out in the midday sun" (Coward 1995:122–123).

The British headquarters administration was at the core of the social world, with male hierarchy strictly determined by rank, and a wife's status reflected by that of her husband. The district commissioner was the top person, officially but also socially, even when away from work (see Tanner 1966:294); his wife then was the top in the corresponding women's hierarchy. (One junior administrator jokingly told me that the British football team so often lost to the Africans because the domineering district commissioner always insisted on deciding all plays and no one liked to contradict him, however stupid he was.)[22] At the bottom of the hierarchy were the British in the public works department, responsible for roads, housing, and other mundane matters, and those in the police. Both were mostly men lacking college educations and therefore lacking the "right" accents, tastes, and manners. Rank and seniority determined income and were published annually, so that everyone knew where everyone stood. There was an upper-middle-class attitude, real or feigned, permeating the behavior of the British administration, a kind of out-dated squirearchy, associated with so-called British country (or county) life and public schools.[23] (Actually, by the 1950s the colonial service was far more middle- or lower-middle- than upper-class, though it often aspired to "higher" mannerisms.) In addition, there was the usual British preoccupation with class, speech forms, manners, and dress, although none of this could entirely surmount the hierarchy of the colonial register of rank and pay. Even so, in general I found nearly all British in the territory trying to assume a genteel facade often above what would have been appropriate back home. At a station like Kilosa, with less than thirty British, one had to work with what was available, "make allowances," and preserve social illusions and pretenses. Local British did make snide remarks about class, speech, education, dress, and manners but absolutely always closed ranks when confronted by the Greeks, Asians, or Africans. Christian missionaries remained totally out of the social web of the British in Kilosa; nor did they seem to have better relations with administrators in other districts I visited.[24]

I encountered some senior administrators who had entered colonial service after an army commission during World War II. Except for senior staff in Dar es Salaam, I rarely met the stereotypical public school, Oxbridge colonial officer-type who figured in so many earlier historical and fictional accounts. I knew some administrators who were not even born in Britain but were continental Europeans who had become "British." Those younger officers I met at Kilosa, men of the postwar generation, were usually college graduates but often products of lower-ranked British schools and red brick universities. They saw the colonial service as a means to fill demands for national service (rather than being in the army) and to provide a temporary adventure before finding a more lasting, humdrum job back home. Few said they thought the colonial service offered a permanent career in the precipitous anticolonial era. The few who later did choose to stay in the early independent African administration soon were disenchanted as they were asked to leave (though most said they did not regret postponing their leaving a life they had found both romantic and challenging).

I have not written much here about British colonial women. There were no unmarried British women in Kilosa town. Those few there were married to senior officials. In general, a woman's standing in colonial society depended on her husband's rank, not on her own character. As mentioned above, the wife of the district commissioner was the key woman at any station, assuming that officer was married (see Strobel 1991:10–15; Gartrell 1984:160). Aside from supervising African servants and spending time with children who had not yet been sent abroad for primary education, such women faced a challenge filling their time.

Most colonial women welcomed the idea of servants, even though by the time I did fieldwork, few colonial women had grown up in homes with any. Colonial wives were never expected to do housework, although light gardening, small household projects, sewing and knitting, and preparing special delicacies such as complex desserts were acceptable labor. Bored, restless, and idle wives posed a real problem to the system, especially at a small station such as Kilosa. Some wives drank, and a few had sexual affairs. Some observers have claimed that colonial wives brought middle-class values and "civilized" standards to a cultural wilderness. Others claimed these wives intensified racism by furthering the everyday distance between European men and African servants, as well as demanding that men spend time at home rather than mingling with natives. It is true that unmarried colonial men spent more time at work with Africans rather than at home (see Tanner 1966; Bujra 2000; Kirk-Greene 2006; Lewis and Foy 1971; Strobel 1991; Callaway 1987:3–20). Even by the end of British colonial rule, women remained relatively peripheral to official, public life at any colonial station (Herbert 2002:23).

The various British administrators and service officers in Kilosa district were all part of the colonial service. These were subject to similar terms of recruitment, salaries, and benefits. Colonial officials fell into two broadly different categories: district administrators responsible for the general governance of the district, and specialized officers responsible for such spheres as the police, prison, post office, public works, and special services such as labor relations, agriculture, forestry, medicine and health, and livestock management and veterinary services. Those supervising the post office, railway, public works, and prisons operated nearly independently of the district headquarters, taking orders from the provincial headquarters and Dar es Salaam. These different branches of the colonial service were often far less cooperative than was stated in theory. Each special services headquarters in Dar es Salaam was protective of its own turf (McCarthy 1982:9). If there was to be any cooperation between these special service officers and the district administration, it was usually the provincial governor who directed this. The police were independent, though required to act if called by the district headquarters, something that rarely occurred except when disorder broke out on the sisal estates. The district administration and the special service departments had a loosely defined interconnection in that such service officers were expected to keep the district commissioner informed of their activities, and the more senior provincial commissioner was expected to deal with any conflicts between local administrators and the specialist officers, securing (compelling) local African cooperation (forced labor), usually implemented through local Native Authorities. The district administration was the ventriloquist voice behind the Native Authority dummy that mobilized local Africans needed to work for government services. For some, "the term 'Native Authority' was a legal fiction meaning 'District Commissioner'" (Apthorpe 1968:19), who had final authority in almost everything (Lewis and Foy 1971:146–147; Lumley 1976; Liebenow 1971:18, 94–96; Cooper 1998:48–49; Rex 1980:135–136; Redmond 1971:162).

The division between the administrative officers and the specialist officers epitomized the classic political scientist's categories of general administrative officers, prefects, and specialists in a single area. There was (as we saw in my account in chapter 1) a British colonial tradition of preferring prefectural-types, the generalists, to head the districts and provinces at the colonial grassroots level. This was a concept originating not from British politics at home but from their policies developed in India. The administrative generalists were thought to have a breadth of vision and generosity of command that surpassed the skills of the specialists. Obviously many specialist officers failed to accept this view of their subordinate status. There was always some tension between these two groups of colonial officials.[25]

Here are a few writers' descriptions of the kinds of broad generalist range of tasks that could confront a district commissioner (DC) or even his subordinate district officer (DO):

> Field officers held the conjoint powers of the executive, as DC's; of the law, as magistrates; and of the "tribal police," as commander. They held to the self-critical doctrine that personal character best resolved the contradiction in role. As executives they must be firm, as judges fair. Such discretion needed reliance on their seniors' support. DC's also had ideology on their side. Their persuasive command was a tool of progress. Trustees of their African wards, they were schoolmasters in modernity. (Lonsdale 2000:199)

> There were petty court cases, there were matters affecting the African courts, there were things connected with the prison. But there was also

road-building, tree-planting, the collection of tax, the exemption of tax from some of the older people or the sick, there were things like trading licenses, matters connected with hygiene and extension of the health service which the medical officer couldn't possibly cope with himself. All this together with endless miscellaneous things connected with schools, churches, and various individual problems that people themselves would bring forward because they rightly regarded the DO as a person to whom to bring their complaints and their problems. (Allen 1979:85)

One assumed a superiority and capacities which make one surprised now that we didn't have a bit more humility. But it induced a sense of responsibility which tended to bring the best out of one rather than the worst. (ibid.:89)

The oft-repeated dictum, "Trust the man on the spot" expressed a set of pragmatic judgements based on long historical experience of the difficulty of controlling the acts of the distant imperial agents. (Berman 2006:76)

The administrators' perception of what was socially and politically possible took precedence over the technicians' judgement of what should be done; the generalist decided whether proposed specialist activities would fit the social framework. (ibid.:86)

Within the district the DC's word is law and his authority unquestioned. (Herbert 2002:13)

Herbert also quotes a Tanganyikan colonial official:

In what other task can you have so much power so early? (ibid.:21)

The "manner" evinced by many district officers was for me, at times, difficult to appreciate, which is probably why my favorite officials as friends were the specialist officers. The key attribute of a district administrator was "prestige," or a pervasive sense of moral ascendency. This was best translated as a constant air of confidence, of never admitting to a mistake, at least not in public. It involved seeing any use of force as a kind of failure because the force of one's prestige alone had not "carried the day." Above all such an official never openly yielded to any demand of an African, even though he might readily grant a favor or a kindness so long as it looked beneficent and not extracted against his will. A further result of such an attitude is that administrators closed ranks and almost never criticized one another, or at least were not supposed to do so. That, too, was probably why I liked the specialist officers better: they readily criticized the administrators.[26]

In 1957–58 the Tanganyika government service was short of officials needed to run local affairs in Kilosa. From time to time services were run by fewer staff than were needed, so officials were overworked and unable to do their jobs properly. Ideally the district headquarters should have been run by a district commissioner and two subordinate district officers. Yet sometimes only two officers (or even one) were present, making governance difficult, at least in monitoring local African affairs in the manner prescribed by the rules. An unexpected illness of a single administrator could set everyone else off schedule. Conditions varied widely from year to year on account of the way the colonial service was set up.

Territorial policy discouraged assigning officers to the same district for more than one tour of duty. Given such a short stay, there was little motivation to learn a local language or the details of native customs. Toward the end of an administrator's tour an officer was not inclined to begin any new projects, since he would not be around to follow them through or even learn how they had turned out. A district might therefore be run by a team of administrators with little experience of the district, or poorly motivated to give their best. New, green recruits in their first tour of duty arrived from time to time, making heavy demands on any senior officer in charge of training them. Newcomers often did not even know much Swahili.

One argument for the policy of rotating officers from district to district was that such transfers over the huge area of the territory produced a more broadly experienced official, better able to assume more supervisory rank, when he was promoted to the provincial or territorial level. In short, this policy created "generalists." Everyone considered postings to be rewards and punishments, signs of how the central administration in Dar es Salaam viewed one's capabilities and past performance. A more challenging or more prominent posting was seen as signaling one's rising success in the bureaucratic system. A posting to a backwater was seen as a sign that one was not viewed as a potential high-flyer in the system (Kirk-Greene 2006:62). Districts such as Moshi, Arusha, Mwanza, or Morogoro, which were populous and wealthy, were prized stations. A few, such as Rufiji, Mpanda, Chunya, and Ngara, were seen as backwaters. Kilosa was a better than average posting but without any real distinction.

The posting policy meant that an administrator had only three years to learn a district, so that during the first few months he was operating with difficulties. Frequent motor tours into the countryside and overnight stays in remote rest houses were thought to provide initial valuable background for grasping a district's character and the "native's point of view." Of course, a senior administrator might be assigned to a district where he had earlier served as a junior officer, but this was not common. Generally each new tour brought confrontation with new surroundings, new ethnic groups, new problems. No district officer was likely to develop deep knowledge of a particular ethnic group in his area during his three years stationed there. His knowledge was fashioned around a generic stereotype of the rural African and formulated around the Swahili language. Given the short time most administrators spent in any one district, most saw the African countryman as a sedentary Bantu language-speaker practicing a mixture of agriculture and herding. A truly exotic-appearing society such as the pastoral-nomadic Maasai (Baraguyu) both fascinated and perplexed most administrators, who saw them as noble savages, much in the spirit of Lawrence of Arabia viewing the Bedouins as backward and vexing savages resisting modern administration.[27] This was reflected in the shabby way most Kilosa administrators (except for the veterinary officer) treated Baraguyu and Kamba.

I rarely heard any British administrators blatantly deride Africans in the way that I heard Boers and Belgians speak, except among those with less education such as some in public works or the police. Yet British conviction of white superiority seemed ever-present.[28] Administrators worked hard to appear as gentlemen, and that precluded any crass demonstrations of racism, though the pervasive and enduring deep-seated racism and ethnocentrism of European Christian culture inevitably colored attitudes (see Pieterse 1992). Racist jokes were common.

Kilosa district was subdivided into seven domains. Most of the area was taken up by four Native Authorities: Kaguru in the north, North Sagara and South Sagara in the center, and Vidunda in the south. One district officer should have been assigned to the Kaguru and the other to the less important Sagara and Vidunda, but short-staffing did not always allow this. The district commissioner oversaw these areas but could himself, if necessary, take up the administrative slack by monitoring some of the Native Authorities. The towns of Kilosa and Kimamba each had weak but growing town councils dominated by the district administration. Even so, African townfolk were more sophisticated and critical than most rural Africans; some had social networks that crossed ethnic boundaries and latched on to educated leaders. Town councils were weak but less tractable than Native Authorities (see Sperber 1970:30). Town councils were chaired by the district commissioner or a district officer and had British representatives from public works and the health service, a supervisor of government properties, and local Africans chosen by district headquarters, including an African *liwali* (a Muslim petty judge). Because of the lack of education and governing experience among local African leaders, important Native Authority and Township policies were formulated by Kilosa headquarters.

The British complained about how Africans lacked governing skills and how much extra work was required by the Native Authorities and town councils. However, it was clear they actually preferred things that way. The annual budgets and accounts of these groups were set up and audited by the district commissioner aided by his district officers. All appointments were reviewed by them. Each month court records and income in taxes, fines and fees were reviewed and audited by Kilosa Headquarters. Despite the public rhetoric about Indirect Rule and African town governments, the final responsibility for most local government was shouldered by British officials, who were loath to relinquish these powers however much they complained. This huge body of paperwork meant that district administrators spent much time stuck behind desks in Kilosa headquarters, even though everyone spoke constantly of how much pleasure there was in getting out into the bush and getting to know the grassroots of the district. Every administrator was committed to making an official visit to every Native Authority headquarters at least once a year. Besides the four Native Authorities and the two towns, the seventh domain of government rule was the sisal estates, where government control was through the labor officer and the police, though these areas were run day-to-day by estate managers. District officers were remarkably free from outside control. Africans and Asians held little credence in any complaints they may have tried to make to provincial authorities (Listowel 1965:108–109), and despite being asked to make reports to their superiors, district officers kept much information from those outside the district (Allen 1979:132).

At the close of colonial rule Kilosa district had a district council headed by the district commissioner, combining European administrators and special service officers, members of the town councils, chiefs of the Native Authorities and other appointed Africans. This new organization was a puppet of the district headquarters, but government hoped to give a semblance of democracy to the conservative cast of the local government, especially Native Authorities, as well as to draw educated Africans into local administrative business. The hope was that this would counteract the growing influence of TANU and the labor unions. Few local educated Africans were fooled politically or saw Native Authority or town council work as lucrative (see Maguire 1969:21–24, 86–108.[29]

In contrast to the district administration, the special service officers spent far more time in the countryside. The labor officer spent many hours visiting the sisal estates checking working and housing conditions of laborers and mediating labor disagreements. He was the British official who dealt with Greeks and the one least likely to know local Africans, since almost no natives of the district worked on the estates. While rural dispensaries were run by the Native Authorities (except for the Protestant mission station), the medical officer was responsible for standards at all medical facilities, as well as proper distribution of local Native Authority medical supplies, checking the activities and qualifications of medical staff and the condition of buildings and equipment. As the only European doctor in Kilosa town, his duties were diverse and complex, as much administration and supervision as actual medical practice (see Ladkin 1953:22). The Asian community had a doctor in private practice who also saw some Africans. In 1957–58 the forestry officer was absorbed with the controversial reforestation project in the Itumba Mountains. His only other concerns were that the Kaguru Native Authority provide him with cheap if unwilling labor for planting seedlings and building a road into the mountains. He avoided Kilosa town and took his job because he liked roughing it in the bush. The agricultural officer supervised local African staff who were supposed to encourage better methods of cultivation, but his main concern was keeping track of marketing local produce at Native Authority markets. The local veterinary officer scouted the area for animal diseases, supervised veterinary assistants, who distributed livestock medicines and advised herders, and regularly visited the cattle markets to check on sales and information about stock and grazing conditions.

None of these service officers was responsible to the district headquarters; instead, they followed policies formulated at the provincial headquarters by the provincial specialty officers. It was obvious that despite the informality of this system, all of these officers needed amicable contact with Kilosa headquarters, not only to articulate their various activities with each other but to call on the district headquarters for the periodic labor of rural Africans through the Native Authorities, which were actually the pawns of the district administrators. The authority of any and all the officers derived from the general authority and power of the Kilosa district administration.

The central and complex task facing British at Kilosa headquarters was "administrating"[30] the African Native Authorities and Kilosa and Kimamba townships. The Ukaguru Native Authority was by far the most important of these organizations (governing over 66,000). The North Usagara Native Authority was nearly as large (59,000), but a large number of that population were not natives but transient estate workers not under the jurisdiction of the Native Authority, as were many in South Usagara (7,000). Uvidunda Native Authority was the geographically smallest and most remote of these (13,000 population). All the Native Authorities presented serious challenges to control, but Ukaguru was the most diverse and complex.

The first need for effective administrators was to speak Swahili. When a new recruit arrived, he almost never had any training in Swahili and was on two years' probation, until he passed an examination in Swahili as well as legal tests to prepare for serving as a magistrate in African cases (Allen 1979:68). If he continued to fail these tests he would be out of the service, though I never heard of anyone who did not eventually pass. I never met any British administrator who could speak an African local language, and certainly none ever existed for Ukaguru. This meant that no administrator ever had full access to the particular aspects of speech and belief characterizing any local culture. Nor could he speak to many women and many older, uneducated Kaguru except through some translator. This provided considerable advantages to adept African translators (see C. Roberts 1969:14–19). It meant that all local Africans could speak to one another in front of the most veteran British administrator and he would not know what they were saying. This language and cultural gap also posed a barrier to most of the outsider Africans posted to work for a Native Authority.

The pattern of local administration had significant temporal rhythms. First of all, reports of Native Authority court cases and financial accounts were sent down to Kilosa headquarters at the end of every month. Toward the end of each month administrators, especially junior ones, spent many long hours, often at night and on weekends, compiling monthly summaries and reports, which were forwarded to provincial headquarters.

Another factor affecting administrative routine was the seasons. The rains came from November through May, with the peak in December through March. The height of the dry season was from June through October. At the peak of the rains, areas in Ukaguru such as Itumba were sometimes unreachable except by foot or bicycle, and even major centers such as Berega and Idibo might be difficult to reach, and sometimes impossible, unless one was willing to leave one's auto and wade waist-deep through streams and hike. At this time transportation to some of the Native Authority centers was irregular, and British administrators relied on Africans driving Native Authority trucks to carry information as best they could. In contrast, the dry season was the time administrators toured. Travel was then far easier, especially since district administrators and specialist officers owned regular autos and not the expensive four-wheel drive Land Rovers. Besides, the early dry season was the time when work was done on local roads. The late dry season was the time of harvests, when taxes and fees were to be paid and markets flourished. It was also when most local Africans had more time free from cultivating their fields, so that was when Africans preferred going to court. This was the time for the British to catch the activities that most interested them. Unfortunately, this meant that most administrators missed seeing how stunningly beautiful areas such as Ukaguru and Uvidunda might be, since they appeared their most verdant at the height of the rains. They also saw the least of the rural Africans during the time when they were working endlessly in their fields. Since the British mainly toured the countryside in the dry season, when Africans had little work but often drank beer and held ceremonies with dances, some British wrongly considered Africans lazy and idle.

Every November district administrators submitted an annual state-ment of the Kilosa district funds and a budget for the coming year, which were sent to the director of audit in Dar es Salaam as well as to provincial administration superiors (Tanganyika 1959b:53; see Lumley 1976). This required laborious work on the cash books kept by local Native Au-thority clerks, books that were not usually well maintained (Tanganyika 1957b:27–33; see Lumley 1976:11–17). Many administrators had given up on local African clerks keeping such accounts in a manner that would satisfy the government auditors, because the rules for managing Na-tive Treasuries were exceedingly, even ridiculously complex (ibid.:1–2). There were 24 different forms used by the Native Authority Treasury, not including receipts issued to local Africans (Tanganyika 1957b:56). Every court clerk, tax collector, and market master kept a collector's cashbook and was subject to monthly audit. Administrators were also urged to make surprise inspections of the actual cash contents of Native Authority Treasury safes (ibid.:46–48).

Government directives unrealistically preached that British admin-istrators were only to supervise and guide, but in fact they tended to do most of the work (see Liebenow 1956b:456). Finally, when a district administrator went on leave or retired he had to submit a full financial report to the provincial headquarters as well as a "Handing Over Note" appraising the situation in the district, both to the incoming district administrator and to the provincial commissioner. Consequently, no administrator undertook any new projects in the months preceding his leave (Kirk-Greene 2006:93). Some administrators felt crushed by pa-perwork, something they had not anticipated when they had signed up for adventure in the tropics (see Liebenow 1971:150). McCarthy describes Tanganyikan budgets as "more public relations statements than financial accounting" (1982:12). He points out that the colonial service survived by deliberately providing obscure reports and accounts so that few could know exactly what went on. Colonial administrators had to learn such jargon to guard their respective turfs from those above. (It was rather like the newspeak language I learned in the US Army, another institu-tion thriving on misinformation.)

District administrators themselves heard some cases that were ap-pealed from the local Native Authority courts. In this they were both prosecutors and judges all in one; they may have even drawn up the local ordinances that sometimes figured in these cases (see Lumley 1976:11–17). Their broad sphere of powers—legislative, judicial, administrative, and policy—inevitably led district administrators into a prefectural attitude of near omniscience and awesome demand for deference from many they encountered—certainly from Africans. Their general opinion and word always trumped that of any of the specialist officers. Given their short stay in any one place, district administrators had only a rough idea of local African laws, customs, and community life. Legal rules and purposes are always ambiguous and disputable (see Levine 1985:42), but district administrators needed some quick and easy way to make sense of local Native Authority cases. Newly arrived district administrators were urged to study past court records to get a feel for the local system, which had scant resemblance to any British jurisprudence (see Lumley 1976:137–138; Lewis, A. 1970). In this sense the colonial legal examination provided poor help in making judgments (see Dryden 1968:17–18).[31] It certainly provided no means for reform or innovation. Many were told that their best preparation for understanding local law and custom was to read the district book (Kirk-Greene 2006:104–105).

British administrators were expected to serve 30 to 36 months before receiving a five- or six-month leave with full pay and some travel allowance. This leave could not be taken in East Africa but only in South Africa or Europe, which were both considered sufficiently civilized to allow the administrators to recharge their moral and intellectual batteries and prevent them from going too "native" (Moffett 1958:332; see Lumley 1976:59). British administrators emphasized their ultimate identities with the life and culture back home, their "Britishness"; settlers and estate managers could spend a lifetime in Africa and would eventually assume a colonial, tropical subculture, but colonial administrators never thought of themselves in this way, even though in fact a lifetime career in the colonial service did create a peculiar subculture. Colonial administrators and service officers always spoke of returning to Britain or Europe and complained about the life they missed. Ironically, some found that they could better settle in South Africa rather than Britain, both because they had actually become accustomed to a warmer climate and because they enjoyed having black subordinates and an exotic environment. Despite their constant complaints, many turned out to be reluctant to abandon the colonial milieu once African independence came. Years after I stopped doing fieldwork in East Africa, I continued to meet former colonial administrators who spoke nostalgically about their days in service.

The colonial administration staffers were keen to preserve their "Britishness" and cultivated mannerisms, clothing, and a view of social proprieties that had to be periodically reinforced by visits home. This motivation was supported by the constant presence of pictures of the queen in all government buildings, from the district headquarters to the lowliest Native Authority. Many were keen to rise at dinners and the cinema or sports events whenever the royal anthem was played. Above all the queen's presence was felt by the annual concern about the publication of the royal honors list (see Cannadine 2001:104–105; J. C. Mitchell 1960:11; Ranger 1983:211–212), a concern sometimes expressed with disparagement, for example referring to the OBE (Order of the British Empire) as "Other Bodies' Efforts" as described above. Any visit from any high British official of important social rank, especially one with a title or royal connection, elicited a flurry of heady excitement. Occasions such as Empire Day or Remembrance Day or a visit from the governor brought special uniforms, plumes, and medals out of steamer trunks and inspired searching out any decent silver and china.

Local British administrators well illustrated what Tidrick rightly describes as "the desire to be powerful and the desire to be good" (1990:198), a love of command and a need to be liked for it (ibid.:198). These were values sanctified in a British school, especially a public (i.e., private) one. Governing was supposed to work because of the personal influence and prestige of these administrators, who were aloof yet also paternal (ibid.:205–208). The ideal district administrator has been described as a blend of country squire, headmaster, and regimental officer (Ranger 1983:221).

Unfortunately, this administrative ideal was based on a false appraisal of how local Africans reacted to British officials. Many Africans reacted in the ways that they thought that the British wanted, much as how in the past some American blacks manipulatively reacted to domineering whites. This did not preclude secret hate and contempt. While the colonial administrators themselves always maintained a personal reserve, decorum, and a stuffy attempt at dignified mien, gesture, and speech, in the hope of awing African underlings, many local Africans saw them as duplicitous, pompous, and hypocritical (ibid.:212). Many Africans told me that they preferred the open brutality of the Germans to the supposedly treacherous politeness and hypocrisy of the British, though I wondered just what they could know, since few were old enough actually to recall the Germans. It was certainly clear to me that many Africans who seemed to get on well with the British really disliked them, though after independence some Africans told me that they wished the British had not left because they took the money and jobs with them. Furthermore, after independence many African bureaucrats behaved even more rudely and pompously than the British. The British cultivation of a Simmelian strangerhood did not always work with Africans (see Levine 1979:23–24). Even so, the British colonial administrators of Tanganyika had the reputation of being more easygoing and open than those in neighboring Kenya and Uganda (Taylor 1963:137–138).

Neither Africans nor British really understood one another, but the working relationships in Tanganyika were far less unpleasant and mean than those reported in many others parts of the empire, and certainly less than in neighboring Belgian and Portuguese colonies. Never did I hear the raw racist or politically menacing comments by Europeans in Tanganyika that I heard from visiting Belgians and South Africans, nor did I ever witness the sheer social nastiness I encountered in Kenya toward the end of the Mau-Mau emergency. It may be that many anthropologists underestimate colonial racism because they mainly worked with Africans without other whites being around (Balandier 1970:46). Colonialism in Kilosa district was ultimately racist, exploitative, and repressive, but it superficially still seemed to present a relatively well-meaning and easygoing, if inept, character, far from that described, often undoubtedly justly, for so many other parts of colonial Africa.

Local British administrators never encountered Africans outside of a domineering relation. At work Africans were subordinates or supplicating subjects, and at home and at leisure Africans appeared as accommodating servants. The most informal encounters were probably in the special services, where common work problems might be discussed with educated African staff. It was extraordinary how very rarely blacks and whites ever casually conversed, even after years of contact. The economic and educational gulf between them was too vast. This gulf was even greater between whites and African women. There was almost no contact at all between whites of any sort, administrative or domestic, and any African women, who remained profoundly insulated from any such exchange.

The larger, outer world of the Kaguru was most deeply influenced by the British colonial administration. That was, as I have repeatedly observed, a world full of contradiction, illusions, and delusions. The colonial administration saw itself as a bastion of British civilized society, though in fact it represented a very peculiar spinoff from that world. It lacked the numbers or infrastructure ever to resemble the world at home back in Britain. The more these expatriates strove to be very British, the more they actually deviated from ordinary British. Even in Dar es Salaam the number of whites was too small to comprise a full society, and up-country at posts such as Kilosa district, the numbers were so small that life was peculiar indeed. Most striking, all over Tanganyika the major and most prestigious persons were employed in government administration, certainly not exactly the case back in Britain. Most peculiar of all, it was a society mainly composed of young and middle-aged men, with only a few women and few old people or children. It was also a society in which no white person did any real manual labor and where nearly everyone white gave orders to a lot of people, at least a lot more orders than anyone white received.

Those at the top of the system prided themselves on ruling well. Given their very small numbers, lack of funds in their budgets, and poor communications, they did remarkably well.

But by the terms of modern Britain or America, they governed ineptly, lacking the means to do little more than maintain some semblance of order in the system and to collect enough taxes to keep it going. That, however, was still quite a feat.

The most peculiar side of British colonial life in Tanganyika hardly seemed odd to those who had been there long. It only struck outsiders who had just arrived, or perhaps readers today who never experienced colonialism. This was a world profoundly dominated by men, not just in administration and business, but in nearly all public affairs. The only large mass of working women were African, and off the radar in most public discussions and in most government reports. It was a social world utterly within a real gender time-warp. Oddly, in this sense, the supposedly modern British began to resemble the supposedly backward Africans. Both were societies where women's voices and visibility were easy to miss, however important they might actually be. The other important difference was that until the last few years of colonial rule, this seemed a land oddly missing any sense of open conflict, contention, and debate. The very nature of colonial rule and the lack of higher education of most Africans muted the fact that this was a society in which a tiny minority ruled, and even oppressed, a huge number of people. It was only toward the end of the 1950s that loud opposing voices were clearly heard, though, of course, a sense of domination and oppression had been there, voiceless, all along and everywhere. Given the constant conflict and debate back in Britain in the 1950s and 1960s, this deceptive order seemed eerie—though by the time I finished my first field trip it was clear to me (though to very few other whites there) that this illusion of order was just that, an illusion. Only toward the end of colonial rule was it clear that not only was there the obvious gulf between the British and those they ruled, but there was almost as big a gap between the British in "the service"—in the colony—and those back home who ultimately made the system possible.

PART THREE

How It Ended and
Where It Went

Independence and After

This book is about the colonial experience in Ukaguru, and therefore by strict standards it should not consider events after December 1961, the beginning of Tanganyikan (Tanzanian) national independence. Yet the end of colonialism was not sharply defined. It lingered for at least two more years. The colonial world of Ukaguru truly ceased when the Kaguru chiefships and Native Authority were dissolved in early 1963 (Tordoff 1965:80).[1] Yet other aspects of colonialism lingered on even after the end of Indirect Rule. Many of the changes that eventually took place can best be understood as outcomes of the earlier colonial system. I briefly mention here a few of the changes that Ukaguru and the Kaguru subsequently underwent.

Tanganyika's transition from colonial territory to African nation-state has often been wrongly described as a great success, a model of painless and constructive social planning (Pratt 1982:249). The transition probably appeared successful to some European and American writers because it was peaceful, and because it provided so little initial independence to local Africans. For the first year it was difficult for many, including me, to believe much had changed. British ran nearly all senior administration. At independence, a few high-level posts in the central administration in Dar es Salaam were held by Africans. All provincial commissioners were British, as were 55 out of the 57 district commissioners (Pratt 1982:272–273; Dryden 1968:6).

At independence, the new president, Nyerere, wrote to every British officer asking each to stay, out of "a sense of mission," even though he soon launched local political appointments that undermined and demoralized them (Kirk-Greene 2006:214). All the district administrators and technical officers in Kilosa were British; some were persons I knew earlier. While these men still performed their tasks, they now did so with a disinterested diligence that was new.[2] They worked as hard as ever but now spoke about pensions, severance pay ("lumpers," from lump-sums), and future plans. Most spoke with a new candor about work. Many local files had been destroyed before independence, but what little remained in the Kilosa district office was now open to me. When I asked to look at Kaguru Native Authority court records at the district office, I was astounded to be handed the entire lot and told, "Take them! They're yours! No one else will want them!" (I still have them.) Unfortunately, these were only a fraction of what should have existed.

There was no longer the old open hostility between white colonial officials and educated Africans, not even those in TANU, though there was almost no socializing. The British who stayed were skeptical about whether Africans were properly trained to govern. They had seriously underestimated the speed with which the empire would be scuttled and were shockingly remiss in preparing anyone (Porter 2007:6; Mueller 1981; see Allen 1979:150–163). It was "a damn disaster" (ibid.:10). The problem was exacerbated by the fact that the British had left the territorial administration often divided against itself; each minister and his department constituted a little kingdom of its own. This continued with the new government (McCarthy 1982:9).

After independence Africans slowly began replacing non-Africans in the central administration, but the severe shortage of trained Africans continued to hamper all levels of administration. Even before independence the few highly educated Africans were being drawn out of local government and sent to high-level policy posts in the growing central administration in Dar es Salaam. This heightened the disparity in capability between African central and local administrations (Tordoff 1965:5–6). There were increasingly poor relations between ministers and lower administrators (Pratt 1971:103). Yet Nyerere never supported the better-trained civil service against the arrogant and often ill-informed African ministers who held their posts through TANU party patronage (ibid.; Kirk-Greene 2006:215, 221–222). These new ministers sometimes imposed poor economic policies even during droughts (Mwansasu and Pratt 1977:2–14).

In 1962, 88 percent of the top administrative posts were held by British (Symonds 1966:180–181). Even at the second highest, level 58 percent of all posts were held by whites or Asians (ibid.:175–176). Salaries were set on a racial basis, with Europeans being assumed to require higher pay than Asians and Asians more than Africans, even for the same positions (ibid.:177). The argument for this was that these non-Africans would leave if their salaries and benefits were cut. As late as the end of 1963, expatriates still held 45 percent of all senior administrative and technical posts (ibid.:193).

At first, Nyerere concentrated on more visible changes at the capital and hedged on what he intended for local Native Authorities (Taylor 1963:207–208). Later, he began placing party members on town councils. On November 2, 1962, the central government reshaped the provincial administrations, replacing the white provincial commissioners with Africans, and renaming the provinces "regions." At the same time, districts were renamed "areas" but still lacked the African staff to replace any white administrators at that level.[3] Even at the new regional levels, the new African heads had to rely heavily on white staff who were far more knowledgeable and educated than they about most technical and practical matters (Tordoff 1965: 66–67). These new regional commissioners found this very demeaning and resented such advice.

At about this time the central government replaced the old Native Authority councils, such as the one at Kilosa, with councils dominated by TANU members and began reforming the local African courts, removing the chiefs from presiding (ibid.:84). Still later, early in 1963, the central government dissolved all Native Authorities and related chiefly offices entirely (ibid.:80). The Kaguru courts were centralized in Mamboya, where a non-Kaguru African with training in legal procedure was put in charge (Georges 1967). I attended his court, which seemed well-run and fair, though hindered by the fact that the magistrate did not understand Chikaguru and had no idea about the social backgrounds of the litigants. He was far better educated than any of those who had run Kaguru courts in the colonial era. He tried to rely on what locals told him about Kaguru custom but also tried to construct a general set of African principles about such notions as bridewealth, property, and the relative rights of men and women. He was Luguru, from a nearby matrilineal ethnic group closely resembling the Kaguru, so he had a "feel" for Kaguru culture. I found him bright, enthusiastic, and seemingly conscientious. Soon Kaguru custom mattered little, because the government banned matrilineal inheritance (Mamdani 1996:133).

With independence, a new form of "police" or political enforcers gradually entered local life, including Ukaguru. This was the Tanganyika Youth League, apparently the brainchild of Nyerere. The Youth League was formed mainly of unemployed young men, most poorly educated. Their job was to enforce local order. Just what they did and how they did it depended on the area where they operated. In sophisticated areas and with educated people, their powers were apparently limited, at least where I saw them. I first saw them in 1963 in Ukaguru, where they swaggered about at markets and settlements where there were court hearings. My very first encounter was at the cattle market at Chakwale, where they tried to intimidate Baraguyu and other non-Kaguru, people with little education or sophistication. I assumed that they saw themselves taking over the job of police, since there were very few if any actual police around in Ukaguru at the time. I later saw them in Dodoma, an area (provincial) headquarters west of Ukaguru. They were holding down a Baraguyu warrior, about twenty years old, and forcibly washing off his decorative red ochre paint and cutting off the long braids that signified his warriorhood (and manhood). The Baraguyu was doubled up and weeping, presumably out of humiliation and not fear. For me, this did not bode well for the prospect of independence bringing dignity or rights to African minorities or outsiders. I did not encounter any other striking Youth League activities before I left toward late 1963, but I was told of other incidents that occurred after I left.

The new African national government was weak mainly because it lacked trained African administrators and technical staff. TANU, the political party that took control, lacked many highly educated members, because the colonial administration had shortsightedly forbidden all government employees and schoolteachers from joining the party. Since this automatically excluded the overwhelming majority of well-educated Tanganyikans, when the new government sent TANU men to administer local areas, these replacements were often ill qualified and inexperienced. Many tried to make up for this through bravado and arrogance.

It was clear that Nyerere would have alienated long-time party loyalists if the old African administrators who had long been kept outside the party were now promoted over party stalwarts, however uninformed or inept. Consequently, early on there was a division between political leadership and many educated Africans, a gap that only slowly narrowed. This demoralized some educated African elites (Court 1976:665), though most with a middle school or university degree could count on a decent job somewhere. Still, half of those elected to parliament had no more than a high school education (Kjekshus 1975:16–20), so legislation was very poorly informed.

Earlier British anti-independence tactics had been aimed at setting local Native Authority administrators, like those in Ukaguru and Kilosa district, against the nationalists. If TANU had local support in Kilosa district, it was mainly among those living outside Ukaguru, those in Kilosa and Kimamba towns, and the masses of newly unionized workers on the sisal estates. Though some Kaguru had been covert TANU supporters, many local government employees had in the past followed British orders to harass TANU. With independence, these men were not always welcomed into better jobs in a new government that was now seen by party loyalists as a pork barrel for rewards. Besides, if old government employees were rewarded with new and better jobs, who would then be the needed schoolteachers, clerks, specialist workers, and secretaries? There was much to forgive and forget politically on all sides (Pratt 1982:252–259). Whether anything was actually forgiven or forgotten was doubtful.

At this time, the needs felt by Kaguru were voiced in ways that still almost exclusively involved the chiefdom and were rarely expressed in terms of the nation of Tanganyika or the district (area) or province (region). To counteract such supposedly narrow loyalties, the national government gradually promoted a vague, generalized "African culture" that was aimed at displacing tribal identity with a national one (Samuel-Mbaekwe 1986:89; Maddox and Giblin 2005:8–10).

Local political and economic affairs were at times difficult because the development plans of the new African government turned out to be huge failures. These discounted or minimized the weaknesses I already mentioned. Furthermore, past history had led planners to overdepend on government and international funding and to underestimate the need for private foreign investment. Nyerere's misguided Fabian socialism went against the realities of Tanganyika's immediate need for funds. Increasingly, Ukaguru became an area with many locals opposed to much that Nyerere and TANU had done. In April 1963, after Nyerere declared a one-party state, the opposition party, ANC (African National Congress), became illegal. Yet many of its members refused to disband. It was vociferously headed by Jackson Saileni, one of the early Kaguru promoters of USA and Umwano and the son of a former Kaguru paramount chief. Saileni, an appealing and quixotic leader whom I personally liked, was declared mad by some government officials, though their attempts to put him in a mental hospital were stopped by a court of law. (I was reminded of comparable attempts by a repressive Soviet government trying to suppress and discredit political dissidents.) It was hardly surprising that this constant harassment drove Saileni into seemingly paranoid behavior (Brennan 2005:263–265).

Besides suffering from poor economic planning, the new nation faced a long string of very poor agricultural years. (Much later, in 1965, there was an outright famine.) Through all this the rural poor were treated ever more badly (Mbilinyi 1973).[4] Nyerere showed little courage for openly making tough, unpopular decisions and confrontations that might jeopardize his party popularity (Pratt 1967:38–55). Instead, he resembled the previous top-rank British colonialists who spoke benevolently in public and then let the lower-level, local administrators do the dirty work it wanted. With African independence, it was still the same old colonialistic ventriloquism, only now it was local TANU party hacks and the thuggish Tanganyika Youth League who did the government's unpleasant jobs, replacing the earlier Native Authorities as "strong-arms" at the grassroots. As with the earlier British, it was a government with "missionizing" plans for modernization and supposed progress, imposing its policies from above onto those poorer and more uneducated below.

In January 1964, the Tanganyika army mutinied. This was part of a greater unrest all over East Africa, with military protests and attempted coups in Zanzibar, Kenya, and Uganda. Nyerere went into hiding and called in British troops to restore order and protect him. Later, his stooges ungratefully blamed the British for these troubles and broke diplomatic relations, calling attention away from their own errors and weaknesses

(Tanganyika Peoples Defense Forces 1993; Parsons 2005; Lawrence 2007). (As with the 9/11 attacks in the United States, this crisis served as an excuse for ever more abrogation of civil rights and condemnation of any political criticism as unpatriotic.) Nyerere became even more anxious about subversion after the army mutiny, and then later a university students' strike led to even more repression.

In 1965 major national elections were held, presumably to rubber-stamp the changes Nyerere had instituted since independence. At this time, Kaguru supported local Kaguru candidates with ties to USA and Umwano, sometimes against the candidates of TANU stalwarts picked by party leaders in Dar es Salaam. At the elections, Ukaguru was one of the areas least supportive of Nyerere and his candidates (Cliffe 1967a; 1967b:47, 227; 1967c:279; 1967d:305; 1967e:357).

By this time, Nyerere's rule seemed to teeter between trying to maintain a phony aura of democracy and the illusion of popular participation (despite a mass of poor, uneducated, and apathetic farmers in the countryside who did not much vote) and at the same time still trying to maintain strong central political control (Saul 1972:114). This was a government with a professed liberal credo of democracy, which it proclaimed in the capital and to foreign observers, and little concern by officials for the realities of the poor, uneducated masses up-country, such as in Ukaguru. Such attitudes were no better than the British delusions and illusions fostered in Dar es Salaam and London in the colonial era. As Saul wryly observes, governments such as Tanganyika's work because "control by the ruling classes has often been a low-key affair, therefore dependent as much on apathy and parochialism among the populace as on the fist" (1972:115). Saul should also have mentioned the illiteracy and lack of information among the Tanganyikan masses, and also the pseudo-liberal verbiage and patriotic cant that insecure governments use to obscure and justify their activities to outsiders.

The fragility of TANU, due to its ethnic, regional and ideological differences, led to a failure by those at the very top to push through necessary but tough decisions that would be unpopular with most in the party.[5] Almost no one ever dared open disagreement with Nyerere's policies, because the president equated political argument with unpatriotic subversion (Bienen 1971:197; Hopkins 1974:236).[6] At the same time, government ministries were involved in serious infighting, personal machinations, backstabbing, and competition in turf wars over funds and power, not so different from the administrative turf wars in British colonial times.

With every year, Nyerere struggled more to promote his unrealistic form of "African socialism." It was at odds with how traditional African societies actually worked, but it also ran against the modern, conservative educations of most of the new African elite bureaucrats. Their educations, mostly embodying Western conservative Christian and capitalist notions, led them to expect middle-class material rewards for their hard personal struggles for a better life and more respect.[7] There was little in their educations that would encourage real socialism. They saw little that was admirable about sharing their new wealth and power with the uneducated masses (though, ideally, this was also a Christian, socialist vision) nor did they care about self-sacrificing for uneducated strangers, for those who were not kin, friends, or fellow tribesmen (another Christian socialist vision neglected). Nyerere's socialist theories culminated in the Arusha Declaration of 1964 (Pratt 1971:78). In it, he claimed that a one-party state was a true democracy (Nyerere 1967a, 1968:261–265).[8] He said that his goals were "No remaining division between 'ruler' and 'ruled'" and "No monopoly of political power by any sectional group" (Nyerere 1967a:137). He seemed to confuse his muddled, sanctimonious and contradictory exhortations with reality (Nellis 1968:14–15). The nation was soon deluged with glib mottos such as *"Uhuru na kazi"* (freedom and work) and *"Ujamaa"* (social sharing). To fulfill this dream of "national socialism," Nyerere first urged and then later ordered compulsory labor and forced villagization of the rural population.[9] African bureaucrats never saw these ideals applying to themselves, even though, under the new ideology, bureaucrats were expected to be satisfied with low salaries and avoid accumulating extensive property (which only led them to more corruption to meet their frustrated "needs"). Rural Africans saw compulsory labor and forced villagization as repetitions of earlier colonial interference in their lives (Mazrui 1967; Resnick 1969:14; Pratt 1976:203; Burke 1964:184–195, 219–228; Ergas 1980).

After the Arusha Declaration, Nyerere's policies increasingly reflected an oppressive paternalism even worse than that of the British, because it was more inept in theory and deeply corrupt in practice (L. Schneider 2004:370–372; Freyhold 1979:78–79; Mapolu 1986:120). The earliest phase of villagization was "optional" and not extreme. As the plan developed and became more widespread, it became ever more violently enforced and resented. When villagization eventually reached Ukaguru, it was especially harsh, forcing people into agricultural settlements that were sometimes in bad locations with poor access to water, fields, or transportation. Houses were destroyed and people were beaten. Some Kaguru surely recalled their earlier displacement, beatings, and forced labor encouraged by the British in order to facilitate the colonial forestry scheme, another project that was said to be for their benefit but never did help them. Africans living close together in these new, large settlements were said in many areas to have suffered an increase in witchcraft fears and accusations (L. Schneider 2004:357; Barker 1974:45). Freyhold, reporting on an area adjoining Ukaguru, claimed that villagers became ever keener to celebrate traditional rituals and festivals, the very traditional ethnic practices that the new government bureaucrats had apparently hoped to discourage. These traditions gave these oppressed farmers a sense of meaning and comfort that alien government policies were taking away (Freyhold 1979: 66). Numerous authorities writing about post-independence Tanganyika describe villagization as brutal and encouraging deep corruption on the part of the officials sent to enforce and supervise these hated policies (Collier et al. 1986:3–4; Bryceson 1988:44–46; Mapolu 1986: 122–125; Freyhold 1979:79, 141; Raikes 1978; L. Schneider 2004:347, 357–359; Ergas 1980:401–402). Ergas writes of the officials enforcing villagization: "The bureaucrats in general are allergic to dialogue with peasants, both by training and by class interests" (Ergas 1980:389). Villagization led to massive food shortages and ruined local economies (Bryceson 1988:42–44; Freyhold 1979:7; Mapolu 1986:122–125; Shivji 1986:3–4). Some Kaguru suspected that they were treated especially badly because their area was one of those that had least supported Nyerere in the earlier elections. Later, enforced villagization of Kaguru cultivators was followed by compulsory creation of pastoral villages for local Baraguyu and Maasai. These too were poorly conceived in terms of the needs of these people. Furthermore, these policies also reflected ethnic prejudices against such people, hardly surprising since the bureaucrats in charge were all from agricultural societies ill-disposed to para-Nilotic pastoralists; see Benjaminsen et al. 2009).

My Last Visits to Ukaguru and Tanzania: 1965–66

By the time of my last visits, Tanganyika had been renamed Tanzania, after it was "united" (the tie has always been problematic) with Zanzibar on April 16, 1964.

At these last visits, I found that the euphoria and enthusiasm of independence had worn off. I found the roads in disrepair, the railway facilities at Kilosa and nearby Morogoro run-down, supplies scarce for the technical services such as schools, medical dispensaries and live-stock services—and where supplies did exist, these were channeled by bribes and favoritism. Many local Kaguru, Kamba, and Baraguyu expressed hostility or indifference toward area and regional governments, attitudes little better than those they earlier held toward the previous colonial regimes. In Ukaguru there was widespread black-marketing (*magendo*) of crops to Asian merchants buying covertly in the bush. Many Kaguru tried to avoid legal sales at government markets, which were now controlled by African officials who offered prices far below what Asian merchants would pay. (Kaguru claimed the market masters illegally and secretly sold to Asians, for a personal profit, some of the produce they had bought so cheap.) Kaguru desperately needed the highest possible prices in a time of food shortages and inflation. They did not see why the national government should pocket the profits from their labor. They were not getting much that was positive back from the new, independent government. This was a period dominated by "a state-employed 'labor aristocracy'" (Saul 1972:121), which itself was underpaid and in need of cash during these high-cost times. Their corruption was probably as much due to poor salaries and galloping inflation as it was because of their greed and hard-heartedness.

I am glad that I did not witness the forced villagization of Ukaguru; that began shortly after I left. Nor did I witness the changes in the main road that ran through the middle of Ukaguru, though I was told that it brought considerable crime and many strangers, at least to the town of Gairo (formerly Geiro), which had replaced Mamboya as the government administrative center for Ukaguru. I have been told that I would no longer recognize Gairo as the sleepy settlement I remembered. It was now a busy truck stop on the main east-west artery.

At the time of my last visits to Tanzania, some whites still directed administrative affairs and technical services, even at fairly high governmental levels, especially in Dar es Salaam and in most big centers, for special services such as medicine, education, forestry, fisheries, and agriculture.[10] Still, by then it was clear that even these last vestiges of the old social order would be short-lived, because hundreds of young Tanzanians could now be found a universities and colleges abroad. A few British made race relations worse. I was appalled to learn that a newly appointed African regional commissioner had been refused admission to the British Gymkhana Club at the regional capital at Morogoro.[11] Later, prominent Africans were denied membership at the Dar es Salaam yacht club.[12] Of course, such clubs were then closed until matters changed. (Only a few brave critics asked why supposedly socialist, self-sacrificing public servants should want to join a yacht club.) Other whites left the cinemas shortly before programs ended, presumably so they would not have to stand when the Tanganyika national anthem was played. Some were even arrested for this. That surprised me, since, during the colonial era, there was always a rush of many audience members (of all "races") out of a theater before "God Save the Queen" could be played on the loudspeakers, and no one was ever even admonished. Some Africans may have been overly sensitive to any presumed slight to their new national dignity, yet nothing could excuse the racist behavior of those in the Morogoro Gymkhana or Dar es Salaam yacht club.

Unfortunately, there were also flickers of racial resentment between administrators after independence, despite the fact that a large number of whites had answered Nyerere's plea and remained behind to serve temporarily in the new government. This was probably predictable, because foreign administrators were all paid far more than most Africans; otherwise they would not have served. This was euphemistically called "hardship pay," though educated Africans rightly wondered what hardship such people had. Social relations between educated Africans and educated British were not much easier after independence. Educated Africans were often uneasy entertaining British socially, not only because most were paid less but also because most African wives were quite unprepared to entertain in a European manner (see Tanner 1966:290–302). In general, too, the lower ranks of British officials (such as those in public works, the railroad, and the police) were sometimes unpleasant about African independence, mainly because the lower their education and rank, the less likely it was that they were going to find new, comparably well-paid posts when they left the territory (see ibid.: 292). They were certainly going to have to give up a life with servants. By 1965 diplomatic relations between Tanzania and Britain had been broken. Even after these relations were resumed, little would be the same, and most inter-racial relations seemed worse than before. The very worst cases of racist conflicts were caused by the boorish conduct of some South Africans, Belgians, and Rhodesians who passed through Dar es Salaam in transit or who visited local tourist resorts. They continued to bring their racist, segregationist attitudes with them along with their other baggage. I had seen them behave very badly before independence, but then such offenses were never punished by the British.

In 1968 I returned to East Africa, this time to Uganda, where I briefly taught at Makerere University. My best African friend from Tanzania joined me, and in Kampala I met many people who spoke about what was going on back in Tanzania. (Most of those friends I knew in Uganda are now dead or have fled the country.) In Uganda I learned about the terrible suffering in Ukaguru and elsewhere due to compulsory villagization, which, of course, I never witnessed. This was still before the HIV/AIDS epidemic, which affected Ukaguru just as it did the rest of East Africa. It was also before the horrors of Idi Amin, whose invasion of northeastern Tanzania led to a war that further hurt the Tanzanian economy. While the war did displace the evil Amin, Nyerere's friend, Milton Obote, returned as president of Uganda and proceeded to become a scourge almost as destructive as Amin, instigating a political system that led to conditions that still have not brought good government to that beautiful country.

Today there is probably little trace of the Ukaguru I knew. The Native Authority and all official recognition of "Kaguruness" are gone. Matriliny is not even legal. By now all of the elders I knew are dead, and probably, due to HIV/AIDS, so are many other younger people I knew, though like me, they are now far from young. The population of Tanzania has probably tripled since I first arrived, so I assume it has also vastly increased in Ukaguru as well. The Berega hospital station, founded by the Christian CMS mission, where I briefly lived, still serves Ukaguru, and recent reports about it indicate that life is still very hard for many rural Kaguru, especially women (Grady 2009a, 2009b). Despite these drawbacks, there are now Kaguru with college educations and some influence. Tanzania's economy and social conditions are now far better than when I was last there, though life is still difficult. The Kaguru are an attractive, tough, and resourceful people who have endured much. They live in a beautiful countryside. They deserve better than what history has so far given them. They were kind and good to me, and I wish them a better future than their past.

CONCLUSION

This study is concerned with one small and relatively remote chiefdom in East Africa. In many ways this system was far more economically and politically undeveloped and insignificant than others that have been described in studies of colonial rule in East Africa. Far more attention has been paid to other peoples and to rich, complex, and populous areas such as the interlacustrine kingdoms of Uganda, the Kikuyu of Kenya, with their violent and tortured relations with British settlers and missionaries, and the prosperous and educated coffee-growing Chagga and Haya of Tanzania (Tanganyika). Ukaguru and its people lacked the drama and flash of these places. Yet the seemingly drab ordinariness of the Kaguru situation may make it more representative of most of East Africa. In any case, I know of no single study of grassroots colonialism in East Africa as detailed as mine, though the total body of literature on some areas and ethnic groups surpasses my work. My study has aimed at being a fuller, broader picture of everyday colonial political life and concerns in one chiefdom. In that I believe it represents a first of its kind. I tried to represent the culture of local colonialism (Dirks 1992:3; Cannadine 1995:194), a pervasively exploitative system (Fanon 1967b:80) with a "somewhat pathological character" (Balandier 1966:56).

I have provided much case material and many anecdotes to create a sense of everyday concerns and events. I related the aims and difficulties of a wide range of local Africans and British involved in the district. I did not provide the views of those few Arabs and Indians involved in the area. Still, I tried to approach a more holistic account of colonial life, of the kind of "plural society" mentioned by Furnivall, Balandier, and Gluckman.

The major subject of my study was the Kaguru Native Authority, the organization embodying Indirect Rule, which the British repeatedly described as the guiding principle behind their local colonial government in East Africa. In discussing Indirect Rule, I tried to show how this led to extensive amalgamation and emphasis on a "tribal" system, on ethnic values and practices that might provide a common base for a people to be plausibly ruled as a coherent group. Such an ethnic group, supposedly deriving from customs and values from the past, developed into a people holding a sense of unity and identity unlikely to have existed in so strong a form in the precolonial era. This new "tribal" or ethnic identity, embodied by Indirect Rule, became a concept utilized by Kaguru and by the British, sometimes in opposing ways. It became an impediment to modern colonial and later national identity and change (see Lonsdale 1992:316–318, 468; Dumbuya 1995:133; Berman 1996:207).[1] This was in contradiction to British claims that such rule would enable Africans eventually to modernize. While Indirect Rule provided a base for local solidarity against the inroads of an authoritarian and meddling colonial government, it did not provide a successful opportunity for leadership by a small but growing African educated elite (Samoff 1979b:53; Fanon 1963:34). Indirect Rule and the Kaguru identity on which it was based did create the Kaguru Native Authority, a loosely workable though "rickety" framework through which everyday affairs and services could be carried out, though without extensive modernization. It was a system where a few Africans and British needed one another (Robinson 1972:118–121, 139), but where most local Africans had little effective voice. If it was at times unjust and conflict-ridden, it does not seem to have been more unjust or violent than what was reported to have existed before colonialism or what immediately followed after national independence. To many Kaguru, living in a system determined by non-African officials was probably no worse than later being oppressed by corrupt and authoritarian outsider Africans, which is what occurred with independence.

In my account of Kaguru local rule I showed that the few British colonial officers engaged in such rule were not the villains sometimes recently portrayed by critics of colonialism. Many struggled to administer as honestly and fairly as they knew how. They saw their tasks as honorable and constructive contributions to stability and order in the district. They claimed they wanted a better life for Africans, though what they actually wanted may not really have been better than what Africans presently had. Nor was it probably what Africans would have wanted, if they could have changed things. After all, these British administrators knew surprisingly little about the African people they governed. Still, what ordinary Africans themselves wanted often seemed misconceived in terms of what was realistic. The British rarely asked Africans what they wanted. Worse, they failed to provide Africans with the proper educational and economic opportunities that would have helped them achieve their aims, or at least think clearly about what those aims should have been. The British record on education was particularly shabby (Lohrmann 2007:70). This was in part because well-educated Africans would not have fit into the conservative model of a traditional African society that best fit the British idea of Indirect Rule. If one were to assign blame for this stagnant system, then responsibility for most of these problems rested at a higher level than local or even territorial government. It rested on policies envisaged in London.

One of the worst aspects of the Tanganyikan colonial regime was that it produced a government that claimed to know what its supposedly ignorant subjects needed and wanted, but actually produced a government distrusted by and alien to those it ruled. It was ultimately alien to most Africans, and it was even viewed skeptically by many British local officials at the grass roots. It was a rule imposed from the top down on Africans and local British administrators alike. This government built some roads, clinics, schools, and courthouses, but these were more symbols of change, since the local people had little part in choosing them. The broad effect was that the "profound paternalism of the colonial state imprinted itself on the popular mind the expectation that these services were an entitlement; yet at the same time the state was perceived as a hostile, alien intrusion" (Young 1988:59). It tried to infantilize a population, even as it claimed to educate. Unfortunately, this baneful situation only intensified with African independence, which was also inevitably paternalistic.

Lower-level British colonial administrators almost never closely followed the many and contradictory directives they received from superiors at the provincial and territorial level. Instead, they diverged to make the local system more workable and bearable for themselves. Few, if any, of these administrators saw Indirect Rule and the resultant Kaguru Native Authority as desirable blueprints to be followed closely. Rather, these were obstructions to pragmatic rule. Yet, however questionable this was, it seemed all that could be expected, since few had the courage or convictions to oppose territorial policies openly or wholeheartedly. The resulting organizational illusions and subterfuges lent a sense of hypocrisy and cant to much of the governmental rhetoric about the mission of colonialism, especially in a place like Tanganyika, which as a mandated territory was theoretically open to outside inspection and was not officially a colony.

My study showed how a very small group of African and British agents maintained considerable order for decades in a large area, poorly articulated with those ruling at the top who claimed to be working toward building a proper government. These officials struggled to do this with small staffs and poor communications. There was little funding, since the territory was expected to support itself (McCarthy 1982:23; Berman 1996:75). The system failed to provide proper political, educational, and economic development, but such changes were never possible, given the small numbers of administrators provided and the lack of external funds invested in the colonial endeavor. Only toward the very end of colonial rule were large metropolitan funds pumped in from overseas.

All these facts contradict any misconceived or hypocritical claims that colonial rule was well thought out and efficient, or that its resulting form of domination was coherent and consistent. What occurred in everyday colonial life at the grassroots level was often at odds with what was presented in the official pronouncements about Indirect Rule in territorial evaluations, and with what was reported from below to those higher up who wrote those evaluations. This was not only inevitable but perhaps for the best at the time, since it thwarted the implementation of many misconceived policies dreamed up by governors and the colonial office. Such administrative "slippage" underscored the fact that official information about what went on locally in a colony rarely corresponded closely with reality (see Berman 1996:33, 80–83, 88–97). Indirect Rule, and therefore the British pattern of colonial rule in East Africa, were based on so many contradictions and misconceptions, so many illusions and delusions, that they could never have worked as they were officially described and praised. Colonialism's inefficiency and impenetrability to those at the top and to those outside provided many opportunistic openings for lower-level rulers, British and African, to find their own solutions outside the official framework. Colonial rule, with its short-comings, did not create a system satisfactory to most of those involved, but then neither did the system before colonial rule, nor did the African nationalist system that supplanted both.

The most dangerous weakness in this system, one that caused griev-ous problems after Tanganyika's sudden independence, was the scandal-ous failure by the British to promote African higher education. There were few Africans, and certainly no Kaguru, with sufficient education to assume high-level posts in administration at the time of decolonization. There were some Kaguru, such as those involved in USA and Umwano, who felt angry that they could not realize their ambitions and dreams, to take part effectively in any government at all. The inadequate educa-tion they did have only further fueled their frustration. These conflicts and distress must have been repeated and compounded all over the new nation. The supposed goal of enlightened colonialism, and certainly the aim reiterated in New York at the United Nations during the era of the Mandate, were to foster modernization and self-rule. Those admirable ends were never honestly pursued by those in power.

My study is an account of illusions and delusions put into action. Much of the local colonial "success" that officials reported as achieved amounted to far less in reality. Yet I also hope my study provides enough ethnographic detail to show that colonialism was more complex, locally varied, and diversely conceived and enacted than has sometimes been claimed. My study's value rests on its descriptive, ethnographic details. I hope it reflects little of the glib, Foucaultian "literary constructions" that have often lately passed for social analyses of colonial life (see Wind-schuttle 1997:121–157). In postwar writings there have been calls for a new and better anthropology of colonialism (e.g., Thomas 1994:17). There have been perceptive analyses of the earlier works by others on colonial topics, though such critics provide little ethnographic reportage of such reality on their own (e.g., Shaw 1995). What we need are more accounts of particular situations in social detail—though unfortunately these are now ever harder to come by. Those who recall colonial life firsthand are dying off. Massive colonial archives and collections of memoirs, diaries, and letters are yet to be fully and properly examined, and some oral history can still be collected.

I believe colonialism will increasingly be judged as less well organized and therefore less well conceptualized by its practitioners than its past critics envisioned it. Up to now, many British steadfastly refuse to acknowledge a mass of discreditable events, to acknowledge how poor their record was (Porter 2007:6–7). Colonialism had a vast impact on the peoples it subjugated, but also on the dominators as well. Its influences were never as clear or coherent as is sometimes claimed. Colonialism is credited with too much rationality and efficiency. Its motives were not entirely malevolent, as some of its critics argue, though, no matter how one views it, one still finds that it was founded on economic exploitation, coercion, and the ethnocentric domination and disruption of one culture and society by another. It was permeated with racism (ibid.:7), with a view of its subjects as "non-adult races" (Davis 1973:385–386). Yet to deconstruct the imposing facade of colonial rule does not lessen colonialism's historical power or importance or the fact that many colonialistic attitudes influenced its former subjects . As Thackeray noted: "The dignity of history sadly diminishes as we grow better acquainted with the materials that compose it" (Sutherland 1970:15).

Reviewing what we have learned about colonial administration and Indirect Rule, several features appear that should make it clear why I used terms such as "illusion" and "delusion" when introducing the issue of colonialism. While force was at the heart of all colonial rule, it was rarely used once the system was in place. This led much colonial literature, especially that published before World War II, to imply that British rule was accepted by most of the empire's subject Africans. This was a major delusion of colonial rule. Colonial rule was always resented by most Africans. It was tolerated because Africans saw little hope of ousting their oppressors. They knew the force behind it. Africans also found ways to get on in a system they disliked. That was because Indirect Rule incorporated many Africans into the system, leading them to believe they had some advantages cooperating with their oppressors. While this system made use of a bureaucracy of white administrators who dominated their African underlings, it provided many loopholes for

Africans to elude British control. This was because the system held so many contradictions and therefore was never what it seemed.

The broad assumption behind this ruling hierarchy was that Africans would communicate helpfully with the British, informing them about what occurred below and then carrying out British orders they received from on high. Since the British deliberately remained distant from the Africans—in part because they thought social distance enhanced authority and respect, in part because they disdained Africans—they did not know well what actually happened on the ground. African underlings consequently had more power than the British thought, because much that occurred out in the bush was not accessible to those British above. The drawback for Africans, at least for the Kaguru, was that they were so poorly educated that they could rarely strategically use the powers they did have to develop broader skills, resources, or influence.

While the British always believed they were better fit to rule than were the Africans, they were in fact not as well trained as they should have been. Anyone who has read about Sir Ralph Furse, who long selected colonial cadets, should know that he established a tradition where he rejected highly knowledgeable and technically skilled applicants. A general "classic" education, class connections, sportsmanship and British illusions about some sense of old-school loyalties, and county-squire living counted more. Even after Furse was gone, some of his nonrational thinking, prejudices, and sentiment persisted. Young is only partly right in his view that colonial administration changed: "The diverse assortment of military officers, adventure seekers and occasional psychopaths who mingled with the early generation of proconsuls was phased out in favor of an earnest cohort of professional functionaries schooled for service" (1988:149).

To the end, recruits for local administration received little proper training in just how to do their jobs. They were schooled in the spirit of service, but practical skills were neglected before they went out to Africa itself. The brief courses taught at schools such as Oxford and London hardly prepared recruits for what they encountered. New recruits continued to be mainly untutored in the languages, customs, and histories of those they would rule. If they did painfully pick up such knowledge once they were there, they were usually transferred to other areas for future service, supposedly to broaden their perspectives. Most recruits did not even know how to examine court cases or how to draw up a fiscal budget. They were expected to pick up these skills on the job and not through formal instruction. What initially mattered was "character." Consequently, one could hardly claim that these rulers were the most fit for administering the system, at least not according to the rational terms that Weber set for a proper modern bureaucracy, where education and technical skills count for so much. The illusions and delusions of British rule were twofold. The rulers did not rule the ruled to the degree they assumed, and the rulers themselves were not as able and all-knowing as they thought. Indeed, they often bungled a good deal and wasted a lot of time and effort during their first tour of duty, learning what could have already been taught. The system was riddled with ineptitude, inefficiency, and miscommunication. However, these British administrators were for the most part deeply honest about money and loyal in upholding middle-class values of morality, values not always held by British settlers or traders or by non-British colonial officials in other parts of Africa. Somehow the system did seem to work, more or less, but more because it was not what it claimed itself to be rather than because it was a well-conceived construction.

There were further contradictions in Tanganyikan colonial rule. While the British administrators at the top were not selected because of any technical or mental skills, gradually many other officers were. These were the officers in the specialized departments that were later added to the system. Those with backgrounds in medicine, veterinary studies, agriculture, forestry, and other fields often had considerable expertise. These new differences in training and understanding between branches of the colonial service were probably the main reasons those in the specialized services were rarely motivated to mesh with administrators in other sectors. Recruits to the administration also began to differ from old-timers after World War II, when ambitious and educated young men who previously would not have considered time in the colonies began to apply. This was because colonial service could be substituted for conscription into military service. In contrast, a shortage of recruits just after the war led to recruitment of military officers who were recently demobilized. These were older men rather than impressionable cadets, and they too contrasted with many already in colonial service. All these factors led to new and wider differences between colonial officials, differences that at times undermined the supposedly common ethos holding the administrative service together.

Differences and rivalries within the colonial administration probably led to another peculiar feature of the postwar system, one that permeated all levels, those of the whites and those of the Africans. That was an increasingly wordy and convoluted, even opaque, red tape—a demand for ever more reports and communication. With every year after World War II, more and more reports, seas of paperwork, were demanded. This seemed as much to legitimate a dubious system and safeguard officials' positions within it as it was to provide useful facts. Reports were increasingly written in a form of bureaucratic newspeak that was difficult for outsiders to translate (and difficult for some insiders as well). Such reports defended each level of administrative turf. Each protected its level from the one below and above, but also served to advance people up the system by reflecting "favorable" attitudes. This mass of reports did not necessarily reflect what was actually happening or what administrators candidly thought. Reports had to be read cautiously and skeptically. Official red tape was its own kind of illusion. As Weber well knew, with time a bureaucracy would become more than the tool it was intended to be, but would instead become a system that perpetuated and defended itself from external criticism and interference. The colonial administration was a bureaucracy, and inevitably far different from Weber's ideal model (see Weber 1938:196–244).

I provide one brief illustration of the bizarre qualities in this system. After Tanganyikan independence, a British friend of mine was still in charge of supervising a budget for the national government administration in Dar es Salaam. His original college training was in medieval history at Cambridge. When I asked how he got into bookkeeping, he explained that obviously there was no use for European medieval history in Africa and he had abilities doing accounts. He was apparently very good at what he did and enjoyed his work, but he had taken an odd and circuitous route into bureaucracy, rather like Chinese mandarins described by Weber who studied poetry and the classics in order to end up as magistrates and administrators. The method long survived in ancient China and surfaced in twentieth century colonial Tanganyika, but it seemed weirdly out of tune with the rhetoric of bringing modernity to a colony supposedly launched toward "progress."

When the British repeatedly spoke of their efficient and competent administrative system, their assertions were grounded on some peculiar methods and assumptions. They were deluded if they saw it as deeply rational or efficient. One did see that Africans were sensible to dissolve Indirect Rule as soon as they could, as well as to replace it with staff who were oriented toward nationalistic and less tribalistic goals. Unfortunately, as my preceding epilogue reveals, these new administrators and different government policies had their own destructive bases.

So far this conclusion has neglected the Africans ruled by this colonial system, even though they were the major subject of this study. I have so far emphasized the British because, in reading the colonial literature, I found that few anthropological works had taken much cognizance of the British who dominated colonial Africans' worlds, perhaps because the British were not visible in most Africans' everyday lives, the lives most anthropologists studied. I now briefly summarize what this study told us about these Africans.

In this study the central feature of African (mainly Kaguru) life involved the conflicts and mixed motives generated by Indirect Rule and the Native Authority it created. This was a system that was both plausible and practical and yet ill-conceived and misguided. It was plausible and practical in the short run because it enabled a very small number of white administrators to rule a large area inhabited by a huge number of black people utterly alien, culturally, to those who tried to rule them. Yet those who advocated Indirect Rule promoted a profoundly contradictory system, one that inevitably held its own seeds of self-destruction and harmful consequences.

The British considered Indirect Rule the best way to teach Africans how to enter the modern world. They thought gradual change under the leadership of traditional (tribal) rulers would make change less disruptive. Even if the changes that had already occurred had made such leaders questionable or even eliminated them, they were rehabilitated, or even created, and African traditions were enlivened or invented. African rural people were considered too backward to be directly confronted with any modern type of government. They were seen as "childlike," both simple and yet potentially dangerous because of their simplicity. Africans were thought to need authoritative teachers. (It was no accident that later, when the "missionizing" and authoritarian Nyerere took over Tanganyika, the informal title he most liked to assume was that of *mwalimu*—teacher—a title that implicitly assumed that most Tanganyikans resembled childlike students.) The Native Authorities spawned by Indirect Rule operated under the assumption that customs and tradition provided the civil order by which Africans would lead peaceful lives under colonial rule. Modernity was tacitly assumed by the British to lead to disorder and disobedience. Presumably, ordinary Africans could not "handle it." Consequently, one doubts that many British colonialists thought Africans would ever govern themselves, at least not for a very long time.

The very means by which Native Authority leaders were selected contradicted modern values, thinking, and goals. Since these "traditional" leaders were appointed and sustained by the British, they were more dependent on the British than on their own people to remain in office. While they were described as spokesmen and teachers of their people, they would have been dismissed if they had spoken out for their own people against most aspects of British rule. They were expected to enforce British policies such as taxation, recruitment of labor, and alienation of land, despite any objections by their own people. They were rarely allowed to institute any new laws themselves, only those devised by the British and those passed off as African tribal customs, which did not conflict with British aims or prejudices. Finally, because they were uneducated, which was part of their characterization as traditional and authentic, they were provided with small salaries, far beneath what they themselves thought they deserved. This inevitably made almost all such officials corrupt, since bribes and extortion were their only means available to enhance their incomes to fit the prestige they wrongly assumed they had. While this was consistent with traditional African ideas about chiefs getting tribute and gifts, it conflicted with British ideas about proper government. Such corruption did, however, fit with British stereotypes of Africans being so flawed that they should not rule without supervision. Some corruption was therefore usually tolerated by the British as an inevitable weakness of African officials.

These images of Africans and African society, conjured up by British assumptions underlying Indirect Rule, reinforced British paternalism and domination and impeded most attempts by ordinary educated Africans to effect change. British preferred "traditional life," a life that was tribal, rural, and uneventful. This was easy to govern because it was not disturbed by modernity and excluded young, educated, restless Africans from assuming power. Local uneducated elders were the ones British consulted about the selection of chiefs and headmen, and these old men had no desire to be displaced by educated youth. Furthermore, educated young men would never have wanted Native Authority posts under the current arrangement. These would have to provide higher wages consistent with modern values and needs, and that was something the British were loath to pay for.

The British preoccupation with rural, traditional Africans led them to underrate the importance of Africans who lived outside the bounds of Native Authorities, those Africans who best epitomized the most modernizing trends in the colony. Migrant African laborers, traders, petty government specialist officials, and townspeople were seen as potential sources of disorder and therefore discouraged from engaging in politics. The British were inept at dealing with such Africans and continually sought to categorize them as some sort of atypical, detribalized people temporarily adrift from the tribal societies in which they no longer dwelled. The British hung on to tribal labels and stereotypes. Doing so, they tried to ignore the demands of "new" Africans. The British preoccupation with Indirect Rule blinded them from thinking realistically about any urban Africans who did not fit their picture of natives living orderly lives bound by customs in rural areas. Time and again this was proved to be a deadly flaw to British thinking about colonial development and the growing importance of changing, modern African leadership. Besides, there was a tribalism outside that of the Native Authorities. It involved the young, educated, and disaffected Africans excluded from these various tribal councils. This youthful "alternate tribalism" was important but short-lived. In Ukaguru it was expressed in Umwano and USA. Soon, however, such tribalistic organizations were replaced by labor unions and national political parties that were more powerful precisely because they transcended tribal boundaries. Some of these leaders had begun their training with unsuccessful attempts to lead more parochial tribalistic movements, the most famous being those involving the Kikuyu in neighboring Kenya. British stereotypes about Indirect Rule and tribalism eventually backfired, producing frustrated and aggressive young leaders who had been excluded from the old system and who correctly saw this earlier system of Indirect Rule and tribal values as an obstacle to modernity—an obstacle to be undermined.

Indirect Rule was envisioned as preventing the turmoil and unrest of modernity. Eventually, the very flaws and contradictions embodied in Indirect Rule spawned changes and tainted ethnicity and tribalism themselves, though, often for the worse, these notions persist even today. Now, tribalism has been conflated with local interest; now, local groups put upon by autocratic centralizing governments still find tribal or ethnic values the easiest rallying points for protest against oppression. Unfortunately, this trend is related to ethnic violence and discrimination as well. No wonder that today tribe and ethnicity have so many negative associations for many modern African intellectuals. To call someone "tribalistic" insultingly suggests that such a person stands in the way of national "progress." The reverberations of Indirect Rule are manifold.

My ethnography of local colonial rule has benefitted from a knowledge of Weberian theory about bureaucratic organizations mainly because this led me to grasp how far both the colonial and postcolonial systems of administration diverged from any such rational model. The reasons for this divergence were economic, political, and cultural and were "rational" only in terms of short-term political expediency and certain deluded pseudosocialistic ideas. They were contradictory with one another and ultimately destructive.[2]

Despite its many flaws, the British colonial administrative system was at first retained by the Africans after independence because Africans needed time to devise a replacement. The changes they finally made, the politicization of the administration and the creation of a one-party undemocratic state dominated by an educated or semi-educated minority, were not the big departures one might at first have thought. Rule was still by a "missionizing" elite who claimed they, rather than the people they ruled, knew what was good for the masses. Like the British earlier, these new African pseudosocialistic leaders had few qualms about enforcing unpopular policies. Like the British before them, they shared little understanding or empathy for those they governed, and they disguised the brutality and corruption of their policies with sanctimonious, nationalistic rhetoric. As Young perceptively observed: "The new states were not simply bureaucratic autocracies, alien to boot, like their colonial predecessors. They were political mongrels legitimated by frequently nationalist ideology, ritual consecrated by periodic electoral ceremonies" (1988:57). Like the preceding colonial government, this was a system embodying delusion and illusion, along with a good bit of self-righteousness and hypocrisy. The past does bend the present to its image. As the old adage goes, the more things seem to change, the more they remain the same. What Heussler depressingly observes about the history of Tanganyika's colonial administration probably applies just as aptly to the black rule that followed with independence: "What was planned did not happen and what happened was not foreseen until it was too late for the planners to do much about it" (1971:60).

This is my final book on the Kaguru, but not, I hope, my last publication about them. The world I have described here is gone, but that world still haunts Tanzania, because many of its features influence its present problems. I have not returned to Tanzania for many years, but I have closely followed events in that country and tried to keep up on publications about it. This study makes no claim to encompass Tanzania, but only to describe one small area in it, and then to show how it was, rather than how it is today, even though I obviously think the past is tied to the present. I hope I have made colonialism and modernization seem more understandable and vivid than more general historical or political studies could do. Most of all, I hope that I have made the Kaguru's past and their part of the world come alive for a moment. Living in Ukaguru and knowing African people were the most important experiences in my life.

APPENDICES

Appendix 1. Population of Ukaguru, Kilosa District (1957), Non-African Population (my estimates)

AREA	INDIANS	SOMALIS	ARABS	EUROPEANS
Lowlands	160	–	200	–
Plateau	30	50	40	4
Mountains	–	–	–	2

The Europeans are missionaries and two reclusive farmers with almost no current relations with African residents of Ukaguru. The Somalis, Indians, and Arabs are all petty traders.

Appendix 2. Estimates of Population Per Square Mile (my estimates)

SUBCHIEFDOM	APPROX. SIZE IN SQ. MI	APPROX. POP. PER SQ. MI.	% OF TOTAL POP.
Mamboya	580	31.0	27.9%
Geiro	170	51.0	13.0%
Idibo	310	48.3	22.2%
Nong'we	255	21.5	8.2%
Msowero	600	**	26.2%

**The large sisal estates make computation of population living by cultivation and animal husbandry impossible to figure. I assume that relatively few inhabitants are Kaguru and that the majority of people in the area are temporary residents on the estates and not subject to the Kaguru Native Authority. I estimate that about 11,000 alien Africans reside in lowland Ukaguru, either on the estates or connected in some way to them. I have not been able to exclude the estate populations from these figures derived from the census. I assume that were I to do so the percentages in the final column of the table would increase considerably.

Appendix 3. Ethnic Population of Ukaguru (1957)

AREA	KAGURU	BARAGUYU	NGULU	KAMBA	GOGO	OTHER	TOTAL
Lowlands							
Msowero	6,670	60	100	–	820	11,344	18,974
Plateau							
Mamboya	17,252	694	216	3	74	431	18,680
Idibo	10,734	520	1,649	1,677	100	195	14,875
Geiro	8,154	170	52	4	139	158	8,677
Mountains							
Nong'we	5,429	2	–	–	25	60	5,514
Total	48,349	1,424	2,017	1,684	1,157	12,188	66,719

(My total used estimates from original census forms and sample forms for parts of the area: I have assumed these are more accurate than the published forms.)

Total	48,249	1,424	1,939	1,889	1,157	12,062	66,720

Appendix 4. Ethnic Population of Ukaguru (1957) by percentages

AREA	KAGURU	BARAGUYU	NGULU	KAMBA	GOGO	OTHER
Lowlands						
Msowero	35.1%	00.2%	00.5%	–	6.4%	57.8%
Plateau						
Mamboya	92.4%	3.7%	1.1%	–	00.3%	2.1%
Idibo	72.1%	3.4%	11.0%	11.2%	00.7%	1.2%
Geiro	93.9%	3.9%	00.6%	–	1.6%	1.1%
Mountains						
Nong'we	98.4%	–	–	–	00.4%	1.0%
Official total	72.3%	2.3%	2.9%	2.9%	2.3%	17.3%

**Appendix 5. Ethnic Populations of Mamboya and Idibo Chiefdoms (1957)
(% given in parentheses wherever significant)**

		MAMBOYA CHIEFSHIP				
HEADMANSHIP	KAGURU	BARAGUYU	KAMBA	NGULU	OTHERS	TOTAL
Mamboya	1,340 (83.1)	229 (14.2)	–	1	42	1,612
Mwandi	1,006 (98.0)	10	–	9	1	1,026
Magubike	1,136 (88.5)	88 (6.9)	–	11	48	1,283
Berega	639 (91.4)	57 (8.1)	–	1	2	699
Mgugu	2,584 (88.3)	198 (6.7)	3	107	34	2,926
Nyangala	1,025 (89.9)	39 (3.6)	–	32	44	1,140
Mloko	657 (83.4)	–	–	–	130	787
Mtumbatu	1,203 (97.4)	–	–	5	23	1,231
Mkundi I	155 (81.5)	–	–	17	18	190
Kitange I	830 (95.0)	24 (2.9)	–	–	11	865
Kitange II	1,711 (93.4)	49 (2.2)	–	15	57	1,832
Maundike I	594 (92.2)	–	–	17	33	644
Maundike II	467 (99.1)	–	–	–	4	471
Njung'wa	694 (98.7	–	–	–	9	703
Msong'we	220 (100)	–	–	–	–	220
Ihanga*	283	–	–	1	3	287
Uponela	1,274 (99)	–	–	–	–	1,274
Ikwamba	1,179 (97.2)	–	–	–	34	1,213
Kifwe	265 (100)	–	–	–	–	265
Total	17,262 (92.4)	694 (3.7)	3	216	493	18,768

*About two-thirds of this population are Kaguru men brought here for forced labor
from elsewhere for a reforestation scheme.

		IDIBO SUBCHIEFSHIP				
HEADMANSHIP	KAGURU	BARAGUYU	KAMBA	NGULU	OTHERS	TOTAL
Idibo	1,578 (77.4)	11 (0.6)	111 (5.4)	266 (13.0)	71	2,037
Chakwale	1,050 (77.5)	32 (3.7)	1	222 (16.4)	49	1,354
Leshata	556 (45.3)	33 (5.9)	529 (43.1)	106 (7.8)	2	1,226
Iyogwe	796 (83.2)	27 (2.7)	–	118 (12.3)	14	955
Chisulwa	155 (43.2)	–	–	196 (55.8)	5	356
Chilama	824 (87.5)	–	–	107 (12.9)	10	941
Chagoale	225 (44.2)	–	–	283 (55.8)	–	508
Talagwe	1,413 (82.8)	65 (3.9)	60 (3.6)	72 (4.4)	23	1,633
Makuyu	1,106 (87.4)	53 (4.0)	3	96 (7.6)	7	l,265
Ndogami	428 (32.8)	71 (5.4)	744 (57.0)	4	46	1,303
Nguyami	1,376 (72.7)	94 (4.8)	220 (11.6)	149 (7.8)	53	1,894
Chibedya	1,225 (87.3)	134 (9.5)	9	30	5	1,403
Total	10,732 (72.1)	520 (3.4)	1,677 (11.2)	1,649 (11)	285	14,863

Appendix 6. Per Capita Holdings of Livestock by Kaguru in Various Areas (1957) (Contrast first five mountain areas with the other plateau areas)

HEADMANSHIP	BOVINES	GOATS	SHEEP	DONKEYS
Uponela	0.34	0.64	0.17	0.01
Mtumbatu	1.58	0.87	0.24	0.06
Kumbulu	0.42	0.90	0.33	–
Chang'ong'we	0.60	0.92	0.54	0.01
Ikwemba	0.34	0.64	0.17	0.02
Idibo	0.22	1.42	0.09	0.002
Geiro	0.57	0.26	0.13	0.016
Berega	0.01	0.98	0.32	0.007
Magubike	–	1.94	0.49	0.01
Maundike I	–	0.82	0.13	–

Per capita holdings by ethnic group for Ukaguru (1957)

ETHNIC GROUP	BOVINES	SHEEP	GOATS	DONKEYS
Kaguru	0.233	0.39	0.11	0.007
Baraguyu	3.03*	0.22	0.09	0.09
Kamba & Ngulu**	0.57	1.86	0.22	0.08

* I estimate that all these government figures for Baraguyu cattle holdings are below actual holdings. I estimate these to be about eight bovines per capita.
**I could not obtain government figures separating these two groups.

Appendix 7. Livestock Holdings in Ukaguru

ETHNIC GROUP	CHIEFDOM	BOVINES	GOATS	SHEEP	DONKEYS
Baraguyu	Mamboya	1,943	391	164	48
	Idibo	1,506	125	46	41
	Geiro	1,214	72	18	79
	Nong'we	–	–	–	–
Total		4,663	588	228	168
Kaguru	Mamboya	3,325	7,346	1,770	193
	Idibo	2,424	4,534	989	23
	Geiro	4,655	2,184	1,079	137
	Nong'we	1,589	5,099	1,696	–
Total		11,993	19,163	5,534	353
Others	Mamboya	455	2,762	768	12
	Idibo	1,654	5,391	636	245
	Geiro	–	30	21	2
	Nong'we	–	–	–	–
Total		2,109	8,183	1,425	259

Appendix 8. Cash Sales in Kaguru Native Authority Markets 1958
(crops in plateau, lowlands, and mountain areas)

Figures to the nearest thousand kilo. Figures below 1,000 kilos not listed. All seven Kaguru Native Authority markets indicated.

	GEIRO	RUBEHO	IDIBO	MAMBOYA	CHAKWALE	KITETE	CHANG'ONG'WE
maize	138	111	17	2	188	–	2
sorghum	17	1	–	–	5	–	–
castor	136	123	4	22	111	1	18
beans	–	–	1	12	4	1	4

Appendix 9. Charter of Establishing the Court of the Chief of Ukaguru

I have followed the form of the government text, capitalizing some words and arranging lines as presented rather than by forming proper sentences.

REGULATION
By the order of His Excellency the Governor, I, Eric George Rowe, the Provincial Commissioner of Eastern Province, have certified that the Court of the Chief of Ukaguru has been firmly established as this:

AUTHORITY
The area of this court will have an authority in this area over the country of Ukaguru.
Cases which cannot be dealt with (Part 13)
This court will not have authority in the following areas:
(a) If a man is accused because he has murdered or any similar case which can receive capital punishment.
(b) All cases which are in regard to marriage management but if it is a local marriage or the bride-price or adultery can be dealt with by the local order. [this excludes dissolution of church marriages]
(c) All cases which are concerned with farms and soil which have been written in the book to follow the Land Registry Ordinance. (This excludes lands alienated from Kaguru.)
(d) All cases which are concerned with witchcraft.
Cases which can be heard (part 15)
This court can fulfil and hear:
(a) Those cases concerning local authorities if they are good and if they are not against the Government.
(b) Regulations and all orders of the local authority which have got power in the area of authority of this court.
(c) Order and other law which the court has been permitted to set-up.
Cases of Legal Claims (Part 12)
By the regulation of this charter this court is allowed to listen to any cases of dispute which can appear in this area of authority or if the one being sued resides in its area. But all cases of dispute concerned with farms and soil are not under the authority of this court, these cases may be heard in this court but the D.C. has the power to change a verdict.
Again disputes concerned with great amounts of money (3000/ or more) will not be listened to in this court, also disputes of not more than sixty cows; but in cases of inheritance the court shall not hear cases of more than 3000/ or sixty cows if the heirs have not come to terms, but if the heirs are in agreement, the court may deal with legacies above 3000/ or sixty cows. If the heirs come to terms there is no limit in the amount dealt with in inheritance matters.

Cases of Breaking the Order (Part 16)

This court has power to judge any African who does not keep law in this area of authority, and if he is reported to have helped any wrong-doer.

The Power of Punishment (Part 16)

In cases of disobedience this court can do the following:

(a) Fine of not more than 1000/ and

(b) to give punishment of imprisonment of people for not more than one year and to give punishment of five sticks not more than eight strokes but not in the following cases only:

> (1) to beat someone severely or because the victim is very young or very old or is not strong or a woman or because the one who is beating has used a dangerous weapon or has great power.
>
> (2) The stealing of cattle, but not any man who is under sixteen years can receive punishment of being beaten in any case of disobedience.
>
> (3) To require a person who is found guilty often to show himself frequently to the court.
>
> (4) To confiscate soil or money and other things if these have been taken and used without justice. The court can give another order including the order of paying if justice is used. But any order in any case must be justly reached after examining the conditions of that case, again, in any case of punishment by imprisonment or sticks, or requiring a frequent wrong-doer to present himself to the court, or confiscation of soil or any articles, it is not good to finish this before the D. C. has been informed.

The court may choose any of the punishments which have been explained in this charter.

APPEAL

Appeals from this court can be sent to the District Council Kilosa. But some cases which have begun at the Courts of Msowero, Idibo, Kibedya, Geiro, Nong'we will be sent to the D. C. or Provincial Local Courts Officer Kilosa. If the Provincial Commissioner will agree, these will be sent to the Appeal Court at Dar es Salaam. But there will be no appeals if the fines in cases of disobedience and dispute are not more than 20, therefore every case concerned with dispute of soil, marriage (but the claim of bride-price only), divorce, to get jurisdiction of children or inheritance will be granted an appeal.

This court will listen to appeals from the following courts: Msowero, Kibedya, Geiro, Nong'we, Idibo.

It has been signed by the Provincial Commissioner 15/2/54.

Appendix 10. District Commissioners, Kilosa District (Kilosa District Book)

The information in the Kilosa District Book is incomplete for some of the administrative entries. For background information I relied on Kirk-Greene (1991), which does not contain information on all the names in the Kilosa District Book.

C. M. Coke, 2 January 1940–3 June 1942

N. C. Varian, 6 July 1942–19 August 1942
  b. 1900, educ. Avoca School, Blackrock, Dublin and Trinity College, Dublin

A. M. LeGeyt, 31 August 1942–31 July 1943
  b. 1902, educ. Victoria College, Jersey, Pembroke College, Oxford

M. G. Lewis, 27 July 1943–1 March 1944
  b. 1905, educ. St. Andrew's College and Rhodes University, Grahamstown, S.A., LL.B.

J. S. Darling, 1 March 1944–19 January 1945
  b. 1911, educ. Largan College, N. Ireland and Queen's University, Belfast, milit. Service 1943–6, lt. col.

P. W. I. Piggott, 18 December 1945–7 July 1946
  b. 1909, educ. Highgate School and Caius College, Cambridge

P. C. Duff, 8 July 1946–17 December 1946
  b. 1922, ed. Wellington College and New College, Oxford, milit. service 1941–2, lt.

D. W. I. Piggott, 18 December 1946–?, see entry above 1945

G. N. Clark, ?–23 January 1949
  b. 1901, educ. Dulwich College and Roy. Military College Sandhurst, milit. service 1939–48, lt. col.

H. M. Alleyne, 23 January 1949–26 May 1950
  b. 1899, educ. Blundells, milit. service 1918–29

M. H. Newman, 26 May 1950–13 October 1951
  b. 1911, educ. St. Paul's, Darjeeling and Bradley Court, milit. service 1934–45, commander R.N.

G. R. A. M. Johnston, 13 October 1951–13 January 1952
  b. ?, educ. Cheltenham College and St. John's College Cambridge
D.S.O, M.B.E., D.F.C.

L. M. Manson, 12 January 1952–30 July 1950
  b. 1920, educ. Merchiston School, S. A., Chatham House School, Ransgate and Royal Military College, Sandhurst, milit. Service 1938–48 major

I. F. Aers, 30 July 1953–15 April 1954
  b. 1921, educ. Dulwich College and Roy. Milit. College Sandhurst, milit. service 1939–48 major

L. M. Manson, 16 April 1954–28 March 1957, see above 1952

W. B. Helean, 20 March 1957–5 July 1958
  b. 1917, educ. Otago Boys' School and Victoria University, Wellington,
    N. Z., milit. service 1939–45, major (desp.)
J. M. Piper, 5 July 1952–28 May 1961
  b. 1918, ed. Canford
G. R. F. Henton, 29 May 1961–?
  b. 1927, educ. Christ's Hospital and St. John's, Cambridge
Assistant District Officers, Kilosa District
D. C. Flatt, 25 November 1938–2 March 1940
P. Bleackley (Cadet), 20 March 1939–30 August 1940
  b. 1915, educ. Merchant Taylor School and Jesus College, Oxford,
    Jurisprudence
R. B. Richardson, 27 August 1940–13 November 1940
  b. 1902, educ. Lansing College and Brasenose College, Oxford
A. G. Rige de Rogli (Cadet), 4 May 1942–2 January 1943
A. G. Harvey (Cadet), 4 May 1942–2 January 1943
L. A. Haldane, 5 January 1943–9 January 1943
  b. 1916, educ. Wellington College and Clare College Cambridge, milit.
    service 1940–2, capt.
P. L. Hairac, 12 January 1943–23 July 1944
R. C. H. Risley, 3 July 1944–5 November 1944
  b. 1917, educ. Winchester College and Oriel College, Oxford
P. C. Duff (Cadet), 14 October 1944–1 November 1944
  b. 1922, educ. Wellington College and New College, Oxford, milit.
    service 1941–2, lt.
R. S. Lloyd (Cadet), 14 October 1944–27 April 1947
  b. 1920, educ. St. Paul's School and Magdalene College, milit. service
    1939–40, major
J. J. McPhillips (contracted), 11 April 1947–?
  b. 1910, educ. St. Malachy's College, Belfast and Dublin, milit. service
    1937–46, major
J. Harris, ?–3 August 1948
  b. 1914, educ. King's College School, Wimbledon, milit. service
    1939–46, major
G. B. Mitchell, 1 January 1950–27 April 1950
  b. 1924, educ. Portsmouth Grammar School and Jesus College
    Cambridge. milit. service 1943–4, R.N. 1944–6
D. J. M. Bennett, 29 January 1950–27 April 1950
E. M. Younge, 3 October 1950–27 July 1951
D. W. F. Tulloch (Cadet). 24 September 1951–2 December 1951
  b. 1928, educ. Marlborough College, milit. service 1946–9, lt.
L. M. Manson, 16 April 1954–28 March 1957, see earlier entries
G. F. M. Woodland, 3 December 1959–?

M. B. Denton, August 1952–May 1953

I. B. Aers, 5 January 1952–30 July 1953, see earlier entry 1953

G. S. Gabb, 15 July 1953–?
  b. 1924, educ. Tunbridge School and Downing College. Cambridge,
  milit. service 1942–5, capt.

A. W. F. Russett (Cadet), 26 August 1953–9 September 1954

W. A. Brooks (Cadet), 3 September 1954–8 March 1955

M. D. Beardmore, 17 February 1955–28 July 1955

M. B. Dyson (Cadet), 1 September 1955–?

D. Fullerton, 9 April 1956–24 November 1958
  b. 1928, educ. Colchester Royal Grammar School, Birmingham and
  St. Catherine's College, Cambridge, milit. service 1946–8, 2nd lt.

R. W. Reardon, 10 July 1956–December 1957
  b. 1934, educ. Wanstead County High School, milit. service 1943–8, capt.

H. M. Magnay (Cadet), 21 August 1958–?

H. F. Lawson, 1 March 1959–15 July 1959

J. Y. Ellis (Cadet), 21 August 1959–25 February 1959

A. Dixon, 5 July 1959–April 1962

J. Redding (Cadet), 5 June 1959–?

B. Jenney ?

J. A. Campbell

Appendix 11. Kilosa District Native Authority Ordinances
[a shortened paraphrase; from Kilosa District Book]

Punishment for infractions of these ordinances cannot exceed 200 sh. fine or 2 months in prison or both.

Ordinances for all Native Authorities in District

No liquor sold before noon

No weapons at beer clubs

Local officials can prohibit all brewing during time of cultivation or famine (though special permission may be given for ceremonies for adolescent initiations, birth-celebrations, marriages, funerals, work-parties, offerings (ancestral propitiation)

No public gambling

No manufacture of firearms or their parts without permission [It was already a territory law that no one could own a firearm without a license]

No felling of trees on slopes which have not been cleared for 15 years

No urination within 20 yards of river

No bathing or washing 3 yards from source of drinking water

Report smallpox, meningitis, and other dangerous diseases

Report all deaths from serious diseases

No moving residence without reporting change to both one's new and old headmen

All taxpayers, unless monthly wage-earners, must plant cassava or potato fields

All those sent by officials to clear roads must do so

No marihuana or Indian hemp

Everyone must reserve enough seed for next year's planting; no one should sell food crops unless that person has enough reserves to supply own household

Everyone should co-operate in killing baboons, wild pigs, and locusts if officials declare these to be a danger to crops

Everyone must uproot and burn all refuse cotton plants

All parents must send their children to school

Ordinances pertaining to Ukaguru Chiefdom only:

No newcomers shall graze or water their livestock without the permission of the local headman [clearly directed against Baraguyu and Kamba]

Appendix 12. Chiefship of Ukaguru, Kilosa District

Court Areas and Headmanships with names of owner-clans in parentheses.
Numbers correspond to areas indicated on Map 6.

I. Mamboya Chiefship of Paramount Chief (Jumbe)

1. Mamboya (Jumbe)
2. Uponela (Ponela)
3. Njungwa (Ponela)
4. Maundike I (Gomba)
5. Maundike II (Njeja Kwama)
6. Chifwe (Nyandwa)
7. Msong'we (Salu)
8. Nyangala (Kami)
9. Magubike (Hehe)
10. Mloko (Sindugu)
11. Mkundi (Limbo)
12. Mwandi (Nyao)
13. Berega (Gowe)
14. Mgugu (Songo Duma)
15. Mtumbatu (Gomba)
16. Kitange II (Nyafula)
17. Kitange I (Jumbe Masa)
18. Ikwamba (Ng'hangafu)
19. Ihanga (Gweno)

II. Subchiefship of Idibo (Ganasa)

20. Idibo (Ganasa)
21. Talagwe (Mukema)
22. Mkuyu (Songo Ng'ombe)
23. Chilama (Gomba)
24. Chisulwa (Gweno)
25. Chogoali (Gomba)
26. Iyogwe (Gomba)
27. Leshata (Limbo)
28. Ndogomi (Gomba)
29. Nguyami (Gomba)
30. Chakwale (Mhako)

III. Subchiefship of Geiro (Jumbe)[1]

31. Geiro (Jumbe)
32. Kibedya[2]
33. Rubeho (Gomba)
34. Nholong'wa (Ng'anga)
35. Chisitwi (Ng'humi)
36. Chisambo (Shomi)

IV. Nong'we Subchiefship (Nyangasi)

37. Nong'we (Nyangasi)
38. Ching'holwa (Njagowe)
39. Kumbulu (Jong'we)
40. Chanjale (Chanjale)
41. Lukando (Logola)
42. Chang'ong'we (Ng'anga)
43. Mtega (Nyafula)
44. Msita (Nyagatwa)

V. Msowero Subchiefship (Nyafula)

45. Msowero (Nyafula)
46. Mvumi (Nyandwa)
47. Mhang'ati (Lulenga)
50. Mkobwe (Kimbilisi)
51. Chiluwa or Makambwe (Ngufa)
52. Kitete (Simba)

48. Luhulwe (Kami)

49. Mhowe (Mhowe)

53. Magole (Mukama)

54. Mkundi II (Nyafula)

Notes:

1. All colonial documents employ the name Geiro. Post-independence documents employ the name Gairo.

2. Formerly the site of a Baraguyu court that was closed in 1957; the number of Kaguru in the area was under 31. Some colonial documents employ the name Chibedya.

Appendix 13. A Very Old and Famous Court Case

This is the oldest case I found recorded for any Kaguru court. It was heard in Mamboya, and I was told it was a very famous dispute. I had to consult local Kaguru to understand what was happening and why Kaguru still remembered it. One could tell little from the record itself. In 1937, an old man named Magome brought his son, Ng'huyu, to the Mamboya Court when it was still presided over by Paramount Chief Justino Saileni. He recounted how in the previous year his son had tried to spear him but had missed. He had taken his son to the paramount chief's court, where the son had been warned to behave and his father persuaded to forgive him. Now the son had again attacked his father, this time with a bow and arrow, again missing him. Some said the son hated his father because the father meddled in a dispute between his son and the son's wife. His son's wife had left her husband because he was abusive. The accused son admitted trying to kill his father, but justified himself because he claimed his father had also wanted to kill him. The Mgugu headman (whose area was under the jurisdiction of the Mamboya Court) testified that the young man was quarrelsome and had also tried to kill him when he tried to settle the dispute. The Mgugu headman had urged the youth to leave the area. The youth moved to Idibo, but he repeatedly returned home to berate his father. The paramount chief's court elders noted that this was not the first time Ng'huyu had been brought to court for violent behavior. They sentenced him to three months in prison.

The entire record was less than three hundred words long. Without knowing this background to the case, and more, the record made little sense to me. I wondered how much sense it had made to the district officer who had read it, and I wondered why Kaguru considered it important. I later learned that Ng'huyu had married his cross-cousin, his father's sister's daughter. This is a preferred form of marriage among traditional Kaguru. It is advantageous to the father, who pays less bride-wealth and has more control of both his son and daughter-in-law than if his son had married an outsider. This woman had two children, but both died young. She had accused her husband of being unfit, implying that his quarreling had probably angered the ancestral dead into taking the children back in order to punish him. Magome defended the wife (his niece) when she was criticized by his son (her husband). Magome remained on good terms with her and on bad terms with his son.

The case was famous because Magome was a model matrilineal elder. He had married his niece to his son and showed intense loyalty to his niece, and therefore implicitly also loyalty to his sister, her mother. His son should always have deferred to his father, and in this case doubly so on account of the fact that his father had arranged a marriage that traditional Kaguru thought especially desirable. Magome had undoubtedly presumed that a cross-cousin marriage would be a stable one, which also had led to favorable arrangements and closer ties to his sister. However, it would also have been true that a son such as Ng'huyu would have always been in a weak position toward his own wife because she was also his father's niece. This also made him especially beholden to his father because of the bride-wealth, which had been raised by his father's manipulations rather than by Ng'huyu himself. Kaguru clinched their interpretation of the case by pointing out that the son had twice failed to kill his father. They argued that two such failed attempts surely showed that the father had supernatural protection from the ancestral dead who endorsed his conduct and disapproved of his son. The case was a kind of parable of reward and punishment for good and bad matrilineal behavior.

NOTES

PREFACE

1. I had earlier met Margery Perham on several occasions when I was a graduate student at Oxford. I even talked with her for about an hour in her office at Nuffield College. At that time, I had already done two years of fieldwork in East Africa. When I questioned her after her lecture, two years later, I doubt that she remembered me. I was never impressed with her views about Africans.

INTRODUCTION

1. Throughout this study I use the term "colonialist" rather than "colonist." A colonist is a person who settles permanently in a colony. A colonialist is a person who works in a colony but does not plan to remain there permanently. The British administrators I write about here planned on leaving when their terms ended. They looked forward to retiring back in Britain.

2. I remember his first words to me as an incoming graduate student: "You're American. I suppose you're Jewish as well." I should add that Evans-Pritchard's remarks were probably a bit calculated to fluster me, since I know he had been earlier told that my background was that of German Protestants.

1. KAGURU AND COLONIAL HISTORY

1. For earlier versions of various sections of this chapter see Beidelman 1962a, 1962b, 1970, 1971b, 1978, 1982a, 1982b:48–98. Throughout this text the word Ukaguru refers to the land where the Kaguru people live. The Kaguru speak a language called Chikaguru.

2. For information on such early raiding see Last 1883b:584–586, 1885:10; Meyer 1909:197, 202; Falkenhorst 1890:107–108; Fonck 1894:295; Schynse 1890:67–69; Pruen 1899:77; Schmidt 1892:10–12; *Church Missionary Intelligencer* 1880:735, 737, 743; Rees 1902; A. N. Wood 1889b:24–26; O'Neill 1878:8; Church Missionary Society, *Proceedings of the Church Missionary Society* 1877:405; 1880:735, 739; Meyer 1909:197, 202; Tucker 1911:30; Beidelman 1970:83–86. Briggs's account suggests that this raiding

continued even into the early twentieth century (1918:76–77). For even earlier but thin accounts of the area see Burton 1860, I:168–169; Speke 1863:48–54; Stanley 1872: 161–170.

3. Establishing of such stations was typical all along the caravan route, not just Ukaguru (Kjekshus 1977a:122–123).

4. Arning gives an annual figure of 100,000 for 1890, though he does not indicate how he determined this (1936:316). Fuchs reports 29,000 inbound in 1903–04 and 38,000 in 1904–05 (1907:19). Schynse reports large numbers (1890:71). Langheld reports 100,000 (1909:38). *Deutsche Kolonialblatt* states that 200 slave caravans passed through Mpwapwa in 1887 (1890:69). Stuhlmann estimates 100,000 passed through Mpwapwa yearly (1894:216).

For descriptions of these caravans and how they operated see Beidelman 1982b; K. M. Cameron 1990:15–30.

5. The first published statement describing Kaguru as matrilineal is by Thurnwald (1950:115), though many earlier writers noted that nephews inherited property and authority.

6. In all official colonial literature the important subchiefdom, headmanship, and settlement are named Geiro. In the postcolonial literature this name has been changed to Gairo.

7. Masingisa seems identical with the powerful chief Sekwao described by Wood in his account of his visit to Geiro in 1889. Yet Wood was told that the Geiro chief was the son of the Sultan of Mamboya, not that he was his elder brother. The accounts seem to vary with which Kaguru group provides them. What is clear is that Jumbe clansmen from Mamboya and Geiro had long and enduring links (Wood 1890:183–185).

Alliances between Baraguyu and Kaguru were not unique to Geiro. Rees (1902) also reports that the local Kaguru leader at Mlali, twenty miles south–southwest of Geiro, had also made blood brotherhood with Baraguyu and was raiding or extorting protection payments from caravans with their help.

The rise of leaders who could control resources is a common feature of similar societies in this cultural area at this time; see Giblin 1996:236–137.

There are reports of chiefs in the west at Mpwapwa, Mlali, and elsewhere, but since those do not involve Kilosa district, I have not investigated them. It is reported that in 1884 there were battles over the chiefship at Mpwapwa between those at the caravan post and the hill Kaguru living outside (Price 1884).

8. Kaguru joking-relations are complex. I discuss them in detail elsewhere (Beidelman 1986:124–134).

Some Gomba claimed that Saidi had married a Gomba woman but later fled the area and made allies with the Baraguyu. Hence, he owed his power to outsiders and not to true Kaguru. Gomba also claimed that because they were the true owners of the Mamboya area, only they should and do make rain there.

9. Peters is also described as securing allegiance from the Kaguru leader at Mvomero in the lowlands to the southeast of Mamboya, though this had little implication for later Kaguru politics. Some sources deny that Peters ever reached the Mamboya area, only Msowero in the lowlands, but Kaguru oral tradition repeatedly states otherwise (Lewin 1915:173).

10. In 1885 the Germans also established a station at Sima just south of Ukaguru (Falkenhorst 1890:47). Earlier a Frenchman named Bloyet established a trading post at Kondoa near Kilosa in 1880, but it was soon abandoned (Müller 1959:117).

11. Oliver asserts that at the smaller, more remote stations missionaries were the key agents for all economic change (1952:69). This would certainly be true for Ukaguru.

12. Stoecker describes Peters as a "psychopath" and a "criminal" (1977:95). He was certainly a very nasty person.

13. At the outbreak of World War I it was estimated that nearly 500 muzzle-loaders were held by Africans in the area (Admiralty 1916:42, 84).

14. The Kaguru did not offer any help to the Germans (Church Missionary Society, *Proceedings of the Church Missionary Society* 1889–90:45, 51–54).

15. In 1889 Hermann von Wissmann recruited 600 Sudanese from Egypt, 850 Shangans (Zulu?) from Mozambique, and 50 Somalis, along with 80 Germans officers and NCOs. He also brought 26 pieces of field artillery and seven naval vessels (Stoecker 1977:99).

16. The early weakness of German control may be appreciated when we remember that in 1888, during Peters's attempt to rule, there were only 56 Germans in all of East Africa (Koponen 1995:78).

17. In a Kaguru oral history of the Mukema clan of Talagwe in northeastern Ukaguru, Wissmann appears to be the German whom the Kaguru named Kasimoto (Swahili, *kazimoto,* fierce work) who toured Ukaguru and Ungulu to pacify raiding Baraguyu/Maasai (Beidelman 1970:85–86).

18. Some Kaguru say that when Senyagwa/Saidi died, his post was offered to a true matrilineal relative named Malanda, but he refused, and so it went to Senyagwa's son, Saileni.

19. For an account of the Kilosa and Morogoro areas in German times see Bald 1970; Fuchs 1907:14–15; Kaundinya 1918:56, 60; Prince 1911:113. For interesting photographs of the Mpwapwa and Kilosa installations see Langheld 1909:278, 285; Fonck 1894:55, 72, 75.

20. In 1906 Governor Count Adolph von Götzen separated district officers from control by the central administration in Dar es Salaam, deeply enhancing district officers' powers (Austen 1968:71). In his comments Meyer clearly means administrative officers in the various outlying districts, not all those employed in all forms of government service. Sperber states that in 1913 the Germans had 510 such employees (1970:29).

21. In 1911 there were only 3,113 Germans in all of German East Africa, and only 4,227 whites total (Henderson 1962:132). Furthermore, Germans were said to lack the social solidarity, the "white tribalism," that was thought to characterize the British (Gann and Duignan 1977:73).

22. These changing borders are somewhat confusing. For the earliest German administrative boundaries see Meyer 1909 I, map preceding 429. For later German and British boundaries see L. Berry 1971:106–109.

23. Stoecker states that a 3-rupee hut tax was introduced in 1898 (1977:109); M. Bates states that a 2-rupee hut tax was introduced in 1897 (1957:26). The first tax ordinance was promulgated in 1897 but was not put into effect until much later (Iliffe 1969:60; Koponen 1995:210). At this early period at least two thousand Africans were killed during tax collections (ibid.:219).

24. German settlers were generally short of funds and consequently paid poorly (Gann and Duignan 1977:157–158). Wages were generally tied to the varying local prices for food (Koponen 1995:658). Government soldiers (*askaris*) were the best paid Africans at 35–50 rupees a month. Junior school teachers got about 15 rupees a month, and common laborers on the estates got 12 to 15 (Koponen 1995:636).

25. While it is true that German officials used African underlings to recruit labor for settlers, there were resentments between the disruptive and mercenary settlers and German colonial officers trying to maintain order. Austen suggests that some German district officers tried to build up local African leaders so as to undermine the power of vexing white settlers (1968:148).

26. By the outbreak of World War I, German East Africa had 24 districts, 19 overseen by civilian administrations, the 2 most affected by *Maji-maji* under military commands, and 3 kingdom-districts with German residencies (L. Berry 1971:106–107). Two of the residency districts became Belgian-ruled Ruanda-Urundi.

27. Henderson reports that over 28 thousand Africans were coerced into being porters and that at least two thousand died of exposure (1962:90). His figures seem too low. Iliffe estimates that several hundred thousand died (1979:250), probably too high. The contrast in these numbers well illustrates how vague our knowledge remains about many sides of African life in this era, a lack of knowledge made far worse by the loss of so many records during World War I.

28. Even so late as 1910 there were only 73 doctors (36 employed by Government) in a colony of ten million people (Beck 1977:2).

29. Chidzero (1961) has written extensively on whether mandate and trusteeship status significantly altered Tanganyika's situation as a "colony" (see Dumbuya 1995). I bring up some of his points later in this chapter and indicate others in chapters 1 and 6.

30. The British felt some nostalgia for the akidas even after they were replaced by appointees under Indirect Rule. The original akidas under the Germans were chosen not for any traditional reasons but because they were literate and able. Furthermore, they were rarely tied culturally or socially to those they oversaw; consequently, they seemed more disinterested as aides in ruling than were chiefs and headmen (Liebenow 1971:90–91).

31. In 1913 the Germans had 510 civil servants to rule seven and a half million Africans, whereas in 1925 the British had 800 to rule four million (populous Ruanda-Urundi was run by Belgians. Sperber 1970:29; Austen 1967:580).

32. Here are two quotes from Cameron that contradict his own policies: "It is ensnaring and dangerous to proceed on the assumption that this or that must have been the tradition and custom of a people; that they must at some time have obeyed this or that authority of their own" (D. Cameron 1930:7); "The Native Authority that is not acceptable to the people and is maintained only because we impose it on them is therefore almost certainly bound to fail, after doing a considerable amount of mischief, and it would have been much wiser in the first instance to have endeavoured in such circumstances at any cost to administer the people directly through our own officers" (D. Cameron 1939:90). This is Cameron pontificating; in retrospect these quotes seem accurate reflections of Cameron's flawed and misconceived system of Indirect Rule. They are certainly accurate appraisals of the Kaguru Native Authority. Unfortunately, Cameron did not seem to take his own remarks to heart.

33. When Cameron first established Eastern Province, its capital was Dar es Salaam, but it was soon relocated to Morogoro, the seat of an earlier German headquarters (Gailey 1974:75). Dar es Salaam was the Territory's capital and therefore was not thought appropriate as the site of a provincial capital as well. Furthermore, Morogoro was more centrally located in the province.

34. This division was well reflected in November 1960 when Kaguru from Mpwapwa and Kilosa districts met on their own to discuss a possible boundary change that

would better reflect their own local kin and clan affiliations. Since this involved a boundary between provinces as well as districts, it triggered sharp admonitions from the British administration (Kilosa District Book; Mpwapwa District Book).

35. Iliffe claims that the Native Authorities constructed larger political units that corresponded to African desires. This seems a totally unfounded assertion. At best, such authorities created units that could be taken over by later African politicians, but there is no good reason to believe that such an aim corresponded to anything that ordinary Africans wanted or even thought about in the 1920s and 1930s. Iliffe's own pandering to TANU (Tanganyika African National Union) policies and current Tanganyikan nationalists' desires to reconstruct a more advanced and radical history are probably the source of this assertion (1979:323–324).

36. J. Willis (1993) provides a good, detailed account of how local British administrators impeded social and economic development in one district.

37. Baines was an eccentric and reclusive Rhodesian who settled in western Ukaguru in 1919 and eked out a meager living for many decades in the western Itumba Mountains south of Geiro (A. Wood 1950:36–37).

38. In 1878 the CMS missionary, the Rev. Dr. Baxter, made abortive farming attempts in the same area. His grim reports were available at the CMS archives but were apparently ignored.

39. Judgments conflict as to whether the United Nations Trusteeship forced the British to be more honest in promoting democracy and self-rule. Chidzero believes that it did (1961:255), while Dougherty argues the reverse (1966:219).

2. UKAGURU 1957–58

1. In 1959 fewer than 15 thousand Africans (out of a population of about nine million Tanganyikans) had incomes of over 10 pounds (25 dollars) a month (Pratt 1976:21).

2. The average Tanganyikan entered primary school at an older age than what we would consider normal in the United States, most being about age eight and some as old as ten. Students at all levels in schools seemed older and more mature in attitudes than in the United States.

Primary school classes were taught in two shifts, two morning grades (I and II) and two afternoon grades (III and IV). Grades I and II provided 15 30-minute periods per week. These involved classes in arithmetic, reading Swahili, and much garden work and some marching and exercise. Grades III and IV provided 20 40-minute periods per week. These involved classes in reading both Swahili and English, general knowledge, Christian religion, and much time in garden work and exercise and marching (George 1960:37–39).

3. Each week in grades V and VI the middle school provided 6 hours of mathematics, 12 hours of English, 2 hours of Swahili, 6 hours of general knowledge, 3 hours of Christian religion, and at least 7 hours of agricultural labor and shop work. Sports time was extra, and soccer was extremely popular. Grades VII and VIII provided 6 hours of mathematics, 12 hours of English, 2 hours of Swahili, 4 hours of general knowledge, 4 hours of general science, and at least 7 hours of farm and shop work. Many students complained about how much farm work and other chores they performed for the school (George 1960:43).

4. After I completed fieldwork in Ukaguru, I stayed with the former headmaster of the middle school who had entered a school for higher government administration in Kenya. Later, in England and America, I met even better-educated Kaguru who

had taken posts in the foreign service. No one, even today, has much economic future in Ukaguru itself.

5. I met a handful of local African Muslims who at first appeared to be Kaguru, but all of these turned out to be Ngulu. In any case, these were not very ardent Muslims. The most prominent, ironically the brother of the African CMS Archdeacon of Berega, ran the largest beer-club in the Idibo area.

3. THE KAGURU NATIVE AUTHORITY

In this chapter, which describes the situation during the colonial and neocolonial period from 1957–62, I sometimes imply the ethnographic present, although all of this system has now utterly disappeared.

1. The other Native Authorities were Usagara North, Usagara South, and Uvidunda. The Sagara (Beidelman 1967a:51–53) and the Vidunda (Beidelman 1965, 1967d:53–57) closely resemble the Kaguru socioculturally.

2. The establishment of district councils was an innovation brought in by the central Tanganyika Territorial administration. The purported aim of this was to modernize local government by slowly de-emphasizing "tribalistic" leaders' prominence through introducing an administrative group based on the district rather than ethnicity.

3. I discuss this council further in chapter 6. Because the council seemed likely to undermine their local hegemony, local Native Authorities generally opposed it. It was set up not only as a purportedly modernizing organization and as a means for more efficient government, but also as a method of combating the African political party TANU (see chapter 6). Despite claims of modernizing, a government anthropologist described it thus: "The plan means the restoration of 'Indirect Rule' as far as the political struggle of the territory is concerned" (Cory 1957).

4. I list these headmen and their clan affiliations in Appendix 12.

5. I do not discuss the subchiefdom of Msowero. Being in the lowlands and inhabited by a large number of transient workers connected to the estates, it was too atypical for me to include in this study of Kaguru.

A court for Baraguyu had been set up at Chibedya (Kibedya), west of Chakwale, in the northernmost part of Geiro subchiefdom. It was closed late in 1958. When I consulted the district files, I found a letter of October 1958 from the provincial commissioner that ordered the Chibedya (Kibedya) Court closed because only 13 criminal cases and nine civil cases were heard in that court during the six months preceding its closing. The commissioner also noted that there were only 291 Baraguyu taxpayers in the area.

6. A map and figures on the size and population of these court areas are available in map 6, table Appendix 12.

7. I list headmen and their clan affiliations in Appendix 12.

8. I qualify these differences with the phrase "in public" because many Kaguru Christians did drink, smoke, and fornicate and even attended dances, but they would lose their jobs at the mission if they were reported to the white missionaries.

9. There had been no recent census in Tanganyika until 1957. Consequently the district administration relied upon rough estimates for their calculations of taxes and fees. Each year's estimate was the projection of figures from the previous year. As a result, expectations for what money was due was largely determined by the local information headmen and chiefs fed to the district headquarters. I had many opportunities

to watch Kaguru collect the 1957 census figures, and I saw that they were very unreliable. I was allowed by the census officers to examine the detailed sample censuses collected in Ukaguru and later stored in Nairobi. It was clear that those were not reliable. More important, the published results of the census involved figures by district, not by chiefship or by headmanship. No other material was available to district administrators. My own access to these materials was due to personal acquaintance with one of the British census officers. Even after the 1957 census, the local British administrators were still dependent upon rough estimates by local Africans to determine the taxes due any headmanship.

10. A collector should issue a receipt immediately on securing a payment. If a collector stole tax money, he would be fined 500 shillings and be imprisoned for three months (African Studies Branch 1951:33).

11. There were many other government regulations that headmen rarely if ever enforced and would not even try to use as leverage against their subjects. Some rules were so unpopular with all Kaguru that no one in the Native Authority would enforce them. It always struck me as amazing that the British thought they were achieving anything by getting such regulations put on the books by unsympathetic Kaguru officials. Just proving that a Kaguru committed such an offense would often pose real problems. Here are some examples of such rules that Kaguru themselves viewed as utterly bizarre and unreasonable: not cultivating so as to cause erosion, not cutting down certain trees even when they were on one's own land, not killing certain wild animals, not burning grassland in order to get new grass, not urinating or defecating in rivers, not bathing near water-points. Such rules existed on the list of laws registered in the Kaguru Native Authority, yet they were clearly entirely the products of British bureaucratic thinking. They made little sense to Africans.

12. The monthly presence of armed police at Chakwale in Idibo subchiefdom made sense. Arabs brought a great deal of money to the market to purchase livestock, and there was always fear of robbery. The monthly gathering there was the largest congregation of people in the entire chiefdom. People had sold cattle as well as handicrafts and beer. Many got drunk. There was a heady mix of Kaguru, Ngulu, Kamba, Baraguyu, Indians, Arabs and a few Europeans and Somalis, who often had misunderstandings with one another, especially those who were drunk. Often assaults, brawls, and robberies occurred.

13. Kaguru usually called a subchief by the English term "headman," or *hedamani*, and called an actual headman *jumbe*. Occasionally, Kaguru would refer to a subchief as *mundewa* (chief), mainly when they wanted to sound flattering. The word *mundewa* was usually reserved for the paramount chief.

14. British administrators told me that they were aware that there were serious discrepancies between reality and various government reports. Given the small number of British staff and the vast difficulties in communication and supervision, they were resigned to this, since they saw no practical way to solve this problem.

In 1957 a local government directive listed 24 forms that could be issued by local Native Authority treasuries, and these did not even include forms for local court clerks dealing with litigation (Tanganyika 1957b:56).

15. The salaries of chiefs in Tanganyika varied widely. The most privileged from the rich and sophisticated areas made one hundred times the salary of chiefs from poor areas such as Ukaguru (Dougherty 1966:213).

16. During colonial rule, British administrators were remarkably uncorrupt in terms of money. This related to the ethos of the colonial civil service (discussed in

chapters 1 and 6). Of course, I do not suggest that Western societies are not also often corrupt. Still, despite their own general uprightness, colonial administrators expected African chiefs to be corrupt and merely set limits on just how far this should go (Tidrich 1990:44).

17. A Tanganyika government memorandum states: "It is not so difficult as it might at first appear to deal with the likelihood of corruption. The first essential is of course to remove as far as possible the temptation to take bribes, and the best way to do this is to see that all the personnel of the court are adequately paid" (Tanganyika 1957a:13). Few quotes could better illustrate how British colonial bureaucratic thinking frequently substituted prim moralistic humbug in place of the actual shambles of colonial reality.

Views on corruption vary widely. A Tanganyika court justice saw all Africans as dishonest: "Those of us who had experience of the natives of Tanganyika were struck by the readiness with which the official vested with a little brief authority set about abusing it for his own personal aggrandizement" (G. Alexander 1936:204).

In contrast, a U.S. political scientist remarks: "The administrative reports show us the principal difficulties: record-keeping, enforcement of decisions, illegal punishments, and bribery. Evidence of corruption was surprisingly small, and the government native courts adviser later wrote that from the African point of view it was nonexistent; some extortion as a European would call it was to be expected from chiefs" (M. Bates 1957:136–137).

18. Court clerks were generally recognized as administrative secretaries running a wide range of local Native Authority business (African Studies Branch 1952:22–23).

19. Kilosa district administrators were well aware that the paramount chieftaincy was not a traditional post, but many British continued to rationalize the usefulness of the post, just as they defended the posts of headmen and subchiefs. For many British administrators all these posts reflected reasonable accommodation both to Kaguru matrilineal politics and to earlier central administration demands that local administrators find some kind of traditional rulers to take responsibility and interpret government to local Africans. These were the Kaguru leaders in the bush to whom British should speak.

20. One of the few times I got a serious infection in the field was from an injection by the Idibo medical dispenser. It was probably from a dirty needle. I paid for the treatment, and the dispenser and I were friends, because I had earlier driven him many miles to a mission hospital for treatment when he had been poisoned by a jealous husband with whose wife he had been sleeping. When I told the dispenser I had got infected from his injection, he refused to acknowledge that this was possible. We remained friends, and he later entertained me at his tribal home when he was on vacation. He continued to provide much help with my study in the chiefdom. My point here is that if I had received an infectious injection, how more likely was it that others were also likely to suffer. I was lucky this was long before the HIV/AIDS epidemic, when dirty injections could be lethal.

4. COURT CASES

1. For example, on March 7, 1962, the subchief of Idibo held his court at Iyogwe, the most distant area from his courthouse at Idibo.

2. The Idibo Court did not always like to give written receipts for small fees. I once saw a man thrown out of the court for demanding a receipt for a small payment.

I assumed that the court did not like to give such receipts all the time because many such payments were pocketed by the chief, elders, and clerk.

3. The Native Authority Handbook states that prisoners should be detained only a few days and be furnished with a mat and blanket. No such treatment was usually given to ethnic minorities, who also had to pay for their food if possible (see Tanganyika 1957b:115). Government directives state that rations must be supplied and that no one should be held for more than three days without a filed explanation. Kaguru courts did not bother with such niceties. It is, however, true that most such abuse involved Baraguyu and Maasai, who would have been difficult to hold onto once freed.

4. The government court memoranda recommended registering a case as criminal when in doubt; but Kaguru preferred the reverse, since then registration fees could be collected (Tanganyika 1957b:61–62). If a civil case was later judged as criminal, the unauthorized fees could be pocketed.

5. Many Kaguru preferred imprisonment to parting with goods in a fine. In 1957 the food and living conditions at the Kilosa prison were not worse than those faced by many free Kaguru. Two anecdotes can illustrate my claims that local prison life might not seem so bad to some Africans. (1) One afternoon I went to the largest African beer club in Kilosa. Hundreds of Africans were sitting around under the trees drinking beer. I bought beer for several, and after we drank for about an hour, they told me they had to leave. They said that they had to return to prison for the curfew. They had been working during the day for Asians in Kilosa town and had been given some free time between work and curfew. They had also received modest payment for their labor. (2) I once complained about a problem with some European tools I had. A Baraguyu friend offered to fix them on the spot and did so. When I expressed surprise, he told me he had learned such skills while he was in prison, where he had been employed out in town to an Indian mechanic. He had enjoyed the training. He also claimed that he had enjoyed a rich urban sex life as well.

Local Government directives on courts and punishment reaffirmed that many Africans preferred going to prison to paying large fines. The money-strapped territorial government invariably preferred collecting fines to bedding and boarding an African in prison (Tanganyika 1957a:33).

6. Kaguru courts could not flog men over 45 years old or under 16. They were supposed to flog men only in private and with a medical person in attendance. The whip was supposed to be clean (Tanganyika 1957b:104–105). Women were never to be flogged. All these rules were broken by Kaguru courts.

One senior British judge in Tanganyika enthused over flogging: "Brutalized men have committed certain brutal crimes, laugh at imprisonment, but recoil from a measure of justice which acts both as retribution for the past and as deterrent for the future" (G. Alexander 1936:191). In fact, flogging seemed no more a deterrent than capital punishment in Texas. It certainly seemed less horrible to many Kaguru than long imprisonment or confiscation of goods. One should also remember that for most of the colonial era flogging was also allowed in many British schools and in British prisons.

7. Sir Donald Cameron, the governor credited with founding the Tanganyika Native Authority system, wrote: "I made it a rule that the Courts should sit in public, i.e. that the sides of the court house should be open for the most part with low eaves, and the audience freely, but with decorum, express their dissent if they think that justice has not been done or native law or custom has been misinterpreted" (1939:175). Simi-

larly, M. Bates writes: "In the smaller courts of the more rural areas, the court might be held under a tree, and the elders and public mixed in a throng as animated and as interested as on market days, with which the court might well, in fact, coincide. The only literate present would be the court clerk, and his record bare and scanty" (1957:135).

8. After three years records were sent on to Kilosa headquarters (see Tanganyika 1957a:80). Apparently they were not kept there indefinitely.

9. Bizarrely, this even banned Kaguru from hearing cases involving local Somali traders, who certainly were Africans but at this time, in 1957–58, were categorized as Asians along with Indians and Arabs (Tanganyika 1957a:21). The law forbade Africans all access to judging Europeans and only allowed Asians and Somalis in African courts if they consented—which, of course, they would not usually do.

10. Kaguru were unacquainted with the details of Tanganyika territorial statutory law. If they had been, many features of it would have perplexed or shocked them. For example, claims to witch-finding (in Kaguru eyes, a good thing) and being a witch (a bad thing) were both crimes punished by up to seven years imprisonment and stiff fines, whereas one who committed incest merited only five years unless the victim was under 12 (then life). Kaguru equated witchcraft with incest, so this would seem confusing to them (Tanganyika 1947:231–232, 160). The vagaries and contradictions in this law probably went back to Cameron's own muddled views on African thought and behavior (1939:198–201).

11. I originally discussed these cases in Beidelman 1961a.

12. Much has been written about Native Courts and law in British East and Central Africa. Most writing is devoted to discussing African customary law and how it was applied. This is not my main concern in this study (see Epstein 1953:28–32; 1954:18; Allott, Epstein, and Gluckman 1969:23–29; Gluckman 1955; 1963; 1965a; 1965b; 1969; Chanock 1985; Roberts and Mann 1991:22, 39; McCarthy 1979:13; Lowbridge 1949:7–13; C. Roberts 1969:350). It is clear that colonial influences on East African law eroded the rights of women (Gopal and Salim 1998:48–69; Boesen 1979:236–248).

13. Jeater reports an early abduction case considered in northern Rhodesia even before regular British-type courts were established. It very closely resembles this and the next case. In both, serious crimes are converted into civil litigation about bridewealth and rights over women, all settled with fines and compensation. I am sorry that Jeater does not cite my two published cases (Beidelman 1961a), since they so closely resemble the fascinating material she reports.

14. This was a strange remark, given that Kaguru herdboys frequently saw herd animals copulating. I think that this was probably a reflection of a general Kaguru dislike of publicly acknowledging that uninitiated people should ever express sexual knowledge. The court did allow the boy to testify.

15. Kaguru did not fine or punish people for false testimony (kusiga). They assumed that with constant questioning and arguing, the court could decide what testimony was believable and what was not. Oaths were not taken in court.

16. There was for a time one Kamba elder assessor, Nzangu, in the Idibo subchief's court, but he resigned. He still continued to enter discussion at court whenever a Kamba was involved.

There was also once a Baraguyu court at Chibedya, a tiny hamlet west of Chakwale and Idibo. It had been closed by the time I arrived in nearby Idibo. British officials told me it had been closed because it was little used.

17. I originally discussed these issues in Beidelman 1966, 1967a.

18. A directive on Native Authorities notes: "The courts often do not appear to appreciate the need to make the punishment fit the crime and tend only to make it fit the criminal's circumstances" (Tanganyika 1957a:9).

19. By local custom, Kaguru or otherwise, any injury involving bloodshed was considered more serious than one in which blood was not spilled (Beidelman 1963c).

20. According to Lindblom, the parents of a dead child should have sexual intercourse, presumably to purify themselves after the death (Lindblom 1920:109). I suspect that Lindblom got his ethnography muddled and that the parents were purified by having sexual relations with someone other than one another. I also suspect that it was only the mother that had to engage in this.

21. Kaguru custom forbids two members of the same lineage from having sexual relations with the same woman or even two different women of the same lineage. Kaguru considered such an act very polluting, and kin of those who did such a thing would have to cleanse themselves by expensive rites of purification or they might be in danger from the angered ancestral dead. It was therefore not just that Kaguru found Kamba customs repulsive, but they found them supernaturally dangerous to themselves.

22. The Gogo were held in contempt by many Kaguru, even though they were culturally fairly similar to them. Gogo were considered even poorer and less educated than Kaguru. This was probably because the main times Kaguru encountered Gogo was when they had fled eastward to Ukaguru on account of famine, which was always more severe in Ugogo.

23. I very rarely interrupted court proceedings. When I did, it was only to ask that a witness or letter be known when the court was clearly trying to prevent people from testifying. I never interfered with any judgment, and my presence never seemed to inhibit the courts from what seemed to be extralegal or illegal actions. I was living in the subchief's hamlet at his invitation and got on well with the court officials, despite my dislike of much that they did and said.

24. While the British repeatedly criticized fining people on the basis of their wealth rather than their actual crimes, they repeatedly showed themselves eager to punish cattle theft (almost solely a Baraguyu, Maasai, or Kamba crime) severely. As early as 1950, the provincial commissioner wrote to Kilosa headquarters: "I do not like the very lenient punishments meted out for cattle theft. These, I admit, are presumably the limits of the jurisdiction of the courts, but in that case I seriously suggest to you that you should either issue an order that all cattle theft cases should go to the A Court of Mamboya or to the District Court of Kilosa" (Morogoro District Headquarters Book). Neither course was taken, but instead the British simply overlooked the Kaguru courts fining Baraguyu and Kamba harshly. Unfortunately, such cases were then not recorded, and as a result the tacit policy amounted to a license for corruption by Kaguru officials.

25. This was in 1957. Such was the authority of Europeans then that the Baraguyu, although armed with a spear, sword, club, and staff, sullenly allowed us, both unarmed, to walk him to a Kaguru headman without any resistance.

26. Official writings disclose how simplistic and delusional British ideas about traditional African societies remained (Tanganyika 1957a:2).

5. SUBVERSIONS AND DIVERSIONS

Some of this appeared in different form in Beidelman 1961d in German, and later in Beidelman 1970 in English. I published initially in German because the material might have seemed compromising to Kaguru officials before independence, when they were still in office. All are now long dead.

1. In 1957 Kaguru in Idibo subchiefdom numbered 10,734 and held 2,434 head of cattle (.22 head per person); Baraguyu numbered 520 and held 1,506 head of cattle (1.42 head per person); Kamba numbered 1,577 and were estimated to hold perhaps 1,600 head of cattle (nearly 1 head per person).

2. The elder was the subject of a biography collected as part of an oral history project organized to promote pride in African grassroots nationalism and resistance to colonialism (Mlahagwa 1973). The author gets Kaguru terms and customs muddled and omits any material negative to this leader's image. He is presented more as a fore-runner of African nationalism than as the intense tribalist that he was. The article claims that TANU and Umwano had cordial relations. This is not how I recall the situation. If there was a common goal for both, it was that both sought to bring down the paramount chief. The secretary of Umwano was also a member of TANU, but generally TANU was opposed to Indirect Rule and to the tribalistic sentiments embodied in Umwano (Kiwanuka 1970:305; M. Bates 1957:337; see Cooper 1994:1538). This is ironic, since TANU had its start through tribal associations (Bienen 1967:25). Mlahagwa's account seems to rely almost entirely on what the elder told him, which was very self-promoting.

3. A dominant clan could appoint a patrilateral kinsman if he was considered outstanding or was in some way useful to the clan. In such cases, such a child (*mwana*) of the clan would be heavily obligated to those who had appointed him. In this case, the man chosen was the son of a man of the Ganasa clan, not a son of a woman, and therefore not a proper matrilineal member.

4. The district commissioner's approval of Umwano surprised me. It struck me as an irresponsible decision encouraging potential ethnic conflict and abuse. I wondered whether the district commissioner's experience as an army officer contributed to this militant decision. He strove to appear gruff, tough, and macho.

5. The government permit held by the general secretary of Umwano was typed in English and could not be read by any of the members, not even the subchief or deposed subchief. At the celebratory meeting I had my field assistant make an oral translation into Chikaguru for the assembly.

6. In a recent article concerning contemporary ethnic violence in Kilosa district, the authors underscore that the Baraguyu/Maasai pastoralists in the area are still the subjects of considerable political oppression by the Bantu language majority, which dominates both local and national government (Benjaminsen et al. 2009).

7. The man did not appeal. The time and effort would not have been worth it to a Baraguyu who could have afforded such a fine, even though it was very high by Kaguru standards.

8. Such hostility toward Native Authorities was a growing problem all over Tanganyika (see M. Bates 1957:336; Austen 1967:602; Austen 1968:255). While Africans wanted to be governed by their fellow Africans, anticolonial rhetoric increasingly became antichief rhetoric (Liebenow 1956a:136–137). The animosity felt by educated Africans toward chiefs seemed widespread (see Liebenow 1971:220; 1991:233; Rotberg 1966:508; Murray 1967:413–419; Montague 1951:21).

9. In 1953 the Tanganyika Government banned government servants from politics and encouraged Native Authorities to enact similar prohibitions (M. Bates 1957:337–340). This ban meant that TANU had a poor supply of well-educated leaders, which led to deep political harm after independence (ibid.:340–341).

10. Perhaps the title was inspired by that of TANU's newspaper *Sauti ya TANU*.

11. This project was officially called the Jakula Softwood Scheme and was begun in 1954. (A more detailed description of the project appears later in chapter 5.) This was part of a 278-square-mile forest reserve originally gazetted (officially promulgated) by the Germans and near Mamiwa, the highest peak in the Itumba Mountains of central Ukaguru. Under British pressure, the Kaguru Native Authority had alienated these additional lands at Mamiwa and nearby Itugi for forestry use. At the time of these disputes, 15 thousand acres had been planted with softwood saplings. The displaced Kaguru were deeply resentful, even though they appeared to have been settled in lower areas to the north of their former homes. While I had formally opposed the brutal recruitments associated with the project, I later visited the scheme and became friends with the forestry officer running it. He professed ignorance about how his labor had been recruited. His own conduct toward his workers was good. I found one of my educated Kaguru friends working as his clerk, one who had lost his previous job for USA. As far as I knew, the softwood project never benefitted any Kaguru. The high-handed district commissioner who had allowed recruitment abuses stayed on in Tanzania after independence, working for the new African Government.

12. This was similar to TANU, which in 1958 had an initial membership fee of 2 shillings and yearly dues of 6 shillings.

13. Such references to god are Christian; traditional Kaguru believed in a supreme being, but this god rarely figured in Kaguru prayer or rituals, which were almost entirely concerned with the ancestral dead.

14. I was told by several reliable Kaguru informants that I should pay particular attention to how USA's president addressed the assembly, because he spoke the purest and most elegant Chikaguru I was ever likely to hear now that so many Kaguru had their speech mixed with Swahili. This must have involved considerable effort on the president's part, since he had spent much of his life at mission boarding schools and in town, where he would have had to use Swahili or English.

15. This same building had previously been used by TANU (Tanganyika African Nationalist Union), and before that by TANU's political opponent, UTP (United Tanganyika Party). This showed how keen the local archdeacon was to gain influence with any political movement that he thought might enhance his and his sons' influence.

16. Readers might ask whether such losses might hurt the archdeacon. The archdeacon had not himself, as a mission employee, engaged directly in any of these ventures, but operated through his two sons. Kaguru told me they suspected that the sons were among those who were to blame for losing the money.

17. The provincial commissioner's office for the area had a record of pushing forestry projects and plans to conserve mountain areas, even in the face of intense resistance by local Africans, the Luguru. The provincial headquarters at Morogoro continued such projects, using force when necessary, and faced violent protests by local Africans and TANU. It had persisted in this despite long and dangerous conflict, so that the prospect of problems in Ukaguru, a much less sophisticated and more poorly organized area, probably did not intimidate them (see Fosbrooke 1959b; Young and Fosbrooke 1960:120–121; Maack 1996:154–165). The Kilosa district headquarters would not resist any strongly advocated policy from the provincial headquarters. Kilosa was a low-rank post in a high-rank province. Forestry projects were a vogue in this period (Sunseri 2007; 2009:118–129).

18. An East African newspaper wrote this:

> Add to Mr. Nyerere's [head of TANU and later the first president of the country] difficulties . . . minor revolts among TANU members in the Kilosa and Masasi Districts. In both cases there were enough local Party men against the candidates chosen for them by TANU in Dar es Salaam for the General Election, for other candidates to announce that they would stand against the approved candidates. In both cases the men who will stand as 'independents' are staunch TANU members who object to the candidates wished upon their constituencies by Dar es Salaam. (*Kenya Weekly News,* Friday July 8, 1960, p. 200)

19. The Tanganyika government had set up an anti-TANU party, the United Tanganyika Party (UTP), which it encouraged Native Authority chiefs to support (Chidzero 1961:201–202). It was government policy to use local Native Authorities to harass African nationalists (D. Bates 1972:233, 266, 277–278). This paralleled the fierce resistance against Native Authority–enforced development projects (Maguire 1969:30).

6. THE WORLD BEYOND

1. I describe conditions in 1957–58, when much was far different from later.

2. All provincial, district, and township population figures came from the final government census taken before independence (East African Statistical Department 1958).

3. By the time I ended fieldwork, Dar es Salaam was no longer part of Eastern Province (Region) but a separate capital area. Before 1952 Morogoro was not even a provincial headquarters; the province then was run out of Dar es Salaam.

4. In terms of offering an avenue for career advancement in the colonial service, Tanganyika was the last in rank of the four top-ranked African colonies, after Nigeria, Gold Coast (Ghana), and Kenya (see Allen 1979:158).

5. Even in 1957 only 4 percent of Africans lived in towns, so that their experiences were unrepresentative of what most Africans such as Kaguru knew. It was townsfolk and estate workers, and not people like Kaguru, who could most sympathize was the nationalist cause (Pratt 1976:21).

6. Martin (1993:127–195) provides useful comparative material on social life in a larger African colonial town. There too sharp distinctions separated whites from blacks, and there was a social hierarchy among Africans far stronger than what I noticed in Kilosa.

7. Schumaker observes that Europeans invariably sought a view from the heights, which was why the district headquarters and administrators' residences were on hills far above the African, Asian, and commercial quarters of Kilosa town (1999:331–332).

8. During my first three field trips I spent a total of at least two months in Kilosa town. Time was about equally divided between staying at a Greek hotel and living with Africans in the African quarter. I probably spent no more than twelve nights in the homes of British administrators. I was the only European ever to live in the African quarter.

9. Vincent observes that in general such smaller towns were sometimes more ethnically diverse than provincial capitals (1974:272).

10. In social practice the British avoided the Greeks and secretly did not even consider them proper Europeans (*wazungu*). This was revealed when a visiting governor infuriated the Kilosa district Greeks by dedicating the new Greek community center

at Kimamba. The governor blundered into saying, "I want to thank the African community, the Asian community, the European community, and the Greek community."

11. My account of Kilosa closely resembles the few other accounts of East African up-country European communities (Sofer and Ross 1951; Tanner 1966; Goldthorpe 1958:131–134).

12. In 1957 local British administrators scoffed at me when I suggested that Tanganyika might be independent in ten years; as it happened, it became independent in five.

13. There is much published about servants in colonial Africa, though most appears as anecdotes in autobiographies and novels. Surprisingly few scholarly articles have been devoted to this topic in a way that provides any sustained analysis (see Allen 1979:61, 116; Bujra 1992:244–249, 253; 2000:7, 24, 41, 76–85, 177; Sofer and Ross 1951:321; Hansen 1989, 1992; Buell 1965: I:500–501; Beidelman 1990; D. Kirkwood 1984:157; Coser 1973, 1974:69–75).

14. When I was at Oxford, several East African friends used to urge me to go with them to a club where a retired colonial administrator served as a bartender. They told me they derived special satisfaction watching such a man serve Africans who were better educated than he. The nature of "personalized" serving as contrasted with simply being employed was especially resented by all Africans with any kind of education.

15. The only real anthropological monograph on African servants deals mainly with relations between Asian masters and African servants in post-independence Zambia. It is useful but provides few insights into how British behaved in colonial times (Hansen 1989). Bujra's sociological/historical account lacks useful case material (1992).

16. When I taught at Makerere University in Uganda in 1968, the area had many refugees from the unrest in neighboring Burundi and Rwanda. As a consequence there were many refugee African chefs highly skilled in French cuisine. These were quickly employed at top wages by local European administrators.

17. When I hired a local Kaguru whom I trained to be a cook, he soon hired several women servants, since he felt that it was unmasculine to fetch either water or firewood (feminine duties for Kaguru), at least when performed in his own neighborhood. He was an amiable worker but never figured out how to do his job. When I left, he returned to farming. On my subsequent field trips I cooked, washed, and ironed for myself for most of the time.

18. Stoler writes that Dutch colonials worried about native women bringing up white or half-white children (1997:217); I met no British who expressed such concern, probably because children were sent abroad once they were of age for schooling. British colonial wives liked having African *ayahs*, perhaps because they grotesquely reflected the British upper-class tradition of having nannies. Such servants failed utterly to convey any class values, whereas British nannies did.

19. There is a huge literature on colonial wives, much of it negative; see Gartrell 1984. Some argue that the arrival of women led to increased sequestering of white households from Africans, since men no longer had to seek outside for company (Strobel 1987:377, 1991:1). Fairer but contrasting accounts of what went on, involving women who spent some time in Kilosa district (and elsewhere) both long ago and when I was in the field, can be found in Lamb and Hohlwein 1983; Latham and Latham 1995. Incidentally, the Lamb in the Lamb and Hohlwein citation is the former wife and daughter-in-law in the Latham and Latham citation.

20. Although I am familiar with writings on sex and colonialism, I never encountered any British man who slept with African household servants, though I did know men who had slept with Africans, female and male. There were rumors and jokes about this. I was assured that it was almost unheard of for a British woman (except some prostitutes during the last war) to sleep with Africans. I remarked that I knew white women who had slept with and married black men in Britain and America, but I was assured that was a different matter from Africa.

After 1909 British colonial governments discouraged sexual relations between colonial administrators and natives (Hyam 1990:157–181). Hyam points out that the most virulent denunciations of interracial sexual relations came from the Christian missionaries (ibid.:157–181). Both Kaguru and some British told me that one district commissioner I knew was having affairs with various African women, including a Native Authority employee in Ukaguru. The rumor was so widespread that it may have been true.

The knowledge African servants had about their masters probably would have appalled many British. Most masters knew very little about the personal lives of their employees, mainly because they were not interested. That servants knew so much about their masters was inevitable. British claimed that they told little about themselves to Africans, but African servants were everywhere—at work, at the club, at home, at shops—and they often gossiped with one another. (See Simmel's wry comments on the perils of interpersonal secrecy, 1950:323 n. 349.)

21. Those Europeans who lived in Ukaguru, such as myself, always had Kaguru or Ngulu as local servants, because more sophisticated Africans would have balked at staying out in the bush. All of the missionaries in Ukaguru who had servants had trained them from scratch in their duties, and that was what I did. This was tougher and more time-consuming than one might assume. Later, after 1957–58, I stayed in Ukaguru and Ungulu with a field assistant or an educated African friend, but I never again employed a servant.

22. Sports were always encouraged. The colonial office long held the belief that sports-mindedness was an attribute of a good recruit to the colonial service (Pakenham 1985:170–174).

23. Callaway 1987:16–17; Tidrick 1990:216–218; Wilkinson 1964:14–17, 22, 38, 88, 90, 101, 104, 106–109; Hyam 1990:71–72, 108, 157–187; Kirk-Greene 1978:212, 1980a:43–44, 1986b:279, 2006:11–18, 39–42, 117, 136–137; Symonds 1986:1–31, 300–301; Brett 1973:37–52, 302; Jeffries 1938:124–125; Lewis and Foy 1971:146; Gann and Duignan 1978a:203; 1978b:3. Actual administrative training was scant (Kirk-Greene 1991, 2006:19, 25, 38, 47, 53; Jeffries 1949; Allott et al. 1969:27; C. Roberts 1969:14–19).

24. One of the oldest jokes that administrators tried on newcomers was to ask them, when on tour, where they wanted to stop for a meal and possible housing. They would ask, "Do you want a bath or a drink?"—that is, a Protestant or Roman Catholic mission station. Visits to missions were never thought to be enjoyable, and this was in a colonial society where, ordinarily, administrators at small outposts relished any new social encounter with fellow English-speaking whites.

25. For a discussion of such conflictual situations, see Berman 1996:73, 86–87, 1112–1120; Allen 1979:64). For a good account of the prefectural concept, see Berman 1996:73–75, 80–81).

26. For an excellent discussion of prefectural values, see Berman 1996:73–75; for a good account of the concept of prestige, see ibid.:203–205; Lonsdale 2000:200. Berman quotes a Kenya administrator commenting on an official's construction of

prestige among Africans: "Good manners are really the basis of good race relations" (ibid.:107). Good manners, especially if they are seigniorial, hardly foster real respect or affection. I am, however, amused to recall that Evans-Pritchard once told me that all one had to remember for doing good fieldwork in Africa was to show good manners to the natives. Besides being a facetious statement, it struck me as ludicrous coming from someone who was sometimes rude and even unkind to people, even strangers.

27. Tidrick writes of the "Maasai-itis" of some British administrators (1990:172; Hammond and Jablow 1970:165). Except for the veterinary officer, none of the British I met in Kilosa cared for the Maasai (Baraguyu), and most saw them as almost outside the sphere of normal social beings. In Kilosa district the British almost never supported them in their disputes with other Africans. British elsewhere in the territory were often charmed by Maasai, much as one might be charmed by exotic lions and elephants rather than real people. I created a sensation by bringing two red-painted, scantily clad Maasai warriors into the New Africa Hotel in Dar es Salaam and having them served sodas. (I recognize that some may accuse me of simply using these Maasai to make a point; yet the Maasai seemed to have had a good time and I certain did.) I too was initially in awe of Maasai and Baraguyu, but after some years and staying many weeks in their camps I found them kindly and sociable. My last days residing in Ukaguru itself were in a Maasai (Baraguyu) camp. The Kilosa administrators' general antipathy toward Maasai might have been changed if any had been able to spend more time in the countryside. They were very hospitable.

28. Nothing I encountered supported Cannadine's perverse and ludicrous assertion that class was more important than race in determining behavior in the British colonial world (2001; see Lyall 2001). It was, however, true that highly educated, upper-class British were more at ease socializing with Africans than were lower-class British.

29. Various local councils were begun as early as 1953, but Kilosa was a late starter in this (Sperber 1970:36; see Liebenow 1956a:133–134).

30. Governor Cameron favored the term "Indirect Administration" rather than "Indirect Rule," and in general local British officials spoke of "administrating," not governing or ruling (Taylor 1963:54). These were simply word games.

31. Initially, due to Governor Cameron's policies, there was no connection between the Native Authority courts and the high court in Dar es Salaam or any other organizations outside the district, which operated essentially in terms of English and not native law. The final appeal for local Africans was the district headquarters. By 1950, however, Africans could appeal Native Authority rulings beyond the district level—but this almost never occurred (Moffett et al. 1952:17–21).

EPILOGUE

1. This was the inevitable outcome of President Nyerere's long animosity toward tribalism, chiefs, and the Native Authorities (D. Bates 1972:253, 266–267, 277–278).

2. The Fleming Report of 1960 recommended that future expatriate recruits be hired on contract without pensions and other benefits, which led to less commitment by the new civil service (Symonds 1966:178).

3. Local administrations were weakened further after independence when many able administrators were sent to Dar es Salaam to man the growing central bureaucracy (Symonds 1966:194).

4. Nyerere's placing TANU stalwarts in local political positions put them in conflict with old-time rural administrators and led to eroding of competent local government. This policy became increasingly adrift from the supposed socialist and idealistic claptrap that was spewed out in Dar es Salaam, especially at the university and in government proclamations. In practice, local administrators became the new bureaucratic bourgeoisie, mouthing the same self-righteous cant that disfigured colonial rhetoric. In contradiction to the message of the speeches, there was an increase in corporal punishment for slackers, forced labor, and confiscation of property and pocketing of fines (Shivji 1976; 1990). A local band of officials motivated by greed and newly won power exploited local farmers and what few African traders remained (Saul 1972:111–121; Samoff 1979a:45, 1979b:52; Ergas 1980:389). This encouraged a new rural black market sale of foodstuffs by poor and oppressed farmers such as those in Ukaguru.

At first contemporary European leftist scholars praised Nyerere's "socialism," though none of these "radicals" had experience living in rural areas (see Samoff 1979b:3). The white supposedly radical faculty at the University of Dar es Salaam had much to answer for in endorsing Nyerere's disastrous and dictatorial policies aimed at Tanganyika's farmers. These "intellectuals" knew nothing about the lives of up-country Africans. Ignorance of African life at the grassroots may account for Pratt's fulsome obituary of Nyerere (1999).

5. TANU was poorly organized and represented far less of the population than it claimed. In the pre-independence election of 1959 it won a landslide, but only 15 percent of the population voted due to limits set on education and income as qualifications (Mwansasu 1977:169–177; Bienen 1967:50–56). Once in power TANU became increasingly cut off from popular rural support and instead went along with Nyerere's unpopular policies of rural collectivization and state controls of trade and industry (Bienen 1967:64–65). Ironically, labor unionizers, African doctors and lawyers, and petty traders, some of the strongest supporters of TANU before independence, were among those most hurt by these policies (Shivji 1976:80, 83; 1990:13–19, 76; Hyden 1969:137–138, 215–216; 1980:103, 113–115). For a depressing history of TANU tracing its changes as it entered government and became a source of power and wealth for some, see Mlimuka and Kabudi (1986).

6. Some of my old friends in TANU proved endearingly naive. For example, one had begun as a labor union organizer and later moved up ever higher in government. He continued to speak out about labor betterment and even possible strikes. He was repeatedly warned and once even sent abroad on a "cushy" post, just to get him out of the way. Eventually he lost his job in government and was even placed in detention for a time. The new government could no more countenance strikes than could the colonial one; it had only promoted labor agitation in order to bring down the colonialists.

7. These new African officials were preoccupied with rules, procedures, titles, perquisites; they became semi-educated "Black Mandarins" embracing protocol to mask ineptitude and lack of moral conviction (West 1965:69–78; Tordoff 1965:85–88, 104–107; Hopkins 1974:116, 136–137, 236; Symonds 1966:180–193; Allen 1979:139; Shivji 1976:90–109). They were contemptuous of ordinary, poorly educated rural folk, though they expected them to work, sacrifice, and endure hardships. Cox aptly writes that dignity cannot be given to common labor when no dignity is afforded those laborers by those that rule them (1970:343). Cox was writing about blacks in the American South, but this was increasingly the situation in Tanganyika, where African bureaucrats preached "freedom and work" to their poor rural fellow countrymen. For valuable surveys on African leadership, see McGowan and Wacirah 1974.

8. After he left office, Tanganyika's last British governor, Sir Richard Turnbull, stated that while Western two-party democracy was admirable, new African states were better suited to a one-party state. Perhaps this was because such an authoritarian government resembled the colonial rule that Turnbull himself had so long directed (Allen 1979:177)

9. The most brilliant and acute criticisms of Nyerere's misconceived notions and their malignant results are by Shivji (1976, 1986, 1990), who taught in Dar es Salaam but also taught and published his strongest criticisms outside the country.

10. One of the last senior Europeans to leave the central administration was a state auditor, a man of impeccable rectitude, who told me that government officials valued him because he was not a native and therefore was disinterested. Even as late as 1965 Europeans held disconcertingly odd positions of trust. At that time I visited Tanzania and sought permission to travel and reside freely up-country. While there was no rule against this, I suspected I would find difficulties (I was right). After many weeks of waiting, I secured an appointment with a cabinet minister to get official permission (which later proved useless). When I reached the ministry, I was told that as a non-Tanganyikan I needed special permission and had to be searched before entering such a high-security building. When I finally gained entry into the minister's section, I was confronted with half a dozen white European women secretaries typing what I presumed to be confidential documents and freely coming and going into files and offices. This did not seem like much apparent concern about security from foreigners. I assume that these were able secretaries; they certainly were "ornamental."

11. Such clubs were quickly closed by the government. Still, clubs of one sort or another remained key premises for doing politics. In 1965 when I spent weeks fruitlessly trying to see a Tanzanian cabinet minister, I regularly saw him "doing business" late at night with other Africans in bars and dance clubs in Dar es Salaam.

12. The fact that newly rich African bureaucrats wanted to join an expensive yacht club was a topic of criticism by Dar es Salaam university students who had unsuccessfully protested the corruption of the government and their own supposedly difficult conditions (Peter and Mwangi 1985:161),

CONCLUSION

1. I here present a sample of diverse sources highly critical of Indirect Rule, noting that it inhibited political and economic development, was unstable, and divided Africans from one another (Robinson 1972:135; Hughes 1969:25; Tanganyika 1954:4; S. Berry 1993:25, 32; Davis 1973:54, 392-499; Bienen 1967:58; Crowder 1968:22; Porter 2007:6-7; Pratt 1982:264-266; Cannadine 2001:139). There was considerable rhetorical humbug supporting Indirect Rule (Balandier 1966:44, 89; Schumpeter 1951:66-67; Crocker 1970:113-117). Indirect Rule was based on "artifice and arrogance" (Hughes 1969:23). Above all, it froze African thinking in a stereotype of the past (Fanon 1967a:34) that later was transformed into some odd national versions of history and tradition (Jackson and Maddox 1998:277; Maddox and Giblin 2005:10; Samuel-Mbaekwe 1986: 88-90).

2. Berman's (1996) brilliant historical study of British rule in Kenya provides a superb Weberian/Marxist analysis of these contradictions and illusions. I read his fine book only after I had completed almost all of my book, but I provide some comparative references to it in earlier chapters. I am deeply grateful to my friend Ivan Karp for bringing this splendid study to my attention.

BIBLIOGRAPHY

Abani, Chris
  2000   *Graceland*. New York: Picador.
Abedi, Sheik Amri
  1963   *African Conference on Local Courts and Customary Law*. Dar es Salaam: Faculty of Law, University College.
Abrahams, R. G.
  1985   Introduction. In *Villagers, Villages, and the State in Northern Tanzania*. R. G. Abrahams, ed., pp. 1–15. African Monograph no. 4. Cambridge: African Studies Centre.
Achebe, Chinua
  1964   *Arrow of God*. London: Heinemann.
  1975[1973]   Colonial Criticism. In *Morning Yet on Creation Day: Essays*, pp. 3–18. London: Heinemann.
Adewoye, O.
  1970   Native Administration in a Mandated Territory: The Tanganyika Example, 1919–1945. *Tarikh* 3(2): 41–50.
Admiralty
  1916   *A Handbook of German East Africa*. London: His Majesty's Stationery Office.
African Studies Branch, Colonial Office
  1951   Methods of Direct Taxation in British Tropical Africa, part 2: East Africa. *Journal of African Administration* 3:30–41.
  1952   A Survey of the Development of Local Government in the African Territories Since 1947, vol. 3: Tanganyika. *Supplement. Journal of African Administration* 5:13–24.
Akpan, Ntieijong U.
  1970   Epitaph to Indirect Rule (1956). In *Problems in the History of Colonial Africa 1860–1960*, Robert O. Collins, ed., pp. 147–150. Englewood Cliffs, N.J.: Prentice Hall.
Alexander, Gilchrist
  1936   *Tanganyika Memories: A Judge in the Red Kanzu*. London: Blackie and Son.
Alexander, Jane
  1983   East and Central Africa. In *Voices and Echoes: Tales of Colonial Women*, pp. 7–53. London: Quartet Books.

Allen, Charles, ed.
1979[1986]   *Tales from the Dark Continent: Images of British Colonial Africa in the Twentieth Century.* New York: St. Martin's Press; later edition. London: Futura Macmillan.

Allott, A. N.
1950   The Extent of Operation of Native Customary Law. *Journal of African Administration* 2:4-11.
1970   *New Essays in African Law.* London: Butterworth's.
1978   The Development of the East African Legal System during the Colonial Period. In *History of East Africa,* vol. 3, D. A. Low and Allison Smith, eds., pp. 348-382. Oxford: Clarendon Press.

Allott, A. N., A. L. Epstein, and Max Gluckman
1969   Introduction. In *Ideas and Procedures in Customary African Law,* Max Gluckman, ed., pp. 1-96. London: Oxford University Press, for the International African Institute.

Alpers, Edward A.
2005   Kingalu, Mwana Shaha and Political Leadership in Nineteenth-Century Eastern Tanzania. In *In Search of a Nation,* Gregory H. Maddox and James L. Giblin, eds., pp. 32-54. Athens: Ohio University Press.

Anderson, Benedict
1991[1983]   *Imagined Communities.* Rev. edition. New York: Verso.

Anonymous
1909   Die Itumbaberge. *Deutsche Kolonialblatt:* 219.

Apthorpe, Raymond
1968   Does Tribalism Really Matter? *Transition* (27):18-22.

Arning, Wilhelm
1936   *Deutsch-Ostafrika, Gestern und Heute.* Berlin: Verlag von Dietrich Reimer.

Asad, Talal
1973   Introduction. In *Anthropology and the Colonial Encounter,* Talal Asad, ed., pp. 10-19. London: Ithaca Press.

Austen, Ralph A.
1967   The Official Mind of Indirect Rule: British Policy in Tanganyika, 1916-1939. In *Britain and Germany in Africa: Imperial Rivalry and Colonial Rule.* Prosser Gifford and William Roger Louis, eds., pp. 577-608. New Haven: Yale University Press.
1968   *Northwest Tanzania under German and British Rule: Colonial Policy and Tribal Politics, 1889-1939.* New Haven: Yale University Press.

Austin, Dennis
1982   The British Point of No Return? In *The Transfer of Power in Africa: Decolonization, 1940-1960,* J. Prosser Gifford and William Roger Louis, eds., pp. 33-54. New Haven: Yale University Press.

Bachelard, Gaston
1969[1958]   *The Poetics of Space (La poétique de l'espace).* Boston: Beacon Press.

Balandier, Georges
1966[1951]   The Colonial Situation: A Historical Approach. In *Social Change: The Colonial Situation,* Immanuel Wallerstein, eds., pp. 34-61. New York: John Wiley.
1970[1955]   *The Sociology of Black Africa (Sociologie actuelle de l'Afrique noir.* New York: John Wiley.

Bald, Detlef
1970   *Deutsch-Ostafrika 1900-1914.* Munich: Weltforum Verlag.

Barker, Jonathan
1974 Ujamaa in Cash-Crop Areas of Tanzania: Some Problems and Reflections. *Journal of African Studies* 1:441–463.
1979 The Debate on Rural Socialism in Tanzania. In *Towards Socialism in Tanzania*, Bismarck G. Mwansasu and Cranford Pratt, eds., pp. 95–124. Toronto: University of Toronto Press,

Barnes, J. A.
1954 *Politics in a Changing Society.* London: Oxford University Press, for the Rhodes-Livingstone Institute.
1969 The Politics of Law. In *Man in Africa,* Mary Douglas and Phyllis Kaberry, eds., pp. 99–118. London: Tavistock,

Bates, Darrell
1961 *A Fly-Switch from the Sultan.* London: Rupert Hart Davis.
1962 *The Mango and the Palm.* London: Rupert Hart Davis.
1972 *A Gust of Plumes: A Biography of Lord Twining of Godalming and Tanganyika.* London: Hodder and Stoughton.

Bates, Margaret L.
1957 *Tanganyika under British Administration 1920–1955,* D. Phil. dissertation, Nuffield College, University of Oxford.
1965 Tanganyika: Changes in African Life, 1918–1945. In *History of East Africa,* vol. 2, Vincent Harlow and Sally Chilver, eds., pp. 625–638. Oxford: Clarendon Press.
1976 Social Engineering, Multi-racialism, and the Rise of TANU, the Trust Territory of Tanganyika 1945–1961. In *History of East Africa,* vol. 3, A. Low and Alison Smith, eds., pp. 157–195. Oxford: Clarendon Press.

Baudet, Henri
1965[1959] *Paradise on Earth: Thoughts on European Images of Non-European Man.* New Haven: Yale University Press.

Baxter. J.
1879 Letter. *Church Missionary Intelligencer,* pp. 532–534.
1880 Letter to Lang (Mamboya, February). Church Missionary Society Archives.
1894 Letter to Baylis (Mpwapwa, 15 November). Church Missionary Society Archives.

Beachey, R. W.
1962 The Arms Trade in East Africa in the Late Nineteenth Century. *Journal of African History* 3:451–467.

Beck, Ann
1977 Medicine and Society in Tanganyika 1890–1930: A Historical Inquiry, *Transactions of the American Philosophical Society* 67, part 3: 1–59.

Behr, H. von
1891 *Von Kriegsbilder aus dem Araberaufstand im Deutsch-Ostafrika.* Leipzig: Brockhaus.

Beidelman, T. O.
1960 The Baraguyu. *Tanganyika Notes and Records* 55:245–278.
1961a Kaguru Justice and the Concept of Legal Fictions. *Journal of African Law* 5:3–20.
1961b Beer Drinking and Cattle Theft in Ukaguru: Intertribal Relations in a Tanganyika Chiefdom. *American Anthropologist* 54:534–559.

1961c   A Note on the Kamba of Kilosa District. *Tanganyika Notes and Records* 57:181–194.

1961d   Umwano und Ukaguru Students' Association: zwei stammespartikularische Bewegungen in einem Hauptlingstum in Tanganyika, *Anthropos* 58: 818–845; republished in 1970 in English translation as Umwano and Ukaguru Students' Association: Two Tribalistic Movements in a Tanganyika Chiefdom.In *Black Africa*, John Middleton, ed. pp. 303–326. New York: Macmillan, 1970.

1961e   *The Social System of Ukaguru: A Study in the Exercise of Power in an East African Chiefdom*. D.Phil. dissertation, Trinity College, University of Oxford, Oxford.

1962a   A History of Ukaguru, Kilosa District: 1857–1916. *Tanganyika Notes and Records* 58 and 59:11–37.

1962b   Iron-working in Ukaguru. *Tanganyika Notes and Records* 58 and 59:288–289.

1963a   Witchcraft in Ukaguru. In *Witchcraft and Sorcery in East Africa*, John Middleton and E. H. Winter, eds., pp. 57–98. London: Routledge and Kegan Paul.

1963b   Kaguru Omens: An East African People's Concepts of the Unusual, Unnatural and Supernatural. *Anthropological Quarterly* 46:43–59.

1963c   The Blood Covenant and the Concept of Blood in Ukaguru. *Africa* 33:321–342.

1963d   Notes on the Vidunda of Eastern Tanganyika: An Ethnographic Survey. *Tanganyika Notes and Records* 65:63–80.

1964   Intertribal Insult and Opprobrium in an East African Chiefdom (Ukaguru). *Anthropological Quarterly* 37:33–52.

1966   Intertribal Tensions in Some Local Government Courts in Colonial Tanganyika, part l. *Journal of African Law* 10:18–130.

1967a   Intertribal Tensions in Some Local Government Courts in Colonial Tanganyika, part 2. *Journal of African Law* 11:25–45.

1967b   *The Matrilineal Peoples of Eastern Tanzania*. London: International African Institute.

1967c   Addenda and Corrigenda to the Bibliography of *The Matrilineal Peoples of Eastern Tanzania*. *Africa* 39:186–188.

1970   Myth, Legend and Oral History. *Anthropos* 65:74–97.

1971a[1983]   *The Kaguru*. New York: Holt Rinehart and Winston. Repr. Prospect Heights, Ill.: Waveland Press.

1971b   Kaguru Descent Groups. *Anthropos* 66:373–396.

1972   The Kaguru House. *Anthropos* 67:1–18.

1974a   Social Theory and the Study of Christian Missionaries. *Africa* 49:235–249.

1974b   Further Addenda to the Bibliography of *The Matrilineal Peoples of Eastern Tanzania*. *Africa* 44:297–299.

1978   Chiefship in Ukaguru. *International Journal of African Historical Studies* 11:223–246.

1980   Women and Men in Two East African Societies. In *African Systems of Thought*, Ivan Karp and Charles Bird, eds. pp. 143–164. Bloomington: Indiana University Press.

1981   Third Addendum to the Bibliography of *The Matrilineal Peoples of Eastern Tanzania*. *Anthropos* 76:864–965.

1982a   *Colonial Evangelism: A Socio-historical Study of an East African Mission at the Grassroots*. Bloomington: Indiana University Press.

1982b The Organization and Maintenance of Caravans by the Church Missionary Society in Tanzania in the Nineteenth Century. *International Journal of African Historical Studies* 15:601–623.

1986[1993] *Moral Imagination in Kaguru Modes of Thought*. Bloomington: Indiana
University Press. Repr. Washington: Smithsonian Institution Press.

1988 Fourth Addendum to the Bibliography of *The Matrilineal Peoples of Eastern
Tanzania*. *Anthropos* 83:558.

1990 Review of Hansen: *Distant Companions*. *Anthropos* 85:226–228.

1991 Review of Feierman: *Peasant Intellectuals*. *International Journal of African
Historical Studies* 24: 693–695.

1997 *The Cool Knife: Imagery of Gender, Sexuality, and Moral Education in Ukaguru Initiation Ritual*. Washington: Smithsonian Institution Press.

1998 Marking Time. *Ethnos* 93(2):1–24.

1999 Altruism and Domesticity: Images of Missionizing Women among the
Church Missionary Society in Ukaguru Nineteenth Century East Africa. In *Gen-
dered Missions*, Mary Taylor Huber and Nancy Lutkehaus, eds., pp. 113–143. Ann
Arbor: University of Michigan Press.

2000a Fifth Addendum to the Bibliography of *The Matrilineal Peoples of Tanzania*.
Anthropos 95:235–236.

2000b Review of Pels: *A Politics of Presence*. *Anthropos* 95:629–630.

Benjaminsen, Tor, Faustin P. Maganga, and Jumanne Moshi Abdallah
2009 The Kilosa Killings: Political Ecology of a Farmer-herder Conflict in Tanzania. *Development and Change* 40:423–445.

Benton, Lauren
2002 *Law and Colonial Culture: Legal Regimes in World History, 1400–1900*. Cambridge: Cambridge University Press.

Berger, John
1979 *Pig Earth*. New York: Pantheon Books.

Berman, Bruce
1996 *Control and Crisis in Colonial Kenya: The Dialectic of Domination*. Athens:
Ohio University Press.

Berry, L., ed.
1971 *Tanganyika in Maps*. London: University of London Press.

Berry, Sara
1993 *No Condition Is Permanent: The Social Dynamics of Agrarian Change in Sub-
Saharan Africa*. Madison: University of Wisconsin Press.

Bienen, Henry
1967 *Tanzania: Party Transformation and Economic Development*. Princeton:
Princeton University Press.

1971 Political Parties and Political Machines in Africa. In *The State of the Nations*,
Michael F. Lofchie, ed., pp. 195–213. Berkeley: University of California Press.

Bissell, William Cunningham
2003 Engaging Colonial Nostalgia. *Cultural Anthropology* 20:215–248.

Blommaert, J.
1997 Intellectuals and Ideological Leadership in Ujamaa, Tanzania. *African Languages and Culture* 10:127–144.

Boahen, A. Ada
1987 *African Perspectives on Colonialism*. Baltimore: Johns Hopkins University
Press.

Boesen, Jannik

1979 Tanzania: from Ujamaa to Villagization. In *Towards Socialism in Tanzania,* Bismarck U. Mwansasu and Cranford Pratt, eds., pp. 125–144. Toronto: University of Toronto Press.

Bozeman, Adda

1976 *Conflict in Africa,* Princeton: Princeton University Press.

Brantlinger, Patrick

1985 Victorians and Africans: The Genealogy of the Myth of the Dark Continent. *General Inquiry* 12:166–203.

Breman, Jan

1990 Introduction: Race, A Class Apart. In *Imperial Monkey Business,* Jan Breman, ed., pp. 1–6. Amsterdam: VU University Press.

Brennan, James R.

2005 The Short History of Political Opposition and Multi-Party Democracy in Tanganyika, 1958–64. In *In Search of a Nation,* Gregory H. Maddox and James L. Giblin, eds., pp. 250–276. Athens: Ohio University Press.

Brett, E. A.

1973 *Colonialism and Underdevelopment in East Africa: The Politics of Economic Change.* London: Heinemann.

Briggs, John H.

1918 *In the East African War Zone.* London: Church Missionary Society.

Brooke, H. J.

1954 The Changing Character of Customary Courts. *Journal of African Administration* 6:67–73.

Brookfield, H. C.

1967 *Colonialism, Development and Independence.* Cambridge: Cambridge University Press.

Brown, G. Gordon, and A. McD. Bruce Hutt

1935 *Anthropology in Action.* London: Oxford University Press, for the International Institute of African Languages and Cultures.

Brown, Richard

1959 Indirect Rule as a Policy of Adaptation. In *From Tribal Rule to Modern Government.* Raymond Apthorpe, ed., pp. 49–56. Lusaka: Rhodes-Livingstone Institute.

Bryceson, Deborah

1988 Household, Home and Nation: Development Politics of the Nyerere Era. In *Tanzania After Nyerere,* Michael Hodd, ed., pp. 36–48. New York: Pinter.

Buchert, Lene

1994 *Education in the Development of Tanzania: 1919–90.* Athens: Ohio University Press.

Buell, Raymond Leslie

1965[1928] *The Native Problem in Africa*, vol. 1. London: Frank Cass.

Bujra, Janet

1992 Men and Work in the Tanzanian Home: How Did They Ever Learn. In *African Encounters with Domesticity,* Karen Tranberg Hansen, ed., pp. 242–265. New Brunswick: Rutgers University Press.

2000 *Serving Class: Masculinity and the Feminization of Domestic Service in Tanzania.* Edinburgh: Edinburgh University Press.

Bull, Bartle
　1988　*Safari: A Chronicle of Adventure.* New York: Penguin Books.
Burke, Fred
　1964　Tanganyika: The Search for Ujamaa. In *African Socialism,* Carl G. Rosberg, ed., pp. 194–219. Stanford: Stanford University Press, for the Hoover Institution on War, Revolution, and Peace.
Burton, Sir Richard F.
　1860　*The Lake Regions of Central Africa,* London: Longman, Green, Longman, and Roberts.
Cairn, J. S.
　1959　*Bush and Boma.* London: John Murray.
Callaway, Helen
　1987　*Gender, Culture and Empire: European Women in Colonial Nigeria.* Urbana: University of Illinois Press.
Cameron, Sir Donald
　1930　*Principles of Native Administration and Their Application.* Dar es Salaam: Government Printer.
　1939　*My Tanganyika and Some Nigeria.* London: George Allen and Unwin.
　1970[1934]　Indirect Administration. In *Problems in the History of Colonial Africa 1860–1960,* Robert O. Collins, ed., pp. 125–141. Englewood Cliffs, N.J.: Prentice-Hall.
Cameron, J., and N. A. Dodd
　1970　*Society, Schools and Progress in Tanzania.* New York: Pergamon Press.
Cameron, Kenneth M.
　1990　*Into Africa: The Story of the East African Safari.* London: Constable.
Cannadine, David
　1995　The Empire Strikes Back. *Past and Present* 147: 80–194.
　1999[1990]　*The Decline and Fall of the British Aristocracy.* New York: Vintage.
　2001　*Ornamentalism: How the British Saw Their Empire.* New York: Oxford University Press.
Césaire, Aimé
　1970　On the Nature of Colonialism (from *Discours sur le colonisme,* 1966). In *African Politics and Society,* O. L. Markowitz, ed., pp. 37–47. New York: Free Press.
Chachage, C. S. L.
　1988　British Rule and African Civilization in Tanganyika. *Journal of Historical Sociology* 1:199–223.
Chanock, Martin
　1985　*Law, Custom and Colonial Experience in Malawi and Zambia.* Cambridge: Cambridge University Press.
Chatterjee, Partha
　1986　*Nationalist Thought and the Colonial World.* Minneapolis: University of Minnesota Press.
Chidzero, B. T. O.
　1961　*Tanganyika and International Trusteeship.* London: Oxford University Press.
Church Missionary Society
　Church Missionary Archives, Executive Conference December 1903, Church Missionary Society, London.

Church Missionary Intelligencer, Church Missionary Society, London.
Proceedings of the Church Missionary Society, Church Missionary Society,
London.

Cliffe, Lionel

> 1967a The Political System. In *One Party Democracy: The Tanzania Elections,*
> Lionel Cliffe, ed., pp. 1–20. Nairobi: East African Publishing House.
> 1967b The Campaigns, pp. 227–253 in above.
> 1967c The Candidates, pp. 254–272 in above.
> 1967d Factors and Issues, pp. 299–327 in above
> 1967e Appendices, pp. 356–465 in above.

Cocks, Paul

> 1995 The Rhetoric of Science and the Critique of Imperialism in British Social
> Anthropology c.1870–1940. *History and Anthropology* 90:93–119.

Cohn, Bernard S.

> 1996 *Colonialism and Its Forms of Knowledge.* Princeton: Princeton University
> Press.

Coke, C. M.

> 1942 Notes on Wakaguru and Wasagara, typescript. Kilosa District
> Headquarters.

Cole, Henry

> 1895 Letter to Baylis (Kisokwa, 25 January). Church Missionary Society Archives.
> 1896 Letter to Baylis (Kisokwa, 23 January). Church Missionary Society Archives.
> 1902 Notes on the Wagogo. *Journal of Institute of Anthropology* 32:305–338.

Cole, J. S. R. and W. N. Denison

> 1964 *Tanganyika: The Development of Its Laws and Constitution.* London:
> Stevens.

Collier, Paul, Samuel M. Wangwe, Samir Muhammed Rachwan, with Albert Wagner

> 1986 *Poverty in Rural Tanzania: Ujamaa and Rural Development in the United Re-
> public of Tanzania.* Oxford: Clarendon.

Collins, Robert O.

> 1970 Indirect Rule in Theory and Practice. In *Problems in the History of Colonial
> Africa,* Robert O. Collins, ed., pp. 83–37. Englewood Cliffs, N.J.: Prentice-Hall.

Colonial Office

> 1951 *Development of African Local Government in Tanganyika.* Colonial 277.
> London: His Majesty's Stationery Office.

Colson, Elizabeth

> 1958 *Marriage and Family among the Plateau Tonga of Northern Rhodesia.* Man-
> chester: Manchester University Press, for the Rhodes-Livingstone Institute.
> 1974 *Tradition and Contract: The Problem of Order.* Chicago: Aldine Publishing.

Cooper, Frederick

> 1989 From Free Labor to Family Allowances: Labor and African Society in Co-
> lonial Discourse. *American Ethnologist* 16:745–765.
> 1994 Conflict and Connections: Rethinking Colonial African History. *American
> Historical Review* 99(5):1516–1545.
> 1997a Review of Mamdani: *Citizen and Subject, International Labor and Working
> Class History* 52:156–160.
> 1997b Modernizing Bureaucrats, Backward Africans, and the Development Con-
> cept. In *International Development and the Social Sciences,* Frederick Cooper and
> Randall Packard, eds., pp. 64–97. Berkeley: University of California Press.

1998   *Decolonization and African Society: The Labour Question in French and British Africa.* Cambridge: Cambridge University Press.

2005   *Colonialism in Question.* Berkeley: University of California Press.

Cooper, Frederick, and Ann L. Stoler

1989   Introduction. Tensions of Empire: Colonial Control and Visions of Rule. *American Anthropologist* 16:699–621.

Cornevin, Robert

1969   The Germans in Africa before 1918. In *Colonialism in Africa*, L. H. Gann and Peter Duignan, eds., pp. 383–419. Cambridge: Cambridge University Press.

Cory, Hans

1957   The Councils and the Native Authority, typescript. Morogoro District Headquarters.

Coser, Lewis A.

1973   Servants: The Obsolescence of an Occupational Role. *Social Forces* 52: 31–40.

1974   *Greedy Institutions: Patterns of Undivided Commitment.* London: Free Press.

Costa, A. A.

1999   Chieftaincy and Colonisation: African Structures of Government and Colonial Administration. *African Studies* 59:13–43.

Cotran, Eugene

1967   The Position of Customary Criminal Law in African Countries. In *East African Law and Social Change*, G. F. Sawyer, ed., pp. 114–125. Nairobi: East African Publishing House.

Court, David

1976   The Education System as a Response to Inequality in Tanzania and Kenya. *Journal of Modern African Studies* 17:661–690.

Coward, Noël

1995[1965]   *The Lyrics of Noël Coward.* London: Mandarin.

Cox, Oliver Cromwell

1970[1948]   *Caste, Class, and Race.* New York: Modern Reader Paperbacks.

Crocker, W. R.

1970[1936]   Indirect Rule: an Elaborate Facade. In *Problems in the History of Colonial Africa*, Robert O. Collins, ed., pp. 111–118. Englewood Cliffs, N.J.: Prentice-Hall.

Crowder, Michael

1964   Indirect Rule—French and British Style. *Africa* 34:197–205.

1968   *West Africa under Colonial Rule.* London: Hutchinson of London.

1978   The White Chiefs of Tropical Africa (1969). In *Colonial West Africa: Collected Essays*, pp. 122–150. London: Frank Cass.

Curtin, Philip

1964   *The Image of Africa.* Madison: University of Wisconsin Press.

Davidson, Basil

1992   *The Black Man's Burden.* New York: Times Books.

Davis, R. Hunt

1973   Interpreting the Colonial Period in African History. *African Affairs* 72 (289):383–400.

Deekes, D.

1896   Letter to Baylis (Mamboya, 26 October). Church Missionary Society Archives.

Deutsch, Jan-Georg
    2006   *Emancipation without Abolition in German East Africa c. 1884–1914*. Athens: Ohio University Press.
Deutsche Kolonialblatt
    1890   non-authored and non-titled item: 69.
Dirks, Nicholas B.
    1992   Introduction: Colonialism and Culture. In *Colonialism and Culture,* Nicholas B. Dirks, ed., pp. 1–26. Ann Arbor: University of Michigan Press.
Doherty, Joe
    1982   Review of James N. Kariuki: Tanganyika's Human Revolution. *Africa* 52:116–117.
Dougherty, Mary Imbriglia
    1966   Tanganyika during the Twenties: A Study of the Social and Economic Development of Tanganyika under British Mandate. *African Studies* 25:197–225.
Dryden, Stanley
    1968   *Local Administration in Tanzania*. Nairobi: East African Publishing House.
Dumbuya, Peter A.
    1995   *Tanganyika under International Mandate 1919–1946*. Lanham, Md.: University Press of America.
Dundas, Sir Charles
    1955   *African Crossroads*. London: Macmillan.
Durkheim, Émile
    1978   Introduction to Morality (Introduction B, la morale, 1920). In *Émile Durkheim on Institutional Analysis,* Mark Traugott, ed., pp. 191–202. Chicago: University of Chicago Press.
East African Statistical Department
    1958   *Tanganyika Population Census 1957*, parts 1 and 2, Nairobi: East African Statistical Department.
Eberlie, R. F.
    1960   German Achievement in East Africa. *Tanganyika Notes and Records* 55:181–214.
Ehrlich, Cyril
    1964[1976]   Some Aspects of Economic Policy in Tanganyika, 1945–1960. *Journal of Modern African Studies* 2:265–277; republished as The Poor Country: The Tanganyika Economy from 1945–1960. In *History of East Africa*, vol. 3, D. A. Low and Alison Smith, eds., pp. 290–330. Oxford: Clarendon Press.
Ekeh, Peter P.
    1975   Colonialism and the Two Publics in Africa: A Theoretical Statement. *Comparative Studies in Society and History* 17:91–112.
    1990   Social Anthropology and Two Contrasting Uses of Tribalism in Africa. *Comparative Studies in Society and History* 32:660–700.
Elton, J.
    1879   *Travels among the Lakes and Mountains of Eastern and Central Africa*. London: Murray.
Epstein, A. L.
    1953   *The Administration of Justice and the Urban African*. Colonial Research Studies 7. London: Her Majesty's Stationery Office for the Colonial Office.

1954 *Judicial Techniques and Judicial Process.* Rhodes-Livingstone Papers 23. Manchester: Manchester University Press.

Ergas, Zaki
1980 Why Did the Ujamaa Village Policy Fail? *Journal of Modern African Studies* 18: 387–410.

Ernst, Klaus
1980 Racialism, Racialist Ideology and Colonialism, Past and Present. In *Sociological Theories of Race and Colonialism*, pp. 450–474. Paris: UNESCO.

Fage, John D.
1967 A British and German Colonial Rule: A Synthesis and Summary. In *Britain and Germany in Africa: Imperial Rivalry and Colonial Rule.* Prosser Gifford and William Roger Louis, eds., pp. 691–706. New Haven: Yale University Press.

Falkenhorst, C.
1890 *Deutsch-Ostafrika,* Berlin: Union Deutsche Verlags Gesellschaft.

Fallers, Lloyd A.
1955 The Predicament of the Modern African Chief: An Instance from Uganda. *American Anthropologist* 57: 290–305.
1956 *Bantu Bureaucracy.* Cambridge: W. Heffer, for the East African Institute of Social Research.
1967 *Law without Precedent.* Chicago: University of Chicago Press.

Fanon, Frantz
1963 *The Wretched of the Earth (Les damnés de la terre,* 1961). New York: Grove Press.
1965 *A Dying Colonialism (L'an cinq de la révolution algérienne,* 1959). New York: Grove Press.
1967a *Toward the African Revolution (Political Essays) (Pour la révolution africaine,* 1964). New York: Monthly Review Press.
1967b *Black Skin, White Masks (Peau noire, masques blancs,* 1952). New York: Grove Press.

Feierman, Steven
1990 *Peasant Intellectuals: Anthropology and History in Tanzania.* Madison: University of Wisconsin Press.

Fenton, C. Stephen
1980 Race, Class and Politics in the Work of Émile Durkheim. In *Sociological Theories: Race and Colonialism,* pp. 143–180. Paris: UNESCO.

Ferguson, James
2002 Of Mimicry and Membership: Africans and the "New World Society." *Cultural Anthropology* 17: 551–569.

Fieldhouse, D. R.
1983[1978] *Colonialism 1820–1945: An Introduction.* London: Macmillan.

Fields, Karen E.
1985 *Revival and Rebellion in Colonial Central Africa.* Princeton: Princeton University Press.

Finley, Moses I.
1976 Colonies: An Attempt at a Typology. *Transactions of the Royal Historical Society* 26:167–188.

Firth, Raymond
1973 Whose Frame of Reference? One Anthropologist's Experience. *Anthropological Forum* 4:145–167.

Fitzpatrick, J. F. J.
    1970   Nigeria's Curse: Indirect Rule (1934). In *Problems in the History of Colonial Africa 1860–1960*, Robert O. Collins, ed., pp. 118–124. Englewood Cliffs, N. J.: Prentice-Hall.

Fonck, H.
    1894   Bericht über meinen Marsch Mpwapwa-Ugogo-Ussandawe-Irangi-Uassi *Mitteilungen von Forschungsreisenden über Gelehrten aus den Deutschen Schutzgebieten* (Berlin) 8: 291–296.
    1907   *Deutsch-Ost-Afrika.* Berlin: Vossiche Buchhandling.

Förster, Brix
    1890   *Deutsch-Ostafrika.* Leipzig: Brodhaus.

Fosbrooke, Henry A.
    1959a   Tanganyika: The Application of Indirect Rule to Chiefless Societies. In *From Tribal Rule to Modern Government*, Raymond Apthorpe, ed., pp. 17–29. Lusaka: Rhodes-Livingstone Institute.
    1959b   Tanganyika: A Note on Successes and Failure in Luguru Adaptation. In *From Tribal Rule to Modern Government*, Raymond Apthorpe, ed., pp. 173–179. Lusaka: Rhodes-Livingstone Institute.

Frankel, S. H.
    1938   *Capital Investment in Africa.* London: Oxford University Press.

Freeman-Grenville, G. S. F.
    1963   The German "Sphere" 1884–1898. In *History of East Africa*, Roland Oliver and Gervase Mathew, eds., pp. 433–453. Oxford: Clarendon Press.

Freyhold, Michaela von
    1976   The Problem of Rural Development and the Politics of Ujamaa Vijijini in Handeni. *The African Review* 6: 129–142.
    1979   *Ujamaa Villages in Tanzania: Analysis of a Social Experiment.* New York: Monthly Review Press.

Friedland, William H.
    1966   The Evolution of Tanganyika's Political System. In *The Transformation of East Africa* Stanley Diamond and Fred Burke, eds., pp. 241–311. New York: Basic Books.

Friedrichsmeyer, Sara, Sara Lennox, and Susanne Zantop
    1998   Introduction. In *The Imperialist Imagination: German Colonialism and Its Legacy*, Sara Friedrichsmeyer, Sara Lennox, and Susanne Zantop, eds., pp. 1–29. Ann Arbor: University of Michigan Press.

Fuchs, P.
    1907   *Wirtschaftliche Eisenbahn-erkundungen im mittleren und nordlichen Deutsch-Ostafrika.* Berlin: Kolonial wirtschaftliche Komitee.

Fuggles-Couchman, N. R.
    1964   *Agriculture in Tanganyika: 1945–1960.* Stanford: Food Research Institute, Stanford University.

Furley, O. W.
    1971   Education and Chiefs in East Africa in the Inter-war Period. *Transafrican Journal of History* 1:60–83.

Furley, O. W., and T. Watson
    1966   Education in Tanganyika between the Wars: Attempts to Blend Two Cultures. *The South Atlantic Quarterly* 65:471–490.

Furnivall, J. S.

1956[1946]   *Colonial Policy and Practice: A Comparative Study of Burma and Netherlands India.* New York: New York University Press,

Gailey, Harry A.

1974   *Sir Donald Cameron: Colonial Governor.* Stanford: Hoover Institution Press.

Gallie, W. B.

1964   *Philosophy and the Historical Understanding.* London: Chatto and Windus.

Gann, Lewis H., and Peter Duignan

1962   *White Settlers in Tropical Africa.* Harmondsworth: Penguin.

1967   *Burden of Empire: An Appraisal of Western Colonialism in Africa South of the Sahara.* New York: F. A. Praeger, for the Hoover Institution on War, Revolution, and Peace, Stanford University.

1977   *The Rulers of German Africa 1884–1914.* Stanford: Stanford University Press.

1978a   *The Rulers of British Africa 1870–1914.* Stanford: Stanford University Press.

1978b   Introduction. In *African Proconsuls. European Governors in Africa,* Lewis H. Gann and Peter Duignan, eds., pp. 1–16. Stanford: Free Press, for the Hoover Institution.

1978c   German Governors: An Overview. In *African Proconsuls: European Governors in Africa,* Lewis H. Gann and Peter Duignan, eds., pp. 467–472. Stanford: Free Press, for the Hoover Institution.

Gartrell, B.

1984   Colonial Wives: Villains or Victims. In *The Incorporated Wife,* H. Callan and S. Ardener, eds., pp. 165–185. London: Croom Helm.

Geiger, Susan

2005   Engendering and Gendering African Nationalism: Rethinking the Case of Tanganyika (Tanzania). In *In Search of a Nation,* Gregory H. Maddox and James N. Giblin, eds., pp. 278–289. Athens: Ohio University Press.

George, Betty

1960   *Education for Africans in Tanganyika: A Preliminary Survey.* United States Department of Health, Education, and Welfare Bulletin No. 19. Washington: Government Printing Office.

Georges, P. T.

1967   The Court in the Tanzania One-Party State. In *East African Law and Social Change,* G. F. A. Sawyer, ed., pp. 25–47. Nairobi: East African Literature Publishing House.

Giblin, James L.

1992   *The Politics of Environmental Control in Northeastern Tanzania 1840–1940.* Philadelphia: University of Pennsylvania Press.

1996   The Precolonial Politics of Disease Control in the Lowlands of Northeastern Tanzania. In *Custodians of the Land.* Gregory Maddox, James Giblin, and Isaia N. Kimambo, eds., pp. 127–151. Athens: Ohio University Press.

Gifford, Prosser

1967   Indirect Rule: Touchstone or Tombstone for Colonial Policy? In *Britain and Germany in Africa: Imperial Rivalry and Colonial Rule.* Prosser Gifford and William Roger Louis, eds., pp. 351–391. New Haven: Yale University Press.

Girouard, Mark

1981   *The Return to Camelot: Chivalry and the English Gentleman.* New Haven: Yale University Press.

Gluckman, Max

1955   *The Judicial Process among the Barotse of Northern Rhodesia*. Manchester: Manchester University Press, for the Rhodes-Livingstone Institute.

1958   *Analysis of a Social Situation in Zululand*. Rhodes-Livingstone Papers 28. Manchester: Manchester University Press.

1963   The Reasonable Man in Barotse Law. In *Order and Rebellion in Tribal Africa*, pp. 178–205. London: Cohen and West.

1965a   *The Ideas in Barotse Jurisprudence*. New Haven: Yale University Press.

1965b   *Politics, Law and Ritual in Tribal Society*. Oxford: Basil Blackwell.

1968   Inter-Hierarchical Roles: Professional and Party Ethics in Tribal Areas in South and Central Africa. In *Local-level Politics*. Marc J. Swartz, ed., pp. 60–93. Chicago: Aldine.

1969   Property Rights and Status in African Traditional Law. In *Ideas and Procedures in African Customary Law*, Max Gluckman, ed., pp. 252–265. London: Oxford University Press, for the International African Institute.

1970   Tribalism in Modern British Central Africa. In *African Politics and Society*, Irving Leonard Markovitz, ed., pp. 81–195. New York: Free Press.

Gluckman, Max, J. C. Mitchell, and John Barnes

1983[1949]   The Village Headman in British Central Africa. In *Order and Rebellion in Tribal Africa*, Max Gluckman, ed., pp. 146–170. London: Cohen and West.

Goldthorpe, J. E.

1958   *Outlines of East African Society: Kampala*. Department of Sociology, Makerere College, University College of East Africa.

Goody, Jack

1995   *The Expansive Moment: Anthropology in Britain and Africa 1918–1970*. Cambridge: Cambridge: University Press.

Gopal, Gita, and Maryam Salim, eds.

1998   *Gender and Law: East Africa Speaks*. Washington: World Bank.

Gordon, Jay

1967   African Law and the Historian. *Journal of African Law* 8:335–346.

Grady, Denise

2009a   Where Life's Start Is a Deadly Risk. *New York Times* (May 24).

2009b   The Deadliest Toll of Abortion by Amateurs. *New York Times* (Science Times, June 2).

Graham, J. D.

1976   Indirect Rule: The Establishment of "Chiefs" and "Tribes" in Cameron's Tanganyika. *Tanzania Notes and Records* 77 and 78:1–9.

Green, Reginald Herbert

1979   Tanzanian Political Economy Goals, Strategies, and Results, 1969–74: Notes Towards an Interim Assessment. In *Towards Socialism in Tanzania*, Bismarck U. Mwansasu and Cranford Pratt, pp. 19–45. Toronto: University of Toronto Press.

Gregory, Robert G.

1962   *Sidney Webb and East Africa*. University of California Publications in History, vol. 72. Berkeley: University of California Press.

Guha, Ranajit

1997   *Dominance without Hegemony: History and Power in Colonial India*, Cambridge: Harvard University Press.

Guillebaud, C. W.
1958 *An Economic Survey of the Sisal Industry of Tanganyika.* Welwyn, U.K.: James Nisbet, for the Tanganyika Sisal Growers' Association.

Gulliver, P. H.
1969 Introduction. In *Tradition and Transition in East Africa,* P. H. Gulliver, ed., pp. 5–38. London: Routledge and Kegan Paul.

Gunzel, Theodor
1966 Memoirs of a German District Commissioner. In Mwanza, 1907–1916, Ralph Austen, ed. *Tanzania Notes and Records* 66: 171–179.

Gwassa, G. C.
1969 The German Intervention and African Resistance in Tanzania. In *A History of Tanzania,* I. N. Kimambo and T. N. Temu, eds., pp. 85–122. Nairobi: East African Publishing House.

Hailey, Lord
1950 *Native Administration in the British African Territories,* part 1: *East Africa: Uganda, Kenya, Tanganyika.* London: Her Majesty's Stationery Office.
1951 *Native Administration in the British African Territories,* part 4: *A General Survey of the System of Native Administration.* London: Her Majesty's Stationery Office.

Halbwachs, Maurice
1980 *The Collective Memory* (*Memoire collective,* 1950). New York: Harper Row.

Hammond, Dorothy, and Alta Jablow
1970 *The Africa That Never Was.* Prospect Heights, Ill.: Waveland Press.

Hannigan, A. St. J.
1961 The Imposition of Western Law Forms upon Primitive Societies. *Journal of Modern African Studies* 4: 1–9.

Hansen, Karen Tranberg
1989 *Distant Companions: Servants and Employers in Zambia 1900–1985.* Ithaca: Cornell University Press.
1992 Introduction: Domesticity in Africa. In *African Encounters with Domesticity,* Karen Tranberg Hansen, ed., pp. 1–22. New Brunswick: Rutgers University Press.

Haynes, Jeff
1996 *Religion and Politics in Africa.* London: East African Educational Publishers, Zed Books.

Headricks, Daniel R.
1981 *The Tools of Empire.* London: Oxford University Press.

Henderson, W. O.
1962 *Studies in German Colonial History.* London: Frank Cass.

Herbert, Eugenia
2002 *Twilight on the Zambezi: Colonialism in Central Africa.* New York: Palgrave Macmillan.

Herdern, Charles
1941 *Military Operations in East Africa,* vol. 1. London: His Majesty's Stationery Office.

Heussler, Robert
1963 *Yesterday's Rulers: The Making of the British Colonial Service.* Syracuse: Syracuse University Press.
1971 *British Tanganyika: An Essay and Documentation on District Administration.* Durham: Duke University Press.

Hill, Francis

    1979–80   Administrative Decentralization for Development, Participation, and Control in Tanzania. *Journal of African Studies* 6:182–192.

Hill, J. F. R., and J. P. Moffett

    1955   *Tanganyika: A Review of Its Resources and Their Development.* Dar es Salaam: Government of Tanganyika

Hirji, Karim F.

    1980   Colonial Ideological Apparatuses in Tanganyika under the Germans. In *Tanzania under Colonial Rule,* M. N. Y. Kaniki, ed., pp. 192–233. London: Longman.

Hirsch, Susan F.

    1998   *Pronouncing and Persevering: Gender and the Discourses of Disputing in an African Islamic Court.* Chicago: University of Chicago Press.

Hobson, J. A.

    1967[1902]   *Imperialism.* Ann Arbor: University of Michigan Press.

Hochschild, Adam

    1998   *King Leopold's Ghost.* New York: Houghton Mifflin.

Holtzman Jon

    2009   *Uncertain Tastes.* Berkeley: University of California Press.

Hopkins, Raymond F.

    1974   *Political Roles in a New State: Tanzania's First Decade.* New Haven: Yale University Press.

Hordern, C.

    1941   *Military Operations in East Africa,* vol. 1. London: His Majesty's Stationery Office.

Hore, A.

    1894   *To Lake Tanganyika in a Bath Chair.* London: Sampson Low.

Hornsby, George

    1964   German Educational Achievement in East Africa. *Tanganyika Notes and Records* 62:83–90.

Hughes, A. J.

    1969   *East Africa.* Baltimore: Penguin Books.

Humphreys, Sally

    1985   Law as Discourse. *History and Anthropology* 1:241–264.

Hunt, Nancy Rose

    1992   Colonial Fairy Tales and the Knife and Fork: Doctrine in the Heart of Africa. In *African Encounters with Domesticity,* Karen Tranberg Hansen, ed., pp. 143–171. New Brunswick: Rutgers University Press.

    1997   Introduction. In *Gendered Colonialisms in African History,* Nancy Rose Hunt, ed., pp. 1–13. Oxford: Basil Blackwell.

Huxley, Elspeth

    1948   *Sorcerer's Apprentice: A Journey through East Africa.* London: Chatto and Windus.

Hyam, Ronald

    1990   *Empire and Sexuality: The British Experience.* Manchester: Manchester University Press.

Hyden, Goren

    1969   *Political Development in Rural Tanzania: Tanu Yajenga Inchi,* Nairobi: East African Publishing House.

1980   *Beyond Ujamaa in Tanzania: Underdevelopment and an Uncaptured Peasantry.* Berkeley: University of California Press.

Hyden, Goren, and Donald C. Williams

1974   A Community Model of African Politics: Illustrations from Nigeria and Tanzania. *Comparative Studies in Society and History* 36(1):68–90

Iliffe, John

1968   Tanzania under German and British Rule. In *Zamani: A Survey of East African History,* B. A. Ogot and J. A. Kiernan, eds., pp. 290–311. Nairobi: East African Publishing House.

1969   *Tanganyika under German Rule 1905–1912.* Cambridge: Cambridge University Press.

1979   *A Modern History of Tanganyika.* Cambridge: Cambridge University Press.

Ingham, Kenneth

1962   *A History of East Africa.* London: Longmans.

1965   Tanganyika: The Mandate and Cameron 1919–1931; and Tanganyika: Slump and Short-term Governors 1932–1945. In *A History of East Africa,* vol. 2, Vincent Harlow and Sally Chilver, eds., pp. 543–593; 594–624. Oxford: Clarendon Press.

Ingle, Clyde R.

1972   *From Village to State in Tanzania.* Ithaca: Cornell University Press.

Jackson, Robert H., and Gregory Maddox

1998   The Creation of Identity: Colonial Society in Bolivia and Tanzania. *Comparative Studies in Society and History* 35:263–184.

Jahresbericht über die Entwicklung der Schutzgebiete in Afrika und der Südsee. Berlin: Mittler.

Jeater, Diana

2000   "Their Idea of Justice Is So Peculiar": Southern Rhodesia 1890–1910. In *The Moral World of the Law,* Peter P. Cose, ed., pp. 176–195. Cambridge: Cambridge University Press.

Jeffries, Sir Charles

1938   *The Colonial Empire and Its Civil Service.* Cambridge: Cambridge University Press.

1949   *Partners for Progress: The Men and Women of the Colonial Service.* London: George G. Harrap.

Jerman, Helene

1997   *Between Five Lines: The Development of Ethnicity in Tanzania with Special Reference to the Western Bagamoyo District.* Somerset, N.J.: Transaction.

Joelson, F. S.

1920   *The Tanganyika Territory.* London: T. Fisher Unwin.

Jones, Thomas Jesse

1970[1925]   *Education in East Africa.* New York: Negro Universities Press.

Kant, Immanuel

1956   Idea for a Universal History from a Cosmopolitan Point of View (Idee zu allgemeinest Geschichte in welt-bürgerlicher Absicht, 1784). In *Kant: Selections,* pp. 415–425. New York: Macmillan.

Kapinga, W. B. I.

1986   State Control of the Working Class through Labour Legislation. In *The State and the Working People of Tanzania,* Issa G. Shivji, ed., pp. 87–106. Dakar: Codesria.

Karp, Ivan

2002 Development and Personhood. In *Critically Modern Alternatives, Alterities, Anthropologies*, Bruce M. Knauft, ed., pp. 62–104. Bloomington: Indiana University Press.

Kaundinya, R.

1918 *Errinerungen aus meinen Pflanzerjahren in Deutsch-Ost-Afrika*. Leipzig: Haberland.

Kelly, John D.

1992 Review of Ronald Hyam: Empire and Sexuality. *Journal of the History of Sexuality* 2:276–278.

Kennedy, Dane

1987 *Islands of White: Settler Society in Kenya and Southern Rhodesia, 1890–1939*. Durham: Duke University Press.

1996 History and Post-Colonial Theory. *Journal of Imperial and Commonwealth History* 24:345–363.

Kennedy, Raymond

1945 The Colonial Crisis and the Future. In *The Science of Man in the World Crisis*, Ralph Linton, ed., pp. 306–346. New York: Columbia University Press.

Kieran, J. A.

1970 Abushiri and the Germans. In *Hadith 2*, Bethwell A. Ogot, ed., pp. 157–201. Nairobi: East African Publishing House.

1971 Christian Villages in North-eastern Tanzania. *Transafrican Journal of History* 1:24–38.

Kiernan, V. G.

1972 *The Lords of Human Kind*. Harmondsworth: Penguin Books.

Killingray, David

1986 The Maintenance of Law and Order in British Colonial Africa. *African Affairs* 88:411–437.

2003 Punishment to Fit the Crime? Penal Policy and Practice in British Colonial Africa. In *A History of Prison and Confinement in Africa*, Florence Benault, ed., pp. 97–118. Portsmouth, N.H.: Heinemann.

Kilosa District Book, Kilosa District Headquarters.

Kimambo, Isaria N.

1991 *Penetration and Protest in Tanzania: The Impact of the World Economy on the Pare 1860–1960*. Athens: Ohio University Press.

King, Anthony D.

1976 *Colonial Urban Development*. London: Routledge

1985 Colonial Cities: Global Pivots of Change. In *Colonial Cities*, Robert J. Ross and Gerard J. Telkamp, eds., pp. 7–32. Dordrecht: Martinus Nijhoff, for Leiden University Press.

Kirk-Greene, A. H. M.

1978 On Governorship and Governors, British Africa. In *African Proconsuls: European Governors in Africa*, Lewis H. Gann and Peter Duignan, eds., pp. 209–264. Stanford: Free Press, for the Hoover Institution.

1980a The Thin White Line: The Size of the British Civil Service in Africa. *African Affairs* 79:25–44.

1980b "Damnosa Hereditas": Ethnic Ranking and the Martial Races Imperative in Africa. *Ethnic and Racial Studies* 3:393–414.

1982   Margery Perham and Colonial Administration: A Direct Influence on Indirect Rule. In *Oxford and the Idea of Commonwealth*, G. Madden and D. F. Fieldhouse, eds., pp. 122–143. London: Croom and Helm.

1986a   Colonial Administration and Race Relations: Some Research Reflections and Direction. *Ethnic and Racial Studies* 9:275–287.

1986b   Introduction (1970). In *Tales of the Dark Continent: Images of British Colonial Africa in the Twentieth Century*. Charles Allen, ed., pp. xii–xiv. London: Futura Macmillan.

1991   *A Biographical Dictionary of the British Colonial Service*. London: Hans Zell.

1999   *On Crown Service: A History of HM Colonial and Overseas Civil Services: 1837–1937*. London: I. B. Taurus Publishers.

2000   *Britain's Imperial Administration, 1858–1966*. New York: Macmillan, for St. Anthony's College, University of Oxford.

2006   *Symbol of Authority: The British District Officer in Africa*. New York: I. B. Tauris.

Kirkwood, Deborah

1984   Settler Wives in Southern Rhodesia: A Case Study. In *The Incorporated Wife*, H. Callan and S. Ardener, eds., pp. 143–164. London: Croom Helm.

Kiwanuka, M. Semakala

1970   Colonial Policies and Administrations in Africa: The Myths of the Contrasts. *African Historical Studies* 3:295–315.

Kjekshus, Helge

1975   *The Elected Elites: A Socio-Economic Profile of Candidates in Tanzania's Parliamentary Election, 1970*. Research Report no. 29. Uppsala: Scandinavian Institute of African Studies.

1977a   *Ecology Control and Economic Development in East African History: The Case of Tanganyika 1850–1950*. Berkeley: University of California Press.

1977b   The Tanzanian Villagization Policy: Implementational Issues and Ecological Dimensions. *Canadian Journal of African Studies* 11:269–287.

Knoff, David, and G. Von der Mahl

1967   Political Socialization in East Africa. *Journal of Modern African Studies* 5(1):13–51.

Koponen, Jahani

1995   *Development for Exploitation: German Colonial Policies in Mainland Tanzania, 1884–1914*. Hamburg: Lit Verlag, for the Finnish Historical Society.

Kuper, Leo

1980   The Theory of the Plural Society, Race and Conquest. In *Sociological Theories: Race and Colonialism*, pp. 239–266. Paris: UNESCO.

Labour Research Department

1926   *British Imperialism in East Africa*, Colonial Series no. 1. London: Labour Research Department.

Ladkin, R. S.

1953   The Medical Officer and Local Government. *Journal of African Administration* 5:21–30.

Laiten, David

1992   *Language Repertoires and State Construction in Africa*. Cambridge: Cambridge University Press.

Lamb, Patricia Frazer, and Kathryn Joyce Hohlwein
    1983   *Touchstones: Letters between Two Women.* New York: Harper and Row.

Lambrecht, Bezirksamtmann
    1903   Über die Landwirtschaft der Eingeborenen im Bezirk Kilossa. In *Berichte über Land-und-Forst-Wirtschaft in Deutsch-Ostafrika,* pp. 391–434. Heidelberg: C. Winter's Universitäts Buchandlung.

Langheld, Wilhelm
    1909   *Zwanzig Jahre in Deutschen Kolonien.* Berlin: Wilhelm Weicher.

Last, J. T.
    1878   Letter. *Church Missionary Intelligencer:* 645.
    1879   Letter to Wright (24 December). Church Missionary Society Archives.
    1880   Letter. *Church Missionary Intelligencer:* 742–744.
    1883a   Letter. *Church Missionary Intelligencer:* 293–294.
    1883b   A Visit to the Wa-itumba Iron-workers and the Mhangaheri, near Mamboia in East Central Africa. *Royal Geographical Society* 5: 81–92.
    1885   *Polyglotta Africana Orientalis.* London: Society for Promoting Christian Knowledge.
    1886   *Grammar of the Kaguru Language, Eastern Equatorial Africa.* London: Society for Promoting Christian Knowledge.

Latham, Gwynneth, and Michael Latham
    1995   *Kilimanjaro Tales: The Saga of a Medical Family in East Africa.* London: Radcliffe.

Lawrence, Tony
    2007   *The Dar Mutiny.* Brighton: Book Guild.

Lessing, Doris
    1961[1950]   *The Grass Is Singing.* Harmondsworth: Penguin.

Levack, Brian P.
    1999   The Decline and End of Witchcraft Prosecutions. In *Witchcraft and Magic in Europe: Eighteenth and Nineteenth Centuries,* Bengt Ankerloo and Stuart Clark, eds., pp. 1–93. Philadelphia: University of Pennsylvania Press.

Levine, Donald N.
    1979   Simmel at a Distance: On the History and Systematics of the Sociology of the Stranger. In *Strangers in African Societies,* William A. Shack and Elliot P. Skinner, eds., pp. 21–36. Berkeley: University of California.
    1985   *The Flight from Ambiguity.* Chicago: University of Chicago Press.

Lewin, Evans
    1915   *The Germans and Africa.* London: Cassell.

Lewis, Anthony
    1970   Law and Policy in East Africa, *New York Times* (Op Ed, January 3).

Lewis, Diane
    1973   Anthropology and Colonialism. *Current Anthropology* 14:581–559.

Lewis, Roy, and Yvonne Foy
    1971   *Painting Africa White: The Human Side of British Colonialism.* New York: Universe Books.

Leys, Colin
    1968   Inter Alia—or Tanzaphilia and All That. *Transition* 34:51–53.

Liebenow, J. Gus
    1956a   Some Problems in Introducing Local Government Reform in Tanganyika. *Journal of African Administration* 8:132–137.

1956b Responses to Planned Political Change in a Tanganyika Tribal Group. *American Political Science Review* 50:442–461.

1971 *Colonial Rule and Political Development in Tanzania,* Evanston, Ill.: Northwestern University Press.

Lindblom, Gerhard

1920 *The Akamba: An Ethnological Monograph,* 2nd edition. Uppsala: Archives d'études orientales.

Listowel, Judith

1965 *The Making of Modern Tanganyika.* London: Chatto and Windus.

Lohrmann, Ullrich

2007 *Voices from Tanganyika: Great Britain, the United Nations and the Decolonization of a Trust Territory, 1940–1962.* Europa-Uebersee-Historische Studien. Berlin: LIT Verlag.

Lonsdale, John

1992 The Moral Economy of Mau Mau: Wealth, Poverty and Civic Virtue in Kikuyu Political Thought. In *Unhappy Valley,* vol. 2, Bruce Berman and John Lonsdale, eds., pp. 315–504. Athens: Ohio University Press.

2000 Kenyatta's Trials: Breaking and Making an African Nationalist. In *The Moral World of the Law,* Peter C. Cose, ed., pp. 196–209. Cambridge: Cambridge University Press.

Loomba, Anita

1998 *Colonialism/Postcolonialism.* New York: Routledge.

Low, D. Anthony

1963–4 Lion Rampant. *Journal of Commonwealth Political Studies* 2:235–252.

Low, D. Anthony, and R. Cranford Pratt

1960 *Buganda and British Overrule 1900–1955 Two Studies.* London: Oxford University Press, for the East African Institute of Social Research.

Lowbridge, A. J.

1949 The Future of Native Courts. *Journal of African Administration* 1:7–18.

Lugard, Lord F.

1928 The International Institute of African Languages and Cultures. *Africa* 1:1–22.

1970a[1920] Principles of Native Administration. In *Problems in the History of Colonial Africa 1860–1960,* Robert O. Collins, ed., pp. 88–103. Englewood Cliffs, N.J.: Prentice-Hall.

1970b[1919] Methods of Native Administration. In *Problems in the History of Colonial Africa 1860–1960,* Robert O. Collins, ed., pp. 163–111. Englewood Cliffs, N.J.: Prentice-Hall.

Lumley, E. K.

1976 *Forgotten Mandate: A British District Officer in Tanganyika.* London: C. Hurst.

Lyall, Sarah

2001 Was the Sahib, Then, Just a Sahib? *The New York Times* (August 25):B7, B9.

Lyne, R.

1936 *An Apostle of Empire Being the Life of Lloyd William Mathews.* London: Allen and Unwin.

Maack, Pamela A.

1996 "We Don't Want Terraces." Power and Identity under the Uluguru Land Usage Scheme. In *Custodians of the Land,* Gregory Maddox, James L. Giblin, and Isaia N. Kimambo, eds., pp. 152–169. Athens: Ohio University Press.

Mackenzie, W. J. M.

1954   Changes in Local Government in Tanganyika. *Journal of African Administration* 6:123–129.

Macmillan, Hugh

1995   Return to the Malungwana Drift: Max Gluckman, the Zulu Nation and the Common Society. *African Affairs* 94:39–65.

2000   From Race to Ethnic Identity: South Central Africa, Social Anthropology and the Shadow of the Holocaust. *Social Dynamics* 26:87–115.

Maddox, Gregory H., and James L. Giblin

2005   Introduction. In *In Search of a Nation,* Gregory H. Maddox and James L. Giblin, eds., pp. 1–12. Athens: Ohio University Press, Athens.

Mafeje, Archie

1971   The Ideology of "Tribalism." *Journal of Modern African Studies* 9:253–261.

Maguire, G. Andrew

1969   *Toward "Uhuru" in Tanzania.* Cambridge: Cambridge University Press.

Mair, Lucy P.

1936   Chieftainship in Modern Africa, *Africa* 9:305–316.

1938   *Native Policies in Africa.* London: Routledge.

1958   Representative Local Government as a Problem of Social Change. *Journal of African Administration* 10:11–24.

1977   District Commissioners. *Royal Anthropological Institute Newsletter* 22:9–10.

Malcolm, D. W.

1953   *Sukumaland: An African People and Their Country.* London: Oxford University Press, for the International African Institute.

Malinowski, Bronislaw

1929   Practical Anthropology. *Africa* 2:22–39.

1930   The Rationalization of Anthropology and Administration. *Africa* 3:405–436.

Mamdani, Mahmood

1996   *Citizen and Subject.* Princeton: Princeton University Press.

2001   Beyond Settler and Native as Political Identities: Overcoming the Political Theory of Colonialism. *Comparative Studies in Society and History* 43:651–662.

Mandala, Elias A.

2005   *The End of Chideyramu: A History of Food and Everyday Life in Malawi, 1860–2004.* Portsmouth, N.H.: Heinemann.

Mannoni, O.

1964   *Prospero and Caliban: The Psychology of Colonization (Psychologie de la colonisation,* 1950). New York: Frederick A. Praeger.

Mapolu, Henry

1986   The State and the Peasantry. In *The State and the Working People of Tanzania,* Issa G. Shivji, ed., pp. 107–131. Dakar: Codesria.

Martin, Phyllis M.

1993   *Leisure and Society in Colonial Brazzaville.* Cambridge: Cambridge University Press.

Martin, Robert

1974   *Personal Freedom and the Law in Tanzania: A Study of Socialist State Administration.* Nairobi: Oxford University Press.

Maunier, René
1949   *The Sociology of Colonies*. London: Routledge.
Mazrui, Ali
1967   Tanzaphilia. *Transition* (31):20–26.
1970   Political Hygiene and Cultural Transition in Africa. In *The Passing of Tribal Man in Africa*, Peter Gutkind, ed., pp. 113–125. Leiden: Brill.
Mazrui, Ali A., and Alamin Mazrui
1979   *The Power of Babel: Language and Governance in African Experience*. Chicago: University of Chicago Press.
Mazrui, Ali Al'Amin [same name as above]
1963   Edmund Burke and Reflections on the Revolution in the Congo. *Comparative Studies in Society and History* 5:121–133.
Mbilinyi, M. J.
1973   Rural Development and Rural Employment Generation: Lessons from Experimentation in Tanzania. *Rural Africana* (19):67–85. East Lansing: Michigan State University.
1979   History of Formal Schooling in Tanzania. In *The Tanzanian Experience*, E. H. Hinzen and V. H. Hundsdörfer, eds., pp. 76–87. London: Evans Brothers, for the UNESCO Institute for Education, Hamburg.
1980   African Education during the British Colonial Period 1919–61. In *Tanganyika under Colonial Rule*, M. N. Y. Kaniki, ed., pp. 236–275. London: Longman.
McCarthy, D. M. P.
1979   Language Manipulation in Colonial Tanganyika, 1919–40. *Journal of African Studies* 6:9–16.
1982   *Colonial Bureaucracy and Creating Underdevelopment: Tanganyika, 1919–1940*. Ames: Iowa State University Press.
McClintock, Anne
1995.   *Imperial Leather: Race, Gender and Sexuality in the Colonial Contest*. New York: Routledge.
McGowan, Patrick J., and H. K. M. Wacirah
1974   The Evolution of Tanganyikan Political Leadership. *African Studies Review* 17:179–204.
Memmi, Albert
1969   *The Colonizer and the Colonized (Portrait du colonisé précédé, 1957)*. Boston: Beacon Press.
Meredith, Martin
2005   *The Fate of Africa*. New York: Public Affairs.
Meyer, Hans
1909   *Das Deutsche Kolonialreich*, vol. 1. Leipzig: Bibliographische Institut.
Miles, Robert
1980   *Racism*. London: Routledge.
Miller, Charles
1974   *Battle of the Bundu: The First World War in East Africa*. New York: Macmillan.
Miller, Norman N.
1969   The Political Survival of Traditional Leadership. *Journal of Modern African Studies* 6:183–201.
Mitchell, J. C.
1960   *Tribalism and the Plural Society*. London: Oxford University Press.

Mitchell, Sir Philip

    1935   Introduction. In *Anthropology in Action,* G. Gordon Brown and A. McD. Bruce Hutt, eds., pp. xi–xviii. London: Oxford University Press, for the International Institute for African Languages and Cultures.

    1954   *African Afterthoughts.* London: Hutchinson.

Mlahagwa, J. R.

    1973   The Headman: Chilongola Jenga. In *Modern Tanzanians:A Volume of Biographies,* John Iliffe, ed., pp. 133–153. Nairobi: East African Publishing House.

Mlimuka, A. K. L. J., and P. J. A. M. Kabadi

    1956   The Study of the Party. In *The State and the Working People of Tanzania,* Issa G. Shivji, ed., pp. 58–86. Dakar: Codesria.

Moffett, J. P.

    1958   *Handbook of Tanganyika.* Dar es Salaam: Government Printer.

Moffett, J. P., and the African Studies Branch, Colonial Office

    1952   Native Courts in Tanganyika. *Journal of African Administration* 4:17–25.

Molohan, M. J. R.

    1959   *Detribalization.* Dar es Salaam: Government Printer.

Moloney, Joseph A.

    1893   *With Captain Stairs in Katanga.* London: Sampson, Low, Marston.

Montague, F. A.

    1951   Some Difficulties in the Democratisation of Native Authorities in Tanganyika. *Journal of African Administration* 3:21–27.

Moore, Barrington

    1978   *Social Bases of Obedience and Revolt.* White Plains, N. Y.: M. E. Sharpe.

Moore, Sally Falk

    1972   Legal Liability and Evolutionary Interpretation: Some Aspects of Strict Liability, Self-help and Collective Responsibility. In *The Allocation of Responsibility,* Max Gluckman, ed., pp. 51–107. Manchester: Manchester University Press.

    1977   Political Meetings and the Simulation of Unanimity: Kilimanjaro 1973. In *Secular Ritual,* S. F. Moore and B. G. Myerhoff, eds., pp. 151–172. Amsterdam: van Gorcum, Assen.

    1978   *Law as Process: An Anthropological Approach.* London: Routledge and Kegan Paul.

    1986   *Social Facts and Fabrications: Customary Law on Kilimanjaro 1880–1980.* Cambridge: Cambridge University Press.

Morogoro District Headquarters Book

Morris, H. P., and James D. Read

    1978   *Indirect Rule and the Search for Justice.* Oxford: Clarendon Press.

Morrison, David R.

    1976   *Education and Politics in Africa: The Tanzanian Case.* Montreal: Mcgill–Queen's University Press.

Mpwapwa District Book, Mpwapwa District Headquarters.

Mueller, Susanna D.

    1981   The Historical Origins of Tanzania's Ruling Class. *Canadian Journal of African Studies* 15:457–499.

Müller, Fritz Ferdinand

    1959   *Deutschland-Zanzibar-Ostafrika.* Berlin: Ruetten and Lorning.

Mullings, Leith
  1976   Women and Economic Change in Africa. In *Women in Africa,* Nancy J. Hafkin and Edna Bay, eds., pp. 237–264. Stanford: Stanford University Press.
Murray, A. Victor
  1967[1938][1929]   *The School in the Bush,* copy of 2nd edition. London: Frank Cass.
Mwakyembe, H. G.
  1986   The Parliament and the Electoral Process. In *The State and the Working People of Tanzania,* Issa G. Shivji, ed., pp. 16–57. Dakar: Codesria.
Mwansasu, Bismarck U.
  1979   The Changing Role of the Tanganyika African National Union. In *Towards Socialism in Tanzania,* Bismarck U. Mwansasu and Cranford Pratt, eds., pp. 169–192. Toronto: University of Toronto.
Mwansasu, Bismarck U., and Cranford Pratt
  1979   Tanzania's Strategy for the Transition to Socialism. In *Towards Socialism in Tanzania,* pp. 3–15.
Myers, Garth Andrew
  2003   *Verandahs of Power: Colonialism and Space in Urban Africa.* Syracuse: Syracuse University Press.
Naalli, Shamshad
  1986   State Control over Cooperative Societies and Agricultural Marketing Boards. In *The State and the Working People of Tanzania,* Issa G. Shivji, ed., pp. 132–154. Dakar: Codesria.
Nairn, Tom
  2002   *Pariah: Misfortunes of the British Kingdom.* London: Verso.
Nellis, John
  1968   A Note on the Policy-Program Dichotomy. *Rural Africana* (4):14–15. East Lansing: African Studies Center, Michigan State University.
Newman, James L.
  1973   Hazards, Adjustments and Innovation in Central Tanzania. *Rural Africana* (19):1–19. East Lansing: Agricultural Development and Employment, African Studies Center, Michigan State University.
Nyerere, Julius
  1967a   Democracy and the Party System. In *East Africa: Past and Present,* pp. 122–149. Paris: Présence africaine.
  1967b   *Socialism and Rural Development.* Dar es Salaam: Government Printer.
  1967c   *Freedom and Unity: Uhuru na Umoja.* London: Oxford University Press.
  1968   *Ujamaa: Essays in Socialism.* London: Oxford University Press.
O'Callahan, Marion
  1980   Introductory Notes. In *Sociological Theories: Race and Colonialism,* pp. 1–36. Paris: UNESCO.
Oldaker, A. A.
  1957   Tribal Customary Land Tenure in Tanganyika. *Tanganyika Notes and Records* 47 and 48:117–144.
Oliver, Roland
  1952   *The Missionary Factor in East Africa.* London: Longmans.
O'Neill, T.
  1878   *Sketches of African Scenery from Zanzibar to the Victoria Nyanza.* London: Church Missionary Society.

Osterhammel, Jürgen
    1997   *Colonialism* (*Kolonialismus*, 1995). Princeton: Markus Wiener.
Oyono, Ferdinand
    1966   *Houseboy* (*Une vie de boy*, 1960). London: Heinemann.
Padmore, George
    1969a[1936]   *How Britain Rules Africa*. New York: Negro Universities Press.
    1969b[1949]   *Africa: Britain's Third Empire*. New York: Negro Universities Press.
Pakenham, Valerie
    1985   *Out in the Noonday Sun: Edwardians in the Tropics*. New York: Random House.
Parker, Henry
    1904   Letter to Baylis (August). Church Missionary Society Archives.
Parsons, Timothy H.
    1999   *The African Rank-and-File: Social Implications of the King's African Rifles 1902–1964*. Portsmouth, N.H.: Heinemann.
    2005   *The 1964 Army Mutiny in the Making of Modern East Africa*. Westview, Conn.: Praeger Greenwood Press.
Pels, Peter
    1994   The Construction of Ethnographic Occasions in Late Colonial Uluguru. *History and Anthropology* 8:321–351.
    1996   The Pidginization of Luguru Politics: Administrative Ethnography and the Paradoxes of Indirect Rule. *American Ethnologist* 23:738–761.
    1999   *A Politics of Presence*. Amsterdam: Harwood Academic Publishers, for Gordon and Breach.
    2001   Creolisaton in Secret: the Birth of Nationalism in Late Colonial Uluguru, Tanzania. *Africa* 72:1–28.
Pels, Peter, and Oscar Salemink
    1999   Introduction: Locating the Colonial Subjects of Anthropology. In *Colonial Subjects*. Peter Pels and Oscar Salemink, eds., pp. 1–52. Ann Arbor: University of Michigan Press.
Perham, Margery
    1931   The System of Native Administration in Tanganyika. *Africa* 4:302–313.
    1961   *The Colonial Reckoning: Reith Lectures 1961*. London: Collins.
    1967a   Some Problems of Indirect Rule (1931). In *Colonial Sequence*, pp. 91–118. London: Methuen.
    1967b   Native Administration in Tanganyika (1931). In above, pp. 24–34.
    1967c   The Indirect Principle in Tanganyika (1930). In above, pp. 12–23.
    1970   A Re-statement of Indirect Rule (1934). In *Problems in the History of Colonial Africa 1860–1960*, Robert O. Collins, ed., pp. 141–147. Englewood Cliffs, N.J: Prentice-Hall.
Perras, Arne
    2004   *Carl Peters and German Imperialism 1858–1918*. Oxford: Clarendon Press.
Peter, Chris, and Sengondo Mwingi
    1986   The State and the Student Struggles. In *The State and the Working People of Tanzania*, Issa G. Shivji, ed., pp. 155–194. Dakar: Codesria.
Phillips, Anne
    1989   *The Enigma of Colonialism: British Policy in West Africa*. Bloomington: Indiana University Press.

Phillips, Arthur
  1955   The Future of Customary Law in Africa. *Journal of African Administration*
  7:151–165.
Pieterse, Jan N.
  1992   *White on Black: Images of Africa and Blacks in Western Popular Culture*. New
  Haven: Yale University Press.
Piper, John
  1960   Letter to Beidelman, my files.
Porter, Bernard
  2007   Trying to Make Decolonisation Look Good. *London Review of Books* 20(18)
  (August):6–10.
Pratt, R. Cranford
  1967   The Administration of Economic Planning in a Newly Independent State: The
  Tanzanian Experience 1963–1966. *Journal of Commonwealth Political Studies* 5:38–59.
  1971   The Cabinet and Presidential Leadership in Tanzania 1960–1966. In *The
  State of Nations*, Michael F. Lofchie, ed., pp. 92–118. Berkeley: University of California Press.
  1976   *The Critical Phase in Tanzania 1945–1968*. Cambridge: Cambridge University
  Press.
  1982   Colonial Governments and the Transfer of Power in East Africa. In *The
  Transfer of Power in Africa: Decolonization, 1940–1960*, Prosser Gifford and William
  Roger Louis, eds., pp. 249–281. New Haven: Yale University Press.
  1999   Julius Nyerere: Reflections on the Legacy of His Socialism. *Canadian Journal of African Studies* 33:137–152.
Price, J.
  1879a   Letter to Wright (Mpwapwa October 4). Church Missionary Society Archives; version republished in *Church Missionary Intelligencer* (1879):530.
  1879b   Letter to Wright (Mpwapwa, October 28). Church Missionary Archives.
  1884   Letter to Lang (Mpwapwa, August 5). Church Missionary Society Archives.
  1888   Letter to Lang (January). Church Missionary Society Archives.
  1890   Letter to Lang (August). Church Missionary Society Archives.
  1891   Letter to Lang (February). Church Missionary Society Archives.
Prince, Tom von
  1911   *Gegen Araber und Wahehe: Erinnerung aug meiner ostafrikanischen
  Leutnantzeit 1890–1895*. Berlin: S. Mittler.
Pruen, S. T.
  1888   Letter to Lang (January). Church Missionary Society Archives.
  1899   Through German East Africa, *Church Missionary Intelligencer*: 97–107.
Putterman, Louis
  1982   Economic Motivation and the Transition to Collective Socialism: Its Application to Tanzania. *Journal of Modern African Studies* 20:263–285.
Raikes, Philip
  1978   Rural Differentiation and Class Formation in Tanzania. *Journal of Peasant
  Studies* 5:285–325.
Ranger, T. O.
  1969   Local Reactions to the Imposition of Colonial Rule in East and Central
  Africa. In *Colonialism in Africa*, vol. 1, L. H. Gann and Peter Duignan, eds., pp.
  293–324. Cambridge: Cambridge University Press.

1976   From Humanism to the Science of Man: Colonialism in Africa and the Understanding of Alien Societies. *Transactions of the Royal Historical Society,* 5th series 26:115–141.

1980   Making Northern Rhodesia Imperial: Variations on a Royal Theme, 1934–1938. *African Affairs* 79:349–373.

1982   Race and Tribe in Southern Africa: European Ideas and African Acceptance. In *Racism and Colonialism,* Robert Ross, ed., pp. 121–142. The Hague: Martinus Nijhoff Publishers, for the Leiden Centre for the History of European Expansion.

1983   The Invention of Tradition in Colonial Africa. In *The Invention of Tradition,* Eric Hobsbawm and Terence O. Ranger, eds., pp. 211–262. Cambridge: Cambridge University Press.

1993   The Invention of Tradition Revisited: The Case of Colonial Africa. In *Legitimacy and the State in Twentieth-Century Africa,* Terence O. Ranger and Oluemi Vaughan, eds., pp. 62–111. London: Macmillan, for St. Anthony's College, Oxford.

Raum, D. F.

1965   German East Africa: Changes in African Tribal Life under German Administration 1892–1914. In *History of East Africa,* vol. 2, Vincent Harlow and E. M. Chilver, eds., pp. 163–207. Oxford: Clarendon Press.

Raum, Johannes W.

1995   Reflections on Max Weber's Thoughts Concerning Ethnic Groups. *Zeitschirft fuer Ethnologie* 120:73–87.

Redmond, P. N.

1971   Review of Heussler: British Tanganyika. *Journal of African History* 2:661–662.

Rees, D.

1900   Letter to Baylis (Mamboia [*sic*], April 10). Church Missionary Society Archives.

1902   History of the C.M.S. in German East Africa, typescript, Church Missionary Society Archives.

1905   Letter (October), Church Missionary Society Archives.

1913   In the Berega Country, *Church Missionary Gleaner* 40 (April):154–155. *Reports of the Tanganyika Mission of the C.M.S.,* Church Missionary Society Archives.

Resnick, Idrian

1969   Prescriptions for Socialist Rural Education in Tanzania. *Rural Africana* (9):13–33. East Lansing: African Studies Center, Michigan State University.

Rex, John

1980   The Theory of Race Relations—a Weberian Approach. In *Sociological Theories: Race and Colonialism,* pp. 117–141. Paris: UNESCO.

Richards, Audrey

1960   Introduction; Some Conclusions. In *East African Chiefs,* Audrey Richards, ed., pp. 13–24, 244–377. London: Faber and Faber.

Roberts, A. D.

1962   The Sub-Imperialism of the Baganda. *Journal of African History* 3:435–450.

Roberts, Andrew

1990   The Imperial Mind. In *The Colonial Movement in Africa,* J. D. Roberts, ed., pp. 24–76. Cambridge: Cambridge University Press.

Roberts, C. Clifton

1969[1937]   *Tangled Justice. Some Reasons for a Change of Policy in Africa.* New York: Negro Universities Press.

Roberts, Richard, and Kristin Mann

1991 Introduction: Law in Colonial Africa. In *Law in Colonial Africa*, R. Roberts and K. Mann, eds., pp. 3–58. Portsmouth, N.H.: Heinemann.

Robinson, R. E.

1949 The Administration of African Customary Law. *Journal of African Administration* 1:138–176.

1950 Why "Indirect Rule" Has Been Replaced by "Local Government" in the Nomenclature of British Native Administration. *Journal of African Administration* 2:12–15.

Robinson, Ronald

1972 Non-European Foundations of European Imperialism: Sketches for a Theory of Collaboration. In *Studies in the Theory of Imperialism*, Roger Owen and Robert Sutcliffe, eds. London: Longman

Rodney, Walter

1980 The Political Economy of Colonial Tanganyika 1890–1930. In *Tanzania under Colonial Rule*, M. N. Y. Kaniki, ed., pp. 128–163, London: Longman.

1982[1972] *How Europe Underdeveloped Africa*. Washington: Howard University Press.

Roscoe, John

1885 Letter to Lang (November). Church Missionary Society Archives.

1888a Letter to Lang (September). Church Missionary Society Archives.

1888b Letter to Lang (December). Church Missionary Society Archives.

Rotberg, Robert I.

1966 The Rise of Nationalism: The Case of East and Central Africa (1962). In *Social Change: The Social Situation*, Immanuel Wallerstein, ed., pp. 505–519. New York: John Wiley.

Rothchild, Donald S.

1954 The Effects of Mobilization in British East Africa. Pittsburgh: *Duquesne University Institute of African Affairs* no. 2.

Sabean, Hanan

2001 Reviving the Dead: Entangled Histories in the Privatisation of the Tanzanian Sisal Industry. *Africa* 71:286–313.

Said, Edward W.

1979[1978] *Orientalism*. New York: Knopf.

1989 Representing the Colonized: Anthropology's Interlocutors. *Critical Inquiry* 15:205–225.

1993 *Culture and Imperialism*. New York: Knopf.

Samoff, Joel

1979a Education in Tanzania: Class Formation and Reproduction. *Journal of Modern African Studies* 17:47–69.

1979b The Bureaucracy and the Bourgeoisie: Denaturalization and Class Structure in Tanzania. *Comparative Studies in Society and History* 21:30–62.

Samuel-Mbaekwe, Iheanyi J.

1986 Colonialism and Social Structure. *Transafrican Journal of History* 15:81–95.

Saul, John S.

1972 The Nature of Tanzania's Political System: Issues Raised by the 1965 and 1970 Elections I and II. *Journal of Commonwealth Political Studies* 10:113–129; 198–221.

Sayers, Gerald F.
  1930   *The Handbook of Tanganyika*. London: Macmillan
Schmidt, Rochus
  1892   *Geschichte des Araberaufstandes in Ost-Afrika*. Frankfurt on Oder: Verlag der Königlichen Hofbuch Druckerei Trowitzsch.
  1894   *Deutschlands Kolonien ihre Gestaltung, Entwicklung und Hilfsquelle*, I, Berlin: Verlag des Verein des Büchsfreunde.
Schmokel, Wolfe W.
  1967   The Hard Death of Imperialism: German and British Colonial Attitudes. In *Britain and Germany in Africa: Imperial Rivalry and Colonial Rule*. Prosser Gifford and William Roger Louis, eds., pp. 301–335. New Haven: Yale University Press.
Schnee, Heinrich
  1919   *Deutsch-Ostafrika im Weltkriege*. Leipzig: Verlag Quelle und Meyer.
  1926   *German Colonization Past and Future*. London: George Allen and Unwin.
Schneider, G.
  1877   *Die Katholische Mission von Zanguebar: Thätigkeit und Reizen der P. Horner*. Regensberg: Manz.
Schneider, Leander
  2004   Freedom and Unfreedom in Rural Development: Julius Nyerere, Ujamaa Vijini and Villagization. *Canadian Journal of African Studies* 38:344–392.
Schumaker, Lyn
  1999   Constructing Local Landscapes: Africans, Administrators, and Anthropologists in the Northern Rhodesia. In *Colonial Subjects*, Peter Pels and Oscar Salemink, eds., pp. 326–351. Ann Arbor: University of Michigan.
Schumpeter, Joseph A.
  1951   *Imperialism and Social Classes* (*Zur Soziologie der Imperialismen*, 1919; *Die sozialen Klassen im ethnisch homogenen Milieu*, 1927). New York: Augustus M. Kelley.
Schynse, A.
  1890   *Mit Stanley und Emin Pascha durch Ost Afrika*. Cologne: Bachem
Scipio
  1965   *Emergent Africa*. London: Chatto and Windus.
Scott, James C.
  1985   *Weapons of the Weak: Everyday Forms of Peasant Resistance*. New Haven: Yale University Press.
  1990   *Domination and the Arts of Resistance: Hidden Transcripts*. New Haven: Yale University Press.
Secretary of State for the Colonies
  1953   Native Courts and Native Law in Africa: Judicial Advisors' Conference 1953. Special supplement. *Journal of African Administration*.
  1955   *East African Royal Commission 1953–1955*. London: Her Majesty's Stationery Office.
Shadle, Brett L.
  1999   "Changing Traditions to Meet Current Altering Conditions": Customary Law, African Courts and the Rejection of Codification in Kenya, 1930–1960, *Journal of African History* 40: 411–432.
Shaw, Carolyn Martin
  1995   *Colonial Inscriptions*, Minneapolis: University of Minnesota Press.
Shivji, Issa G.
  1976   *Class Struggles in Tanzania*. London: Heinemann.

1986   Introduction: The Transformation of the State and the Working People. In *The State and the Working People of Tanzania,* Issa G. Shivji, ed., pp. 1–15. Dakar: Codesria.

1990   *State Coercion and Freedom in Tanzania.* Human and People's Human Rights Monograph Series no. 8. Roma, Lesotho: Institute of Southern African Studies, National University of Lesotho.

Simmel, Georg

1950   *The Sociology of Georg Simmel,* Kurt H. Wolff, ed. and trans. Glencoe: Free Press.

Sklar, Richard L.

1993   The African Frontier for Political Science. In *Africa and the Disciplines,* Robert H. Bates, V. Y. Mudimbe and Jean O.Barr, eds., pp. 83–110. Chicago: University of Chicago Press.

Smith, Andrea

1994   Colonialism and the Poisoning of Europe towards an Anthropology of Colonists. *Journal of Anthropological Research* 50:383–393.

Smith, Edwin W.

1955   The Earliest Ox-Wagons in Tanganyika, part 1: *Tanganyika Notes and Records* 40:1–44.

Smith, Woodruff D.

1978   *The German Colonial Empire.* Chapel Hill: University of North Carolina Press.

Sofer, C., and R. Ross

1951   Some Characteristics of an East African European Population. *British Journal of Sociology* 2:315–327.

Southall, Aidan

1970   The Illusion of Tribe. In *The Passing of Tribal Man in Africa,* Peter Gutkind, ed., pp. 28–59. Leiden: Brill.

1992   Twinship and Symbolic Structure. In *The Interpretation of Ritual,* J. S. La Fontaine, ed., pp. 73–114. London: Tavistock Publications.

Spear, Thomas

2005   Indirect Rule, the Politics of Neo-Traditionalism and the Limits of Invention in Tanzania. In *In Search of the Nation,* Gregory H. Maddox and James L. Biglin, eds., pp. 70–85. Athens: Ohio State University Press.

Speke, John Hanning

1863   *Journal of the Discovery of the Source of the Nile,* London: William Blackwood.

Sperber, K. W. von

1970   *Public Administration in Tanzania.* Munich: Weltforum Verlag.

Stanley, Henry Morton

1872   *How I Found Livingstone.* London: Sampson Low, Marston, and Searle.

1879   *Through the Dark Continent.* New York: Harper.

Stephens, Hugh W.

1968   *The Political Transformation of Tanganyika 1920–67.* New York: Praeger.

Steward, D. E.

1965   "It Is Better Not to Be Sulky." *Transition* 23:26–27.

Stoecker, Helmuth

1977   German East Africa 1885–1906. In *German Imperialism in Africa,* Helmuth Stoecker, ed., pp. 148–161. Atlantic Highlands, N.J.: Humanities Press International.

Stoler, Ann Laura, and Frederick Cooper
1997 Between Metropole and Colony: Rethinking a Research Agenda; Sexual Affronts and Racial Frontiers. In *Tensions of Empire: Colonial Culture in a Bourgeois World,* Frederick Cooper and Ann Laura Stoler, eds., pp. 1–56. Berkeley: University of California Press.

Strobel, Margaret
1987 Gender and Race in the Nineteenth- and Twentieth-Century British Empire. In *Becoming Visible—Women in European History,* 2nd edition, Renate Bridenthal, Claudia Koonz, and Susan Stuard, eds., pp. 375–396. Boston: Houghton Mifflin.
1991 *European Women and the Second British Empire.* Bloomington: Indiana University Press.

Stuhlmann, F.
1885 Ueber die Luguruberge in Deutsch-Ostafrika. *Mitteilungen aus Deutschen Schutzgebieten:* 109–226.
1894 *Mit Emin Pascha ins Herz von Afrika.* Berlin: Verlag von Dietrich Reimer.

Sunseri, Thaddeus
2002 *Vilimani: Migration and Rural Change in Early Colonial Tanzania.* New York: Heinemann.
2007 "Every African a Nationalist": Scientific Forestry and Forest Nationalism in Colonial Tanzania. *Comparative Studies in Society and History* 49: 881–913.
2009 *Wielding the Ax: State Forestry and Social Conflict in Tanzania, 1820–2000.* Athens: Ohio University Press.

Sutherland, John
1970 Introduction. In William Thackeray: *The History of Henry Esmond,* pp. 7–34. Harmondsworth: Penguin Books.

Swartz, Marc J.
1960 Bases for Political Compliance in Bena Villages. In *Political Anthropology,* Marc J. Swartz and Arthur Tuden, eds., pp. 89–108. Chicago: Aldine.
1968 Process in Administrative and Political Action. In *Local-level Politics,* Marc J. Swartz, ed., pp. 227–242. Chicago: Aldine.

Symonds, Richard
1966 *The British and Their Successors.* Evanston: Northwestern University Press.
1986 *Oxford and Empire.* New York: St. Martin's Press.

Tagart, E. S. B.
1931 The African Chief under European Rule. *Africa* 4:63–76.

Tanganyika
1947 *The Laws of Tanganyika Territory.* London: Watnought (Government Printer).
1954 *Local Government Memoranda no. 1.* Dar es Salaam: Government Printer.
1957a *Local Government Memoranda no. 2 (Local Courts).* Dar es Salaam: Government Printer.
1957b *Local Government Memoranda no. 3, parts 1–3 (Local Treasuries).* Dar es Salaam: Government Printer.
1961 *Baraza za Wenyeji.* Dar es Salaam: Government Printer.

Tanganyika Peoples Defense Forces
1993 *Tanganyika Rifles Mutiny: January 1964.* Dar es Salaam: Dar es Salaam University Press.

Tanner, Ralphe S.
1955 Law Enforcement by Communal Action in Sukumaland, Tanganyika Territory. *Journal of African Administration* 7:159–165.

1965   Crime and Punishment in East Africa. *Transition* 21:35–38.
1966   European Leadership in Small Communities in Tanganyika Prior to Independence: A Study of Conflicting Social and Political Interracial Roles. *Race* 7:289–302.

Taylor, J. Clagett
1963   *The Political Development of Tanganyika.* Stanford: Stanford University Press.

Temu, A. J.
1980   Tanzanian Societies and Colonial Invasion 1875–1907. In *Tanzania under Colonial Rule,* M. H. Y. Kaniki, ed., pp. 86–127. London: Longman.

Thielew, Graham
1986   The Tanzanian Villagization Programme: Its Impact on Household Production in Dodoma. *Canadian Journal of African Studies* 20:243–258.

Thomas, Nicholas
1994   *Colonialism's Culture.* Princeton: Princeton University Press.

Thompson, A. R.
1968   Ideas Underlying British Education Policy in Tanganyika. In *Tanzania: Revolution by Education,* Idrian N. Resnick, ed., pp. 15–32. Nairobi: Longman Tanzania.

Thurnwald, Richard C.
1950   *Black and White in East Africa.* New York: Humanities Press.

Tidrick, Kathryn
1990   *Empire and the English Character.* London: Tauris.

Tignor, Robert L.
1971   Colonial Chiefs in Chiefless Societies. *Journal of Modern African Studies* 93:339–359.

Titmuss, Richard M.
1964   *The Health Services of Tanganyika.* London: Pitman Medical Publishing.

Tordoff, William
1965   Regional Administration in Tanzania. *Journal of Modern African Studies* 3:63–89.
1967   *Government and Politics in Tanzania.* East African Political Studies 2. Nairobi: East African Publishing House.

Trollope, Anthony
1964[1868]   *The Last Chronicles of Barset.* New York: Norton.

Tucker, A.
1911   *Eighteen Years Uganda and East Africa.* London: Arnold

Turner, Bryan S.
1987   A Note on Nostalgia. *Theory and Society* 4:147–156.
1988   *Status.* Minneapolis: University of Minnesota Press.

Turshen, Meredith
1984   *The Political Ecology of Disease in Tanzania.* New Brunswick: Rutgers University Press.

Twining, Lord
1959   The Last Nine Years in Tanganyika. *African Affairs* 58:15–24.

Tyler, J. W.
1967   Education and National Identity. In *Tradition and Transition in East Africa,* P. H. Gulliver, ed., pp. 14–174. London: Routledge and Kegan Paul.

Vincent, Joan
1974   The Changing Role of Small Towns in the Agrarian Structure of East Africa. *Journal of Commonwealth Politics* 12:261–275.

Wallerstein, I.

1951   *Social Change: The Colonial Situation*. New York: John Wiley.

1970   The Colonial Era in Africa: Changes in Social Structure. In *Colonialism in Africa*, vol. 2, L. H. Gann and Peter Duignan, eds., pp. 300–421. Cambridge: Cambridge University Press.

Weber, Max

1938   *From Max Weber*, H. H. Gerth and C. Wright, ed. and trans. London: Routlege and Kegan Paul.

1969   *Economy and Society (Wirtschaft und Gesellschaft, 1922)*, vol. l, G. Roth and C. Wittich, eds. New York: Bedminster Press.

Weinrich, A. K. H.

1971   *Chiefs and Councils in Rhodesia*. London: Heinemann.

Welbourn, F. B.

1961   *East African Rebels*. London: SCM Press.

West, Richard

1965   Tanganyika. In *The White Tribes of Africa*, pp. 40–61. London: Jonathan Cape.

White, C. M. N.

1959   Indirect Rule. In *From Tribal Rule to Modern Government*, Raymond Apthorpe, ed., pp. 195–198. Lusaka: Rhodes-Livingstone Institute.

White, James Boyd

1984   *When Words Lose Their Meaning*. Chicago: University of Chicago Press.

White, Luise

1986   Prostitution, Identity and Class Consciousness in Nairobi during World War II. *Signs* 11:255–273.

1997   Cars Out of Place: Vampires, Technology and Labor in East and Central Africa. In *Tensions of Empire: Colonial Culture in a Bourgeois World*, Frederick Cooper and Ann Laura Stoler, eds., pp. 436–460. Berkeley: University of California Press.

2000   *Speaking with Vampires: Rumor and History in Colonial Africa*. Berkeley: University of California Press.

White, Paul

1956[1941]   *Doctor of Tanganyika*. London: Paternoster Press.

Whiteley, W. H.

1969   Language Choice and Language Planning in East Africa. In *Tradition and Transition in East Africa*, P. H. Gulliver, ed., pp. 105–125. London: Routledge and Kegan Paul.

Widenthal, Lora

1997   Race, Gender, and Citizenship in the German Colonial Empire. In *Tensions of Empire: Colonial Cultures in a Bourgeois World*, Frederick Cooper and Ann Laura Stoler, eds., pp. 263–283. Berkeley: University of California Press.

Wilkinson, Rupert

1964   *The Prefects: British Leadership and the Public School Tradition, A Comparative Study in the Making of Rulers*. London: Oxford University Press.

Willis, Justin

1993   The Administration of Bondei 1920–60: A Study of the Implementation of Indirect Rule. *African Affairs* 92:53–64.

2002   *Potent Brew: A Social History of Alcohol in East Africa 1850–1999*. London: Heinemann.

Willis, Roy
    1981   A Colonial Ritual in Retrospect. *Royal Anthropological Institute News* 45:8.
Windschuttle, Keith
    1997   *The Killing of History.* New York: Free Press.
Winter, E. H.
    1955   *Bwamba Economy.* Kampala: East African Institute of Social Research.
Winter, E. H., and T. O. Beidelman
    1967   Tanganyika. In *Change in Traditional Societies,* vol. 1, J. H. Steward, ed., pp.
    57–204. Urbana: University of Illinois Press.
Wissman, Hermann von
    1889   *Unter deutscher Flagge quer durch Afrika vom West nach Ost.* Berlin: Walther
    and Apolant.
Wood, A. N.
    1888   Letter to Lang (October). Church Missionary Society Archives.
    1889a   Letter to Lang (October). Church Missionary Society Archives.
    1889b   Itinerating in Usagara, 1888. *Church Missionary Intelligencer:* 24–31.
    1890   Journal of Rev. A. N. Wood. *Church Missionary Intelligencer:* 183–185.
Wood, Alan
    1950   *The Groundnut Affair.* London: Bodley Head.
Woodroffe, I.
    1957   The Relationship between Central and Local Government in Africa. *Journal
    of African Administration* 9:3–15.
Wright, F.
    1957   The Relationship between Central and Local Government in Africa. *Journal
    of African Administration* 9:3–15.
Wright, Gwendolyn
    1991   *The Politics of Design in French Colonial Urbanism.* Chicago: University of
    Chicago Press.
Wright, Marcia
    1968   Local Roots of Policy in German East Africa. *Journal of African History*
    9:621–630.
Young, Crawford
    1988   The African Colonial State and Its Political Legacy. In *The Precarious Bal-
    ance: State and Society in Africa,* Donald Rothchild and Naomi Chazan, pp. 25–56.
    Boulder: Westview Press.
    1994   *The African Colonial State in Comparative Perspective.* New Haven: Yale Uni-
    versity Press.
Young, Roland, and Henry Fosbrooke
    1960   *Land and Politics among the Luguru of Tanganyika.* London: Routledge and
    Kegan Paul.
Zimmerman, Andrew
    2006   "What Do You Really Want in German East Africa, Herr Professor?"
    Counterinsurgency and the Science Effect in Colonial Tanzania. *Comparative
    Studies in Society and History* 48:419–461.

INDEX

T. O. BEIDELMAN is Professor of Anthropology at New York University. His publications include *The Cool Knife: Metaphors of Gender, Sexuality, and Moral Education in Kaguru Initiation Ritual; The Moral Imagination in Kaguru Modes of Thought* (IUP, 1986); *Colonial Evangelism: A Socio-historical Study of an East African Mission at the Grassroots* (IUP, 1982); and *The Kaguru: A Matrilineal People of East Africa.*